TRANSNATIONAL CRIME CINEMA

TRANSNATIONAL CRIME CINEMA

Edited by Sarah Delahousse and
Aleksander Sedzielarz

EDINBURGH
University Press

Edinburgh University Press is one of the leading university presses in the UK. We publish academic books and journals in our selected subject areas across the humanities and social sciences, combining cutting-edge scholarship with high editorial and production values to produce academic works of lasting importance. For more information visit our website: edinburghuniversitypress.com

© editorial matter and organisation Sarah Delahousse and Aleksander Sedzielarz, 2023, 2024
© the chapters their several authors, 2023, 2024

Edinburgh University Press Ltd
The Tun – Holyrood Road
12 (2f) Jackson's Entry
Edinburgh EH8 8PJ

First published in hardback by Edinburgh University Press 2023

Typeset in 10/12.5 pt Sabon
by IDSUK (DataConnection) Ltd, and
printed and bound by CPI Group (UK) Ltd,
Croydon, CR0 4YY

A CIP record for this book is available from the British Library

ISBN 978 1 3995 0567 3 (hardback)
ISBN 978 1 3995 0568 0 (paperback)
ISBN 978 1 3995 0569 7 (webready PDF)
ISBN 978 1 3995 0570 3 (epub)

The right of Sarah Delahousse and Aleksander Sedzielarz to be identified as editors of this work has been asserted in accordance with the Copyright, Designs and Patents Act 1988 and the Copyright and Related Rights Regulations 2003 (SI No. 2498).

Every effort has been made to trace the copyright holders, but if any have been inadvertently overlooked, the publisher will be pleased to make the necessary arrangements at the first opportunity.

CONTENTS

List of Figures   vii
Notes on Contributors   viii
Acknowledgements   xi

    Introduction   1
    Aleksander Sedzielarz and Sarah Delahousse

SECTION I   TRANSCRIPTION

1. Illuminating the Black Film: The Weimar Origins of the Argentine *Policial*, the Curious Case of 'El Metteur' James Bauer and Crime as Transnational Signifier   23
Aleksander Sedzielarz

2. Retracing Mafia Locality   44
David Rodríguez Martínez

3. Funhouse Noir: Escapist Expressionism in Samuel Khachikian's *Delirium*   61
Ramin Sadegh Khanjani

SECTION II   TRANSGRESSION

Part I On the Boundaries of Nation and Ideology: Criminal Heroes at the Discursive Limits of Genre, Gender and the Body

4. Crime without Borders: Marginality and Transnational Power in Jacques Audiard's *Un prophète*   79
Julianna Blair Watson

5. Three Crime Films by Jia Zhangke: A Transnational Genealogy of Social and Personal Turmoil 93
Eren Odabasi

6. Tit for Tat: Avenging Women and Self-fashioning Femininity in Malayalam Cinema 107
Rohini Sreekumar and Sony Jalarajan Raj

Part II Modes of Transgression vis-à-vis State Repression and Violence

7. Communist Noir: The Hunt for Hidden Traitors, Saboteurs, Spies, Revisionists and Deviationists in Albania's Revolutionary Vigilance Films of the 1970s and 1980s 125
Jonida Gashi

8. The Case of the Spanish *Gialli*: Crime Fiction and the Openness of Spain in the 1970s 140
Fernando Gabriel Pagnoni Berns

9. The Short Arm of the Law: The Post-dictatorship Crime Film as a Barometer for Justice in Contemporary Argentina 155
Jennifer Alpert

SECTION III TRANSVALUATION

10. Franchising the Female Hero: Translating the New Woman in Victorin Jasset's *Protéa* (1913), France's First Female Spy Film 183
Sarah Delahousse

11. *Shirkers* (2018) Lost and Found? Tracing Transsensorial Trauma in a True-crime Road Movie 199
Jiaying Sim

12. Gated Crimes: Neoliberal Spaces and the Pleasures of Paranoia in *Las viudas de los jueves* (2009) and *Betibú* (2014) 218
Jonathan Risner

13. Ensemble of Experts: *Relentless* as 'Nigerian Noir' 237
Connor Ryan

Postscript: Desires for Transit and Mobile Genealogies of Popular Cinema 253
Aleksander Sedzielarz and Sarah Delahousse

Index 257

FIGURES

1.1	Adolf Schlasy's name in lights in *Turbión* (1938)	28
1.2	Illustrated guns as criminals in the spotlight in the title sequence of *Con el dedo en el gatillo* (1940)	29
1.3	Orlacian hands creep towards Professor Brodart in the mirrored lamp in *Explosivo 008* (1940)	33
1.4	Ilse Gonda dances on the tables of front row spectators in *Explosivo 008* (1940)	34
1.5	An explosive link to Europe in the form of a book on Recalde's desk as he plots to kill Brodart in *Explosivo 008* (1940)	36
10.1	Protéa's Climactic Scene in a World Special Films Corporation advertisement, *Moving Picture World*, 22 November 1913, 905	192
10.2	Protéa Advertisement, *The Moving Picture World*, 8 November 1913, 641	194
11.1	Sandi Tan lying on the grass in *Shirkers* (2018)	200
11.2	Close-up of boardgame in *Shirkers* (2018)	200
11.3	Film reels preserved in an air-conditioned room in *Shirkers* (2018)	208
12.1	Still from *Las viudas de los jueves* (2009) contrasting the interior of a country with a neighbourhood of a lesser economic class	224
12.2	Image from *Betibú* (2014) in which Ronnie watches news footage of looting on the television as protests against the Argentine government unfold	225

NOTES ON CONTRIBUTORS

Jennifer Alpert is a Lecturer at Harvard University. She is currently working on a book project, titled *Collective Reconstructions: Genre and Historical Trauma in Argentinean Cinema*.

Fernando Gabriel Pagnoni Berns is a professor at the Universidad de Buenos Aires, Argentina (UBA) in the Facultad de Filosofía y Letras. He has published chapters in *To See the Saw Movies: Essays on Torture Porn and Post 9/11 Horror*, edited by John Wallis (2013), *Critical Insights: Alfred Hitchcock*, edited by Douglas Cunningham (2016) and *Dreamscapes in Italian Cinema*, edited by Francesco Pascuzzi (2015), among others. He is also the author of *Alegorías televisivas del franquismo: Narciso Ibáñez Serrador y las historias para no dormir (1966–1982)* (2019).

Sarah Delahousse teaches at York College-CUNY. She is the author of 'Reimagining the Criminal: The Marketing of Louis Feuillade's *Fantômas* (1913–14) and *Les Vampires* (1915) in the United States', published in *Studies in French Cinema*.

Jonida Gashi is Chair of the Department of Art Studies at the Institute of Cultural Anthropology and the Study of Art (Academy of Albanian Studies) in Tirana, Albania. She is also one of the founders of the DebatikCenter of Contemporary Art. Her article 'Cinema on Trial: The Films of the Albanian Communist Show Trials' appears in *Visual Past: A Journal for the Study of Past Visual Cultures*.

NOTES ON CONTRIBUTORS

Ramin Sadegh Khanjani is a filmmaker whose publications have appeared in *Film Monthly* and *Film International*. He is also the author of *Animating Eroded Landscapes: The Cinema of Ali Hatami* (2014).

David Rodríguez Martínez is a PhD Candidate at the University of Minnesota-Twin Cities. His essay 'The Noir Sensibilities of Pizzolatto's *Between Here and the Yellow Sea*' was published in *Great River Review*.

Eren Odabasi is an Assistant Professor of Global Cinema in the English Department at Western Washington University. His scholarly articles have appeared in *New Review of Film and Television Studies*, *Post Script* and *The Global South*.

Sony Jalarajan Raj is an Assistant Professor in the Department of Communication at MacEwan University in Edmonton Canada. He co-edited the essay, 'Ruling the Men's Den: Crime, Outrage and Indian Women Gang Leagers in Screen', with Rohini Sreekumar and Nithin Kalorth that appeared in *The Companion to Gangster Film*, edited by George S. Larke-Walsh (2018).

Jonathan Risner is an Associate Professor in the Department of Spanish and Portuguese at Indiana University-Bloomington. He is the author of *Blood Circuits: Contemporary Argentine Horror Cinema* (2018) and he has published articles in journals such as *Journal of Latin American Cultural Studies*, *Hispanófila*, *Studies in Spanish and Latin American Cinemas* and *Studies in Gothic Fiction*.

Connor Ryan is a Lecturer in the Department of Film and Television at the University of Bristol. His work has been published in *Journal of African Cinemas* and *Black Camera: An International Film Journal*.

Aleksander Sedzielarz is an Assistant Professor in the School of English at Wenzhou-Kean University.

Jiaying Sim is an Assistant Professor of Humanities and Social Sciences at Digipen Institute of Technology-Singapore. Her work has appeared in *Journal of Chinese Film Studies*, *The Center for Asia and Diaspora* and *Screen Bodies*.

Rohini Sreekumar is an Assistant Professor in the Department of Media Studies at St Joseph College, Devagiri in Calicut Kerala, India. She is co-author of essays that have appeared in *The Companion to Gangster Film*, edited by

NOTES ON CONTRIBUTORS

George S. Larke-Walsh (2018) and *Filmurbia*, edited by David Forrest, Graeme Harper and Jonathan Rayner (2017), among others.

Julianna Blair Watson is an Assistant Professor of French and Francophone Studies at Santa Clara University. She has published in journals such as *Studies in French Cinema*, *Black Camera*, *Francosphères* and *Essays in French Literature and Culture*.

ACKNOWLEDGEMENTS

We would like to extend our immense gratitude to Gillian Leslie and Sam Johnson for their support and guidance in bringing our collection to print. We would also like to acknowledge Qi Wang for her encouragement and belief in this project.

Aleksander would like to thank Anirban Baishya for his support from earliest stages of the project and during the publication process. He thanks Linda Zhang, Koel Banerjee, Kurt Mosser, and Hongwei Chen for their generosity in sharing their ideas and putting us in touch with colleagues as the collection took shape. He would also like to thank Suchitra Mathur, Matthew Tchepikova-Treon, Olga Tchepikova-Treon, Wendy Truran, Dzmitry Tsapkou, Tom Ue, Mikkel Vad and Ian White for their contributions and insights to the book as it developed.

Sarah would like to acknowledge Baudoin Delahousse for his unwavering support. She would also like to thank her colleague, Heather Robinson, for advising her to take on editing a collection, Richard Abel for introducing her to Jasset's *Protéa*, and Jason Sperb and Cynthia Erb for their expertise and interest in this collection.

Lastly, we would like to recognise our contributors for their scholarship and their commitment to our collection. We could not have asked for a more brilliant and dedicated group of scholars, and their work provides invaluable new perspectives on transnational cinema.

INTRODUCTION
TRANSNATIONAL CRIME CINEMA

Aleksander Sedzielarz and Sarah Delahousse

'Every origin of morality from the moment it stops being pious . . . has value as a critique'
                        Michel Foucault, 'Nietzsche, Genealogy History'

'Before the judge, we all "can't help ourselves"'
              A criminal at Hans Beckert's *ad hoc* trial in Fritz Lang's *M* (1931)

Through an investigation of crime as a fundamental modality of cinema worldwide, *Transnational Crime Cinema* establishes a genealogical method in studies of popular film within critical transnationalism. Building upon the critical orientation of transnational film studies, its chapters provide rigorous accounts of the political, economic, and historical processes entangled in the production, circulation, and reception of crime films most frequently treated through the lens of genre.

More than simply a genre or collection of genres, the association of crime and cinema has deep historical roots in cinemas throughout the world and the studies of crime and cinema in this volume present granular analyses of how, in Will Higbee and Song Hwee Lim's words, transnational cinema 'negotiates with the national at all levels' (2010: 12). Extending and deepening Higbee and Lim's initial formulation of critical transnationalism, chapters in *Transnational Crime Cinema* investigate crime 'within . . . narrative and production process, across film industries, [and] . . . in academia' to interrogate how 'filmmaking activities negotiate with the national ... from cultural policy to financial sources, from the multiculturalism of difference to how [film] reconfigures the nation's image of itself' (Ibid.: 18).

The book joins several recent collections that seek structural interventions in cinema that go beyond interpretations of narrative or aesthetics with the aim of preserving the constellations of meaning in genre and form that so provocatively appeal to audiences internationally in the context of everyday life. These include Christopher Breu and Elizabeth A. Hatmaker's *Noir Affect*, Hervé Mayer and David Roche's *Transnationalism and Imperialism: Endurance of the Global Western Film*, as well as the earlier volume *Global Neorealism: The Transnational History of a Film Style* (edited by Saverio Giovacchini and Robert Sklar).

Our volume investigates the cultural politics, modes of production and aesthetic regimes of crime cinema to find in crime a primary transitive and transformative cultural field of cinema within and between nations. Demonstrating the promise of the 'critical transnationalism' articulated by Higbee and Lim, the collection self-reflexively brings together scholars working in the Anglophone academy with international scholars working outside of the United States and Europe. All contributors are grounded in approaches that are 'polyphonic in their linguistic use' (Higbee and Lim 2010: 18). Studies in the volume begin from crime as defined by local cinema and as it reveals social transformations of power. Many of the film studies' subfields and local cinemas represented in this volume also do not share the ready access to globalised capital – both economic and symbolic – that characterises studies of popular film that begin from the United States or Europe. Instead of looking upon film form or genre from a hegemonic Euro-American production industry standpoint, these studies of crime cinema begin from local and regional history and film history to identify transnational systems and structures within histories of production and reception. Each chapter is linked by a common interest in the ways that crime reveals the 'concrete-specific' of transnational power dynamics (Ibid.: 10). As such, the body and capital are central and recurring concerns that are analysed along lines of the symbolic-linguistic and the political economy. Above all, the contributors share a common understanding of the transnational as processes of cultural transformation (occurring variously in alignment with and in resistance to globalised neoliberal capital) – ongoing processes that also provoke countermeasures that reify ideologies of nation.

Furthermore, studies in this volume take up a genealogy of crime cinema framed by three dominant conceptual points of interrogation: transcription, transgression, and transvaluation. Chapters in each section emphasise one of these three prominent historical dimensions of processes of cinematic transnationalism in a given film, filmmakers, genre cycle or generic lineage. 'Transcription' encompasses processes of both textual translation and bodily inscription in film production, audience experience, and film study to attend to intersections of language, body, and material practice. 'Transgression' focuses on political tensions and shifts that disrupt the boundaries of nation or the prescribed limits of national ideology – for example through interventions in cinema by political movements such as feminism, queer politics, or anti-imperial, anti-colonial or anti-racist agitation that open constructs of the nation to sudden change. This section also includes popular genre representations of murder, revenge, and violence that assign transgressive politics to criminality as part of the cultural process of negotiating impending social change. Finally, chapters in the 'Transvaluation' section engage in critiques of transactional dimensions of transnational cinema with a focus on how systems of globalised or neoliberal capital underwrite national history and ideology. The title of this section denotes the transformation of economic value in what Steven Shaviro identifies as the conditions of the 'real subsumption of labor under capital' as cinema constitutes forms of affective labour in which 'value is, all at once, produced, realized, and consumed' (2010: 47–48). Chapters in this section highlight cinema's production and circulation of (and as) capital, economic exploitation on film, and filmic markets involved in processes of the exploitation of labour.

Before the Law

A sequence from a crime film on which a reader might first meditate upon beginning this volume: the excruciatingly long slow pan as Hans Beckert scans the gallery of criminals that crowd the recesses of the distillery waiting to judge him for his crimes. Thus begins the iconic conclusion of Fritz Lang's *M* (1931) and one of the most memorable moments in the career of a transnational filmmaker who often chose crime as his preferred subject matter. Accentuating mystery, detection, guilt, and justice through synchronised diegetic sound effects, the film self-consciously straddles the eras of silent and sound cinema and offers key critical standpoint – a face of Janus in film – around which the past and future of crime cinema respectively unfold. The scenes that follow from Beckert's arraignment by the criminal court trace many of the numerous points of contact between cinema and crime that foreground this volume. As the camera proceeds to position the audience as witness, member of the crowd, and within Beckert's point of view, the spectator feels an uncomfortable sliding of identifications between both sides of the judgment as criminal being judged by an audience of other criminals.

Something like the mirror and reverse image of the premise of victimhood and redemption that underlies melodrama, crime films based in culpability and condemnation parallel melodrama as a perennially popular mode throughout the history of cinema. Crime narratives also engage in the revelation of a moral occult through conflicts between good and evil, suffering, and victimhood that is a key characteristic of melodrama (Brooks 1976: 5–8).[1] Nonetheless, this sequence in *M* makes an important difference explicit. Rather than an embodied mirroring of pathos, the audience shifts between being uncannily installed in the point of view of the criminal – under suspicion or standing in judgment – and feeling the thrill of the chase with the pursuers or the detective. As Lang's camera places us back with the crowd, we sense that the film audience is ultimately a part of the court that has been convened seeking justice – extending the mass of the lumpenproletariat visualised onscreen out into the mass audience of cinema.

Beckert's testimony reminds us of another possible identification that the spectator might slip into. The accused states that he is running from a crime that is within him or, as Beckert says, 'I shadow myself'. Apprehension runs through the audience that guilt or innocence may not be a matter of choice. After all, if the criminal psyche is a state that exists beneath the level of individual choice or comprehension, so too, of course, might be that of innocence.[2] These disparities of experience, which cinema fosters through its singular durée – shifting through rhythmic continuities and breaks between cinematography, mise en scène, cuts and soundtrack – will be basis for the genealogies of transnational crime film that constitute this volume. Further dissecting Lang's film glimpses this method as a way of connecting filmic detail to the contradictions of transnationalism that inflect ideologies of nation and international flows of cinema.

Moving back to the beginning of the sequence in Lang's film, evidence and charges are delivered by the figure of justice as a blind man. In secular modernity, as clearly indexed in the divisions of class and power of Weimar Germany as it appears onscreen, the human no longer stands in judgment before a divine but before an inscrutable law not unlike that imagined in Franz Kafka's parable a little more than a decade earlier. The contortions of Peter Lorre's outraged face communicate that justice will find us and will be served in a way that is cut to the measure of our crimes. Whether the small everyday dishonesties and regretful lapses in which we wonder, 'why did I do that?' or the secrets of trivial crimes committed and never detected – or thoughtlessly pondered but never committed – our crimes might just be the best-kept secrets from which we shield our ego as we all 'shadow' ourselves in one way or another. Thus, the series of identifications that begins with the criminal's point of view ends with a member of the criminals' court consummating the exchange between criminal and criminal by stating outright the burden of guilt that audience and accused share – that before the law, we are helpless and not in control: 'we know . . . before the judge, we all "can't help ourselves."'[3]

Of course, the shifting of identification between the audience and Beckert is brief and transient. We could never be Hans Beckert. His crimes against the most innocent are the most heinous imaginable. After the sequence ends, rather than merely submitting him to judgment before patriarchal law in the Weimar court, his case finally comes before the mothers. The film holds the ostensibly inviolable laws of nature over and above those of the mere human. While the film unsettles the audience by glimpsing the inscrutable depths of moral corruption in a modern city, the satisfaction of *M*, much like many other crime films that came before it and many that would come after it, comes from an affirmation of justice, even if, in crime films like *M*, justice is withheld and deferred. We continue to both desire and fear the justice of the court of the popular (the dreadful but efficient forces of the lumpenproletariat) while the judgement of the state offers no punishment that truly satisfies.

The final coda of the film is itself a meditation on the way that the crime film enters the inner life of the spectator beyond merely invoking moral prerogatives. After an off-screen voice states that Beckert will be tried 'in the name of the law', a shot-reverse-shot series shows the chambers of the court and then cuts to the mothers staring at the audience. The film cuts to a black screen. The blackness is both visual and internal to the viewer: our 'shadow' eradicates the safe voyeurism from which the spectator watched the crimes unfold in the film. The final series of cuts finally places in the audience all of the heavy burden of simultaneously being criminal, victim, detective, and judge. The truncated judgment, the breaks in film grammar, and the final transition into the bleak interiority of the spectator offers a fitting monument to films obsessed with crime as both paranoia and pathology. As an early sound film in a budding globalised industry of synchronised sound cinema, the film presents a grim picture of the proleptic relationship between justice and public spectacle in the age of mass media that will be developed in chapters throughout this collection.

Questions of Genre: Genealogies of Cinematic Crime

While the well-known scene of the ad hoc trial convened at the end *M* has served as a prototype for many future films of crime, detection, policing, and vigilante justice, the film was produced from within a greater field of lurid cinematic attractions in already established crime genres worldwide. Lang had, of course, already written and directed films of criminal syndicates and criminal masterminds for more than a decade before directing *M*.

As Dudley Andrew has brilliantly expounded, cinema as an international medium can best be described through the concept of 'jetlag' or *décalage* (2010: 60). The asynchronous worldwide movement of cinema genres, styles, and production techniques find perfect expression in Lang's crime films as they display the transnationalism of cinema that Andrew describes through cosmopolitan and national phases: producers, directors, scenarists, set designers, and lighting technicians trained in the German studio system adapted techniques and genre conventions as they fled Germany before the war (Ibid.: 65–68). Always bearing traces of being slightly out-of-sync within the national industry into which they had been absorbed, these reshaped the aesthetic of crime film studio productions in France, Spain, Argentina, and, eventually, Hollywood. Following one of many of the international lineages of Hollywood crime film through the processes of transcription, transgression, and transvaluation that form the conceptual framework of chapters in this collection, one finds Hollywood crime cinema indeed belatedly taking on memorable aesthetic codes that French critics would classify as *noir* (some of the intricacies of this transnational circulation of cinematic production from exiled German filmmakers are described in Chapter One of this volume).

To be sure, genre is the most frequent signpost by which we identify the worldwide travels and transmissions of local culture but to predicate studies of the specificities of social realities exposed by representations of crime upon generic variations, commonalities, or differences would be to fetishise the filmic text rather than explore the complexities of its commodity form. In much the same way, Rick Altman describes the tendency for books on a particular genre to 'begin by specifying the corpus of films that they will treat' revealing an assumption that 'genre is located neither in the authors nor in the audience but in the texts themselves taken as a group' (1999: 84–85). Following Altman, the analysis of a disparate range of crime films in this collection reiterates that genres are not one thing, but multiple. This collection is an encounter with crime in cinema in a way that maintains the multiplicity of genre – preserving the complexity and incommensurability of logics of categorisation as a key critical approach in the study of popular narrative cinema.

In writing on genres as 'multiple things', Altman conceives of genres through the transnational formulation of 'constellated communities' and views popular genres as 'heirs apparent' of the public sphere and imagined communities (1999: 198). Insofar as crime films stabilise into durable genres in a particular place and time, the fact that a crime film consolidates into a gangster, noir, revenge, or heist film can indeed introduce a granular and layered history that complicates a simplistic nation of cinema as media and a naive equivalence of nation with state. Rather than simply a collection of aesthetic attributes, genres are shifting classification systems of production and reception that capture shifts in audience within the particular political economy of a given film production industry. Genres can also reveal the setting of limits on what defines national ideology and, perhaps more importantly, what is excluded or expelled from the nation. As Altman writes, 'like the notion of nation, the very idea of genre exists in the singular only as a matter of convenience – or ideology' (Ibid.: 86).

While genre provides a heuristic to mark movements from the national into the transnational in the way that Altman describes above, crime films also expose the limit condition of genre as a means of analysing the relationship between cinema and audience. Throughout the collection, films under examination promiscuously accrue genre and subgenre (including, horror, revenge, comedy, documentary) and consistently refuse to obey even the law of genre: that law, which Jacques Derrida reminds us, defines what is inside by what is excluded (1980: 55–57). Thomas Leitch begins his introduction to *Crime Films* by describing crime films as 'this genre that is not a genre' (2002: 1–2). While tracking stable genres or describing their hybrid forms may provide seemingly coherent snapshots of constellated or imagined communities, a much larger problem arises from this approach as culture appears at once cosmopolitan and dematerialised. Despite Andrew's buoyant testimony to the contrary in his 2009 essay, in attempts to integrate the producers, audiences, theatres and critics of cinema disarticulated by globalised liberal capitalism back into a world, the ideal supersedes the real and the map exceeds the territory. As Pheng Cheah notes, such theories only track the flux of individual points of reference while reducing 'politico-economic processes' to 'cultural-significatory practices' (1998: 298). However, under conditions of neocolonial globalization, in which transnationalism risks recapitulating colonialism, engaging in a genealogy of genre recognises that culture is inseparable from local and national political agency as well as from the terms of economic dependency or self-determination.[4] Following Cheah, and frequently deploying genealogy as developed by Michel Foucault, chapters in this collection attempt to read cultural-significatory processes from within politico-economic processes. In addition to transcription, our collection introduces transgression and transvaluation as structuring concepts to frame chapters of the text that use common approaches to link the process and practices of the transnational discursively, bodily and dialectically. The fundamental incoherence of crime films as a category internationally, thus, becomes critically rich grounds for interpreting core questions of knowledge, capital, and agency in the transnational cultural exchanges that cinema brings into view.

As Dudley Andrew's nonsynchronous and multiphasic account of transnationalism implies, tracking the geographical mobility of film – for example, by outlining salient strains of crime films (however influential and significant) – merely creates a map: an exercise in tautology that reveals little to nothing about the transnational (or the nation). In the era of global cinema, Andrew calls for films that regenerate the belated and phantasmic qualities of cinema to keep us 'politically agile' (2010: 820). However, instead of predicating this quality upon aesthetic effects produced through the genius of filmmakers, this volume proposes that films about crime have always most clearly exhibited processes of transcription, transgression, and transvaluation that have coevolved alongside globalising capital that has radically altered the public, the state and the institutions of cinema. Andrew summons metaphors of crime and surveillance to illustrate how the globalised capital of the digital marketplace have eradicated circuits of exchange that we are to presume were previously in a state of equilibrium relative to general inequity in world systems:

> Anticipation of new work (scanning the horizon for new waves) is inversely proportional to the increased speed with which films and information about them has become available. The coastal patrols and customs agents of vigilant governments are unable to outwit today's image traffickers; one can presume that all films are simultaneously and everywhere available to those who care. (2010: 834)

To turn this formulation on its head, chapters in our volume probe the image as trafficked, stolen, prohibited, or otherwise delegitimate (or delegitimised) to observe film in a disarticulation of history and discourse rather than reified under national or global ideology.

As a collection with a focus on films that feature dramatic conflicts that reveal the law as it is defined by those outside of it, Foucault's genealogical method has far more to offer in probing films about crime than a method based in analysis of genre. In adopting what he calls a 'pragmatic approach' to genre, Rick Altman is very much in agreement with Foucault in discarding a search for origins of an event (object or text) as a study of history and instead making discursivity the site of critical analysis. Altman sees genres as momentary points of ephemeral stability in cycles of power and domination in which once nomadic cultural actors 'become property owners, and thus authors, map-makers, and intenders'. Writing that pragmatics' understanding of the multiple and competing levels in which use determines meaning reveals 'an ongoing remapping process that alternately energises and fixes human perception' (1999: 212). Underscoring these similarities in Foucault's genealogy and Altman's fluid pragmatic approach to denaturalising genre, chapters in our volume begin with seemingly stable crime genres but ultimately bring into view the institutional power that from which meaning has derived and thereby moves towards the moments in which crime is defined as it is represented.[5] Here Altman's notion of 'use indeterminacy' (Ibid.: 209) – as opposed to textual determinism – which studies works of genre from within a discursive analysis that engages in 'extracting . . . textual structures from the institutions and social habits that frame them' (Ibid.: 211), echoes what Foucault describes as 'domination' in which multiple levels of deferral of historical events and series glimpse the moments of discursivity that produce the subject: a subject that appears, *ex post facto*, as territorialised and nationalised within a matrix of globalised capital (Foucault 1984: 84–86).

Guided by Foucault's genealogy – and setting aside the tendency to theorise the common origins of crime films by making comparisons of conventions, aesthetics, or audience – chapters in this volume do not attempt to survey of the vast and intricate variations of interrelated crime film genres around the world. Instead, contributors keep questions of genre in suspension so that, rather being an analysis of transnational genres that share crime as a feature in common, each chapter instead presents genealogies films in which crime appears as a singular and overdetermined source of ideology, or what Altman calls 'convenience'. Ultimately, just as Foucault describes, the challenges to an unwavering faith in morality delivered by onscreen crime bring crises of knowledge surrounding justice, the state, the victim and the criminal as these terms come to exist within a dynamic and unstable relativity.

As cinema built on extreme experiences of the immoral, or profound dilemmas of morality, crime films are predicated on what Michel Foucault calls 'disparities' (1984: 79) – the accidents, inconsistencies, errors, and lies that disturb and destabilise presumptions of identity and unity (of the self, nation, or culture). Rather than revealing coherent cultural or national values, the event of crime gathers the as-yet-unorganised 'facts' of popular culture and provides grounds for critique of ideological unity. In Foucault's words, disparity 'shows the heterogeneity of what was imagined consistent with itself' (Ibid.: 82). Here it is important to note that genealogy counteracts the continuity that historical narratives retrospectively place on events and qualities associated with a given film. The point, instead, 'is to identify the accidents, the minute deviations – or conversely, the complete reversals – the errors, the false appraisals, and the faulty calculations that gave birth to those things that continue to exist and have value for us' Ibid.: 81). Onscreen crime is fabricated from these deviations. Although this occurs most clearly and overtly when crime is rendered as distortions of morality, these deviations occur, in embryo, in every narrative, acoustic, and visual cue through which crime cinema raises the suspicions of the audience. In this collection, interpretations of these deviations bring us profoundly close to the ongoing negotiation of shared and opposing systems of value within and between societies.

In this spirit, we might also ask how Michel Foucault would have read the above scene in *M*. Without a doubt, the scene would have intrigued the philosopher of the prison and morality (although Foucault clearly would have preferred to be called a historian, or course). At many points, Foucault's essay examining Nietzsche's genealogy of morals reads like a thumbnail sketch of the arguments about right and wrong between criminals in the improvised court in Lang's film: 'the concept of goodness is not specifically the energy of the strong or the reaction of the weak, but precisely this scene where they are displayed superimposed or face-to-face' (1984: 84). Later in the essay, Foucault gives what is probably the best description of the thrill an audience experiences in crime drama that was ever written by a philosopher: 'the law is a calculated and relentless pleasure, delight in the promised blood, which permits the perpetual instigation of new dominations and the staging of meticulously repeated scenes of violence' (Ibid.: 85). Rather than the law of bar exams, civil and criminal codes or judicial appointments, Foucault is describing the law as a recursive gestalt – precisely as it is mirrored in the mass entertainment of crime film. Of course, in this text, Foucault concerns himself with the events domination and violence that gives shape to entire epochs (he notes the Protestant Reformation as one example). Nonetheless, he critically eschews the grand narratives of the 'suprahistorical' and confines his investigations to what often seems to be accidental and arbitrary as is also the case in the studies of our collection, which probe examples where moral complications emerge both in tensions between time, place, and language, as well as in the intrinsic ambiguity of such chronotopes (Ibid.: 86–87, 93).

For the reasons elaborated above, genealogy gives the collection a basis for an analysis of crime films that is far more capacious and rigorous than genre, but it also brings the body into the critical activity of examining popular film. In looking at the disruptions of ideology, nation, and culture, this approach finds unities and limits inscribed in, on, and through the body. In the experience of domination and violence, the nonlinear facts of history surface in the constructivity and performativity of gender: the bodies of the spectator and the collective bodies of the audience form yet another dimension of analysis for chapters in this volume as the body onscreen and offscreen are never individuated apart from, or defined entirely within, a society but, as Foucault describes, are 'the inscribed surface of events ... [and] the locus of a dissociated self (adopting the illusion of a substantial unity)' (1984: 83).[6]

Habeas corpus: you shall have the body. *Corpus delicti*: the body of the crime. Longstanding principles of criminal law surround the body of both criminal and victim. Apropos of a cinematic mode that is cousin to melodrama, studies of crime film are most fundamentally about bodies. As the exegesis of the final scenes of *M* makes clear, in moments of violence in the domination and subjugation of bodies and in the commission of crimes, as well as in their premeditation and aftermath, audiences physically participate in onscreen crime either as hidden voyeurs, installed in the point of view of the criminal, or standing in judgment, although the rules of the game of interpretation are not defined at the outset they derive from an active inscription of events on the body of the viewer. An interpretation of the disparities of these works of popular culture is, thus, as Foucault writes, an 'appropriation of a system of rules, which in itself has no essential meaning, in order to impose a direction, to bend it to a new will, to force its participation *in a different game*, and to subject it to secondary rules' (1984: 85). Not only are the rules nebulous and evolving with our own feelings of right and wrong, but, while we participate in this interpretative game, we are simultaneously involved in another order of power and domination within an unfolding historical process of subject and state.

There is, thus, an urgency to conducting the genealogy of the crime film, even if the subject of the analysis seems 'unpromising' or 'without history'.

Foucault reminds us that these sentiments and sensations are the imperatives of a genealogical analysis that dismantles master narratives of history grounded in the representative schemes of ideology (colonialist, nationalist, or globalist). Insofar as the moral stands for the ultimate 'emergence of different interpretations, they must be made to appear as events on the stage of historical process' (1984: 86). In other words, at their most penetrating, the insights on crime films in this collection and their interplay with complex moral systems do the documentary work of describing historical processes through events that tell us how history is inscribed in bodies onscreen and in the audience. As a whole, the collection builds an account of crime film at a level below organised conceptions of morality – revealing affective states of difference between the audience (what it sees, hears, and feels), the acts of crime on screen (the event in history as ideology), and the periodic collapse of one into the other (we may feel we are just observers and, simultaneously, we cannot help ourselves as we sit before the judge).

Effective Histories of Immoral Image: Cinema and/as Crime in Film History and the History of Cinema

The procedure of genealogy is one that does not postulate causes (or origins) but instead leads to inspecting historical detail as always contingent in what Foucault calls 'effective history'. (1984: 88) Thus, the task of genealogy, as chapters in the collection invoke, is to 'record the singularity of events' by seeking them 'in the most unpromising places, in what we tend to feel is without history – in sentiments, love, conscience, instincts' (Ibid.: 76). The crime film's dramatic shifts of identification and the ignition of passion and pathos – these bring to light events from which to reconstruct tacit movements of power and domination that gave rise to popular sentiments of (and fixation on) the just, right, good, and evil that crime cinema demands of its audience. This affective range, which parallels the deeper questioning of self and society that an audience experiences in crime cinema, is described in Foucault's effective history as the 'origin of duty' and the 'guilty conscience' that signal occluded values surrounding 'morality, asceticism, justice, and punishment' (Ibid.: 78).

Rather than establishing a consistent method derived from Foucault that the reader will return to in each chapter, we draw upon a constellation of philosophers, historians, and critics that undergird the genealogical – rather than generic – approach to crime cinema shared by many of our contributors (genre studies and analysis also appears at points in chapters throughout but, again, not as a suprahistorical frame but, rather, in the sense of collecting genres as effects – or evidence – in the investigation of the relation of crime to the social). Indeed, not only was Foucault reanimating what could be found earlier in Nietzsche's fascination with the popular, but, in laying down a philosophical and historical method that would be called genealogy, he created a critical counterpart to many ongoing studies of morality, justice, and crime that have creatively engaged popular media. Foremost among these are the mythologies through which Roland Barthes meditated upon popular genres and their relation to nation and history. In the American context, Robert Warshow and John Cawelti collected artifacts of violence, horror, and moral outrage in popular culture to reflect upon complexities of national identity. The genre-bound and script-like narrative sketches of Jorge Luis Borges' *A Universal History of Infamy* created a gallery of legendary individuals in the depths of moral turpitude. Borges' hybrid experiment comes closest to the spirit that unites chapters in our volume in that it frequently borrows from cinema in the retelling crime narratives out of fragments of transnational accounts that toe the line between historical fact and folklore (at least two of these accounts also resurfaced in films of criminals and gang warfare).

'Effective history', is thus understood as perceiving in seemingly arbitrary signs of popular discourse the terms of what Foucault calls 'descent' rather than origin, provides a critical lens for understanding crime films while also analysing the social, political, and economic context within which the radical moral questions that drive crime narratives are raised (1984: 81). Rather than looking for the unities that might confirm stable notions of nation – whether imagined among the public, institutionally imposed, or some combination of the two – 'the analysis of descent permits the dissociation of [identity] . . . and [frees] a profusion of lost events' (Ibid.: 81). Contributions to this volume engage in an analysis of the effects of history through the event of the popular crime film productions in relation to local or regional commercial film consumption. Crime films find mass appeal in events that, at least momentarily, upset the moral order and energised by audience affect that ranges from curiosity to outrage (in an example in this volume, Jiaying Sim's study of *Shrikers* exhibits this effect across three national contexts). Popular crime films are based on events in the cultural memory of one city, state, or community that deviate from established moral codes (one set of examples analysed in this volume comes from Eren Odabasi's genealogy of Jia Zhangke's recent crime trilogy). These are moments in which we view morality as a process of descent and ostensible accidents are revealed to be that which 'gave birth to those things that continue to exist and have value for us'. These lost events, thus, become significant by destabilising morality to open up a space of critique.

Also inspired by Foucault's genealogy, Lee Grieveson's research on public perceptions of the immorality and policing of early twentieth-century cinema shows that in the American context criminality and cinema were part of a shared discursive formation in which new publics formed around cheap amusements. Cinema was linked to crime as a medium that was an inextricable part of social change and the management of bodies as transnational capital produced shifts in immigration and labour and as the nation rapidly industrialised and urbanised. The press and public officials portrayed the mass public that avidly consumed cinema outside of their long hours of labour as being at odds with existing hierarchy and order of the state. Reform movements aimed to define and police the ungovernable medium.[7]

Criminality lurked in both the cinematic environment and the subject matter of early film. Grieveson uncovers characterisations of cinema in the press as 'a school for crime' and a 'breeding places for vice' (2004: 16, 18). As one example that indexes the links between cinema, immorality and the commission of crime, Grieveson notes that reporters calling for regulation of cinema in the early 1900s who exhorted the public to see cinema as a 'moral danger' and presented early nickelodeons as a 'moral heart of darkness' (Ibid.: 11). Probing further into the unstable moral content of the films, the reports describe the audience viewing films featuring attacks on police, a burglary, and a mutiny on display at a cinema.

Even worse than the lurid images and the squalid settings of exhibition was the power that cinema seemed to have over audiences. Social reformers of the period viewed the cinema as possessing something like a contagion as the moving pictures so deeply impressed the audience psyche that they would mimic the criminal and acts they saw onscreen (Grieveson 2004: 64–5). Grieveson writes that cinema stood apart from other cheap amusements of the time as:

> the first form of mass entertainment and culture for an emerging mass public, attracting audiences, particularly lower-class immigrant groups and women . . . experiences at moving pictures in nickelodeons were regarded as particularly dangerous . . . because images were seen to be linked closely to imitative responses from 'suggestible' audiences and . . . the ill-lit space of the nickelodeon provided what [was described as] described as 'a cover for familiarity and sometimes even for immorality'. (Ibid.: 13)

Although restricted to the early twentieth century in the United States, Grieveson's examples show concerns that recur in the exhibition of cinema throughout the world in which cinema itself is viewed with suspicion: the question of the morality of the content of film is invoked as part of discourses surrounding mass publics and how state and elite institutions could discipline bodies and masses into a nation. As Grieveson writes, 'regulating and shaping cinema [is] enmeshed with the broader 'panoptic' projects of modernity, those epistemological and institutional practices that effectively centred on a 'policing' of bodies and populations, characterised by increased surveillance, analysis, and codification aimed ultimately at ensuring a productive, effective, loyal, disciplined, and 'governable citizenry' (Ibid.: 18). Nonetheless, as Richard Abel discovered in his earlier research on this same period, which scoured many of the same print sources, the transnational is always already present when the unstable and ongoing question of defining the nation is raised.

Abel finds in the moral panic over cinema an ongoing conflict in the substrata of transnational capital. According to Abel, linking crime and cinema, and thereby asserting the need for regulatory control at a national level, became a tactic for a market takeover. In the face of a competitive film industry abroad and its highly successful exports, foreign films were associated with the 'risqué, deviant, and morally suspect' (1999: 78). Extending Abel's inquiry beyond circuits of transnationalism between Europe and the United States, examinations of crime and film in this volume ask how the linking of cinema and crime in attempts to stabilise and propagate the nation are inflected and fragmented by political and economic aims of imperialist, settler colonialist and globalist projects. The transcription section of our collection begins within the frame of early cinema and move into contemporary formations of capital and state. Moreover, studies probe what happens when locally evolved genres make contact with these ideologies in adapting or resisting American and Eurocentric crime genres and details how these hybrid crime films challenge and subvert their hegemonic counterparts to offer alternative articulations of crime and justice. As noted in its idiosyncratic resistance to genre, cinematic spectacles of crime disobey both aesthetic conventions and the structures of social normativity. That is, onscreen crime has historically permitted a fluidity and, at times, provided a license for fundamentally transgressive representations that are neither subsumed by transnational capital nor consolidated within a particular national ideology but undercut both.

Book Sections and Chapters

The division of our book into three section headings outlines generic and narrative modes through which crime cinema reveals relations of production as it generates sociocultural, political, and emotional affect. The chapters in the collection show rather than operating through the power of suggestion – as the overzealous regulators of early cinema assumed – that crime cinema activates public discourse over the sources and uses of power that divide the masses from power. Following Wendy Brown's notion of democracy as an aspiration towards a political state where people rule themselves together, crime cinema takes a key place among modern narrative forms from early twentieth century into the twenty-first because it exhibits friction and tensions between the masses and power; it is most fundamentally a visual storytelling form deriving suspense and drama from the politicization and policing of and for the masses. As visualised in the final trial in *M*, this can occur through a total democratisation in medium and style in which the audience experiences either identification with a criminal or anxiety surrounding the conversion of the audience into the mob. Or, conversely, crime cinema can make an audience privy to the hidden sources of power, cronyism and corruption that comprise the discourse that gives shape to both space and place and democratic, collective and autocratic power, as is shown in chapters examining *Gomorrah* (2008), *Touch of Sin* (2013), and *Betibú* (2014) in this volume. These studies show that the sensory register of crime cinema cuts across boundaries of nation, culture, and language (especially as these are entangled in ideologies of neoliberal modernity). Cinematically, crimes of kidnapping, torture, assassination and genocide appear as transgressive spectacles of violence-embracing protagonists that belong to both the putatively illegitimate regimes of criminal organisations and state agents violating (or establishing) their popular mandate.

Reconsidered as a coding of material and structural relations between mass audience and power, crime cinema provides a film history that can be read as a self-reflexive horizon for the transnational mediation – and mediatisation – of national identity. Chapters in this collection trace the development of transnational crime cinema through cinematic predecessors, including those indicated above, and, thus, offer a model for the analysis of crime films globally by way of neglected cultural genealogies. These show that cinema has historically exposed and mediated anxieties over the stability and cohesion of the nation state. Cinematic representations of crime also visualise the cultural processes through which the public comes to legitimise (or reject) state authority as well as to make exceptions for the ways that democratic processes are silenced, suppressed or perverted under capital. Just as plots of crime become isomorphic with cinematic plots, crime films render collective political, economic, psychological and sociological conflict into commodity form, especially as morality becomes a function of fetishised objects (loot, mark, or dame, for example), and the human is reified into a materialisation of labour (such as henchman, moll, hitman, or dealer). The studies in this volume also enrich the history of film by uncovering transformations in cinematic representation. Beginning in silent studio productions and early sound film, chapters in the collection demonstrate that crime cinema extends back to the sociocultural origins of the medium as an unstable transnational technology of transcription and transvaluation. Much as crime narratives disrupt the imagined communities of nation, crime narratives recode the geography of place by introducing irreconcilably globalist exchange into intimately local crises – bringing a simultaneously micro- and macrocosmic vision of cities, states and regions into view.

Case studies in 'Section One: Transcription' take on the translations of language and transformations of discourse by which crime narratives travel through circuits of cinematic intertextuality. Part One, 'Translations of the Genre Cycles and Crime Aesthetics', links recombinations of genre through the translation of cinematic style and form in Argentina, Italy, India, and Iran.

In this section's first chapter, Aleksander Sedzielarz reveals the genesis of the Argentine crime film (*policial*) in the migration of directors, cinematographers, and below-the-line film technicians from central Europe in the 1930s. As these filmmakers reengineered popular musicals and comedies with haunting stagecraft and lighting, they inscribed a paranoia and violence brought from Europe on the verge of war onto the dreamlike musicals and comedies of their adopted home. In Chapter Two, David Rodríguez Martínez's tracks a reinscription of noir within neorealist style in films set a half century apart in in Southern Italy to find that noir accesses 'myths [that] create and are the foundation of social realities'. Rodríguez Martínez's analysis of Luchino Visconti's *The Earth Trembles/La terra trema* (1958) exposes tensions surrounding the rapid development of capital through class division and the exploitation of labour. The chapter then turns to a later resurgence of twenty-first century noir aesthetics in Italian mafia film that reorders local experience of place in response to globalization. In the final chapter in this section, Ramin Sadegh Khanjani poses the formalism that critics have ascribed to Samuel Khachikian's films against the mise en scène and cinematography that Khachikian in what Khanjani describes as a 'transfer of expressionism' at the heart of Khachikan's anti-realist approach to filmmaking. While Khachikan's formal embellishments effectively magnify 'the sinister undercurrents of . . .plot' and heighten 'the uncanny mood', Khanjani ultimately finds that the director – an Armenian-Iranian whose father had survived the Armenian genocide – constructed fantasy worlds of crime intentionally absent of politics in his pursuit of a sublime aesthetic for the national cinema of Iran.

'Section Two: Transgression' contains case studies of cinematic aesthetics that indulge audiences in transgressions of cultural normativity as well as in the onscreen transgression of real and imagined boundaries of nation. The section is divided into two parts, 'On the Boundaries of Nation and Ideology: Criminal Heroes at the Discursive Limits of Genre, Gender and the Body' and 'Modes of Transgression vis-à-vis State Repression and Violence'. In the first chapter of Part One, Julianna Blair Watson analyses Jacques Audiard's *Un Prophète* (2009) from within the context of recent transnational French-language cinema to identify crime as a cultural site of ongoing contestation of the reification of race and nation. Watson identifies a new archetype for an Audidarian hero in the Franco-Arabic Malik, who contests contradictory national ideologies of integration, and she proposes that this criminal hero deploys more general forms of disintegration to 'accrue his own power and push those who have been in the centre to the periphery'. In Chapter Five, Eren Odabasi writes on Jia Zhangke's experimentation with spectacles of violence and generic conventions drawn from Hong Kong action and martial arts cinema. His study reveals the director turning to crime film conventions to express latent ethical quandaries as transnational capital has ruptured both material economies and the economy of the image in contemporary mainland China. In Chapter Six, Rohini Sreekumar and Sony Jalarajan Raj analyse female revenge narratives in Malayalam crime cinema to track emerging femininities that span the domestic and public sphere. They establish key female revenge dramas Malayalam that feature protagonists who are vastly different from the female heroes of classic Bollywood crime films and describe an ongoing 'self-fashioning' as an expression of power in the face of the ongoing crises of violence against women.

From within matrix of ideological revolutionary activities in Albania that were launched in parallel with the Chinese Cultural Revolution, Jonida Gashi examines a strain of revolutionary vigilance films from 1970s and 1980s Albania to begin the second part of the section on 'Transgression' in Chapter Seven. As Gashi describes, these films 'staged a *danse macabre*' between the declared enemies of the people, ordinary Albanians suspected of hiding vestiges of bourgeois ideology, and the secret police agents of the *Sigurimi i Shtetit*. Gashi analyses how these crime films upturned the relationships between detective, criminal, and law of conventional crime narratives while also detailing plots of suspense that drew audiences into a tantalising mystery while they became active in a larger revolutionary project in which justice was sought in 'consultation with the people'. Chapter Nine revisits the Argentine *policial* with Jennifer Alpert exploring shifts from subdued expressions of morality and accountability in the period of the most recent military dictatorship. Alpert's chapter then reviews films that stage direct confrontations with state violence in the period of redemocratisation and more recent dramatic appeals to justice by retribution in response to official discourses that expose impunity for or complicity with state terrorism. Alpert finds that Argentine crime films balance appeal to foreign audiences with urgent concerns that are distinctly national as they construct 'allegorical fictional worlds in which the line between morality and crime becomes effaced'. Exploring the aesthetic and thematic mirroring of Italian crime film trends during the years of liberal economic policy in Franco's dictatorship, Fernando Gabriel Pagnoni Berns describes a neglected subset of Spanish *gialli* films of the 1970s in Chapter Eight. Berns connects these crime-oriented transnational productions to Spain's rising consumerism and the disintegrating fascist government's dependence on flows of touristic capital.

Section Three, 'Transvaluation', contains chapters that explore cinema as a commodity that codes relations of production established through globalised finance, neoliberal capital, and materialities of labour. Chapters in this section examine the unusual commodity form that cinema takes as it circulates an anti-social and anti-establishment cultural symbolic of crime in a globalised marketplace. The films examined in the four chapters in the section on 'Transvaluation' also referentially and diegetically project the conversion of cinema's value in (and as) discourse into capital via routes of hypermediated commodity exchange and how, since the late nineteenth century, crime films as cinematic commodities have offered audiences a fluid reimagining of place and identity that is predicated upon contradictions in how crime films appear to interrogate social fractures emerging from capitalism: films construct spaces of coherent spectatorial interiority and collectivity but thereby intensify the transnational accumulation and trade of surplus value. Sarah Delahousse's chapter is an examination of the transatlantic marketing of Victorin Jasset's, *Protéa* (1913), the first in a series of films that featured the first female spy character in French cinema. Her comparative historiography of films and print sources in Chapter Ten uncovers an economic marketplace in which the film's exchange value arose from adaptions of early feminisms for a transnational audience. Jiaying Sim's chapter on Sandi Tan's *Shirkers* (2018) takes readers on an investigation of a cinematic theft in a film that shifts between documentary and true-crime drama and throws boundaries of nation and identity into chaos. The third chapter of this section examines the transnational commodification of cinematic spectacles the uncanny and states of unease induced by neoliberal capital, Jonathan Risner writes on the appeal of paranoia in the Argentine productions, *Las viudas de los jueves* (2009) and *Betibú* (2014). Discussing the marketable thrills of a cinematic sensorium of fear experienced in suburban spaces onscreen, Risner proposes a startling paradox of spectatorship paralleling neoliberal capital in South America (and beyond) in which viewers seek the confined spaces of crime to indulge in endless pleasures of paranoia. In the final chapter, Connor Ryan explores crime genres within transnational economies of knowledge, taste and capital in contemporary Lagos. Through an interpretation of Andy Amadi Okoroafor's crime film *Relentless* (2011) from within the context of its production, Ryan identifies a 'performance of cinematic expertise' through which Nigerian filmmakers showcase the 'global' scale of their creative achievements while rendering the Lagos through markers of genre conditioned by Nigeria's asymmetrical experience of globalisation.

Notes

1. In her Afterword to the volume *Noir Affect*, 'Melodrama, Noir's Kid Sister, or Crying in Trump's America', Paula Rabinowitz describes the 'tears, swelling music, self-sacrifice, and suppressed rage' of melodrama as the affective flip-side of the overt aggression and perverse desire that figures [film] noir's emotional impact' (2020: 266).
2. Describing the features of the kind of 'affective negativity' presaged in this scene in *M* through selected examples of "noir's global efflorescence," Christopher Breu and Elizabeth A. Hatmaker write that 'by tarrying with . . . negative affects as they appear in the stories of two-time losers, violent criminals, and death-haunted subjects can a truly transformational politics become possible . . . noir works in an inverse way to both model empathy with the down-trodden, excluded, and abandoned, and demand

that we engage and value the negativity of their affects. Ironically, however, such noir affects are only available to us through the production of a surreptitious form of positive affect, one that asks us to identify with the abject, the criminal, and the loser' (2020: 4, 7). Reappearing throughout the chapters of this volume, the 'noir affect' that Breu and Hatmaker identify is one of several key forms of spectatorial engagement in transnational crime films.

3. In the hands of another transnational filmmaker, who also began his career in the German studio system and finally settled in Hollywood, these shifting identifications are rendered in two parallel tracks of metacommentary on criminality (and morality) in the film. In Alfred Hitchcock's *Shadow of a Doubt*, Charlie struggles to suppress his criminal identity and warped morals while true-crime fans and small-town moral exemplars Joe and Herb blithely playact as murderers. Both Hitchcock and Lang exemplify what Thomas Leitch calls 'the obsessive focus' of crime films 'on the fluid and troubling boundaries' among categories of 'criminals, crime solvers, and their victims' (2002: 15).

4. In writing on Satyajit Ray's detective fiction, Suchitra Mathur finds an embeddedness and deferral of transnational structures of political economy within texts so that the ostensible generic lineage of crime narratives conceals a 'dual mimicry' that reveals 'nationalist discourse competing with colonial discourse for hegemonic control' resulting in 'a transformative appropriation of both discourses' (2006: 104–108).

5. The fact that crime in cinema exceeds representation and is, instead, a metacinematic presentation of the boundaries and limits of civic and political discursivity of film – with genre as a primary register of this discursivity – is central to understanding commonalities in Foucault and Altman. In short, crime opens a discursive space for cinema to bring the rules of both genre and society under doubt. The micro-scale struggles for cultural hegemony that play out in Altman's descriptions of genres and cycles are captured by Foucault's formulation: 'Rules are empty in themselves, violent and unfinalized . . . The successes of history belong to those who are capable of seizing those rules, to replace those who had used them, to disguise themselves so as to pervert them, invert their meaning, and redirect them against those who had initially imposed them; controlling this complex mechanism, they will make it function so as to overcome the rulers through their own rules' (1984: 85–6).

6. Judith Butler sees Foucault's notion of the body as intervening in an aporia exclusive of the woman and established in the origins of Western philosophy. She notes the entanglement of bodies in cultural and historical practices that constitute discourse in what she describes as the '*schema* of bodies as a historically contingent nexus of power/discourse' (1993: 33). See also Margaret A. McLaren, *Feminism, Foucault, and Embodied Subjectivity*, esp. 83–110.

7. Grieveson's more recent history of the systematization of media by the elite of liberal capitalism/imperialism could be seen as further elaborating the way in which cinema became an accessory to the cultural, and frequently moral, justifications for power could serve as a critical lens to understand the political and economic conditions that films in this collection contend with).

Works Cited

Abel, Richard. 1999. *The Red Rooster Scare: Making Cinema American, 1900–1910*. University of California Press.

Barthes, Roland. 1957. *Mythologies*. New York: Hill and Wang.

Borges, Jorge Luis. 1975. *A Universal History of Infamy*. London: Penguin Books.

Brooks, Peter. 1976. *Melodrama and the Melodramatic Imagination: Balzac, James, and the Mode of Excess*. New Haven: Yale.

Breu, Christopher, and Elizabeth A. Hatmaker. 2020. 'Introduction'. In *Noir Affect*, 1–27. Edited by Christopher Breu and Elizabeth Hatmaker. New York: Fordham University Press.

Brown, Wendy. 2015. *Undoing the Demos: Neoliberalism's Stealth Revolution*. New York: Zone Books.

Butler, Judith. 1993. *Bodies that Matter: On the Discursive Limits of 'Sex'*. New York: Routledge.

Cawelti, John G. 1975. 'The New Mythology of Crime'. *Boundary 2* 3.2: 324–357.

Cheah, Pheng. 1998. 'Given Culture: Rethinking Cosmopolitical Freedom in Transnationalism'. In *Cosmopolitics: Thinking and Feeling Beyond the Nation*, 290–328. Pheng Cheah and Bruce Robbins. Minneapolis: University of Minnesota Press.

Derrida, Jacques. 1980. 'The Law of Genre'. *Critical Inquiry* 7.1: 55–81.

Foucault, Michel. 1984. 'Nietzsche, Genealogy, History'. In *The Foucault Reader*, 76–100. Edited by Paul Rabinow. New York.

Giovacchini, Saverio, and Sklar, Robert, eds. 2011. *Global Neorealism: The Transnational History of a Film style*. Jackson, MS: University Press of Mississippi.

Grieveson, Lee. 2004. *Policing Cinema*. Berkeley: University of California Press.

Higbee, Will, and Song Hwee Lim. 2010. 'Concepts of Transnational Cinema: Towards a Critical Transnationalism in Film Studies'. *Transnational Cinemas* 1.1: 7–21.

Leitch, Thomas. 2002. *Crime Films*. Cambridge: Cambridge University Press.

Mathur, Suchitra. 2006. 'Holmes's Indian Reincarnation: A Study in Postcolonial transposition'. In *Postcolonial Postmortems*, 87–108. Edited by Christine Matzke and Susanne Muehleisen. Amsterdam: Rodopi.

Mayer, Hervé, and David Roche. 2022. *Transnationalism and Imperialism: Endurance of the Global Western Film*. Bloomington, IN: Indiana University Press.

McLaren, Margaret A. 2002. *Feminism, Foucault, and Embodied Subjectivity*. Albany: State University of New York Press.

Rabinowitz, Paula. 2020. 'Afterword: Melodrama, Noir's *Kid Sister*, or Crying in Trump's America'. In *Noir Affect*, 261–274. Edited by Christopher Breu and Hatmaker, Elizabeth. New York: Fordham University Press.

Shaviro, Steven. 2010. *Post Cinematic Affect*. Winchester: John Hunt Publishing.

Warshow, Robert. 1964. *The Immediate Experience: Movies, Comics, Theatre and Other Aspects of Popular Culture*. Garden City, NY: Anchor Books.

SECTION I

TRANSCRIPTION

1. ILLUMINATING THE BLACK FILM: THE WEIMAR ORIGINS OF THE ARGENTINE *POLICIAL*, THE CURIOUS CASE OF 'EL METTEUR' JAMES BAUER AND CRIME AS TRANSNATIONAL SIGNIFIER

Aleksander Sedzielarz

The Early Beginnings of the Argentine Crime Film: Something Sinister Enters Argentina's Dreamworld of Song and Dance

The crime film or *policial* arrived somewhat belatedly in Argentina. With the introduction of sound synchronization technologies into local film production in 1933, Argentine audiences remained enthralled with local musicals that combined comedy and romance. While some of these films contained depictions of class conflict and petty criminality in Buenos Aires, most audiences came to the cinema to see the musical performances of rising celebrities like Libertad Lamarque and Carlos Gardel or the antics of comedians Tita Merello and Luis Sandrini. The fact that filmmakers built their careers and reputations in studio musicals is confirmed by the biographies of the directors that scholars cite as two of the first *policiales* produced by the country's two top studios in this period: 1937's *Outside the Law/Fuera de la ley* (Manuel Romero) and 1940's *With His Finger on the Trigger/Con el dedo en el gatillo* (Luis Moglia Barth) (Peña 2012: 55–56, 84). The director of the first, Manuel Romero, began his career writing lyrics for Carlos Gardel's first feature – the 1931 tango comedy *The Lights of Buenos Aires/Las luces de Buenos Aires* (Adelqui Migliar) – which was filmed at Paramount's Joinville foreign-language studio in France. The director of the second, Luis Moglia Barth, had his biggest hit with the 1933 film *¡Tango!* – the star-studded musical promoted as Argentina's first sound film.

In even the most hard-boiled of the early *policial* films, the soundtrack is still the main attraction. Eminent poets and songwriters were employed as librettists to compose *liberetto* (or *libro*) theme songs that might turn the film into a hit in a film industry with growing transnational ties to Hollywood that was anchored in the promotion of films through soundtracks and singers (Borges 2018: 64–65). In early *policial* films, these songs are typically performed in shows staged within film that offered the audience the vicarious pleasure of a musical attraction justified by the morality tale of the narrative. The well-known production duo of songwriter Homero Manzi and poet Ulyses Petit de Murat began their work in screenwriting with the *policial Con el dedo en el gatillo*. Manzi had earlier written lyrics for the tango '¡Salud Salud!' (Performed by Ada Falcón) featured in the 1938 *policial*, *Downpour/Turbión* (Antonio Momplet). In one of the most fascinating later cases of music getting top billing in an Argentine crime film, tango composer Lucio Demare collaborated with writers Carlos Olivari and Sixto Pondal Ríos on the 1944 *policial Death by Appointment/El muerto falta a la cita*, directed by Belgian-French filmmaker-in-exile Pierre Chenal. Before moving to Argentina, Chenal was highly regarded for directing a strain of dark crime narratives in France (including the 1939 film *Le Dernier Tournant*, based on the James Cain novel, *The Postman Always Rings Twice*).

Pierre Chenal's *El muerto falta a la cita* was released at a moment when the *policial* had just begun to reach maturity in Argentina. Chenal's film exemplifies how *policiales* produced in the mid-1940s would smoothly integrate elements of musical, comedy, and suspense in a way that would lead to their retrospective recognition as a distinct form of Argentine noir.[1] In the case of film noir in the United States, Paula Rabinowitz argues that 'rather than reflecting' violence and destruction that awaited a placid and complacent public, noir film 'prefigures them, encodes them, and makes them intelligible'. She writes that 'cultural sensations coalesce around spectacles of crime' (2002: 16). Argentina's earliest *policial* films have very much the same eerie quality of conjuring a latent sense of general foreboding but were not set against the backdrop of American Cold War ideals of prosperity and security. As techniques and style migrated from Europe, crime's cinematic signifiers arrive in translation. Rather than being produced through solely processes of mimesis – whereby the filmic image and sound would represent Argentine social realities – a transnationally constructed 'prefiguring' marked the diegesis of these films along with an encoding of Argentine national cinema in European sensations of violence and destruction. Despite the fact that the genre conventions of Argentine studio films diverged greatly from the gritty depictions of depraved lives on the margins best suited to modes of lighting and composition inherited from expressionist stagecraft – and despite the fact that Argentina seemed distant from the grim violence that would overtake Europe in World War II – Argentine film studios adopted crime as an affective mode that transgenerically absorbed musicals, comedy, and diverse elements of popular culture. Ultimately, with the first uneven steps towards the initial Argentine *policial* films, a disturbing quality of menace had quietly entered Argentine cultural life that would establish deeper roots in Argentine cinema in the coming decade.

The dark look of European cinema entered Argentine cinema through the influence of camera technicians that had initially worked in German cinema. The collaborations that shaped this aesthetic formed in unexpected ways. This chapter explores one example in which a veteran filmmaker of Jewish descent acted as mentor for a younger protegee who was also moonlighting as a propagandist for the Nazi Party. These two filmmakers, as well as later directors and camera operators living in exile from Europe, brought cinematographic techniques borrowed from earlier avant-garde movements that later also became associated with the noir films produced in the United States. These included a syntax of camera angles that created distortions of proportion and perspective, as well as concepts of set design and lighting that had been established in Weimar-era films. The most dramatic changes to cinematography were introduced through an approach to light and shadow through manipulations of key lighting and backlighting, as well as through techniques of lens diffusion.[2]

The darker elements of European film aesthetics entered Argentine filmmaking at a time when studio productions were a dreamworld of song and dance: becoming a cinema with regional and global reach through newly integrated synchronised sound technologies, the Argentine film industry was rapidly growing through close relationship with radio and recording industries (López 2017: 320–328). Argentine studios aspired to the great heights of Hollywood musical productions, but films were also produced under the strict censorship of the authoritarian government that had consolidated power in the late 1930s in what is known as the 'Infamous Decade'.[3] Acting like 'fortunetellers', as Rabinowitz puts it, the techniques and design that had migrated into Argentine cinema from Europe would introduce a new mode of filmmaking suited to cinematic representations of state authority, mass violence, and collective trauma. Becoming the basis of Argentina's *policial* film, European approaches to cinematography, lighting, and mise en scène would supply Argentine filmmakers with a cinematic language to tell stories of catastrophic violence in the years to come.

From Transnational Technique to National Affect: A Brief History of the Early *Policial*

French transplant Pierre Chenal was a relative latecomer to the Argentine *policial*. The first notable European involved in the origin of *policial* films was John Alton. Born in the Austro-Hungarian border town of Sopron and immigrating to New York in 1919 after living in Transylvania as an adolescent, Alton worked for MGM in Los Angeles and then across Europe before coming to Argentina in 1932 as a consultant for the creation of the Lumiton studios (Alton 2013: xxi). In 1935, with Alton as cameraman, director Luis Saslavsky created what was possibly the first Argentine crime film, *Crime at Three O'clock/Crimen a las 3*, for La Pampa studio.[4] Alton eventually moved to the United States and worked as cameraman on several key noir films, most prominently the 1947 film *T-Men* (Anthony Mann). After *Crimen a las 3*, Luis Saslavsky directed another precursor to the Argentine *policial* film, *The Flight/La Fuga* (1937), which Saslavsky's friend Jorge Luis Borges praised (Peña 2012: 67). As a cameraman for the latter film, Saslavsky opted to work with another cameraman from Europe. Despite the personal or ideological conflicts that such a choice might have presented to the Jewish-Argentine director, Saslavsky selected Gerhard Huttula (credited as Gerardo Huttula in Argentina), a German expatriate working for the Nazi Party abroad. While working with Saslavsky on *La Fuga*, Huttula was also the cameraman for Romero's *Fuera de la ley*, which Fernando M. Peña describes as the 'first important *policial* film' (Ibid.: 56). Peña attributes *Fuera de la ley*'s influence on later Argentine cinema as owing to the 'density of the theme' and the ambience created by Huttula's lighting techniques (Ibid.: 56). Huttula worked for three different directors in the one year that he lived in Argentina (he also shot the film *Mateo*, directed by Daniel Tinayre). The fact that the cinematic style remains relatively consistent across all of the films that he shot for Argentine studios attests to his lasting influence on the cinematography of the Argentine *policial*. Huttula also filmed all three films at the same time as he was working on film projects for the Nazi Party's Foreign Organisation, the Nationalsozialistische Deutsche Arbeiterpartei/Auslands-Organisation (NSDAP/AO), in Argentina. Huttula directed the propaganda film *Far from the Land of the Ancestors/Fern vom Land der Ahnen* for the NSDAP/AO. Making appeals to German nationals moving abroad to retain their German citizenship, *Far from the Land of the Ancestors* exuberantly depicted Germans settlers in rural Argentina as highly industrious and as faithful to Adolf Hitler.[5]

Huttula divided his time creating a multi-reel propaganda film of German goods and cultural influences and scenes of the sunny Argentine countryside – replete images of hard-working farmers, as well as singing and hiking Hitler youth – and devising cinematography for narrative feature films that constructed a dark and disturbing atmosphere. Huttula's film production in Argentina thus presents a schizophrenic picture of a man of whom little is known. Huttula's labour for the Nazis perpetuated a malicious ideology of empire, assimilation, and, ultimately genocide, but he spent his spare time painting with light, to borrow Alton's phrasing, creating fantastic worlds of immersive contrasts inspired by the diversely rich art and theatre that underpinned urban life in the Weimar Republic. The latter, of course, would eventually be portrayed as dangerously degenerate and corrupt by the former.

All three studio films that Huttula worked on in Argentina exhibit the same characteristically lugubrious camera and lighting techniques: deep shadows cutting across the mise en scène, uncanny close ups of objects, long cross dissolves marking the passage of time, and medium-long exterior shots in fog or shadow that feel tight and confined. Finding themselves in the same place at the same time (and both being native speakers of German), Huttula likely found himself under John Alton's tutelage while working on Saslavsky's *La Fuga*, for which he was credited as 'cameraman' and then continuing on with work at Alton's Lumiton studio where he made *Fuera de la ley*.[6]

James Naremore summarises Alton's own account of the composition of such shots and its origins in German theatre:

> [Alton] thinks of the photographic image as theatrical or stagelike space, filled with dramatic highlights and cast shadows. The technique of 'mystery lighting' . . . derives from a long-standing tradition of gothic stage plays and magic shows that illuminate sinister figures from below. (2008: 173)

As Peña's description of Huttula's impact on the *policial* also reflects, local films with such a look – both the stagelike and claustrophobic in their composition of cinematic space, as well as well as the feeling of mystery inspired by high contrasts between dark and light – had not been experienced by audiences in Argentina until the late 1930s. The Nazi filmmaker's borrowed camera and lighting tricks introduced a darkness into Argentine cinema that quickly took hold with a string of new *policial* films, emerging from late 1937 and continuing well into the 1940s, that shared a common visual aesthetic. Argentina's particular brand of crime films was, thus, initiated through a strange brew: a collaboration between a Jewish master filmmaker and a Nazi-affiliated apprentice – a combination that may have only been possible in the cultural life of Argentina in the late 1930s.

While Argentine audiences were primed for a cinema that offered tawdry spectacles of crime, a rich collection of filmmaking talent was in exodus from German studios and made its way into the world of Argentine film production in the late 1930s. As Fernando González García outlines, filmmakers Adolf Schlasy and James Bauer also eventually came to Argentina from Barcelona where they had been part of a larger network of exiled Jewish-German film producers that included Max Nosseck, Arnold Lippschitz, and Erwin Scharf (2013: 25–26).[7] After *Fuera de la ley*, the 1938 *policial* film *Turbión* was directed by Spanish director Antonio Momplet who had worked closely on the film with the wildly popular composer Francisco Carnaro – but again, the lighting of the film was left up to a veteran of German cinema, Adolf Schlasy. The title credits indicate that lighting had become an attraction in and of itself in a way that even approached the importance of musical sequences. While Carnaro's name is displayed prominently at the beginning of film's credits as the author of the film's score, Adolf Schlasy's name is listed in large letters at the top of a title card under his technical role – 'Illumination' (credited as 'Adolfo Schlasy'; Fig. 1.1).

The next year, director James Bauer, a German director in exile from Europe, released *The Mystery of the Grey Lady/El misterio de dama gris*, a highly unusual *policial* that was Bauer's first attempt at a producing a crime film in Argentina. The curators of the Mar de Plata International Film Festival in 2014 described the film as a 'curious film that involved the actors in the theater'. ('Festival Internacional de Cine' 2004: 198). With a Brechtian touch of calling into question the boundaries of stage, screen, and life – as well as, one suspects, a flourish of wit characteristic of the comedies that Bauer had directed in Germany – Bauer clearly sought to shake up the field of *policial* cinema in his adopted home with the now lost film.[8]

In the same year, Homero Manzi and Ulysses Petit de Murat began work on *Con el dedo en el gatillo*, a *policial* that seems fully Argentine by design. No European exiles were employed in the credited production crew and the premise

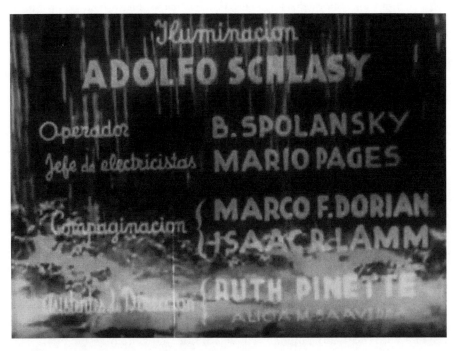

Figure 1.1 Adolf Schlasy's name in lights in *Turbión* (1938).

of the film came from a powerful moment in recent Argentine national history. Manzi and Petit de Murat were closely connected with proletarian art circles in the Boedo neighbourhood of Buenos Aires. While loosely portraying an episode of violent class struggle set in Buenos Aires, the film evokes the true history of arrest execution of anarchist Severino di Giovanni in 1931. As if showing that Argentines had stolen the limelight from their European predecessors, or at least that they had fully embraced their dramatic lighting techniques, the title cards show an illustration of a spotlight in the dark illuminating firearms posed metonymically as criminals (Fig. 1.2). Peña writes that Manzi was interested in cinema as a mass political phenomenon and the creation of 'a national affect' (2012: 85–86). Manzi later wrote lyrics for the songs of the film *Guerra gaucho* (1942), The film was based on an epic poem by Leopoldo Lugones who was a supporter of forms of authoritarian nationalism and was Manzi's attempt the creation of a national melodrama. Nonetheless, despite being consummately Argentine, the earlier *Con el dedo en el gatillo* makes a remarkably strong statement against nationalism with a depiction of martyrdom of internationalist anarchist advocates for the Argentine working class.[9]

Figure 1.2 Illustrated guns as criminals in the spotlight in the title sequence of *Con el dedo en el gatillo* (1940).

The Plot Thickens: The Mysterious James Bauer

> The most curious issue about this film is its director, Belgian James Bauer, of whom very little is known. What we do know is that: before the arrival of Nazism to power he directed films for Biograph in Berlin; from 1934–1935 he worked as a director's supervisor in Barcelona for Orpheum Studios; in 1937 he directed an Argentine-Paraguayan co-production . . . a semi-documentary film which was left unfinished because of trouble with a woman. Between 1938 and 1940 he lived in Buenos Aires where he directed *Singing Comes My Love*, *The Mystery of the Grey Lady* . . . and . . . *Explosivo 008*.
>
> Description of 'Explosivo 008' in the catalog of the 19th Festival Internacional de Cine de Mar del Plata, 2004

In 1940, Cruz del Sur studios released Bauer's *policial* film *Explosivo 008*. The film is a crime comedy featuring a love triangle involving a prosecutor who hears sinister voices, the prosecutor's wife, and a scientist working on top-secret explosives who is in an affair with the prosecutor's wife. The film's visual aesthetic – as well as its portrayal of Buenos Aires' crime circles – recalls Momplet's *Turbión*, suggesting that Momplet and Bauer were continuing to develop films together in a collaboration that began at Unión-Film in Barcelona in the mid-1930s (González García, 2013 17–18). In 1937, Bauer travelled from Barcelona to South America to produce what was planned as the first feature filmed in Paraguay, a film that would never be completed: *Paraguay, Land of Promise/Paraguay, tierra de promisión*. The production schedule for the film in South America in 1937 included close collaboration with musician Remberto Giménez and guaranteed Bauer's passage away from a Spain becoming entrenched in a civil war and from a continent on which anti-Semitic persecution was growing on all sides.

A brief dispatch about the Buenos Aires film studio production plans for Bauer's *Singing Comes My Love/Cantando llegó el amor* published in *Cine-Mundial* in 1938 describes Bauer as 'el metteur alemán' (1938). The sentence just before the mention of Bauer's film discusses the arrival of well-known Spanish director Antonio Momplet in Buenos Aires where he would be working under contract for the Rio de la Plata studio. The dates and studio described in the article indicate that the film is *Turbión*. The placement of the two news items in sequence suggests that the simultaneous arrival of Bauer and Momplet was linked. Nonetheless, describing Bauer as a 'metteur-en-scène' – essentially in charge of putting together scenes before the camera (set, lighting, and so on) – shows that Bauer was not regarded as having achieved the same level of artistry as the *auteur* Momplet.[10] Two years later, Bauer was credited with the role of 'dirección y encaudre' (direction and framing) for *Explosivo 008*, revealing that he had risen to the level of a director in charge of both stage direction and camera work in Argentine studios.

Before coming to Argentina, Bauer was already adept at creating hybrid crime comedies. For example, he directed the 1932 film *The Escape to Nice/Flucht nach Nizza*, which was based on a detective novel by Hans Mahner-Mons. Bauer had also directed films in a range of genres for major Berlin studios. Bauer's earliest films had a dark streak rooted in the gothic stagecraft of the Weimar era also described by Alton. He had directed the 1920 film *The Mask of Death/Die Maske des Todes* and the 1927 film *Witches' Night/Walpurgisnacht*. Bauer was also no stranger to controversy. In 1929, he directed the film *Incest/Blutschande*, which was the subject of anti-Semitic attacks in the *Deustche Zeitung* for the way that the film undermined what the newspaper writer claimed were German morals (Prawer 2005: 97).[11] In his biggest-budget films at Emelka studios, Bauer worked with set designer Ludwig Reiber who had worked on German crime films featuring fictional detective Stuart Webbs in the early 1920s. Reiber was also the art director who had worked with a young Alfred Hitchcock on his first films in the mid-1920s.

In Spain, Bauer joined a large number of German filmmakers in exile that settled in Barcelona beginning in the mid-1930s. In 1935, Bauer had directed his first film for the Spanish studio Unión-Film: the crime film, *Don't Kill Me!/¡No me mates!* Advertisements for the film also gave an alternate title, 'Los misterios del barrio chino'. Set in Barcelona's Chinatown, the film taps into an orientalist and xenophobic imaginary linking overseas Chinese communities to mystery, crime, and corruption. The fact that such tropes had long been a common premise for crime films is seen in earlier Hollywood productions like 1929's *Welcome Danger* – the first film featuring Harold Lloyd's recorded dialogue. Although no print of *Don't Kill Me!* exists, Augusto M. Torres calls the film a 'parody of the detective genre' (much like Lloyd's *Welcome Danger*) and relates that the director was experienced in directing hybrid crime comedies (2004: 284).[12] González García documents Bauer's continued projects among German filmmakers coming to Spain from Germany to evade Nazi Party restrictions on Jewish filmmakers working in domestic production (2013: 18). González García also indicates that Bauer is German (not Belgian) and other biographies put Bauer in Hamburg as a theatre director from early on in his life and career.[13] The bizarre aspect of live performance in the later, *The Mystery of the Grey Lady*, also supports the fact that Bauer had his professional start in early twentieth century German theatre. In 1936, Bauer joined a new studio venture in Spain, Asociación de Productores, S.A, and began a film based on a detective story by Frank Arnau – with Adolf Schlasy working on the film as cameraman. The film was interrupted by the onset of the Spanish Civil War (Ibid.: 20–21).

The restored *Explosivo 008* glimpses Bauer's activities within Argentine cultural life and makes it possible to fill in lapses in the historical record. Just as considering the passage of Huttula's cinematic style into Argentine film history highlights how unexpected transnational encounters embed themselves in film aesthetics, moments of apprehension and doom in *Explosivo 008* expose the anxieties that Bauer carried with him as he fled Europe just before his death. The film thus stands as a monument to transnational figures like Bauer as they continued to navigate life and business as stateless persons.[14] A patchwork of ostentatious sequences inspired by and, at times, directly borrowed from Weimar-era films, there are some indications that the film was conceived as a project approaching the scale of a prestige picture that would elevate Bauer to become a recognisable director in Argentine cinema. Besides consisting of elaborate sets and special effects, as well as intriguing on-location shoots (these include scientific laboratories fully equipped with electrified gizmos and an outdoor weapons testing range), the film also had to be cut from an original duration that was deemed too long after making a dismal premiere in Buenos Aires. The shortened film also had a changed title, changed from 'Dr Recalde, Penalista', or 'Dr Recalde, Criminal Lawyer', to the title that the film is now known by.[15]

As a mashup of crime and science fiction at the intersection of European and South American culture, *Explosivo 008* shows Bauer selecting, adapting and translating Argentine cultural forms into cinematic material with which he already had great experience. As with almost all films of the Argentine classical studio era, the opening credits list a tango, 'Juramento', as a main attraction of the film. The sequence is written by legendary songwriters Francisco Carnaro and Luis César Amadori and performed by the up-and-coming star Maria de la Fuente. However, popular science drives the plot of the film (by all accounts, Bauer also wrote the script for the film), with an intriguing premise built upon top-secret invention of the explosive that is the namesake of the movie from which the narrative unfolds into subplots featuring inept criminals who attempt to steal the invention but do not understand its volatile properties.

Explosivo 008 is a story of adultery and jealousy leading to crime. Dr Recalde is an attorney who is haunted by voices and descends into a criminal underworld. In eerie horror and science fiction sequences interspersed with comedy, musical interludes, and courtroom scenes, Dr Recalde tries to underhandedly destroy his wife's suitor, Professor Brodart. An opening scene in a courtroom invokes an aura of mystery and dread as a murderer recounts a justification for a crime of passion before a court. The camera cuts to Dr Recalde as he confirms that the situation of the accused is something that 'he understands well'. The first scene ends on the utterance of the word 'murder'. The next scene opens with camera placement partially occluded by the shadowy forms of lab equipment in the foreground while Mrs. Recalde argues that her scientist paramour must liberate her from her relationship with her husband and that now – as he is distracted by the conclusion of this important trial – is the time.

Each scene creates a sensation of suspense through Bauer's established style as the camera slowly dollies, pans, and zooms to keep the audience fixed on the characters faces with increasing intensity. The film employs an effect similar to a sound-bridge in which cuts between scenes occur where a section of dialogue culminates – as with the word 'murder' in the opening scene – creating emotional crescendos before changes of scene. The set design and lighting amplify these camera and editing effects to subtly exhibit stylistic nuances shared by Weimar suspense, horror, and science fiction, and key inspirations for the film seem to be Fritz Lang and F. W. Murnau. With a manicured goatee and combed back hair on an oblong head, Recalde (played by Juan Sarcione) even looks strikingly like the evil spy Haghi from Lang's 1928 *Spies*. However, transposed into Argentine musical comedy, the film feels bifurcated into two separate affective registers: the husband's simmering jealousy that leads to ominous crimes and, in parallel yet distinctly separate comedy sequences, a romance between a married woman and her scientist lover.

In a sequence that stands out in the first of these registers, a would-be assassin enters the scientist's laboratory at the behest of Recalde. The drama culminates with a shot that presents the murderer through a series of images depicting hands drawn toward the act of strangulation. Brodart sits at his desk while hands creep towards him through a series of cuts in a way that is optically dazzling and inspired by the uncanny cinematographic effects of Robert Weine's 1924 *The Hands of Orlac* and F. W. Murnau's 1921 film *The Haunted Castle*. The camera captures disembodied hands as projected shadows and transformed by a reflection in a convex mirror (See Fig. 1.3). The struggle that follows takes place entirely in the dark between black silhouettes of figures in

Figure 1.3 Orlacian hands creep towards Professor Brodart in the mirrored lamp in *Explosivo 008* (1940).

the darkened lab. Despite a scene tightly composed to create a feeling of suspense, the fight between shadows concludes with an episode that feels like a spectacle from staged professional wrestling. Brodart body slams the criminal into a vat of acid, police abruptly enter, and they tell the criminal to put his hands up. His hands up but squirming in pain from the acid burning his backside, the criminal bellows 'Help! Help! The water is burning me!'

A song and dance sequence earlier in the film features Ilse Gonda – who appears in the title credits as a soloist dancer. The sequence begins with a group of dancers in synchronised performance led by Gonda clothed in a silk robe and the following scene segues into Gonda's risqué solo ballet. In a racy outfit consisting of a sequined leotard, tights and a top hat, Gonda struts across the stage and then onto the tables of men in the front row of the audience. The costume seems to be lifted from – or quoting – Marlene Dietrich's lounge performances in *The Blue Angel* (Fig. 1.4). The film's protagonist is bemused, gazing at the dancer with increasing pleasure before the scene cuts to the dancer entering a dark dressing room where she is accosted by a criminal with a gun. Dr Recalde is held up by the criminal at the door, but the two recognise each other and arrange to meet at a bar where they agree upon a plan to attack the scientist.

Figure 1.4 Ilse Gonda dances on the tables of front row spectators in *Explosivo 008* (1940).

Despite the overt attempts to interject comedy into dramatic scenes like the encounter between Recalde and the criminal, the sound design of the film further undermines the genre conventions of Argentine musical comedy and augments the sinister atmosphere created by the lighting and camerawork. Recalling *M*, the attorney is haunted by voices that recur throughout the entire soundtrack. The voices are presented as a disembodied whisper inside the protagonist's head during otherwise quiet moments at three separate points in the film repeating the words, '*Mujer . . . ladron . . . matar* [woman . . . thief . . . kill]'. The otherworldly quality of the voiceover, linking the words form a dark undercurrent throughout the film that compromises the comedic tone of the film. The result is a confusion of affect – a cruel laughter – where slapstick sequences are followed immediately by moments of bleak nihilism.

Taking into account Bauer's urgent itinerary out of Europe, his erratic pattern of production work beginning in Spain, as well as his impending death, one is left with the sense is that something more serious is struggling to push its way out of the film's generic conventions. On the one hand, at the level of the film's protagonist and namesake – driven towards murderous insanity – and, on another level, in anticipation of the mass violence that Brodart's work on explosives of unprecedented power for the Ministry of War will eventually lead to. These two troublesome undercurrents collide in a scene in which the Recalde's secretary finds a book on her employer's desk and looks befuddled while a dramatic crescendo of strings punctuates the score. The attorney is studying the scientist's trade in weapons of mass destruction as he plots to kill him (Fig. 1.5). The close-up of the cover, with the words 'Switzerland' and roman numerals for '1940', visually ties the scientist's experiments to the escalating war in Europe. By the time that the film was released in 1940, Czech and Polish lands had already been invaded and occupied at the end of the previous year and Switzerland would be faced with defending itself from both Germany and Italy.

In a time of the restrictive film censorship that continued through the period of the 'Infamous Decade', as well as ostensible Argentine neutrality, *Explosivo 008* not only introduces dark subject matter through formal techniques drawn from Weimar cinema, but the film's pastiche of borrowed images ultimately brings flashes of Europe onto the Argentine screen. Moreover, lighting techniques better suited to the horrors settling upon Europe at the time that the film was produced upset the film's coherence. While local films continued to support national ideologies that posed Argentina as the ultimate exception within world history – separate and autonomous from the violence and chaos spreading internationally– Bauer's blending of imported elements of filmmaking with national cinema shows the early *policial* as a terrain of transnational crossings.[16]

Figure 1.5 An explosive link to Europe in the form of a book on Recalde's desk as he plots to kill Brodart in *Explosivo 008* (1940).

Conclusion: Crime as Transnational Signifier or Mass Enlightenment through Paranoia in an Age of Science and Technology

Explosivo 008 traverses two wholly different cultural worlds. Rich with elements of wit and musical comedy familiar to Argentine filmgoers, the film welds European film aesthetics onto Argentine sensibilities about plot and dialogue. The crime plot – based in subjective dilemmas arising from paranoia, obsession, and madness – offers a mode of translation (sometimes poor or partial) for transferring European quandaries into Argentine cinematic codes. In the process, the film renders objectively volatile and violent world events into an atomised entertainment commodity. Transnational *policial* films prepared the way for Argentine cinematic forms that could grapple with state violence in Argentina in years to come. Nonetheless, representations of crime were not merely something imported but also tapped a deeper vein of cultural production that had existed in Argentine urban culture since the middle of the nineteenth century. In fact, crime fiction had already allowed Argentine writers to fluidly cross the boundaries of nation and disrupt ideologies of nationalism in the early decades of the twentieth century. Filmmakers coming from Europe found a ready audience for crime films in Argentines whose cultural lives straddled local nationalisms and global cosmopolitanism.

Crime narratives proliferated in the urban Argentina in the decades before the first *policial* films were produced. *Policial* fiction was already at its height when Jorge Luis Borges and Adolfo Bioy Casares released the crime fiction parody *Seis problemas para don Isidro Parodi* under the pseudonym H. Bustos Domecq in 1942. The stories in the collection wittily play with the form of serial crime stories that were published in the early twentieth century Argentine popular press, as well as those imported in syndicated translations from abroad. Borges' first crime parody, 'Leyenda Policial', is a genteel take on the stories that writer Roberto Arlt rendered in a much rawer form in the same period. The ultimate – and perhaps most seductive – irony of Borges and Bioy Casares project of intellectualising *policial* stories was that the stories showcased non-elite knowledge honed through experience: cynicism, suspicion, and paranoia that had become a way for ordinary Argentines to face ongoing government corruption and a hostile world in which justice was never guaranteed. Throughout the mid-to-late 1920s, Arlt – a writer more directly in touch with the working class – composed short newspaper pieces on crime that included research and writing drawn from police blotters that he viewed while working at the newspaper *El Mundo*. In 1932, Arlt successfully transformed a *policial* narrative into the opening of the play *Trescientos millones*, which debuted at the proletarian-arts oriented theatre company *Teatro del Pueblo*. The play launched him to fame as a playwright.[17] Arlt's drama and fiction explores knowledge produced through deep cynicism and opposition to authority – sentiments that resonated with a working class that survived on paranoia and toughness.

While locating crime narratives as a vital for channel for communicating with a mass audience in the ways outlined above, Borges delighted in the *policial* because it brought order and coherence to a wildly heterogeneous Argentine cultural life that national ideologies could not tame. In Borges' own words:

> Facing a chaotic literature, the *novela policial* attracts me because it was a mode of defending order, of searching for classical forms, of valorizing form. For every person that is dazzled by the crime genre, there is another that is instead enlightened. (Lafforgue, et al.: 47)

A caper, a plot, suspense, a mystery, a con – what better way to captivate an audience while also offering them the upper hand in the form of the intelligence of an investigator solving the problems of the modern world? While Borges was perpetually drawn to crime as a narrative mode that could intervene within a national literature that felt incomplete and disconnected from tradition, he was neither the first nor the last Argentine intellectual to turn to crime – the *policial* crime narrative had been central to paradigms of Argentine storytelling since the nineteenth century.

In *La ley y el crimen: Usos del relato policial en la narrativa argentina (1880–2000)*, Sonia Mattalía traces the Argentine crime narrative back to Eduardo Holmberg who is generally considered the founder of both the Argentine *policial* and local forms of science fiction. Mattalía writes of Holmberg's invention of Argentina's own form of crime fiction as a form *policial* play (Holmberg himself described his first story as a 'a *policial* toy'). Mattalía points out that this 'didactic' function anticipates the aspects of crime narrative that writers like Borges would exploit. She writes that Holmberg began a narrative tradition in which crime was an intellectual flourish deployed in popular fiction consumed as mass entertainment but that it could ultimately be an edifying – and even educating – force in the lives of a modern audience:

> To educate in crime [was] a manner of giving lessons to the people . . . the idea of entertainment was one of the aspects that signaled the integration of genre in the process of the aesthetic of automation of the nineteenth century . . . crime begins to be presented as a work of art, exempt from verdicts or punishment . . . [mean]while it is relegated to the [status of] 'vulgar crime' in the news pages of periodicals and reemployed as a game of pure intelligences. (Mattalía 2008: 69)

As Mattalía points out, the emergence of Argentina's first domestic crime fiction with Holmberg's 1896 book *La bolsa de huesos* also occurred at a moment that witnessed the marvels of the development of film technology in Argentina and worldwide: 'the notion of the 'toy' also refers to the machine, in this case unifying scientificity of technique with the gratuity of the object . . . talking dolls . . . automatons . . . marvelous machines formed part of the technical imaginary . . . [which] would be fed soon afterwards by the technical imagination created by cinema' (Ibid.: 69). Even more than crime fiction, crime film blends knowledge and imagination through the catharsis of immersive technologies of entertainment.

At a time in which discourses of popular science were just as widely disseminated as crime narratives, James Bauer's *Explosivo 008* thus perfectly expresses a tension about knowledge at the core of Argentine society at the time: film weighs scientific knowledge against criminological knowledge. Both of these popular discourses converged in an early twentieth-century Argentine society that was composed of a transnational mix of recent and first-generation immigrant families from Italy, Spain, Germany, Poland, and elsewhere – each bringing their own languages, as well as folk tales and folk wisdom. Crime and science were thus the great equalisers in an urban society in which most were still in the process of becoming Argentine (an identity which was itself also in formation).[18]

The Argentine *policial* also always retained a trace of the foreign. A key example of this was Horacio Quiroga's mystery fiction at the turn of the twentieth century, beginning with the 1904 book *El crimen del otro*, which was intimately connected with, and compared to, Edgar Allan Poe. The foreignness of Roberto Arlt's name – with Italo-German origins that made it difficult for Argentines to pronounce – and questions over his mastery of textbook Spanish make ethnic hybridity central to his texts but also turned him into an everyman of the Argentine immigrant working class. In his fiction and critical writings, Jorge Luis Borges always maintained a connection with G. K. Chesterton – the British mystery writer that he highly admired. The Francophone psuedonym that Borges and Bioy Casares selected for their crime narrative protagonist, H. Bustos Domecq, overtly connects crime narratives to the circulation of the work of crime writers alongside foreign capital. In all of these precursors to the *policial* film, geographical displacement entailed writing for a public that spilled beyond the boundaries of the imagined nation.

More than simply a variety of strange tales, the ever-present influx of foreign capital and culture is marked in the Argentine *policial* as an element of crime. A symbolic connection to global print markets circulating in translation in Argentina, crime becomes the basis for an ongoing negotiation and dialogue between local Argentine modes of knowledge and an ostensibly cosmopolitan worldview. As Fabián Gabriel Mossello and Marcela Melana note in a recent volume revisiting Argentine crime cinema:

> The discourse of crime . . . has a grand development in Argentina . . . The protohistory of the genre . . . coincided in our country with the consolidation of the nation and the aesthetic projects of Romanticism and Positivism, not only were translations from French, English, and North American writers . . . [but in the] first crime writing . . . influenced by those outside models, writers that were conscious that they were attempting a new type of literature passed along through the logic of an . . . emerging . . . mass public . . . and cultivated it to have an impact on readers that was much more fluid (and profitable) than other literary practices. (2019: 7–8)

The aesthetic and formal hybridity of *policial* narratives reflects their function as an active site of and between the global and the national. Moreover, since its inception as a border-crossing commodity loaded with locally determined significance, the *policial* has transmitted a desire towards a universalising Argentine culture as capital, wherein Argentine concerns might register within the historical consciousness abroad.[19] Once it takes root in cinema, the transnational signifier of crime also absorbs existing cinematic conventions transgenerically and gains the capacity to join diverse and conflicting cultural discourses – creating a heterogeneous, democratised pastiche. Crime also lends itself particularly well to a free play through which it integrates popular film genres, initiating a transgeneric operation glimpsed in the paradoxical combination of levity and gravity in Bauer's film.

Although established in Argentina via the wartime exile of directors from Weimar Germany, films like *Explosivo 008* expose a compelling prehistory of the Argentine *policial*. Forcing a remapping of the promiscuous encounters and interconnected relationships that produced the first series of *policial* crime films in the late 1930s – and which culminated around 1940 – the film shows Argentine cultural life of the period as a rich nexus of identities and ideologies. Early Argentine crime film thus reveals an obscured cinematic history in which film reconnects cultural worlds dispersed by war, migration and exile.

Notes

1. In 2016, the San Francisco Noir Festival held first US screenings of so-called Argentine noirs restored by UCLA. ('Argentinian Noir, Restored with Support From The HFPA, Shines At Noir City Festival', HFPA, 3 February 2016).
2. John Alton's book *Painting with Light*, contains extensive sections on 'Mystery Lighting' and 'Criminal Lighting' (Alton 2013: 44–93). Alton first worked as a camera operator for Ernst Lubitsch's first film for an American studio, as well as for German director Curtis Bernhardt on *The Man Who Murdered/Der Mann, der den Mord beging*. The subsequent year Alton moved to Argentina.
3. Peña describes the steps that filmmakers had to take to appease one of the government's main advocates of censorship, Matias Sanchez Sorondo, during the period from 1935 to 1940 (Peña, 2012: 83).
4. Saslavsky was well-connected with both the Argentine literary circles and Hollywood elite. A correspondent for an Argentine film journal in Los Angeles in the 1930s, Saslavsky crossed paths Josef von Sternberg, Ben Hecht, and Orson Welles. He also worked as a consultant on the 1933 film *Night Flight* (Clarence Brown) (Saslavsky 1983: 115–119, 60–62).
5. Prints of the four reels of the film are held by Museo del Holocausto de Buenos Aires.
6. Alton came to Argentina after being recruited by Argentine investors while working at Paramount's Joinville Studio in France. According to Alton's account, almost all of the aspects of setting up the studio were left up to him as the only person with sufficient expertise. Alton stayed on in Argentina after marrying Argentine journalist and aviator Rozalia Kiss (Alton 2013, xxii–xxiv).
7. From the dates and professional complied by Fernando González García in his article on Jewish-German exiles in the Barcelona film industry it is likely that Antoni Momplet arranged for Bauer and Schlasy to immigrate to Argentina and helped them establish themselves in the Buenos Aires film industry (González García: 17–21).
8. Others describe it as 'the strangest film' ever made in Argentina. See *Crónica loca de maravillas, curiosidades, rarezas y misterios de la Argentina*, a kind of Argentine

Guinness Book of World Records, describes the '*corte policial*' film: 'In a crucial moment . . . a man stands up and harshly criticises the way in which [the film] has come to a conclusion' (146).

9. As a story of an Italian Argentine fugitive bomber working for leftist factions, *Con el dedo en el gatillo* was conceived in outright opposition to growing nationalist movements that were forming political alliances with the Italian right. Interrupting what Matt Losada describes as the 'perpetuation of national fantasy' through cinema, in which 'a commercial, politically docile industry was reproducing canonical images of national identity' (2019: 31), the film subverts this canon describes by playing both sides – visibly condemning the criminal to death, while also casting doubt on relentless authorities who eliminate a criminal whose actions may be justified because they are rooted in the unification of exploited workers.

10. For an explanation of connotations of the term *metteur*, see Gaudreault, 2011: 73–80. See also the distinction that André Bazin makes between *auteur* and *metteur* in '*De Sica*: *Metteur*-en-scène' (Bazin 2005: 63).

11. *Incest* was also shown in some American theatres under the title *Paragraph 173*. An article in *Variety* calls it 'one of the better German pictures' and 'discreetly directed' (1929: 38).

12. According to Augusto M. Torres, there was no 'James Bauer' working on *Don't Kill Me!* but Bauer was rather a pseudonym for the Spanish filmmaker Pedro Puche while he worked at Orphea Studio (2004: 284). In a chapter on anarchist cinema in 1930s Spain, Jesse Cohn corroborates Torres' account, writing that Puche would revisit the noirish Chinatown setting of the earlier film with the 1937 film *Barrios Bajos* (2015: 360–364). *A Companion to Spanish Cinema* (Jo Labanyi and Tatjana Pavlović, eds.) also attributes ¡*No me mates!* to Puche (stating that the film starred Puerto Rican singer and dancer Mapy Cortés).

13. The extensive website of silent film memorabilia collector Thomas Staedeli describes Bauer's origin working in theatre in Hamburg (Staedeli 2015).

14. Under the Reich Citizenship Law of 1935, individuals of Jewish descent were stripped of their citizenship (Majer 2003: 80–81). Bauer's Belgian identity in Argentina may have resulted from forged papers he attained to make the transcontinental voyage.

15. The description of the film for the Mar de Plata Film Festival catalog notes the cut in length, the name change and comments that the film was a 'disaster' (2004: 198).

16. For comprehensive examples of films expressing the exceptionalism of Argentina from political movements of both the right and left, see De Lucia (2016).

17. Adriana Bergero's reading of the play explores the way that Arlt crafted urban tales of scandal and corruption into powerful forms of knowledge for the working and middle classes (Bergero 2008: 216).

18. In *The Technical Imagination: Argentine Culture's Modern Dreams*, Beatriz Sarlo examines discourses of popular science in Argentina's most widely read periodicals in the early twentieth century – and contemporaneous with the rise of serial crime fiction. Sarlo notes that Arlt, and Quiroga, are seminal figures in the dissemination of popular science. The fact that both are also writing crime fiction epitomises the entanglement of the two in the public imagination (see Sarlo 2008: 58–79).

19. Through examples from early tango film posters, Adrián Pérez Melgosa points out the attraction of nationalist and populist narratives, as well as desires for a cosmopolitan modernity that universalised Argentine experience (Melgosa 2017).

Works Cited

Alton, John. 2013. *Painting with Light*. Berkeley: University of California Press.
'Argentinian Noir, Restored with Support From The HFPA, Shines At Noir City Festival'. *HFPA*, 3 February 2016. <https://www.goldenglobes.com/articles/argentinian-noir-restored-support-hfpa-shines-noir-city-festival> (last accessed 28 February 2022).
Bazin, André. 2005. '*De Sica: Metteur*-en-scène'. In Hugh Grey (trans.), *What Is Cinema?: Volume II*, 61–76. Berkeley: University of California Press.
Bergero, Adriana. 2008. *Intersecting Tango: Cultural Geographies of Buenos Aires, 1900–1930*. Pittsburgh, PA: University of Pittsburgh Press.
Borges, Jason. 2018. *Tropical Riffs: Latin America and the Politics of Jazz*. Durham, NC: Duke University Press.
Cohn, Jesse. 2015. *Underground Passages: Anarchist Resistance Culture, 1848–2011*. Edinburgh: AK Press.
De Lucia, Daniel Omar. 2016. 'Se vienen los bolches!!! anti comunismo y anti izquierdismo en el cine argentino hasta el golpe de 1976'. *Pacarina del Sur: Revista de pensamiento crítico Latinoamericano*. http://pacarinadelsur.com/home/pielago-de-imagenes/1496-se-vienen-los-bolches-anti-comunismo-y-anti-izquierdismo-en-el-cine-argentino-hasta-el-golpe-de-1976
Festival Internacional de Cine. 2004. *Catálogo Official*. Mar de Plata, Argentina: Festival Internacional de Cine.
Gaudreault, André. 2011. *Film and Attraction: From Kinematography to Cinema*. Urbana, IL: University of Illinois.
'German Pictures'. *Variety*, 13 November 1929, 38.
González García, Fernando. 2013. 'Exiliados judíos del Tercer Reich en el cine español: 1933–1936', *Secuencias: revista de historia del cine* 37.1: 9–33.
Labanyi, Jo and Pavlović, Tatjana. 2016. *A Companion to Spanish Cinema*. Oxford: Wiley Blackwell.
Lafforgue, Jorge, and Rivera, Jorge B. 1996. *Asesinos de papel: ensayos sobre narrativa policial*. Buenos Aires: Colihue.
Losada, Matt. 2018. *The Projected Nation: Argentine Cinema and the Social Margins*. Albany, NY: State University of New York Press.
Majer, Diemut. 2003. *'Non-Germans' under the Third Reich*. Baltimore: Johns Hopkins University Press.
Mossello, Fabián Gabriel and Melana, Marcela. 2019. *Policial como transgénero*. Córdoba, Argentina: Eduvim.
Mattalía, Sonia. 2008. *La ley y el crimen: Usos del relato policial en la narrativa argentina (1880–2000)*. Madrid: Iberoamericana Editorial.
Melgosa, Adrián Pérez. 2017. 'Cosmopolitan nationalisms: Transnational aesthetic negotiations in Early Latin American Sound cinema'. In *The Routledge Companion*

to *Latin American Cinema*, 135–149. Edited by Marvin D'Lugo, Ana López and Laura Podalsky. London: Routledge.

Peña, Fernando Martín. 2012. *Cien años de cine argentine*. Buenos Aires: Editorial Biblos.

'Preguntas y respuestas'. *Cine-Mundial*. August 1938, 404.

Prawer, S. S. 2005. *Between Two Worlds: The Jewish Presence in German and Austrian Film, 1910–1933*. New York: Berghahn.

Sarlo, Beatriz. 2008. *The Technical Imagination: Argentine Culture's Modern Dreams*. Stanford, CA: Stanford University Press.

Saslavsky, Luis. 1983. *La fábrica lloraba de noche*. Buenos Aires: Editorial Celtia.

Staedeli, T. 2020. 'James Bauer 1884–1940'. *Gallery of the German Film 1903–1945*, <http://www.cyranos.ch/smbauj-e.htm> (last accessed 28 February 2022).

Sueiro, Victor. 2007. *Crónica loca: maravillas, rarezas, curiosidades y misterios de los argentinos*. Buenos Aires: El Ateneo.

Torres, Augusto M. 2004. *Directores españoles malditos*. Madrid: Huerga y Fierro.

2. RETRACING MAFIA LOCALITY

David Rodríguez Martínez

INTRODUCTION: CRITICAL DEBATES SURROUNDING REALISM IN
FILM NOIR AND ITALIAN NEOREALISM

In his introduction to 'American Cinema' in the compiled works of the *Cahiers du Cinéma* from the 1950s, Jim Hillier explains that 'what *Cahiers* felt much American cinema (and much Italian cinema) offered, and French cinema did not, was what Roger Leenhardt called a 'direct engagement' with reality' (1985: 1). He goes on to suggest that the critical position of *Cahiers'* group of French critics and future filmmakers goes against much of the scholarly debate surrounding American cinema to this day because films produced in Hollywood are often dismissed as escapist fantasy. *Cahiers* often approaches films in isolation to emphasise what they believe constitutes the definitive work of auteurship, a status only given to filmmakers whose work best represents the power of cinema to evoke truths about life unconstrained by the confines of entertainment industries. The practice of singling out themes and ideas may be problematic when discussing the entirety of national cinematic output, but the type of work singled out in *Cahiers* better helps us contextualise the current output of realist Italian crime films and suggests the relevance of *film noir's* aesthetics in film historiography as a style that breaks away from Hollywood escapism by incorporating cinematic realism – a style more generally associated with its transnational, postwar counterpart, neorealism. *Cahiers'* understanding that realism functions as a state of mind allows us to make sense of the dissonance brought on by war and fascism (Hillier 1985: 203); that postwar disorientation leads to the melding of *noir* and neorealism as a means to provide social commentary through mafia representation.

If, like *Cahiers* most prominent critic André Bazin, we are to understand neorealism as a cinema of social action, then neorealist aesthetics are always in service of its non-diegetic claims to reality and not vice-versa (1967: 21). This assertion allows scholars to expand the canon of neorealism, including post-Mussolini crime films, and thus our understanding of their ability to function as an instrument of social change, and as a reflection of societal realities. The socio-political realities of postwar Italy – a liminal stage in which the promise of communist ideology is undercut by the government's embrace of capitalist investment and its accompanying urbanisation – results in elements of *film noir* in certain Italian films because this aesthetic fusion more accurately exposed the realities of many Italians as citizens transitioning from subjectivity under fascism to that of the capitalist Christian Democrats toward the end of the 1940s and into the 1950s. The failure of Italian society to crystallise around communist ideology, as early neorealist films would have it, may reflect why Italian postwar films that incorporate *noir* aesthetics do more to further the realist claims of neorealism because these films are not stuck within the vacuum of potentiality; in short, they seem more prepared for a discussion of a society organising around the logic of capitalism and class antagonism.

Because of its transhistorical quality, the discourse on *noir* aesthetics has recently shifted to its impact on cinematic representation in various global contexts. Here, it is worth pausing to consider my use of the term *'noir* sensibility', and the implications of film *noir's* multiple rhetorical usages. By subverting tropes of individual and national prosperity, a *noir* sensibility forms as a reaction against the coherence and supposed sturdiness of national identity, and that affective response creates its now ubiquitous dark and cynical worldview. A sensibility emerges from *noir's* portrayal of insecurity, despair, displacement and doom. This is best summed up in Edgar G. Ulmer's 1945 classic, *Detour*, when Al Roberts (Tom Neal) suggests, 'fate or some mysterious force can put the finger on you or me for no good reason at all.'[1] We can take the idea of *noir* realism a step further by suggesting that life reflects *noir* aesthetics (Rabinowitz 2002: 16).[2]

Neorealist *Noir*

For the purposes of this chapter, I focus on the impact of the *noir* sensibility in Italy, observing organised crime and capitalist greed in Luchino Visconti's *The Earth Trembles/La terra trema* (1958) and Matteo Garrone's *Gomorrah/ Gomorra* (2008). The comparison is not meant to signal similitude in their political aims. After all, the two films engage with different historical contexts. But they are both grounded in the neorealist impulse to document regional specificity using a particular set of principles and cinematographic techniques, and I hope that this dialectical discussion of crime films and neorealism will demonstrate how in Italy, contemporary crime films deromanticise criminal representation by fusing *noir* and neorealist aesthetics that defy periodisation.

Although the term neorealism is mainly linked to a specific visual representation (of Italy), its combination with noir in the form of 'Italian neorealism *nero*' provides an opportunity for understanding transnational crime films in various global contexts that emphasise the particular dangers of regional crime that exists within the larger system of global crime (Fay and Nieland 2010, 87).[3] Many of these films focus on organised crime's ripple effect within communities as opposed to a sole focus on the rise and fall of a singular and often larger-than-life gangster.

The grouping of neorealism and *film noir* by aesthetic features still has merit if we accept that parameters of genre are never static. This leaves room for the varying traits of the films that are branched together under the umbrella of *noir*, and it more clearly reveals the dual paths of neorealism (the *neorealismo nero* strand) and its critically touted counterpart of proper neorealism.[4] It is not that neorealism lacks aesthetics; it is that the films categorised as neorealist seem more unified by social criticism than by film form. I argue that neorealism has some aesthetic parameters, that if anything, are made apparent when these parameters are broken. Consider the following oft-cited features that Marcus establishes in *Italian Film in the Light of Neorealism* (1987). She assembles a list of conventions that includes some featured in *Gomorra*, such as non-professional actors, and 'implied social criticism', but for the purposes of my discussion of *Gomorra*, I would like to highlight those that are more related to aesthetic features: 'location shooting, lengthy takes, unobtrusive editing, natural lighting, a predominance of medium and long shots, respect for the continuity of time and space, use of contemporary, true-to-life subjects'(Marcus 1987: 22). These aesthetic features are a means to convey realism, but they only correlate as a movement if they appear throughout a series of films. There are few neorealist films not predominantly shot on location. Location sets steep viewers in Italy's postwar milieu, which in turn lends itself to long shots and natural lighting. Consider, for example, Antonio, the protagonist of *Bicycle Thieves/Ladri di biciclette*, plastering posters of Rita Hayworth (from *Gilda*) as the camera reveals just how exposed his bicycle is to theft by providing a deep-focus shot of the narrow street in the background. The bike indeed gets stolen as the untraceable thief quickly goes into the middle of the street and blends into the busy crowd, still framed in the background. In that film, as in De Sica's other iconic neorealist film, *Umberto D* (1952), vehicles and people seem to be moving in a controlled and chaotic fashion that is reminiscent of Dziga Vertov's 1929 modernist classic, *Man with a Movie Camera*. The neorealist bent of filming individuals in groups relates to the question of how these films provoke affective responses.

neorealism's aesthetic features make sure that we do not experience the individual isolated from the crowd; instead, spectatorship always exists in relation to the crowd. We are moved because we see that these individuals are part of a larger social order in turmoil. Despite these previously mentioned shared features, and there are others, Marcus points out that a 'shared moral commitment united filmmakers "from above" dissolving their petty stylistic differences into basic agreement on the larger issues of human concerns and general world view' (Ibid.: 23). I would argue that those petty stylistic differences might not always be so petty but instead shed light on a theoretical approach to the representation of Italian postwar society that has room for conventions and aesthetic practises more commonly associated with film *noir*. In this, Garrone's filmmaking style in *Gomorra* is a groundbreaking example of the push to focus on Mafia representation without losing sight of realism.

The aesthetic qualities of film *noir* do not need to exist evenly in every crime film for us to accept that a *noir* sensibility exists in various postwar new wave cinemas. Through a penchant for focusing on individuals as they pertain to communities, *neorealismo nero* reveals the fact that not every individual will achieve the pinnacle of success. That truth – which is not necessarily observable via the objective image but palpable through reflection on a subjective (in this case, existential) level – grounds *neorealismo nero* in a fatalistic film style.[5] A *noir* sensibility lends realist cinema a discourse that clearly addresses the friction between the idea that everyone can achieve success and the reality that most do not. This manifests on multiple levels, but one of the key aspects of criminal failure is in the 1940s postwar fear of a broken patriarchy and a shattered, nostalgic way of life. It is not that noir can only discuss myths instead of social realities; but that these myths create and are the foundation of social realities, especially when we consider individuals in relation to society.

Claiming that there is a uniquely *noir* presence in neorealism is difficult without a tangible and feasible demonstration of Italian cinema's relation to film *noir* that is rooted in close analysis, and I hope that my discussion of *La terra trema* and *Gomorra* will clarify this theoretical discussion. For Visconti, crime becomes a means to express class divide and the ensuing onset of modernity at the end of Mussolini's reign, and for Garrone, the Camorra, a crime organisation that controls Italy's Southwestern region of Campania, is a disparaging reminder of capitalism's entanglement with organised crime. I analyse Visconti's 1948 masterpiece, *La terra trema*, in conjunction with *Gomorra* because I hope to reveal how the film encapsulates the problem of aesthetic purity in neorealism and the dialectical representation of capturing pre- and post-fascist Italy. Visconti and Garrone, following coeval trends in *noir* narration from their respective eras, were both aware of the potential for stories of crime to function in Italian cinema as a platform with which to discuss the social unrest occurring in Southern Italy. Other than providing some of the language and conventions, *noir* provides a realism that stems from a visual concern of mapping local space, an act which is done to make up for the lack of particularity that spreads throughout urban centres. Both filmmakers respond to this dilemma of homogeneous globalisation with an excessive need to coordinate space on a local level.

La terra trema and the Half-life of Fascism

Due to the eventual creation of a non-communist, non-revolutionary Italy in the 1940s, *La terra trema* accurately reflects the half-life of fascism that lingers into postwar Italy through the eventual stabilising of the bourgeoisie via rapid industrialization in the late 1940s and well into the 1950s.[6] The film deals with the neorealist impulse of depicting what post-fascist Italy was and what post-fascist Italy could or should be. Moreover, it does not often occupy a place of contention within neorealist scholarship in regard to its use of the conventions typically associated with the movement; with a cast void of professional actors, the film is a prime example of aesthetic immersion into the intricacies of life in the fishing village of Acci Trezza, off the coast of Sicily. But *La terra trema* is also brutally humanist,[7] and it prefigures neorealism's gradual movement away from communist aspiration because it depicts, expressionistically, the potential of collective solidarity encumbered by the reality that it did not coalesce into a revolution. By focusing on the everyday lives of the labourers and their families, the film portrays this village as seemingly untouched by urbanisation and the broader influence of capitalism. But film production does not exist in a vacuum, and it is difficult not to read the wholesalers as capitalists who blur the line between criminal and legitimate activity. Grounding a documentary impulse in narration, the film explores the experience of Antonio Valastro in relation to the local fish wholesalers who exploit the community's lack of resources. As a young fisher who has travelled beyond Sicily with the military, Antonio aspires to a level of personal gratification and economic stability that the previous generation did not seem to understand. No longer willing to toil night and day for a living that amounts to a pittance, Antonio cuts out the wholesalers; to achieve this goal, he must refinance his family's house and rely on the household members for the manufacturing of the sardines they catch. This attempt at economic freedom backfires when his boat is ravaged by a storm. As a result of his failed uprising coupled with pressure from the wholesalers, the community ostracises Antonio and his family, and the Valastros slowly descend into abject poverty.

In an textual explanation during the credit sequence, Visconti makes a point of explaining that this is a distinctly Sicilian film (not even Italian) with actual labourers and non-professional actors, thus conveying a regional focus that steeps our spectatorial vision in authenticity: we are guided toward the understanding that we are not watching an escapist or romanticised portrayal of life on the sea; instead the film amplifies the labour of fishing by opening with a panorama shot of the village as the fishermen return home with their catch before sunrise. It is worth noting that the narrative voice over in the opening sequence does not always objectively describe the action on screen. Early on, he declares that 'the wholesalers buy cheap what costs the fishermen dearly.' Later as the fishers haggle with the wholesalers, the narrator asserts that 'fear for hunger haunts the fishermen; it haunts their sleep.' These extradiegetic assertions demonstrate how the initial objective focus on fishing-as-labour quickly gives way to the ideological underpinnings of the film.

Visconti introduces the tension between objectivity and ideology by dramatising Antonio's conflict with the fish wholesalers who control the local economy via ownership of the fishing vessels and the means to sell packaged fish regionally. In one particularly effective scene, an uncut panning shot presents an argument that unfolds between the fishers and the wholesalers. As a medium shot, the camera gives us just enough detail to invoke a sense of disorder while maintaining its main focus on Antonio's younger brother, who the camera follows through the crowd. As the boy eventually leaves the quarrel, the shot widens and provides a deep focus that shows him fleeing this scene. On a narrative level, this long take sets up the tension that will spill over into the next encounter. The wholesalers are clearly underpaying, but this time Antonio throws the wholesalers' scales into the sea. His exclamation, 'this is what I do to the scales! I throw them into the sea!', may shed light on a neorealist belief in the potential of postwar communism, but it also undercuts the purported objectivity of the film. The film criticises a rising bourgeois class; the wholesalers use the scales to maintain the status quo of class division. In reference to the aesthetic project of reportage, are we supposed to believe that the actual fishers in their day-to-day lives espouse Marxist rhetoric to the extent that Antonio does? Or should we accept that there is a place in neorealist aesthetics for the incorporation of melodrama in seemingly unfettered screenwriting? Without Antonio's crafted and contrived rhetoric that relies heavily on didacticism, the film would be unable to articulate with nuance the exploitation it hopes to shed light upon. The wholesalers represent a greedy, property-owning class that has collectively agreed to keep the price of fish low, increasing their profits on the market.[8]

Because of the film's allegorical representation of class antagonism, we might suggest that with *La Terra Trema*, like *Ossessione* before it and his masterpiece that blurs the lines between neorealism and new wave, *Rocco and his Brothers/Rocco ei suoi fratelli* (1958), Visconti uses something more similar to film *noir*'s penchant for fatalism as a means to express the difficulty in assessing Italy's postwar future.[9] After all, in *La terra trema*, external forces (such as the storm that destroys Antonio's boat) are against the family, and as in film *noir*, space seems to be an active player in the outcome of the plot. Antonio's desire to improve his life leads to his downfall mainly because he makes the fatal error of going out while the storm is forming.

There is a more overt nod to *noir* sensibility and transnationality that takes place when Cola, Antonio's brother, decides that he can no longer suffer for the sake of his family's integrity. After the storm, a man whose face we never clearly see but who presumably has Mafia ties recruits Cola. The shadowy figure of a man, sporting a nice fedora and trench coat, may represent what Fay and Nieland call 'Americanization': 'In the most pejorative sense, Americanization is an unwanted culture foisted upon countries whose economies and armies simply cannot compete with American power and whose citizens act more like consumers' (2010: xii). We assume that he is connected to regional organised crime. But the man's expensive clothing and lack of facial recognition allow him to be read symbolically, and he is coded by visuals of Hollywood gangsters whose media presence and representation stems from Mafia stereotypes. He comes to Aci Trezza to recruit teenagers. For what? Potentially smuggling, potentially a tireless life on the black market, but it is his means of recruitment that links explicitly to mafia representation. The man piques Cola's interest with a surplus of Lucky Strike cigarettes that equates him with monetary abundance, and thus capitalism. Cola cannot help but be seduced by the sheer amount of cigarettes. He gives one to about every teenage male he sees, and they follow him to a rendezvous. The scene may shed light on Visconti's scepticism of an economic recovery aided by the United States at the expense of Italian autonomy. In the film, Cola never returns and we have no idea what impact the man with the Lucky Strikes has on the community other than that his presence destabilises the integrity of a family whose roots are deeply steeped in Aci Trezza's local culture.

Without communal support and without the funds to fix his boat, Antonio is forced to go back to the wholesalers. This second to last scene reveals the starkest movement away from reportage, but its affective stylisation helps solidify our spectatorial and ideological stance against the exploitation of fishers. When Antonio is forced to return to the wholesalers' office in search of work, they are villainised on a level of caricature. At the office, Antonio and his brother are greeted by one of them who mockingly quips, 'look who's here! Hunger drives the wolf from its lair.' Inside, the wholesalers laugh endlessly at the pitiless Antonio as they continue to mock him with jokes suggesting the uselessness of communism. Antonio is forced to sign a contract to work on the wholesalers' new fleet that has room for more fishers (and we should assume that it also means that the profits get stretched thin). As the debacle unfolds, the camera places the wholesalers in front of a slightly faded etching of Mussolini's name on the wall. The medium shot gives equal weight to the name and to one of the wholesalers as if to suggest that they were previously supporters of fascism. Hence, Antonio's revolutionary aspirations have amounted to nothing.

Fascism has transitioned into a postwar society in which people are starving and the means of production are still out of the hands of the labourers.

This scene uses decidedly more stylisation and acute awareness of characterization in order to reveal an anti-fascist and pro-communist stance. But instead of reifying escapism and celebrating potentiality, through the wholesaler's excessive malice and through Antonio's failure, we as spectators should realise that injustice could be avoided only if we could stand together in solidarity. Notably, Antonio and his brothers seek work amongst the other fishers when they first lose their boat. The pivotal sequence shows what happens when everyone pulls to their own side and avoids unification. Had the town stood with Antonio, the loss of his boat would have only amplified the unjust conditions under which they all live. Therefore, if all unite and take up arms against the wholesalers, they could collectively maintain a fleet of vessels. Instead, we are left with an understanding that fascist ideology still lingers into postwar Italy. As evidenced in the time lapse between *Ossessione* and *La Terra Trema*, the revolutionary humanism present in early neorealist films quickly gives way to a longing for what could have been and a realisation that fascism did not just decay but also melted into the fabric of a liberal democratic society that was eager to replace one form of control with another in the form of exploitative participation in capitalism.

Garrone's Revision of Mafia Representation in *Gomorra*

One of the many unsettling scenes in *Gomorra*, a bleak, multi-narrative crime film, opens with a medium shot of a boy wearing a bulletproof vest that evidently was not meant for a child. The vest covers his entire torso much like a sack and the dim lighting only reveals three-quarters of his body; the rest is consumed by a dark silhouette. A boy named Luigi (Luigi Caputo), visibly shaken and sweaty, has no choice but to respond when asked, 'Come closer . . . You a tough guy? Show me how tough you are.' The ironic lines are spoken off camera with a tinge of menace. The camera pans left into a closeup of a man's arm pointing a gun at Luigi. That alone is enough to imbue the scene with tension, but it is even more disturbing when the man's face comes into view, revealing O'Lungo (Salvatore Russo), one of the killers from the film's opening scene in which a series of murders occur at a tanning salon. He shoots Luigi at close range, sending him to the floor, sprawled out on his back as if he were already dead. Fortunately, he is not, but the next scene reveals a group of boys waiting in line to face the same fate. Among them is Totò (Salvatore Abbruzzese), the protagonist of one of the six stories that unfolds over the course of the film. When Totò is up, he walks alone toward the camera out of a shadowy expanse into the centre of a space that appears to be part of an abandoned sewer system. The man who approaches him is also in the shadows; the vents from above the sewer provide high-contrast lighting that obscures both of their facades. 'Now you're a man', O'Lungo tells Totò, patting him lightly on the back of his head like the prepubescent boy he actually is. The next scene shows Totò looking into the mirror. When the camera reveals his chest, there is no sign of hair; there is, however, a large bruise where the bullet left a mark. The practice of shooting boys at close range is a rite of passage that cements their affiliation with the Camorra.

With its focus on gun violence and the rise and fall of criminals, *Gomorra* may seem to have more in common with Hollywood and *gialli* gangster films than with Italian neorealism. But the film's attention to Neapolitan regional details, notably the postwar housing project known as '*Le vele*' *di Secondigliano* in the suburbs of Naples, puts it squarely in line with crime films from the neorealist period that have come to be known as *neorealismo nero*. Its wandering camera, non-professional actors, location shooting, and milieu ties it directly to neorealism, a movement rooted in a belief that the images on screen could not have occurred elsewhere in any other historical moment other than Italy. In this section, I demonstrate how *Gomorra* relies on techniques used in neorealism to create a sobering crime film. The film exposes the relationship between the personal and global impact of organised crime and sheds light on the larger social issues of class antagonism and the excess (waste) of global capitalism. Neapolitan particularities serve the purpose of highlighting global tensions that mark the Camorra's sprawling yet fragile network.

It should be noted that the Camorra is not the Mafia, but because of its ubiquity in popular culture, as a genre, mafia films are always in dialogue with all organised crime in Italy. The film attempts to show how invasive and extensive their criminal empire is by weaving together five stories that unfold chronologically in combination with scenes from each of the others. All these stories are foregrounded before the opening credits with a scene that introduces the brutality of the Camorra and the film's reliance on dualities. The film opens within a tanning booth. The intensely bright blue lights and confinement of the camera within the booth suggest the extremity of their criminal lifestyle. In this brief scene, *camorristi* are relaxing, pampering themselves, only to be murdered at close range by a few of their others. There is little lingering on the violence; instead, violence becomes commonplace and on screen appears to be part of their everyday life, de-romanticised and de-fetishised, as is often the case in Hollywood mafia films. Shot in close quarters and culminating with Raffaello's upbeat 2007 pop song 'La nostra storia', the murders forewarn the danger Camorra affiliation poses to the protagonists of the following five stories. The resulting tension that emerges between this bloodbath-turned-epigraph and the slow-pace thereafter sets the unnerving tone for each individual story.

The film's straightforward presentation of five stories loosely linked together creates a narrative structure that defies conventional placement in the canon of mafia films by immersing viewers into the everyday life of those surrounded by organised crime. Opening with Don Ciro's (Gianfelice Imparato) story, the film immediately demonstrates how the Camorra are entrenched in the socio-economic conditions of *Le Vele* and its surroundings. His job is to distribute a stipend to families who have been loyal to the Camorra even though many are serving lengthy jail sentences. Totò's story, introduced above, follows suit. I will expand upon both hereafter as these two seem most intricately connected to each other and to neorealism. Transitioning from children to teenagers, the third story introduces us to Marco and Ciro, two misfits who seem to be a mash-up of cliches and movements. They venerate the fictional Tony Montana (Al Pacino), emulating his bravado and recreating classic sequences from *Scarface* (1983), while their loosely connected exploits contain the episodic whimsy of early French New Wave. Suggesting that Camorra's reach goes beyond the type of crime associated with the mafia, the fourth and fifth stories highlight the tension between legal and illegal economic practises. With its emphasis on corporate toxic waste disposal, the fourth storyline highlights the tension between the imagined gangsters of Hollywood and the unglamorous life of many *camorristi* who have monotonous day jobs. The story introduces viewers to the Camorra's legitimate front with Franco (Toni Servillo) and Roberto (Carmine Paternoster), whose job it is to dispose of toxic waste for Northern Italian corporations that are themselves transnational corporations. Essentially, Franco scours the countryside in search of quarries and other non-urbanised spaces that could serve as toxic dumping sites.

The fifth story, Pasquale's (Salvatore Cantalupo), highlights the impact of globalisation on our conception of Italian culture. In it, Pasquale, an expert tailor, is approached by Xian (Zhang Ronghua), a Chinese factory owner who insists that he 'has to get into haute couture right away'. At first hesitant, Pasquale eventually agrees to teach Xian's employees the intricacies of tailoring haute couture knock-off dresses. But Pasquale has long been employed by a factory owner with ties to the Camorra, and they will not stand for any outside competition, something Xian knows all too well. This character study quickly turns into a crime story when Pasquale has to be transported to the Chinese factory in a trunk because, as Xian reassures him, 'it is best for both of us because it is dangerous.' That danger proves closer than Pasquale and Xian could have imagined when they are ambushed in a drive-by shooting. This story exposes the interconnectedness of consumerism, the Camorra and globalisation.

With Don Ciro's plight as one of Camorra's consiglieri who has no intention of harming anyone, and Totò's coming of age story as a boy forced to plot against his best friend's mother, Garrone upends the notion that all involved in organised crime are the type of criminals that spectators are accustomed to viewing. If the film hints at any lightheartedness, it comes from Don Ciro's ironic interactions with *Le Vele's* tenants. We never see him brandishing a gun or threatening violence. Instead, the residents treat him like a super that cannot provide for the building's tenants. Don Ciro's job is to keep tenants happy (with money), all the while assuaging their concerns or avoiding them entirely. We are first introduced to Don Ciro next to an elderly man who complains that he cannot live on the measly stipend he receives. The exchange is awkward. The man demands more money because he cannot afford to support his family and pay rent on this small stipend. Neither can he work, and he seems to rely entirely on the Camorra, who provide the only monetary safety net to these residents. Upon receiving the same 500 he previously contested, the man grumbles, 'do they know I have served them loyalty for 40 years?', and, 'My wife is in jail.' Next, Don Ciro stops at Maria's house, and what normally would be a quick exchange becomes a domestic scene in which Don Ciro helps Maria deal with the mess resulting from a busted kitchen pipe.

The domesticity of Don Ciro's interactions with Maria seem out of place in a film depleted of warmth. Don Ciro seems not to have a violent bone in his body, which begs the question: how does a man like him end up peddling handouts for the Camorra? The question is best answered by observing the film's five-plot structure. Alone, viewers do not get a sense of how interwoven criminal and non-criminal life is in this region, but together the stories build off each other's new revelations of the Camorra's reach, providing social commentary through observations of loose ends that rely on the entirety of the film's structure for a full understanding of their individual significance. To answer the question from a viewer's perspective, of: *Don Ciro! How could you?*, look no further than the storyline that most clearly underscores the film's neorealist point of view, which also happens to be a child's point of view.

The first storyline after Don Ciro introduces us to a child named Totò. Taking delivery orders from his mom who runs a small corner store within *Le Vele*, he carries the grocery bags out of the tight quarters, and his mom commands, 'hurry up and don't get lost.' The question seems puzzling at first; how could he get lost within an apartment complex? Once he steps out, her command is imbued with maternal concern for his well-being; when sheltered Totò is a boy, but once out in the open, he is exposed to a steady flow of illegal activities. En route to supply Señora Carmela with her day's groceries, Totò runs into his best friend, Simone (Simone Sacchettino). It is hard to tell which of these two boys is younger, but Simone is already projecting masculine tropes he has learned from observing older *camorristi*. Totò greets him and looking back and forth, Simone responds with, 'I'm working . . . They arrested Vitale and Bon Bon.' The neorealist penchant for spontaneity is in full effect here. Framing children with long takes as they wander in and out of spaces that may contain unscripted, or loosely scripted, action can be seen in films such as *The Children are Watching Us/I bambini ci guardano* (1944), *Shoeshine/Sciusià* (1946), *Ladri di biciclette*, and most pointedly, at the end of Rossellini's war trilogy with his transnational classic, *Germany Year Zero/Germania anno zero* (1948).

In *Gomorra*, shaky closeups of a still innocent Totò turn, uncut, into deep-focus shots of busy men and shadowy figures moving to and fro in the background – disconcertedly paired with a cacophony of unrecognisable male voices. The circular motion of the camera's medium shot of Totò coupled with sounds that cannot be located on screen create a dizzying effect that amplifies viewer concern for this boy's well-being. While Totò waits for Señora Carmela to bring back change from the grocery delivery, a film cut finally does happen after he peers over his shoulder. The camera seems to follow his gaze, jumping to a disconcerting scene down below: two men dealing an array of drugs to a group of men below a rusted balcony with outstretched arms. The classic montage sequence switches back to a wide-eyed and pensive Totò who is clearly intrigued, taking it all in with a gaze of curiosity that only a child's face could provide. After finishing his deliveries, the next scene shows Totò on a large blow-up banana in a small above-ground pool atop one of *Le Vele*'s many terraces. As he splashes water on other kids, accentuating his childlike nature, the camera moves up to a man on the lookout for *carabinieri* (Italian law enforcement). It then hovers up to another terrace showing an armed man and further up still, revealing another. The layering here is crucial for spectatorial understanding of childhood in *Le Vele*, and the scene closes with a long shot of the entire complex. Garrone's establishing shot reversal, coupled with a penchant for starting most scenes up close and slowly moving outward, creates a sense of inescapability and speaks to the larger critique of the Camorra's entrenchment in all aspects of society. This technique shows us what Totò is up against and sheds light on Don Ciro's own past. One can only assume that Totò at least has a strong chance of ending up like Don Ciro, or like his imprisoned father, and hopefully not like the many slain men that appear throughout the course of the film. As my introductory comments on this film suggest, he does end up joining the Camorra, in no small part because many of the men who surround him do as well.

Fittingly, the pool scene transitions to the film's most sobering storyline: that of Marco (Marco Macor) and Ciro aka Sweet Pea (Ciro Petrone), two teenagers whose understated murder at the end of the film occurs without any sense of glory, bravado, or heroics as if often the case with mafia cinematic representation. This story is both transnational and didactic because their trajectory unfolds dialectically as the antithesis of the gangster's rise and fall. By not allowing them to achieve success to begin with, Garrone undercuts the glamour associated with mafia films and instead imbues *Gomorra* with fatalism and realism – touchstones of *neorealismo nero*. In their introduction, Marco yells at the top of his lungs in a hula shirt, 'I'm the best! Number one!' He then pulls the trigger of an unloaded handgun. Off screen but in the same room, Ciro responds, 'Go Marco! Who do you think you're dealing with?' Marco continues: 'I'm number one. Tony Montana', as Ciro yells, 'the world is ours', echoing Marco's hubris.

As their re-enactment ends, Marco ad-libs, 'Shit Colombians. They're everywhere.' They are both playing Tony Montana in this ironic recreation of *Scarface's* baroque final scene in which Tony dies, but not before killing swaths of men, alone and armed with an absurd amount of firearms.

The 1983 version of *Scarface* seems somehow void of extradiegetic nativism and here Garrone uses intertextuality to add realism to their storyline. Marco's words echo the type of xenophobic rhetoric that gained traction in the Berlusconi years. There is an odd misstep in representation with Marco and Ciro that could be defined as representational transference that occurs because these teenage boys identify with Tony Montana as if he were Italian, overlooking the fact that Brian De Palma's 1983 adaptation of the original film transfers Tony's nationality to Cuba. Genre tropes and stereotypes clearly impact the cinematic imaginary of these teen boys. In their eyes, Tony has always been Italian, linking him directly to tropes that Hollywood solidified with its 1930s gangster cycle.[10] It is worth shedding light on the lasting impact of Hollywood mafia representation, if only to help us better understand the histrionics of these two unhinged teenagers.[11] Instead of taking place in a decadent Miami mansion, this scene unfolds in a hollowed out mansion that belonged at one point in time to an actual relative of the Camorra, and it was labelled 'Hollywood', replicating the mansion in De Palma's version (Antonello 2011: 382). But here, noir visuals outweigh the gaudiness of classic gangster films as the boys are literally playing in the dark, lit only by hazy light coming in from a broken window. More disturbing still, the boys seem not to be playing when, in the empty jacuzzi, Marco concludes, 'that it has to be all ours now. The whole world, Miami, all of it.'

The film makes a mockery of Marco and Ciro's attempt to become gangsters and suggests the vacuity of a rags-to-riches narrative.[12] In one of the more visually memorable scenes, instead of firing endless rounds at rivals gangs all while keeping immaculate suits intact, the boys strip down to their underwear and fire off rounds into the barren Neapolitan shoreline, in one instance, firing off a grenade launcher that lands on a crumbling shipwreck. The contrast between Marcos' bravado – that money, killing, revenge and girls are the things he likes – and their faux gangsterism renders them cringeworthy. Garonne has succeeded in creating a cautionary tale where others have failed by focusing on representation that has no appeal whatsoever.[13] The rest of their storyline unfolds episodically: they rob black immigrants at gunpoint; they come along a stash of guns (those used when they wreak havoc along the Mediterranean shoreline); they hold up an arcade after running out of coins, and lastly, they are hired in a set-up that leads to their unceremonious demise. Through Marco and Ciro, the tension between real and fake criminals sheds light on the film's tension between noir and neorealism. In the closing shots of the film, the teens, thinking they are the ones performing a hit, get ambushed by Zi' and other *camorristi*.

Ironically, these men who have made it like Tony Montana are nothing more than middle-aged criminals who grumble about needing to take time out of their day to murder the teenagers. Unlike Tony, who never seems to be working, their daily life of crime seems like menial labour and the boys are just one more task to check off. After being ambushed, one of the hitmen complains, 'a lot of time wasted on some snot-nosed kids', as he moves the bodies into a dump truck in sandals. From there the bodies are tossed into the ocean.

The unceremonious nature of Marco and Ciro's execution and disposal immediately calls to mind Franco and Roberto's falling out. As Franco's mentee, Roberto begins to realise that their labour is not confined to quarries and abandoned industrial storage when an old woman offers him a carton of peaches that Franco eventually tosses entirely out the window. After an argument in which Roberto claims to be morally superior to Franco, Franco espouses one of the many criticisms of neoliberal capitalism and the inevitable excesses that world economies produce. Franco justifies his role in the Camorra by stating that he brought them (poor Italians and those not living in urban centres) into Europe and saved them. This line is curious and the film offers no immediate way of contradicting Franco's statement, but it may be interpreted as a suggestion that those who exist outside of urban spaces and outside of the burgeoning consumer class had no economic hope in a neoliberal system that subsumes all means of labour. Their only means of profit is to monetise their land as spaces for corporate waste disposal, which in turn leads to their physical degradation.

Conclusion

The attempt to dislodge neorealism from its potential to discuss life beyond its initial postwar moment by denying certain films a place in the canon is an exercise in teleology that overlooks the strand of *noir* present from the inception of the movement with Visconti's *Ossessione* (1943) that continues beyond the 1940s and 50s. By placing greater emphasis on aesthetics than on periodisation, this chapter begins to address the need to revise critical conceptualisation of national movements. But the use of neorealist aesthetics in a variety of genres and eras deserves further consideration. Notably, *noir* aesthetics pervade a few films by De Santis and Lattuada that resist catagorisation, such as De Santis's *Tragic Pursuit/Caccia tragica* (1947) and *Bitter Rice/Riso amaro* (1949), and Lattuada's *The Bandit/Il bandito* (1949) and *Mafioso* (1959), a dark comedy a presupposes the rise of satire in neo-noir cinema. *Gomorra* is an example of the apotheosis of *neorealismo nero*, an understudied transnational development that explains the rise of realist depictions of organised crime in contemporary Italian cinema. *Neorealismo nero* portrays postwar Italian political and social uncertainty rather than speculating on the possibility of what Italy could become, as is the case in Rossellini's emblematic neorealist drama, *Rome Open*

City/Roma citta àperta (1945).[14] The refusal to recognise the underbelly of our skewed perception of nationhood is what *noir* explores. Films that incorporate a *noir* sensibility demand that we not turn away from the shortcomings of our personal and collective identities. From this perspective, at the first screening of *Ossessione,* Vittorio Mussolini's fabled 'this is not Italy' interruption reifies the very fact that Visconti's tale of betrayal, murder and class antagonism indeed portrays the reality of what Italy would go on to encounter with technological advancements, urbanisation and the transference of fascist practises to capitalist and cultural institutions.

Notes

1. The original script mentions fate, or providence, which suggests a link between noir fatalism and puritanism.
2. Paula Rabinowitz (2002) best explains this mutually beneficial relationship when she states that '*Film noir*, rather than reflecting these changes, in my view, prefigures them, encodes them, and makes them intelligible' (16). Her analysis of *noir* as an embedded facet of American society in *Black & White &* Noir creates a theoretical space to discuss *film noir* by observing the cultural ramifications of its sensibility.
3. I adopt the term *neorealismo nero* from Jennifer Fay and Justus Nieland's *Film Noir: Hard-Boiled Modernity, and the Cultures of Globalization* (2010). Observing the increasing use of *noir* aesthetics in mid-century Italian cinema referred to in the book as 'neorealism *nero*', they state that these films 'dramatised in the noir fashion the crise of displaced persons, returning soldiers, and black markets in Italy's cities' (87).
4. As film historian Carlo Celli (2007) points out in *A New Guide to Italian Cinema*, 1940s postwar Italian Crime films apply introspection to neorealist visuals resulting in, for example, a new application of the long take, a technique used in *film noir* that partly indicates its separation from Hollywood's 1930s gangster cycle (82).
5. Although it exists in other contexts, fatalism is nonetheless a defining feature of *film noir*. I refer to fatalism as an overarching characteristic of a noir sensibility that manifests through various tropes, such as the femme fatale. Fatalism exists in noir's portrayal of insecurity, despair, displacement and doom. We might see fatalism not as a stylistic feature, but as a way of understanding relations within the world of *film noir*: personal relations, communal, or even a character's relationship to space, and time, become part of an affective regime in which power structures and social stability are beyond their reach.
6. In *Class, Crime, and International Film Noir: Globalizing America's Dark Art*, Dennis Broe (2014) explains that many urban industries arose from fascist infrastructure. He connects the Christian Democrats to Italian life under fascism: 'by embracing the *ceti medi*, the petit bourgeoisie, the Milanese class that had helped bring Mussolini to power and that much later brought Italy Berlusconi . . . urged accommodating the wishes of business and fashioned a center-right coalition' (117).

7. The term references Karl Schoonover's (2012) *Brutal Vision: The Neorealist Body in Postwar Italian Cinema* and also implies the affective nature of experiencing neorealist cinema.
8. The practice of dropping prices to increase market share reappears in *Gomorra* vis-à-vis the Camorra's seemingly legal and seemingly legitimate corporate waste management enterprise.
9. This use of crime narratives to focus on reality and not potentiality is why scholars such as Angelo Restiro (2002) in *The Cinema of Economic Miracles: Visuality and Modernization in the Italian Art Form* view Visconti's *Ossessione* not as precursor to neorealism but as a film that indicates the limitations of an aspirational neorealist project, and as a film that begins the dialectical path of *neorealismo nero*.
10. In the first essay for *Mafia Movies: A Reader*, Dana Renga (2011) clarifies the connection between Mafia representation on and off screen: 'With Mafia then, it all comes down to representation; however, with real consequences. Therefore, life imitates art, but only up to a point' (8).
11. In his seminal essay, 'The Gangster as Tragic Hero', Robert Warshow's (1948) conceptualisation of the gangster as an imaginary figure that represents 'what we want to be and what we are afraid to become' establishes one of the most important gangster conventions: a gangster must always be successful/strive for success (584).
12. In *Public Enemies, Public Heroes: Screening the Gangster from Little Caesar to Touch of Evil*, Jonathan Munby (1999) elaborates on this paradox of the gangster film by explaining how an air of censorship produced films in order to 'advance the moral message "crime doesn't pay"', yet inadvertently portrayed glamour (1). Thus, in the inherent drive toward consumerism, audiences registered a different message- crime may not pay off overall, but it sure is tempting. Audiences have always been drawn to make-it-or-break-it narratives, however subversive they may be (the iconic Tony Soprano of the *eponymous* show comes to mind and is arguably referenced in the film).
13. Here, Renga's (2011) assertion that Italian mafia films often focus on peripheral characters whereas Hollywood often highlights major players is crucial in asserting *neorealismo nero's* distinct narration (8).
14. A primary example of the ideological friction between potentiality and reality is evident in the figurative 'openness' at the end of *Rome, Open City* as the children of Italy's rebellion march back into Rome after witnessing the historical and bleak squashing of the rebellion under Nazi-mandated occupation.

Works Cited

Antonello, Pierpaolo. 2011. 'Dispatches from Hell: Matteo Garrone's *Gomorrah*'. In *Mafia Movies: A Reader*. Edited by Dana Renga, 377–385. Toronto: University of Toronto Press.

Bazin, André. 1967. 'An Aesthetic of Reality: Cinematic Realism and the Italian School of Liberation'. In *What is Cinema?*. Vol. 1, 16–40. Translated by Hugh Gray. Berkeley: University of California Press.

Broe, Dennis. 2014. *Class, Crime, and International Film Noir: Globalizing America's Dark Art*. Basingstoke: Palgrave Macmillan.
Celli, Carlo, and Cotinno-Jones, Marga. 2007. *A New Guide to Italian Cinema*. New York: Palgrave Macmillan.
Fay, Jennifer, and Justus Nieland. 2010. '*Film Noir* and the Culture of Internationalism'. In Film Noir, *Hard-Boiled Modernity, and the Cultures of Globalization*, 1–123. New York: Routledge.
Hillier, Jim. 1985. *Cahiers du cinéma – the 1950s: Neo-realism, Hollywood, New Wave*. Cambridge, MA: Harvard University Press.
Marcus, Millicent. 1987. *Italian Film in the Light of Neorealism*. Princeton: Princeton University Press.
Munby, Jonathan. 1999. *Public Enemies, Public Heroes: Screening the Gangster from Little Caesar to Touch of Evil*. Chicago: University of Chicago Press.
Naremore, James. 1998. *More than Night*: Film Noir *in Its Contexts*. Berkeley: University of California Press.
Nicholls, Peter. 2009. *Modernisms: A Literary Guide*. Basingstoke: Palgrave Macmillan.
Rabinowitz, Paula. 2002. *Black & White &* Noir: *America's Pulp Modernism*. New York: Columbia University Press.
Renga, Dana. 2011. 'The Corleones at Home and Abroad'. In *Mafia Movies: A Reader*. Edited by Dana Renga, 3–31. Toronto: University of Toronto Press.
Restiro, Angelo. 2002. *The Cinema of Economic Miracles: Visuality and Modernization in the Italian Art Form*. Durham, NC and London: Duke University Press.
Schoonover, Karl. 2012. *Brutal Vision: the Neorealist Body in Postwar Italian Cinema*. Minneapolis: University of Minnesota Press.
Shiel, Mark. 2006. *Italian Neorealism: Rebuilding the Cinematic City*. London: Wallflower Press.
Warshow, Robert. [1948] 1991. 'The Gangster as Tragic Hero'. In *The Oxford Book of Essays*. Edited by John Gross, 581–6. New York: Oxford University Press.

3. FUNHOUSE NOIR: ESCAPIST EXPRESSIONISM IN SAMUEL KHACHIKIAN'S *DELIRIUM*

Ramin Sadegh Khanjani

To a good number of genre cinema fans to whom pre-revolution Iranian cinema has mostly been swathed in mystery, the mini-retrospective on Samuel Khachikian's films at Il Cinema Ritrovato in 2018, titled 'Tehran Noir', was a thrilling revelation. Although Khachikian's career survived the 1978 revolution and the ensuing sea-changes, even in Iran he was chiefly regarded as a historical figure and his reputation was founded foremost on pictures he made at the peak of his career in the mid-50s to early 60s, the same period on which the 'Tehran Noir' retrospective focused. The eclipse of Khachikian's cinema in later years, however, gives no excuse to understate his instrumental role in formation and evolution of Iranian cinema. He was probably the first Iranian filmmaker who turned the director's name into a recognisable brand, which could draw throngs into the theatre. Most of this was achieved through a group of films that were at the core of a historical cycle of crime films in Iranian cinema of the early 1960s. Indeed, this cycle was instigated by Khachikian's films, the lucrative box-office receipts of which prodded other fellow filmmakers to tread the same territory, although with technically inferior results. In 1963, crime films constituted one-third of output of Iranian cinema (Omid 1995: 352). This phenomenon, however, died off shortly after. New trends forced Khachikian out of his habitual zone into territories that proved damaging to his cinema.

For all their technical bravura – despite shortages of means – and cinematic zest that earned the director popularity and plaudits, Khachikian's crime films have consistently been panned for being removed from the realities of the country – this predominant touchstone of film criticism in Iran – and therefore guilty of an underlying escapism. A review of *Anxiety/Delhoreh* (1962) – one of Khachikian's best achievements, even by director's own admission – for instance goes as far as claiming that the box office returns of Khachikian's film are analogous to the grosses of foreign films since the film, due to its imitative nature, does not qualify as laying the foundation of a national film industry (quoted in Omid 1995: 349).[1] This quality, which can clearly be seen across the career of Khachikian, is probably best exemplified by *Delirium/Sarsam* (1965), a film ending Khachikian's contribution to the abovementioned cycle of crime films on a note of failure (though by no means did it remain his last exercise in the genre). The film's failure at the box office was, in part, a result of an improper release time (Omid 1995: 376) as well as a shift in public taste that heralded a brand-new cycle of light-hearted melodramas dominating the Iranian film market. But it was also attributed to the director's over-reliance on shock effects and a convoluted plot-line often described as shallow, superficial, and overwhelmed by style (Ibid.: 376). This domination of style over so-called 'substance' indeed should be seen as the boon and bane of Khachikian's cinema, laid on thick in *Delirium* by a overweening director believing that his name and signature style are box office sure-fires (Omid 1995: 376). Through a close inspection of *Delirium*, this chapter will underline the essence of the director's style – presented in this film in an amplified form. I will also further illuminate the pedigree of Khachikian's vision of crime films and its influences from international cinema, which went beyond mere plagiarism. I will explicate how, through selective absorption and implementation of elements attributed to film noir, Khachikian forged his own strain of the genre and, via this transnational configuration, expanded the traditional vision of noir.

The critical response to *Delirium* was harsher than Khachikian's earlier crime films. The reviewer in *Setare-ye Cinema*, for instance, lambasted the film as 'a bastard and a doomed film' (quoted in Omid 1995: 376). Probably in view of this, *Delirium* has hardly been studied and received less attention than his preceding crime films. What is notable about *Delirium* is that at its very core lies a mystery in the manner of detective novels. Hence, the visual elements often associated with film noir and present in Khachikian's earlier films are employed herein to boost the excitement and surprise inspired by its serpentine narrative. Khachikian's fascination with mystery, just as his other tendencies cropping up across his output, was apparently going to back to his childhood, when he was taking joy in reading police novels. It was the central mysteries of these novels that enthralled him, even if stories sounded fatuous (Baharlou 2016: 44). The film, befitting its title, is best characterised by its convoluted plot and barrage of mysterious incidents.[2] In fact, a compact blurb like this can hardly do full justice to the film's – at first viewing, at least – puzzling narrative:

A journalist named Shahram Madadpoor (Abdollah Butimar) accidentally learns of the death of his stepbrother, Abdollah, who was involved in illegal affairs. He is then invited to a hotel to meet a guy who introduces himself as Abdollah's neighbour. Handing him deeds to the deceased brother's property and his will, he suggests that flustered Shahram should visit Abdollah's house in the north of the country and scour it for stashed valuables. Driven by professional intuition and personal curiosity, Shahram sets off. En route, he experiences curious incidents including his car being stolen and an attempt on his life. Later, he meets two mysterious ladies, both of whom he suspects of having links to previous incidents. He eventually finds himself in a car with one of them. The drive to his destination alludes to the bloom of a romantic relationship. Arriving on a stormy night, he drops by the gendarmerie station to introduce himself and is warned by the officer in command to stay leery of unexpected developments. From the moment Shahram arrives at the house, the sequence of incidents continue to confuse him. It does not take him long to meet the two ladies once again amidst this mystery-laden landscape and, along the way, learn the truth about the death of his brother.

Owing to the richest vein of his career, Khachikian had been widely seen as an expert in making thrillers, crime and suspense films. Conceivably motivated by the popularity of Hitchcock amongst Iranian critics, Khachikian's films even elicited a comparison between him and the British master of suspense, though Khachikian flatly rejected this by claiming that he had only seen four Hitchcock films (Baharlou 2016: 46). In view of Hitchcock's contribution to American film noir, using 'Tehran Noir' as the title for Khachikian's mini retrospective should be regarded as broadening of this association. Apparently, an association between this specific historical movement and the selected Khachikian's films must have been inspired by similarities in theme of crime, visual style (low-key lighting), and even to some extent costuming. More to validate this analogy is the fact that at least two of Khachikian films – *Faryad-e Nime-shab/Midnight* Cry (1961) and *Osyan/Rebellion* (1966) – were unofficial remakes of American noirs, *Gilda* (Charles Vidor, 1946) and *The Desperate Hours* (William Wyler, 1955), respectively. With a plot likewise organised around a crime, *Delirium* can similarly be seen as extension of Khachikian's experiments in transnational noir.[3]

Coined by French film criticism, 'film noir' has conventionally described a group of American films from the 1940s and early 1950s. Seen by some critics and film historians as a genre, noir has also alternatively been defined as a school, a style or a historical cycle. Whichever the case, there seems to be more agreement as to recurrent elements and features that amount to the essence of film noir. The foremost of them is a visual style that embodies the blackness of the French term: predominance of high-contrast low-key lighting, often accompanied by high and low camera angles and a greater depth of field. The noir visuals are harmonious with their dramatic content; they illustrate a diegetic universe fraught with crime, corruption, deceitfulness and decadence. Enmeshed in this dark and devious network are characters ranging between morally-ambiguous to utterly corrupt, but markedly distinct from the morally upright traditional heroes. The stock characters of film noir such as femme fatales and private eyes have been discursively written about. Oozing with violence, despair and gloom (literally and metaphorically), the world of film noir is also likened to a confusing and unsettling dreamscape – as a result of structure and ordering of the plot – navigated by their lonesome and 'vulnerable' protagonist. In examining Khachikian's film, I will come back to some of these features.

Among other things, the American film noir is often viewed as being closely tied to and reflective of the contemporaneous society. These films are described as presenting a 'perspective' that is 'realistic' and even 'could pass for an excerpt from a documentary' (Borde and Chaumeton 1996: 24). As with many other discussions surrounding this genre, there are arguments to the opposite.[4] All the same, the notion of social relevance of film noirs seem to have gained a wider acceptance, and the argument becomes more robust when it comes to the second phase of the film noir after the end of WWII (Schrader 1996: 55). It is believed that at this phase, film noirs, while maintaining elements of style as their defining feature, remained wed to 'the post-war semi documentary' (Porfirio 199: 77) and, in doing so, 'weld[ed] seemingly contradictory elements into a uniform style' (Schrader 1996: 56). For one thing, this incorporation of realistic impulse manifested itself in taking cameras out of studios and instead shooting in 'realistic exteriors', which ended-up becoming 'a permanent fixture of film noir' (Ibid.: 55).

For all ostensible similarities in overall themes and visual treatment, Khachikian's crime films mark their difference from their presumed models (American noir) in their widely criticised alienation of social realities. This manifest lack of interest on director's part in realities is one reason that Ehsan Khoshbakht, the curator of Khachikian retrospective, invalidates his comparison with Hitchcock (2017: 79). In this regard, *Delirium* outperforms Khachikian's previous crime films, maybe with the exception of *Yek Qadam ta Marg/One Step to Death* (1961), and exhibits the least effort in imbuing its diegetic world with local colour. This made the film a bigger target for the director's detractors. Nevertheless, by the same token, the film more transparently demonstrates the kernel of the director's style, which, despite having the veneer of a crime film, has more profound affinities with fantasy (owing to both incongruity of the depicted world of crime with the daily lived experience and evocation of an eerie mood).

Unlike Khachikian's earlier films, the story of *Delirium*, for the most part is set outside the city, in a country-side mansion. In its departure from setting the story in an urban space, *Delirium* deviates from one major criterion Hamid Reza Sadr identifies in Iranian crime film of that period, which, in his opinion, stemmed from the enforced policy of forming an urban class 'as the social base for the [royal] regime' (2006: 100). Setting *Delirium* in a remote place, engulfed in an air of fear and perturbation, additionally bestows upon film an almost Gothic inflection. The dramatic situation itself has a ring of horror films. Shahram has to stay in the house and witness all mysterious, potentially life-threatening goings-on. This is justified on instructions from the police who claim they have to leave Shahram alone in the house, so that malefactors could be caught red-handed. Notable here is an affinity between this dramatic situation and the premise of a haunted house-style of films, especially those in which a character makes a wager on staying overnight in such houses and experiencing its full terror. The film even seems to exploit this inclination through Shahram's impression of this looming abode as at one point he asserts: 'It's scary. Reminds me of Dracula films', which also appositely adds a layer of reflexivity.

With all mysterious appearances and disappearance, play of shadow and light and taxidermy on display in its main area, the mansion approximates an 'old dark house' which, in true spirit of the 'recognisable mise-en-scene' of a Gothic film, 'destabilise[s] the viewer and convey[s] a sense of seclusion and isolation' (Edwards and Höglund 2018: 3). But remember that Gothic elements were also closely associated with movies from another historical period, which as I will argue would be relevant to this discussion: Weimar cinema. The influence of Weimar cinema, and especially the group of films often designated – even if erroneously – as expressionist films, on American film noir is probably the most discussed and agreed upon genealogical attribute of the latter group of films (Durgnat 1996: 39, Schrader 1996: 56). Porfirio, for instance, refers to Weimar cinema as one of the four main impulses (together with French Poetic Realism, Gangster films and Hard-boiled novels) the convergence of which gave shape to American film noir (Schrader 1996: 77). Janet Bergstrom describes the 'visual language that menaces the characters while it seduces the spectators' as one of the main aspects of the legacy of Weimar cinema channelled into film noir (2014: 38).

In considering a link between Khachikian's cinema and film noir, it would be constructive to pay attention to the director's avowed sources of influence. One particular title he has mentioned in different interviews as having a major impact on him can be put under the rubric of film noir, but one that does not exhibit the conventional iconography of noir. *Spiral Staircase* (Robert Siodmak, 1946) is a film replete with Gothic elements, not least of which is the mansion which – just as *Delirium*, or even more so – hosts most of the film's screen time. Set in the early 20th century, the diegetic world in *Spiral Staircase* – categorised by Raymond Durgnat as a 'plain clothes Gothic' – is a far cry from the contemporary urban settings habitually associated with film noirs (1996: 51).

Attempting to trace Khachikian's film to an older tradition would not seem a far-fetched effort, when we listen to his words of praise for Fritz Lang's

Die Nibelungen (1924) as a definitive influence on him in his childhood years (Baharlou 2016: 26). This might further clarify why, of all films, Khachikian singles out a title that has clear association with the realm of Gothic and indicates it as the film that drove him into making crime films (Saberi 2001: 44). Khachikian's pioneering role, hence, seem to be much indebted to what noir films inherited from German expressionist cinema, a visual style characterised not least by lighting. This is unequivocally acknowledged by Khachikian in one interview in which he maintains that his preference for crime films flows from the fact that they better lend themselves to a creative handling of lighting and 'play of light and shadow' (Saberi 2001: 45). Also relevant here is a note made by Hasan Hosseini about Khachikian's cinema. Citing Khachikian from another interview, he critically points at the director's propensity for ignoring or disrespecting the distinction between horror, thriller and crime films (Hosseini 2021: 137). Nonetheless, this also hints at the fact that Khachikian's obsession with style overrode generic distinction; that is to say Khachikian's vision conflated into a unified territory every genre amenable to his treasured lighting scheme and other stylistic preferences.

The chiaroscuro lighting and expressive style that became a trademark of Weimar films on the international market, to a great extent, served to evoke an unearthly mood and depict a world of fantasy. But one can even claim that the twisted plot of *Delirium* also aligns itself with an 'uncanny feeling of not quite knowing what is going on, a lack of casual logic and stories with twists and turns that double up on themselves' (Elsaesser 2016: 18) as a characteristic element of expressionist films. In *Delirium*, Shahram expresses his bafflement by saying that he feels he is losing his mind, which not only reminds us of the disorientation experienced by film noir protagonists, but also harks further back to the profusion of visions of insanity in Weimar cinema. That said, the whole affair in Khachikian's film turns out at the end to be less complicated than how it appears on the screen and lacks a true *unheimlich* experience that informs some landmarks of German expressionist cinema.

German expressionism is believed to be indebted to Max Reinhardt's stage performances, reputed for their creative signature uses of chiaroscuro lighting, which matched the murky realm of German Romanticism – another major influence on this film school – as well as German sensibilities at large (Eisner 2008: 47, 113). The artistic cross-pollination, as it were, curiously has a parallel in Khachikian's artistic career. Starting up with directing for the stage, Khachikian demonstrated a fascination with expressive use of lights early on in his theatre plays and then carried this fixation into cinema. The way in which Khachikian bridged his theatrical and filmic career makes him stand out from his colleagues pursuing the same path. It was natural for the fledgling Iranian cinema of the 1950s to be highly reliant on theatre talents, including both actors and directors. However, as a consequence of this career transition from theatre to cinema, many films from this period were plagued with theatricality and resembled a recorded stage play, not least owing to that directors' lack of familiarity with the potential of cinema and cinematic tools. Although Khachikian had a background in theatre, he ironically deployed his arsenal of theatrical tools into his film in such a way that it infused the burgeoning cinema with an energy and vitality mostly absent in his peers' films. It can even be argued that Khachikian's theatrical productions were already looking forward to cinema and showed an ambition on his part to work in an art form that could give him a broader scope of working with stylistic elements.

The common denominator of Khachikian's theatrical beginnings and cinematic career is the expressive use of light, which is the same fundamental element of both Weimar expressionist cinema and film noir. Khachikian's desire to employ lighting for dramatic effects is present from the outset of his career in *A Girl from Shiraz/Dokhtari az Shiraz* (1954), even if in an awkwardly obvious and theatrical fashion.[5] It would not be an overstatement to describe lighting as the backbone of Khachikian's directorial style – or at the least that of the praiseworthy portion of his output. He was quoted as expressly saying that he gets inspiration from lighting (Saberi 2001: 46), calling light 'the second actor of cinema' (Ja'fari 1990: 11) and went as far as claiming that 'no other Iranian director has a better understanding of light than me' (Ibid.:10–11). In interviews, Khachikian himself referred to his preferred lighting style as 'crime film lighting' to further reinforce the idea that crime films – as popularised through film noirs – and their atmosphere of suspense have been optimal material for his preferred treatment of light. Khachikian's concept of 'crime film lighting' as he elaborates on by using examples from his own films in which he pivots on using lights that are limited, focused and also mobile (and hence, mutable) (Baharlou 2016: 41).

Across Khachikani's films, lighting can effortlessly be noticed as source of adding a punch and sudden suspense to the scene, often shown in sudden bursts. The simplest example of that could be the commonplace scenes of lightning and storm, which in *Delirium* marks the arrival of Shahram into his destination. Khachikian often uses this concept to suddenly illuminate faces of the characters from below to a grotesque effect. This technique approximates what Naremore terms 'mystery lighting' of film noirs, but also identifies its parentage in older tradition in Gothic stage plays (1998: 173). It also resonates with Lotte Eisner's idea of *Stimung* (mood), which Weimar filmmakers expressed by associating light with 'vibrations of soul' (2008: 199). In a similar spirit, light in Khachikian films appear to be a disquieting element or a source of premonition. In *Delirium*, even the sole presence of light is often meant to inspire frissons. For instance, upon arriving at the presumably vacant mansion, Shahram is surprised to find the lights on, or later he notices light in the window of neighbouring house similarly assumed to be vacant. The expressive use of light together with an animated camerawork – Khachikian himself described camera movement as 'the breath of the mise-scène' (Baharlou 2016: 60) – and in conjunction with dynamic editing – for which he was always responsible – constituted a rhythm he had declared early on to be missing from the works of Iranian directors trained in theatre (Khachikian 1955a: 6). This rhythm, however, often borders on a frenzied quality, which demonstrates itself as Khachikian's signature. This quality leads Hosseini to aptly describe shock effects as the foundation of Khachikian's films and the principle around which every stylistic and narrative element is organised (Hosseini 2021: 131, 136). This is on full display in *Delirium* because its mystery narrative is structured around a constant stream of surprises – resulting from following Shahram's point of view – and cues (false and otherwise) that are delivered as audio-visual shocks. Sudden and quick camera movements, fast zooms or cut-zooms (swift axial cuts) join in to jostle the audience, while the soundtrack – carefully repurposed from foreign films – amplifies the visual punch. It can thus, be argued that this intensified expressivity magnifies the sinister undercurrents of the plot and, in doing so, heightens the uncanny mood.

Additionally, disappearances and reappearances in the plot eventually connect to the notion of coming back from the dead and weave an uncanny feel into the overall mood of the film. This gimmick had been tried by Khachikian in *Anxiety* and apparently his obsession with it persevered as he used it for spinning yarns in *Delirium* and later in *A Man in the Mirror/Mardi dar Ayeneh/* (1992). Though this narrative device alone does not make *Delirium* qualify as a horror, it plants a pseudo-supernatural element at the heart of the film, which thickens in – mostly pictured at night – sets of the mystery-shrouded mansion.[6]

In Khachikian's films, sets are by no means as stylised as those in Weimar cinema (and in that they are closer to film noir). His crime films show a combination of using studio sets and real locations (especially for exteriors). What is interesting about *Delirium* in this respect is the fact that the gestation of the film is tied to its sets; according to Khachikian, he decided to use the sets built for *Escape/Farar* (Abbas Shabaviz, 1963) to shoot another film before it was torn down (Baharlou 2016: 84). In an interview regarding his previous film, *Strike/Zarba* (1964), Khachikian was complaining about limited choices of location in Studio Azhir Film, which resulted in his films looking similar (quoted in Omid 1995: 362). Hence, using new sets must have presented itself as an opportunity to add visual variety to this film, such as the expressive use of houses. However, it is not the first instance of houses in Khachikian films exuding a supernatural feel. The run-down house of *The Storm in Our City/ Tufan dar Shahr-e Ma* (1958) is described by the character as a haunted house, and the mortal fight between the madman at large and the freakish custodian in the opening sequence further solidify this image. In *Delirium*, the director seems to have one gone one step further and transformed the mansion into a veritable spook house.[7] Watching *Escape* – a drama about a fugitive thief who holes up in an apartment and takes the family hostage – one can hardly recognise the sets as being shared with *Delirium*. This can be exemplary of Khachikian's different approach and vision which, through his trademark use of low-key light and dynamic camera, fully transformed the place and, in this way, set it apart from the stagey and drab interiors of other Iranian crime films of the period.

However, unlike expressionist cinema, the fantastic impulse in *Delirium* is bereft of a dark tone. The absence of a dismal worldview is quite unexpected considering the fact that Khachikian's father was a survivor of the Armenian genocide. Indeed, his hair-raising stories of horror and survival captured young Samuel's vivid imagination and, by the director's own admission, later 'charged' him to intensify crime elements of his films (Baharlou 2016: 45). One might then wonder what has resulted in the dilution of this vision. Khoshbakht opines that, by making his films in a cinematic tradition dominated by melodrama, Khachikian allowed this latter genre to amply permeate his cinema (2017: 78). This can partly account for Khachikian's world of crime being painted with lighter, more tender shades.

This altered version of the crime world exhibits itself in the main character of *Delirium* and his exploits. Shahram, the inquisitive reporter, can be described as confused and disoriented facing an 'incoherent world' (Porfirio 1996: 92), just as many central characters in film noir. But, significantly, he is completely stripped of existential angst or moral ambiguity that give film noir protagonists their peculiar flavour. Shahram easily succumbs to feminine charm despite being tipped off by the officer in command and disconcerting string of incidents. Yet, his dalliance, unlike the noir hero, never results in him steering away from the straight and narrow. The perversion of dynamics of film noir also shows itself in presentation of femininity, which is in fact a bifurcated one, divided between two women who are both seductive, but only one of them corresponds to a femme fatale and the other one – Nasrin – ends up coming to the aid of Shahram and eventually reveals herself to be an undercover police detective.

The dalliance between Shahram and Nasrin provides film with a breather and a shift of tone. In fact, the scenes taking place in daytime demonstrate the romantic attraction between the two and provide a temporary break from the director's treasured lighting style. This upbeat romance, in tandem with bursts of comedy, infuse *Delirium* with an air of levity. They push the film away from the dark realm of noir and, together with dilution of reality and a narrative structured on surprise effects, bring it closer to a cartoonish parody of crime mystery noirs such as Tex Avery's *Who Killed Who* (1943). Just as many film noirs (Borde and Chaumeton 1996: 24), the diegetic world of *Delirium* has a dream-like quality to it thanks to its meandering plot, but what is missing is a realistic grounding, a moral ambiguity and an air of gloom that translates itself into a 'mood of pessimism'; this last one is, even in Porfirio's opinion, more essential in qualifying a film as a noir than visual style or a crime story (Ibid.: 80). To cap it all, the film culminates in a jaunty and energetic chase sequence in the broad daylight. As such, *Delirium* exhibits hybridisation of different sources of influence. This quality has been disparagingly highlighted in the review of the film in *Setare-ye Cinema*, which defined the film 'a hotchpotch of thrills and suspense and scuffle and melodrama and sex and pedagogy' (quoted in Omid 1995: 376). *Delirium* therefore, best exemplifies Khoshbakht's description of Khachikian's cinema as a 'recycled' one, based on appropriation and variation (2017: 78), which in effect, gives his films a syncretic quality. Although this quality was already noticeable in films like *Storm in Our City*, unlike the eclectic structure of the former film, various impulses in *Delirium* coalesced into a unified mood.

We can ponder what has caused Khachikian to avoid a realistic presentation in his crime films. The first thing coming to mind could be the infamous censorship, which stringently controlled Iranian films with inordinate stipulations. Not surprisingly, the guidelines – laid down in 1950 and intensified in 1958 – were unsparing on the presentation of crime. According to the guidelines, not only films in which 'the criminal characters do not get punished' (Sadr 2006: 66), but even those with 'scenes that severely disgust, annoy and affect spectators' (Naficy 2011: 186) would be banned. In practice, inasmuch as these stipulations were vague and open to interpretation, it was entirely up to censorship board members to whimsically decide on how films deviate from the guidelines (Ibid.: 186). Khachikian himself had already experienced brushes with censorship. The theatrical run of his comedy, *The Messenger from Paradise/Qased-e Behesht* (1958) was interrupted 5 times on various grounds ('Samuel Khachikian va' 1958: 6) and several scenes of *Storm in Our City* had to change (Omid 1995: 303). This all happened despite Khachikian's lack of interest in politics and efforts to avoid any involvement in it (Ja'fari 1990: 11). Khachikian himself acknowledged the excessive limitation regarding representation of the police in Iranian film, who should not even be shown 'unkempt or how they really were' (Baharlou 2016: 79). The imposed restrictions aside, Khachikian himself had a high opinion of law and the police, even claiming it as one motivation for making crime films and selecting police officers as protagonists (Ja'fari: 14). That said, one still might discern a subversive note in how police are presented in *Delirium*, though one played in a playful and delicate manner. It includes casting Reza Beyk Imanverdi, the actor who was typecast as a fiendish gang-member in Khachikian's previous films, in role of Captain Baharlu, the officer in command.[8] There is also Nasrin, the undercover detective, who not only has a false air of a femme fatale about her, but also engages in a real romantic relation. In both cases, the choices seem to be primarily motivated by an intention to make the audience not trust any character at first blush; yet, the implications are inevitable. This playfulness – together with the fantastical mood – also seems to have given the director some leeway to treat lightly the moral edification that was decreed by legal guidelines and also almost ingrained in Iranian film industry of period. The didactic tone afflicting Khachikian's earlier attempts – *Crossroads of Events/ Chahar-rah-e Havades* (1955) in particular – fades away in *Delirium*, and yet, this avoidance of overt lecturing is far from the moral ambiguity characterising American noirs.

Furthermore, let us not forget that Khachikian belonged to an ethnic and religious minority (Armenian and Christian) that even had an air of foreignness about their lifestyle. As such, Khachikian probably could not fully relate to the dominant social culture.[9] Arby Ovanessian – the avant-garde theatre and film director who is also of Armenian heritage – believes that being alienated from Iranian culture defined a generation of Armenian-Iranian filmmakers – notwithstanding all their pioneering technical contributions to Iranian cinema – to which Khachikian belonged ('Baztab-ha-ye' 2004: 56). In his view, the mood evoked by Khachikian's films is very similar to one experienced in an exclusively Armenian social club in Tehran ('Baztab-ha-ye' 2004: 70). Khachikian himself sounded cognisant of this fact and even put part of the blame on Farsi being his second language, claiming that his Farsi scripts lack the depth of his writings in Armenian (Baharlou 2016: 131). One would hazard to say that in some way the fictional world of crime novels was a more familiar territory to Khachikian than the daily lives of many common Iranian people.

Probably more significant in this respect is the director's own anti-realist tendencies and his inclination towards formalism. In a book-length interview dedicated to an overview of his career, there are multiple assertions pointing at Khachikian's aversion to a realistic representation. For instance, he says: 'In my opinion cinematic imagery should be exaggerated to fit the big screen of cinema; otherwise one can [simply] sit on a chair on the street and observe the real life' (Ibid.: 27). Elsewhere, he remarks: 'I believe that it's better not to approach and touch the reality [. . .] in my opinion, whatever the story demands is real' (Ibid.: 75).

Even though Khachikian did not see himself as a formalist, he emphasised on the significance of form to the cinema saying that 'without a [proper] form cinema would be wanting' (Ibid.: 59). He even perceived his care for the form as the reason for his films being critically described as 'westernised' (Ibid.: 46). He expressly mentioned that the message and the content were secondary to him (Ibid.: 64), and, even while watching films, he was more conscious of their formal structure than storyline (Ibid.: 37). An echo of this can be found in Parviz Sayyad's review of *Strike*, which denigrates the film as 'inhuman cinema' (quoted in Amini 1993: 68), and, given the dominance of form, this could even be extrapolated to all his crime films including *Delirium*. As a result of the characters' lack of depth, the low-key lighting, which in film noirs also underscored 'vulnerability of [. . .] heroes' (Porfirio 1996: 85), mostly operates in Khachikian films as stylistic flourishes. The vulnerability is arguably there in *Delirium* but shorn of a humanistic weight.

The scarcity of the overt signifiers of the realities of life in his society certainly did not cut much of a popular figure of Khachikian for Iranian critics who were searching for a cinema of quality, but one with a distinct national character. Khachikian's crime films were denounced for lack of 'originality and honesty' (quoted in Omid 1995: 349). Originality was something of immense value in Iranian critics' minds, probably due to Iranian cinema's commonplace practices of brazenly lifting from non-Iranian films. Interestingly though, Khachikian himself seemed to have subscribed to the same discourse and joined the chorus of call for originality and films with an Iranian 'spirit' through a prescriptive article serialised in *Setare-ye Cinema* magazine. For instance, in this article, he dismisses the possibility of making cowboy films in Iran altogether because of cowboys not existing there (Khachikian 1955b: 6). Could it be said that his biases towards crime films and their stylistic features were so big that in practice resulted in his films countering his arguments?

Approximating the fantasy of a haunted house, *Delirium* indeed epitomises all these tendencies of Khachikian, that is, love for form and style, laxity with story and a remove from reality. *Delirium* also epitomises the main problem of his cinema which perpetuated itself across his filmography. As Khoshbakht contends, in Khachikian's cinema, a 'plenitude of ideas and dynamism escalates to a level that transforms the film into a runaway roller-coaster' (2017: 82). This sums up the main quality of *Delirium* crystallised in its string of confusing effects that make the film a ne plus ultra of Khachikian's 'shock-effects-based' cinema. Khachikian himself sounded contrite about *Delirium* and described it as one of his 'empty' films (Baharlou 2016: 85), therefore implicitly validating the criticism against him about ignoring social realities (the coveted substance).

That said, to realise how the perception of social relevance could be misguiding, it would be instructive to look at how the preceding *Strike* has been perceived as a better film in Khachikian's career, even a high mark, for its social undertones. The film has even been retrospectively praised for using 'poverty as the main theme' and therefore showing that 'Khachikian has gradually moved away from the abstract world of his previous films' (Amini 1993: 66). Even the characters of *Strike* are described as 'deeper' in their motivations and 'more relatable' (Ibid.: 66). This view of social relevance is quite skin-deep because what Khachikian had essentially done in *Strike* was to pick one trope of Iranian melodrama (love between a poor girl and an affluent boy) previously deployed in his own *A Girl from Shiraz* and use it as a framework for his crime story.

For all the accusations of indulging in fantasy, Khachikian's crime films, like other crime films of that cycle, still have some social resonance. Despite all limitations imposed on them, these films seem to carry an overtone of 'violence and anxiety' marking them as the zeitgeist of the 1960s (Sadr 2006: 99), which could, in turn, explain their reception and popularity with Iranian audiences of the period. This, however, was not of much concern to the apolitical Khachikian who, as *Delirium* demonstrates, was mainly driven by showing off his competency in developing a cinematic form as his signature: a form that was based on repurposing a visual style associated with film noir, just as film noir repurposed stylistic elements of German expressionist cinema.

Reassessing expressionism in cinema, Thomas Elsaesser believes that rather than limiting it to a particular period movement in the history of cinema, the term needs to be viewed as a 'toolbox' (2016: 30) and a 'transferable design' (Ibid.: 35) that lends itself to appropriation in different manners at any given moment in the history of cinema. It seems that Khachikian has been among the notable users of this toolbox for the sake of formal embellishment. Despite having a common premise of criminal activities, Khachikian's films seem to have applied stylistic elements of film noir to erect a façade only partially similar and, in effect, take this toolbox back to limn a fantasy world, but one devoid of darkness and pessimism. In fact, the rosy fantasy – best exemplified by *Delirium* – is in part resulting from elements coming from local traditions (here, popular Iranian melodrama, which was nevertheless similarly scoffed at by Iranian highbrow critics). As such, Khachikian's crime films testify to transferability of the design of expressionism across different periods of history of cinema and national boundaries and demonstrate how it can be interpreted transnationally in unexpected ways.

Notes

1. The transliteration of Persian (Farsi) titles of films, books and articles conforms to the IJMES system, except for the vowel 'اِ' having been transliterated as 'e'. Also, I chose to transliterate the field-specific cognates (like 'cinema') as their English spellings.
2. The missing parts and ellipses in the circulating bootleg copy of the film intensify this quality.
3. Here 'transnational' does not signify the mode of production or circulation. Rather, it has to be construed as transference of foreign genres or styles into a different cultural terrain.
4. Higham and Greenberg, for instance, claim that the world shown in noir films is 'as sealed off from reality as the world of musicals and Paramount sophisticated comedies' (2006: 28). In addition, James Naremore is of the conviction that most celebrated noirs of the 40s are not 'starkly realistic' (1998: 174).
5. A review of the film, for instance, finds fault with the use of light in a scene in which a strong spotlight illuminates the main character and moves with her, while her surrounding is pitch-black ('Dokhtari az Shirāz' 1954: 20).

6. It must be mentioned that Khachikian had dealt with fantasy only in a hybrid and not a pure form (the dream sequence in *Storm in our City* and oneiric trip to the Inferno in the co-directed *A Party in Hell/Shab-neshini dar Jahannam* (1956). Also, despite the fact that Khachikian never made a horror film per se, he edited one of the rare attempts in making an Iranian horror film, *The 29th Night/ Shab-e Bist-o-nohom* (Hamid Rakhshani: 1990). Ironically, during the screening, it was Khachikian's name that was spotlit in advertisements.
7. Khachikian later used once more a country house to stage another story dealing with mysterious murder and disappearances in *The Man in the Mirror*.
8. Later, he went on to become one of most popular superstars of Iranian films, cast almost exclusively as protagonists.
9. To reify this point, Hosseini refers to the fact that Khachikian, unlike many Iranian families of that period who used to dine sitting on the floor, always ate at a table (something which was viewed as a Western habit) (2021: 137).

Works Cited

Amini, Ahmad. 1993. *Sad Film-e Tarikh-e Cinema-ye Iran*. Tehran: Moassese-ye Farhangi Honari-e Sheyda.

Baharlou, Abbas. 2016. *Parvande-ye Yek Jenayi-saz: Samuel Khachikian*. Tehran: Nashr-e Ghatreh.

'Baztab-ha-ye Farhang-e Armani Dar Cinema-ye Iran: Goft-o-guyi ba Hozur-e Arby Ovanessian, Zaven Qukasian va Robert Safarian'. 2004. In *Aramane Va Cinema-ye Iran*, 34–73. Tehran: Muze-ye Cinema-ye Iran.

Bergstrom, Janet. 2014. 'Warning Shadows: German Expressionism and American Film Noir'. In *Film Noir*, 38–57. Edited by Homer Pettey and R. Barton Palmer. Edinburgh: Edinburgh University Press.

Borde, Raymond and Etienne Chaumeton. 1996. 'Towards a Definition of Film Noir'. In *Film Noir Reader*, 17–25. Edited by Alain Silver and James Ursini. New York: Limelight Editions.

'Dokhtari az Shiraz'. 1954. *Setare-ye Cinema*, 9 June 1954.

Durgnat, Raymond. 1996. 'Paint It Black: The Family Tree of Film Noir'. In *Film Noir Reader*, 37–51. Edited by Alain Silver and James Ursini. New York: Limelight Editions.

Edwards, Justin D. and Johan Höglund. 2018. 'Introduction: International B-Movie Gothic'. In *B-Movie Gothic: International Perspectives*, 1–14. Edited by Justin D. Edwards and Johan Höglund. Edinburgh: Edinburgh University Press.

Eisner, Lotte. 2008. *The Haunted Screen*. Berkeley: University of California Press.

Elsaesser, Thomas. 2016. 'Expressionist Cinema – Style and Design in Film History'. In *Expressionism in the* Cinema, 15–40. Edited by Olaf Brill and Gary D. Rhodes. Edinburgh: Edinburgh University Press.

Higham, Charles and Joel Greenberg. 1996. 'Noir Cinema'. In *Film Noir Reader*, 27–35. Edited by Alain Silver and James Ursini. New York: Limelight Editions.

Hosseini, Hasan. 2021. *Rahnama-ye Film-e Cinema-ye Iran*. Tehran: Rowzaneh-kar.

Ja'fari, Mohammad. 1990'. Bu-ye Chamanzar va Seda-ye Ab Elhambakhsh-e Kargardan-e Film-ha-ye Jenayi: Goft-o-gu ba Samuel Khachikian'. *Mahname-ye Cinemayi-e Film*, July 1990.
Khachikian, Samuel. 1955a. 'Cheguneh Mitavan Navaqes-e Film-ha-ye Farsi Ra Raf' Kard: Qesmat-e Sevom'. *Setare-ye Cinema*, 21 January 1955.
Khachikian, Samuel. 1955b. 'Chegooneh Mitavan Navaqes-e Film-haye Farsi Ra Raf' Kard: Qesmat-e Haftom'. *Setare-ye Cinema*, 27 April 1955.
Khoshbakht, Ehsan. 2017. 'Tehran Noir: Thriller-ha-ye Samuel Khachikian'. *Mahname-ye Cinemayi-e Film*, September 2017.
Naficy, Hamid. 2011. *A Social History of Iranian Cinema. Volume 2.* Durham, NC: Duke University Press.
Naremore, James. 1998. *More than Night: Film Noir in Its Contexts.* Berkeley: University of California Press.
Omid, Jamal. 1995. *Tarikh-e Cinema-ye Iran.* Tehran: Rowzaneh.
Porfirio, Robert G. 1996. 'No Way Out: Existential Motifs in Film Noir'. In *Film Noir Reader*, 77–93. Edited by Alain Silver and James Ursini. New York: Limelight Editions.
Saberi, Iraj. 2001. 'Khodahafez Samuel: Goft-o-guyi Montasher-nashodeh ba Samuel Khachikian'. *Mahname-ye Cinemayi-e Film*, November 2001.
Sadr, Hamid Reza. 2006. *Iranian Cinema: A Political History.* London: I. B. Tauris.
'Samuel Khachikian va *Qased-e Behesht*'. 1958. *Setare-ye Cinema*, 23 November 1958.
Schrader, Paul. 1996. 'Notes on Film Noir'. In *Film Noir Reader*, 53–63. Edited by Alain Silver and James Ursini. New York: Limelight Editions.

SECTION II

TRANSGRESSION

Part I
On the Boundaries of Nation and Ideology: Criminal Heroes at the Discursive Limits of Genre, Gender and the Body

4. CRIME WITHOUT BORDERS: MARGINALITY AND TRANSNATIONAL POWER IN JACQUES AUDIARD'S *UN PROPHÈTE*

Julianna Blair Watson

INTRODUCTION

In Jacques Audiard's 2009 film *Un prophète*, Malik El Djebena (Tahar Rahim), the Franco-Arabic protagonist, is sentenced to six years in prison for attacking police officers. Once there, he is forced to murder an Arab-Muslim inmate, Reyeb, for the prison's Corsican mafia leader, César Luciani (Niels Arestrup).[1] Malik is literally told to kill Reyeb or be killed. Once the deed is done, he comes under César's protection and begins working for the Corsicans – a group who are French citizens, but largely marginalised in France – who use and abuse Malik. Although protected by them, the Corsicans relegate Malik to the metaphorical edges of their world, othering him just as his association with them makes him an 'other' to and isolates him from the Arab-Muslim prison gangs. Yet at the same time, Malik uses the prison to learn how to be a 'better' criminal so that upon his release from prison in the film's end, he undoes the Corsican faction and emerges a powerful gangster.

Malik's trajectory – he enters prison a weak and petty (ethnically coded) criminal but emerges an organised crime boss – is perhaps in itself not such an unfamiliar story. Many French critics have likened it to *The Godfather* and even more so to De Palma's *Scarface*. The only real critique of *Un prophète* when it was released was that this film made Malik a 'hero' or a 'model', especially for the male youth in France's stigmatised banlieues, much like *Scarface*'s Tony Montana is for these young men (Durand-Souffland 2010, np).[2] Unlike Tony Montana and other classic gangster stories, though, Malik never learns the 'moralistic lesson . . . [that] crime doesn't pay' (Langford 2005: 21, 138).[3] So what makes Malik different from these other criminal anti-heroes? The answer lies in how he ascends to power, which is, ironically, what initially makes him an easier target for the Corsicans. Malik lives in a France in which people of Arabic descent generally occupy the periphery and are, thus, excluded socially and politically from belonging to the nation.[4] It is Malik's very marginality, to which both French society and the other prisoners relegate him, that allows him to cross metaphorical borders in the pursuit of power. Added to his various exclusions is Malik's own uncertainty as to his origins: Audiard, in fact, intended to deliberately obscure Malik's background (Busch 2015: n.p.), which only serves to further prevent Malik from any clear belonging.[5] Malik's ambiguous and obscured identity, his lack of categorical identification, helps him subvert the structures of (Corsican/French) domination to which he was subject and manipulate within and across these linguistic, cultural, ethnic and national borders to secretly build a transnational criminal enterprise. Malik's marginality, linked as inextricably as it is to his ambiguous ethnicity and fluidity within and across nations, cultures and languages, then introduces fault lines into the binary between the 'integrated' French nation and its outside.

In making *Un prophète*, Audiard used prison as a general metaphor for society (Kaganski 2009 : n.p.). The metaphor, as I read it more specifically, interrogates the continued marginalisation of France's immigrants and populations of colour – as they tend to overlap in the French imaginary – and the few strategies available to them to find a path, not just to survive, but to thrive in a society that pushes them farther away from the centre. In *Un prophète*, Malik's strategy is problematically linked to criminality but nonetheless suggests that a viable strategy requires a thinking outside of borders in any previously conceived sense. Malik's criminality, while literal in the film, is read here as a metaphor that represents a resistance to French authority that denies him a place in society. The metaphor extends to the film's Corsicans: although marginalised themselves by French society, in their treatment of Malik, Audiard's Corsicans represent an iteration of the French nation-state structure that pushes othered populations further away from the centre. Malik takes advantage of his peripheral position to establish criminal networks with other groups on the margins in France – the Muslims, Arabic, black and what the film calls 'gitan (gypsy, likely Roma)' populations, and even the Corsicans to a lesser extent – to become the head of his own operation. Malik pivots, thus, along what diaspora studies scholar Avtar Brah calls 'intersecting loci' of dominated and dominating (Brah 1996: 125) in order to deftly manoeuvre the space of the prison and create a criminal space that moves across, within, and outside of – and thereby undoes – the centre/periphery dichotomy.

In the introduction to their edited volume on transnationalism, Ato Quayson and Girish Daswani note that this concept supersedes – transcends – the borders of the closely related concept of diaspora (Quayson and Daswani 2013: 4). Quayson and Daswani further highlight that transnationalism also exceeds and transcends borders, rendering them 'irrelevant', as transnationalism and its communities, unlike those of diaspora – defined by Avtar Brah as a dispersion from a centre with a 'settling down elsewhere' (Brah 1996: 181) – can be based on what they call an 'elective identity:'

> transnational communities . . . may not be derived primarily or indeed exclusively from the forms of co-ethnic and cultural identification that are constitutive of diasporas, but rather from elective modes of identification. All such groups come to share strongly held objectives and communal values that are nonetheless quite different from the co-ethnic identifications that are taken to define diasporas. (Quayson and Daswani 2013, 4–5)

Malik's transnational community centres around an elective identity dependent upon, problematically, criminal objectives and values – drug dealing, smuggling, illegal gambling, kidnapping, and murder – that not just transcends, but transgresses borders.[6] As his marginalisation becomes tied to criminality, Malik is able to circumvent and transcend borders, embodying, thus, a transnational criminal, not just in that he engages with criminals from multiple national backgrounds, but also in that he himself engages with multiple national and ethnic identities: he is seemingly French of Maghrebin, that is, North African, origins – he is both French and not, Maghrebi and not.[7] But in the French nation, there is no room for multiple national identities, you are French and nothing else.[8] Malik's lack of clear national belonging disturbs, thus, the French nation-state by operating outside of their strict conception of borders and belonging. In other words, thanks to his transnational criminality, Malik navigates within and across, circumnavigates – and thereby undoes – juridical, national, linguistic, ethnic and cultural borders. Malik transcends the traditional notion of the periphery to become, in the end, a pivotal, central, axis upon which turns a transnational criminal enterprise.

Marginalisation and Dis-integration in the Nation

Marginalised protagonists who engage in crime are not so unfamiliar in Audiard's cinema.[9] In 2015, Audiard won the Palme d'Or for his film *Dheepan* in which a group of Sri Lankan immigrants – unknown to each other but posing as a family – flee a civil war only to land, undocumented, in a French banlieue, which becomes a territory just as – if not more – hostile as the one they fled. The titular character Dheepan, just like Malik, differs from the traditional Audiardian hero on the periphery: the two are Audiard's only ethnically coded protagonists, an ethnic coding that automatically places them even farther on the edges of French society. While *Dheepan* features a Sri Lankan Tamil protagonist, who flees a civil war under false papers and lives on the margins in a Parisian banlieue, his similarities with Malik largely stop there. Apart from the undocumented nature of his immigration, Dheepan flees any criminal association or behaviour. It is only at the film's end, when Dheepan's fake 'wife' – with whom he has developed a real relationship in the meantime – is threatened, that Dheepan resorts to a murderous violence to protect his now real loved ones. Further, Dheepan could embody a transnationality through his act of immigration and through his mere presence on French soil. Yet, because he retains deep ties to Sri Lankan communities in France, to the Tamil language and thus to his roots, Dheepan is more representative of the Sri Lankan diaspora than of transnationalism as Quayson and Daswani intend it. Malik, however, has no clear origins or belonging and does not embrace any ethnic, national or cultural identity, except for that of criminality, one which he adopts willingly and eagerly. Malik's criminal identity manifests a different type of transnationality through virtue of its transgression of borders in order to amass more power for criminal ends.

In his work on camps, encampments, and ghettos, Michel Agier makes the connection between 'hors-la-loi' and 'hors-lieux' (Agier 2013: 83), that is, those who are 'outlaws' are also outside, denied, (the centre) spaces to which the rest of society has access. Although he works principally on the space of the refugee camp, he includes the prison among those spaces similar to the camp as characterised by hostility, violence, rejection, and racism (Ibid.: 31–37). Agier cites Foucault's description of 'spaces outside of all space, 'noting three common traits: extraterritoriality, exception, and exclusion' (Ibid.: 66–67). The vulnerable and isolated Malik lives in what Agier calls the simultaneous confinement and extraterritoriality – outlawed – space of the prison, that is, outside spaces delimited by borders. The prison is, thus, a space typically already on the margins; yet, in this already peripheral space, Malik is relegated even further outside a centre: he is othered by the two principal prison gangs – the Corsicans and the Arab-Muslims. Malik, already excluded by society, becomes doubly excluded in prison.

As to the Corsicans – represented in the film as political prisoners – they are peripheral within France as their small Mediterranean island puts them apart from mainland France and in the national imaginary are not considered as French as those on the mainland. They are both French and not. They are French citizens, but there are some who have been fighting for independence and the right to a separate language, one that sounds closer to Italian than French.[10] The Corsicans, in a way therefore, marginalise themselves from greater French society through their separatist, nationalist movement. Their desire to be outliers of the French nation, indicates an equal desire to become their own nation, their own centre and their own outsiders even as France treats them as such.[11] *Un prophète*'s Corsicans create their own centre within the confined space of the prison to counter the social peripheralization by the French nation but still generate their own periphery and exclusions.

Integration, while linked inextricably with the French notion of 'one and indivisible' – where the French Republican model of 'political unity' does not allow for 'distinct ethnic or cultural minorities' (Favell 1998: 70) – has largely been understood in ethnic terms. This association of integration with ethnicity has led scholars from a variety of fields to criticise the French integration policy as one that inherently leads to a *disintegration* of the 'social fabric of the lower sections of French society: in particular, its connection to racism' (Favell 1998: 186–187). In other words, the popular imagination holds that, racially speaking, any 'visible minorities' cannot be fully integrated into French society.[12] The Corsicans' marginality within French society does not prevent them from acting as France does towards its 'visible minorities', treating Malik as the ethnic object whom they use for their menial tasks, whom they push him to the periphery of their centre. The gang members talk about Malik in front of him in Corsican, but he still understands certain words such as 'Arab'. They tell Malik in French that his job is to 'fais l'Arabe [to do the Arab work, subtitled as the 'shit work']' that is, to clean up after and serve them; they consider him an outsider, an outlier, one who does not belong. In what is a potent visualization of Malik's disintegration, the Corsican gang files one after another past a guard, and as they each tell him their last name, we hear 'Luciani, Vittori, Santi, Corleone . . .' and lastly, we hear Malik say 'El Djebena'. Not only does he literally come last, but this position, combined with the stark contrast in surnames reinforce Malik's more isolated, liminal position. Yet, Malik will take this imposed dis-integration and societal exclusion and turn it on its head to accrue his own power and push those who have been in the centre to the periphery while becoming the locus of a multi-ethnic, multi-peripheral crime syndicate.

Incarceration and Immobility on the Margins

In one of the first shots of *Un prophète*, an iris opens on Malik's handcuffed hands as if to suggest an even tighter, more restricted space around this young man. Once Malik has arrived in prison, he must strip naked to be searched for contraband. In a wide shot, the audience sees him stand on an 'X' as he lifts first one foot, then the other upon the guard's orders. The film's early sequence establishes a very corporeal immobility for Malik; in the already freedom-limiting space of the prison, the French nation owns his body's movements. Similarly, in her article on the film when she notes that the prison officials throw out Malik's threadbare shoes, Megan C. MacDonald claims, 'Malik's relationship to the ground is marked as rotten, according to the guards . . .

This limited mobility is compromised from the start' (MacDonald 2012: 566).[13] Malik's immobility marks him with literal isolation from the film's beginning: once newly dressed with prison-provided tennis shoes, he is framed alone in the courtyard while other inmates are grouped together, inmates who quickly rob him of his new shoes.

At the same time, Malik's spatial and social marginality is confounded and compounded by his own uncertainty about his identity and his origins: when a prison official asks Malik whether he spoke French or Arabic with his parents, he says he does not know and when asked which of the two was his first language, Malik's response is 'Les deux [both].'[14] He is equally unsure of any religious or ethnic affiliation; when asked 'Vous êtes pratiquant? [Are you religious]', Malik's response is a simple 'Quoi? [What?]' The prison official specifies: 'Votre religion . . . vous avez un régime alimentaire spécifique ? . . . – Non, rien de spécial . . . – Vous mangez du porc ? . . . Non, euh oui. [Your religion . . . any dietary requirements? – Nothing unusual . . . – Do you eat pork? . . . No. Yeah]'. Malik does not even understand what is being asked of him here; he may speak Arabic but the Muslim religion or an Arabic association are not actively part of Malik's identity.

Problematically though, when Ginette Vincendeau asked Audiard about perpetuating the stereotype of Arabs as criminals, his response is, as she rightly notes, somewhat evasive in that he claims he was 'careful to define him at the outset not as an Arab, but as a vagrant' (Vincendeau 2009: 20). Audiard both does and does not do this, in particular in that the Corsicans and Arab-Muslim gangs both assume that Malik has Maghrebin origins and that he likely comes from one of the three North African countries – all former French colonies – of Tunisia, Morocco, Algeria, although it is never clearly stated which country or if he in fact comes from the larger Francophone Arab diaspora. His lack of a self-identification or clear belonging to any particular language, nation, ethnic group, or religion (read Islamic) certainly contributes to blurred origins. Yet, in his first sequence, Malik code-switches between French and Arabic with his lawyer and Malik's – and the film's – first fully audible dialogic words are in Arabic. As Malik and his lawyer continue speaking, the two men seamlessly mix the two languages: 'C'est du darahim? – C'est du darahim pour moi [It's money? – It's money for me]'('Darahim' is a reference to Arabic currency).[15] Even from his first appearance in the film and arrival in prison, Malik inhabits, and is both inside and outside, two languages, multiple cultures and nations, both France and an indeterminate North African country or the larger Francophone Arab diaspora.

Although Malik does not identify as any particular nationality or ethnicity, prisoners and authorities alike view Malik as Arabic. When César and his gang are looking for a 'frère (brother)' of the Arab-Muslim inmates to kill Reyeb, they approach Malik, and when Malik first approaches Reyeb, Reyeb assumes

Malik speaks Arabic. Everyone but Malik identifies him then as being of Arabic descent, based first and foremost upon what Avtar Brah calls 'the look': 'For some, identity is inscribed on the body and out of a plethora of identities, usually the one associated with the "look" is prioritized by those looking at the body' (Brah 1996: 3). Malik's body is therefore already inscribed by outside forces with a marginalised ethnicity, one which others see but one which he neither claims nor seeks to flaunt nor hide. Yet, Malik's belonging remains unclear even after he comes under Corsican protection. At one point, César wants Malik to ask a favour of the Arab-Muslim gang because César believes they will better negotiate with him because of an association with Arabic. Malik is doubtful though because he says, 'pour eux, je suis Corse [for them, I'm Corsican]'. Being othered by the two major groups within the prison – who are themselves othered by the French nation-state -, Malik belongs to both, and yet, neither group. Through the triple exclusion (he is neither French, nor Corsican, nor Arab) and his own uncertainty, Malik is nothing, and being nothing, he can, at will, be anything.

Transnationalism and Diaspora Power

The Corsicans' reproduction of the structures of the French state become manifest from their first appearance through the trope of surveillance.[16] The film's first shot of the Corsicans shows them looking, surveilling, down into the yard; they see and know all in a Foucauldian-like panopticon. Malik learns of their all-seeing, all-knowing power when he tries to speak to the warden, ostensibly to avoid having to commit the murder assigned to him. Yet, it is not the warden, but the Corsicans, who come to his door. They throw a plastic bag over his head as they say, 'L'administration, c'est nous aussi [We are also the administration]'. Their violent omnipotence puts Malik in the dominated position as they limit his actions and force him to go only where they want him to, to commit murder. Later in the film, Malik is allowed to leave the prison, thanks to César's machinations, for 12-hour permission days. As he repeatedly steps outside, the camera frames him in a medium shot. His legs and feet, unseen in these repeated shots, underscore that his movements, and his body are controlled by others, by outside forces; his mobility, ability to move as, where, and when he pleases remains under César's and the Corsicans' control to some extent.

Yet, the Corsicans' belief in their own omnipotence is part of what enables Malik's betrayal. After Malik hears '[dirty] Arab' in Corsican, the audience hears Malik repeat the phrase as the camera cuts to Malik alone in his room with a French to Corsican dictionary. Unbeknownst to the Corsicans, and in part because they pushed him to the edges of their group, Malik teaches himself Corsican. Yet, when Malik tells César he understands Corsican, although angered at first, César tells him that he is to observe the other Corsicans for any potential treachery: 'Tu seras mes yeux, mes oreilles. Tu les surveilles [You will be my eyes, my ears. You watch them]'. Malik is then able to listen in moments of what I call linguistic clandestinity: he uses the marginal position to which he has been relegated against the group to secretly listen to them even while openly in their presence. Malik flips then the panopticon on its head; he subverts and perverts it, in that he engages in secret surveillance out in the open in what is more of a pan-*auditoricon*, where he can hear – and understand – all without the speaker's knowledge.

In a semi-Foucauldian echo, Avtar Brah notes that power exists both within and across diasporas: 'power is performatively constituted, and both dominated and dominating come about through "multiple, intersecting loci of power"' (Brah 1996: 125, 183). Power, position, and subjectivity are always shifting in a space occupied by different diasporas, shifts that are only further complicated and entangled when criminality is introduced into the mix. The various marginalised criminal groups – Corsicans, North Africans, black, Roma – occupy various positions of power along what Brah calls the 'multi-axiality of power' (Ibid.: 189), with both minorities and majorities shifting positions dependent upon the axis. Malik sits at the locus of this multi-axiality, shifting between minority and majority positions, as he slowly accrues enough power to become the locus of a multi-ethnic, multi-diasporic transnational criminality. Malik finds himself then, in a way, swinging along Brah's diasporic 'multi-axiality of power', on the border between two panopticons, one in which he is dominated, object of power – 'Arab' to the Corsicans – and the other in which he is dominating, exerting secret power through his multi-lingualism, now the clandestine watcher (listener) of the Corsicans. Thanks to his successful manipulation, pivoting as it were, of his peripheral position and linguistic adeptness, he begins to accrue power, which he will use to fight his way out of, across, the periphery to create his own axis of power.

Malik is able to secure his power grab through another linguistic transgression. Near the film's end, César tasks Malik with killing his traitor, and Malik's friend Ryad comes to visit him. César enters the holding room where Malik and Ryad are talking. Malik, deciding what move to make, speaks to Ryad in Arabic to inform him of the plan to undo the Corsican faction. Malik is now the one able to speak openly without concern of being understood. Here, Malik's use of Arabic, a language normally on the margins of French society, pushes the French-speaker to the edges of the conversation, the dominating language has become dominated. Malik's translingual and transcultural obscured identity is undoing the peripheral position put upon him by the French nation. Shortly thereafter, César is framed alone on a bench as Malik looks down on César from an indoor stairway, mirroring the image of the Corsicans watching at the film's beginning. Malik is now the one watching, the one with more power to see and know.

This does not become clear to César, however, until after Malik has staged his coup: César is once again framed alone a bench, as the Arab-Muslims walk into the yard, Malik among them. César nods to Malik to join him and as Malik does not move. As César tries to approach Malik, Malik whispers something in Arabic to another prisoner, two of the Arab-Muslims walk over, and knock César to the ground, who then gets up and goes back to his bench alone. Malik has firmly secured himself along the dominating axis of power while forcing César and the Corsicans onto that of the dominated. Malik's fluidity in language and code-switching between Arabic, French, and Corsican here indicates his ability to navigate and simultaneously engage multiple languages, nations and cultures. Through Malik, the film underlines then an ability that inversely mirrors contemporary France's inability to do the same. The Corsicans, as substitutes for the French nation-state, remain enclosed in a hermetic world and through this exclusion of those they treat as others they lose power. Malik, on the other hand, transcends borders of all kinds, enabling him to take that power from the Corsicans (France) precisely because he does not, will not, exclude.

A Criminal Undoing of Borders

What best enables Malik to begin to work within and across these groups' 'borders' is his own lack of 'fixed originary absolutes' (Brah 1996: 196), that is, a resistance to clear ethnic, linguistic, or national identification. Malik's identity, because it lacks clear or fixed origins and can change from one moment to the next, from one context, language, culture to another, is able to become a new locus around which assemble so many peripheries. Yet, Malik is not interested in identifying with one group or another out of any ethnic, linguistic, national, or racial affiliation, but, as he says more than once, he forges alliances based on what he can get out of it. Malik may join forces with the Arab-Muslim group in the end, but the audience is given to believe that the latter is a group of devout religious men, while Malik, perhaps – likely – from the same region, has no such affiliation. When Malik's friend on the outside, Ryad, is abducted by Latif 'L'Égyptien' as retaliation for some drug business going wrong, Malik engages the help of Jordi, whom the film calls a 'gitan (gypsy, likely Roma)', on the inside and enlists the help of the Arab-Muslim gang and their connections on the outside to secure Ryad's release. When Ryad later wants to kill Latif 'L'Egyptien' as revenge for kidnapping him, Malik says that is for later, for now they will conduct drug business with him. While Malik is still pivoting along the axis between dominated (by César) and dominator, his decision here – one which Ryad begrudgingly obeys – shows his clever working across cultures, languages, national backgrounds to achieve his criminal ends.

Malik then succeeds in building his own criminal enterprise through establishing relationships with other diasporic figures within and outside of the prison. He begins drug deals and a partnership with Ryad, Jordi and Latif 'L'Egyptien', the only somewhat prominent black character in the film. Ryad, like the Arabic-Muslim gang, is presumably, though never clearly stated, of North African descent, just as Jordi the 'gitan [gypsy]', is likely but not definitively Roma, and Latif 'L'Egyptien' may or may not be from Egypt or from the Francophone Sub-Saharan African diaspora. Malik's lack of clear origins become a microcosmic reflection for all of the those represented in the film and treated by French society as 'visible minorities'. These men come to embody various individual diasporas, which 'of whatever character, must not be perceived as a discrete entity but rather as being formed out of a series of contradictory convergences of people, ideas, and even cultural orientations' (Quayson and Daswani 2013: 4); their own mixed, vague nature enables them to assemble around Malik's growing power axis. With the exception of the Corsicans, where each of these men are from is never stated explicitly, they could be from any of these places, none, or all of them at once. Little by little, Malik manoeuvres then not just across linguistic lines, from Corsican to French to Arabic, but across ethnic, religious, and national lines that begin to undo these very borders. The combined non-distinctive, implicit, contradictory nature of the various diasporas and marginalised ethnic groups facilitate these criminals' collective power to transcend the borders and exclusions imposed by the French nation-state.

Malik works not just from his own marginality but within and across other marginalities to produce this transnational crime syndicate that transcends, transgresses – and thereby undoes – juridical, linguistic, national, cultural and ethnic boundaries. Malik finds himself more than just pivoting along this axis of power but becomes the pivotal locus himself, his criminality being both the mechanism for and result of crossing 'borders'. He becomes the hinge, the moving axis, upon which these other groups criminally assemble as Corsicans, Maghrebis, Roma and black diasporic characters are all working together under him: 'His real tomorrow is slyly suggested through black limousines that follow . . . united behind him in a new enlarged multi-ethnic, interracial conglomerate, a business empire in the making' (Radovic 2010: 20). Malik's transnational criminal community is, together, their own centre, one comprised of a composite of peripheries that operates within but also without, outside, the traditional centre/periphery dichotomy as their transnationalism renders irrelevant this very distinction. Malik's axis power will not be an iteration of the Corsican one – itself a repetition, reproduction of the French nation. Rather, through his central position upon which pivot multiple ethnicities, nations and languages, Malik represents a transnational hinge that no longer operates in terms of centre and periphery, in which multiple (former) peripheries work outside the social, ethnic, and political borders imposed by the nation. In the film's final sequence, Malik is being released for good after he orchestrated César's downfall by not killing César's rival as requested but manipulating the rival so that the Corsicans 'se bouffent entre eux [kill each other]'. As he steps out of the prison's walls for the last time, Audiard cuts to Malik's feet, isolated in the shot. Framed in a close up, Malik takes first one step then the other, as Audiard emphasises Malik's new mobility through his position as the linchpin of a transnational, multi-ethnic criminal syndicate where the mobility-limiting centre no longer has any power over his movements.

Conclusion

Upon the release of *Dheepan* in 2015, French film critic Stéphane Delorme excoriated Audiard for the film, claiming that Audiard fails to engage in political cinema because he treats minorities as such, as minorities: 'La politique commence quand on arrête de s'intéresser aux familles, aux communautés, aux minorités en tant que telles, mais qu'on s'intéresse à tous [Politics begin when we stop taking an interest in families, communities, minorities as such, but take an interest in everyone]' (Delorme 2015: 13). Perhaps Delorme has a point. But leaving aside the potential problem that his argument could contribute to minority invisibility, to a whitewashing in French cinema, *Un prophète* highlights the ways in which the French state and society continue to treat its minorities, its diasporic subjects, 'en tant que telles [as such]', apart from other communities. Yet, as its critique in *Les inRocks* underscores, 'Soit dit en passant, monter un casting 50 % arabe pour un film de genre et pas pour un film-dossier sur l'immigration, c'est un geste très fort, plus fort que tous les tracts ou scénarios antiracistes [By the way, establishing a 50 per cent Arabic cast for a genre film and not for a film on the issue of immigration is a very strong gesture, stronger than all the antiracist pamphlets or scripts]' (Babana-Hampton 2010: 275–277). Until France treats its immigrants and populations of colour in ways where they do not feel marginalised and isolated, the more political move is for cinema to insist upon highlighting those inequalities.

Notes

1. The film's Corsicans refer derogatorily to the Arab-Muslim gang as 'les Barbus [the Muslims, literally the bearded ones].' I therefore rely on Megan C. MacDonald's language of 'Arab-Muslim'; the film never clearly defines these men as one, the other or both, but rather, as MacDonald underlines, 'The hyphen between Arab and Muslim is like a feedback loop here, one term feeding into another as if automatically, foreclosing other possibilities, such as belonging in the nation, or living in a nonsurveillance state' (2012, 566).
2. See also Radovic, 2010; Vincendeau, 2010.

3. See also Klein 2011.
4. See Fassin 2013; Khosrokhavar 2016; Mbembe 2007.
5. See also Vincendeau 2009, 2010.
6. The theme of North African criminality in France is also represented in Rachid Bouchareb's 2010 film *Hors-la-loi* which tells the story of three Algerian brothers living in France during the Algerian War of Independence in the 1950s–1960s. The brothers, who strongly identify as Algerian, that is, who have clear identities, also resort to criminal acts that cross borders. Yet, they largely use criminal means for political ends. Malik's motives, on the other hand, are purely apolitical. However, I read Malik politically: although he does not engage in crime for political ends, his being is political as it disturbs the French body politic.
7. See also MacDonald who claims that 'Malik is defined by [the Maghreb] no matter how physically mobile he is' (2012, 572).
8. See Favell 1998; Mbembe 2007; Noiriel 2001.
9. See Austin 2008, Vincendeau 2009, 2010.
10. See Range 2003; Sanchez 2008.
11. See Franc-Valluet 1998; Johannes 1998; Range 2003; Sanchez 2008.
12. I owe my use of 'visible minorities' to Luc Bronner (2010, 4). See also Glissant and Chamoiseau 2007; Noiriel 2001.
13. MacDonald's (2012) article about *Un prophète*'s connection between humanism and capital addresses similar questions of mobility through readings of Saint-Exupery and Agamben. MacDonald's emphasis is on currency and the biopolitical, while my emphasis is on Malik's mobility as a product of a criminality inextricably linked to transcending and undoing boundaries. Further, MacDonald's principal focus is on currency as a form of mobility. I am looking more at his literal ability to move around space, whether dictated by others or of his own will. However, as he accrues power, there is an equal gain in social mobility, both tied, as MacDonald underscores, to increases in currency and capital.
14. All translations of film dialogue are taken from the DVD subtitles. All other translations are the author's own.
15. Although the French gives 'daharim', the English subtitles provide simply 'money'. However, as MacDonald points out, this is a reference to the currency dirham, a currency still used in several Arabic-speaking and, notably, North African countries.
16. Fassin 2013; Khoskrovahar 2016; Mbembe 2007 all speak about the additional surveillance that populations of colour receive in France, particularly as compared to their white counterparts.

Works Cited

Agier, Michel. 2013. *Campement urbain: du refuge naît le ghetto*. Paris: Éditions Payot.

Austin, Guy. 2008. *Contemporary French Cinema: an Introduction*. 2nd edition. Manchester: Manchester University Press.

Audiard, Jacques, dir. 2009. *Un prophète*. Culver City, CA: Sony Pictures Classics, 2010. DVD.

Audiard, Jacques, dir. 2015. *Dheepan*. Criterion Collection, 2017. DVD.

Babana-Hampton, Safoi. 2010 'Actualités cinématographiques.' *Nouvelles Études Francophones* 25.1: 275–277.

Brah, Avtar. 1996. *Cartographies of Diaspora : Contesting Identities*. New York: Routledge.

Bronner, Luc. 2010. *La Loi du Ghetto: Enquête Dans les Banlieues Françaises*. Paris: Calmann-Lévy.

Busch, Gerhard. 2015. 'Jacques Audiard looking back on *Un prophète* (2009).' *The VPRO Cinema Collection*. Available at: https://www.youtube.com/watch?v=XYxXljkZqlE&t=121s.

Delorme, Stéphane. 2015. 'La loi de la jungle: Audiard & Co.' *Cahiers du Cinéma* 714: 6–13.

Durand-Souffland, Stéphane. 2010. 'Un prophète, "une fiction extrêmement documentée".' *Le Figaro*. <https://www.lefigaro.fr/cinema/2009/08/26/03002-20090826ART-FIG00011-un-prophete-une-fiction-extremement-documentee-.php> (last accessed 17 February 2022).

Fassin, Didier. 2013. *Enforcing Order: An Ethnography of Urban Policing*. English edition. Cambridge: Polity Press.

Favell, Adrian. 1998. *Philosophies of Integration: Immigration and the Idea of Citizenship in France and Britain*. London: Macmillan.

Foucault, Michel. 1975. *Surveiller et Punir: Naissance de la prison*. Paris: Éditions Gallimard.

Franc-Valluet, François-Pierre. 1998. *Corse Quel Avenir: L'indépendance?* Paris: Raymond Castells Éditions.

Glissant, Édouard and Patrick Chamoiseau. 2007. *Quand les murs tombents: l'identité nationale hors la loi*. Paris: Éditions Galaade.

Johannes, Franck. 1998. 'Jean Glavany, président de la commission d'enquête sur la Corse. "Trop de gouvernements ont cru que l'on pouvait acheter la paix civile".' *Libération*. <https://www.liberation.fr/france/1998/09/11/jean-glavany-president-de-la-commission-d-enquete-sur-la-corse-trop-de-gouvernements-ont-cru-que-l-o_248018/> (last accessed 17 February 2022).

Kaganski, Serge. 2009. 'Un prophète.' *Les inRockuptibles*. <https://www.lesinrocks.com/cinema/un-prophete-25500-24-08-2009/> (last accessed 17 February 2022).

Khosrokhavar, Farhad. 2016. *Prisons de France Violence, radicalisation, déshumanisation: surveillants et détenus parlent*. Paris: Éditions Robert Laffont.

Klein, Amanda Ann. 2011. *American Film Cycles*. Austin: University of Texas Press.

Langford, Barry. 2005. *Film Genre: Hollywood and Beyond*. Edinburgh: Edinburgh University Press.

MacDonald, Megan C. 2012. 'Humanism at the limit and *post-restante* in the colony: The prison of the postcolonial nation in Jacques Audiard's *Un prophète* (2009).' *International Journal of Francophone Studies* 15, nos. 3–4: 561–580.

Mbembe, Achille. 2007. 'La France peut-elle réinventer son identité?' *Ligue des droits de l'homme-Toulon*. <https://histoirecoloniale.net/Achille-Mbembe-la-France-peut-elle.html> (last accessed 17 February 2022).

Noiriel, Gérard. 2001. *État, nation et immigration : vers une histoire du pouvoir*. Paris: Belin.

Quayson, Ato, and Girish Daswani. 2013. 'Introduction – Diaspora and Transnationalism.' In *A Companion to Diaspora and Transnationalism*, edited by Ato Quayson and Girish Daswani, 1–26. Hoboken, NJ: Blackwell Publishing.
Radovic, Rajko. 2010. 'A Bandit Apart.' *Film International* 8, 3: 14–20.
Range, Peter Ross. 2003. 'France's Paradox Island Corsica.' *National Geographic* 203.4: np.
Sanchez, W. Alejandro. 2008. 'Corsica: France's Petite Security Problem.' *Studies In Conflict & Terrorism* 31, 7: 655–664.
Vincendeau, Ginette. 2010. 'Between the Walls.' *Sight and Sound* 20, 2: 16–18.
Vincendeau, Ginette. 2009. 'Within A Closed World.' *Sight and Sound* 19, 11: 20.

5. THREE CRIME FILMS BY JIA ZHANGKE: A TRANSNATIONAL GENEALOGY OF SOCIAL AND PERSONAL TURMOIL

Eren Odabasi

INTRODUCTION

Jia Zhangke's works have been widely studied within the context of the Sixth Generation in Chinese cinema thanks to his emphasis on globalisation and urbanisation in contemporary China as well as his preference for a realistic, unpolished style indebted to documentary aesthetics (Gateano 2009, Wagner 2013). However, Jia's cinematic language has evolved in unexpected ways, particularly following the release of his 2013 film *A Touch of Sin* (*Tian Zhu Ding*). In this highly stylised crime drama, Jia openly experimented with genre elements, borrowing extensively from Hong Kong triad films while also paying homage to several classics within the wuxia tradition. This shift towards violent, formally ambitious crime stories continued with Jia's two subsequent films, *Mountains May Depart*/*Shan He Gu Ren* (2015) and *Ash is Purest White*/ *Jiang Hu Er Nü* (2018).

In this study, I offer an alternative reading of Jia's films from a genre-oriented perspective, prioritising his growing interest in the conventions of the crime genre over the meditative, naturalistic cinematic language that characterised his early work. First, I trace the genealogy of references and intertextual elements that inform the three films listed above, identifying several sources of inspiration ranging from Johnnie To to King Hu. Second, I analyse the narrative structure of each film, exploring how Jia utilises multi-episodic storytelling strategies to combine crime film conventions with social commentary. Finally, I situate the films within the socioeconomic contexts surrounding their making, delving further into their status as transnational co-productions with financial involvement from French and Japanese partners (two influential national cinemas, each with a rich and distinctive tradition of crime films of their own). I argue that, despite their cultural and political specificity, Jia's films have gradually attained a transnational character in terms of both thematic preoccupations and production processes, thanks to the injection of crime genre codes into the director's oeuvre.

To simply state that Jia's films have become increasingly transnational as his stature as an internationally celebrated auteur improved would be repeating the obvious. Jia's films often bear clear markers of transnational production practices such as funding from a wide range of European and Asian financial institutions; the artistic collaboration of cinematographers, sound designers and other key crafts personnel from a variety of countries; and extensive play on the international film festival circuit, which consequently leads to global circulation in theatrical or ancillary settings. In her influential essay on the plurality of cinematic transnationalism, Mette Hjort (2009) defines the prominent concept of transnationalism as the 'shorthand for a series of assumptions about the networked and globalised realities that are those of a contemporary situation', and distinguishes between marked and unmarked transnationality. Cases where 'the agents who are collectively [a film's] author (typically directors, cinematographers, editors, actors, and producers) intentionally direct the attention of viewers towards various transnational properties that encourage thinking about transnationality' are marked instances (Hjort 2009: 13). On the other hand, Hjort also recognises that 'some forms of cinematic transnationalism are invisible at the level of work-immanent analyses and can be brought to light only through contextualizing research focused, for example, on issues of production' (Ibid.: 14). All three of the Jia Zhangke films I analyse in this study are clearly marked instances of transnationalism; however, unpacking several layers of this rather salient aspect of Jia's work can provide a fresh lens through which these much acclaimed and discussed films can be re-evaluated. I argue that the pronounced transnationalism of Jia's work is partially attributable to the director's interest in the crime film as a genre and that this recognition of affinity with genre conventions is crucial to understanding Jia's films.

Defining Crime Films

Since Jia Zhangke's work is not regularly included in the transnational crime film canon, it is necessary to explain why I consider his recent films under this rather broad and contested category. The definition of the crime film I use in this study is shaped by the theoretical works of Thomas Leitch and Nicole Rafter. In his canonical account of the crime film as a genre, Leitch identifies three key components observed across a range of films in order to claim generic distinctions. According to Leitch, 'the most powerful generic claims are based on mise-en-scène', and 'almost equally powerful as a generic marker is intent' while 'weaker genres are based on typological situations, characters, or presentational features' (2002: 9). As Leitch argues, crime film is a weak genre category because it lacks an 'instantly recognizable mise-en-scène . . . or the singleness of intent of the horror film or parody' (Ibid.: 10). The characteristic and recurring elements of a diverse roster of crime films are often typological situations or events (rival gangs dealing with a conflict, investigations about murders or disappearances, team building leading up to heists and so on) and certain character traits (particularly occupational ones). This relative 'weakness' of the crime film as a genre brings a certain degree of conceptual flexibility and increases the inclusivity of the phrase as an umbrella term that encompasses multiple genres and sub-genres. The three films by Jia that form the main case studies for this article all include easily identifiable markers of the crime film in terms of plotting and characterisation, even though their mise en scène or the primary reactions they aim to elicit from their audiences may not be directly shaped by the notion of crime.

Leitch also makes a key distinction between 'crime as an isolated event' versus 'crime as a metaphor for social unrest', and argues that the former category is related to thriller as a clearly defined genre category where the latter category is 'the province of the crime film' (Ibid.: 13). In this formulation, crime is never committed or presented solely for its own sake in films that belong to the extensive category of the crime film. Instead, screen portrayals of criminal activity act as a metaphor for social turmoil, ethical ambiguities, or broader sociopolitical issues. Crime plays a significant role on a thematic level in terms of societal critique regardless of whether it is central to the plot of the film or not. As I shall demonstrate below, Jia's body of work (the entirety of his filmography, and not only his crime films from the 2010s) offers a sophisticated chronicle of China's transformation in the 21st century, with a particular emphasis on the high cost of rapid urbanisation and globalisation for working class citizens excluded from narratives of continuous growth and increasing privilege. In his recent films, Jia uses criminal activity and characters who commit crimes as markers of a shift in the cultural fabric of Chinese society. He is interested in how the distribution (and redistribution) of power between different segments of society changes over time, and crime, with its obvious connections to notions such as power, influence, and control, functions as a tool for Jia to explore such themes in his films.

Nicole Rafter makes a similar observation about the connection between individual crimes and wider social upheaval in her study of several canonical crime films (2000). She observes that crime films as a category (as opposed to a genre) encompasses several more clearly defined sub-genres such as courtroom dramas, gangster movies, and detective films (2000: 5). This plurality of genres within the category expands the list of works that can be considered as crime films in one way or another. Similarly, the three films analysed in this study are realised with various cinematic sensibilities; *Ash is Purest White* is a gangster story while *Mountains May Depart* is a romance where elements of crime are interwoven into a love triangle. But all three films can be considered under the broad category of the crime film despite the different genre conventions they follow.

While selecting some canonical films as her case studies from this vast pool of crime films, Rafter notes that 'the degree to which a film says something important about the relationship between crime and society' is a significant consideration. Rather than emphasising primarily audiovisual codes or narrative conventions of crime films, Rafter pays due attention to thematic and ideological implications of crime in a diverse roster of films. More specifically, Rafter focuses on movies that 'provide useful points of entry for discussing crime films' implications for the politics of everyday life' (Ibid.: 7). As mentioned above, Jia's crime films are deeply invested in social commentary of this kind, establishing a strong connection between the increasing prevalence of criminal activities and the socioeconomic developments that redefine Chinese society after the opening of the economy to global capitalism.

Another essential aspect of the crime film canon for Jia's recent output is the prominence of themes like devotion to a specific cause or way of life, virtuousness, and respect for hierarchical group dynamics. These concepts are closely linked to the notion of *jianghu*, a set of principles frequently explored in well-known Hong Kong and Chinese crime films by directors such as John Woo and Johnnie To.[1] Film scholar Stephen Teo, writing on the crime film tradition in Hong Kong cinema, explains *jianghu* as a group of 'precepts such as the notion of *yi* (the sense of righteousness), loyalty, and bonding' (2007: 5). Jia's films often feature protagonists who uphold a strict code of honour even when they are confronted with situations where this same code of honour comes at a great personal cost for them. This notion of following the 'righteous path' even in times of personal or professional crisis is an integral part of the crime film conventions Jia follows. But even when the righteous and loyal characters are not those that are involved in criminal acts, such as Shen Tao in *Mountains May Depart*, the *jianghu* principles borrowed from an extensive crime film corpus shape the personalities and actions of Jia's protagonists.

These principles, which have appeared as key character traits in many crime films made in and outside Chinese-speaking territories, carry additional resonance in the context of Jia's work. Since Jia's films often depict a society in transition and reflect on modern China in relation to its traditional roots, it is possible to interpret *jianghu* as an intergenerational concept and compare old and new codes of honour in the underworld as well. Criminals in Jia's films often struggle to uphold the traditions of their profession and find themselves in a dilemma; a costly and irreversible choice between respecting tradition as required by the rules of their milieu and overthrowing those age-old customs in search of upward class mobility. This thematic arc is obviously not exclusive to Jia's oeuvre. For instance, Kelvin Ke Jinde, writing about the Hong Kong triad and gangster films made in the twenty-first century, observes that 'the post-millennial gangster must be deferential, respectful, and always mindful of his place and position. It is a political culture that privileges a hierarchy of seniority and the status-quo' (2019: 494). This much has been true for all gangsters in countless crime films for several decades. But he goes onto state that a new quality that distinguishes the twenty-first century gangster is 'the clash of social mobility and social harmony', with characters who show more interest in entrepreneurship than criminal activities often being drawn back into a life of crime as their socioeconomic ambitions are crushed by the strict rules of the underworld (Ibid.: 494). Like these post-millennial Hong Kong gangsters, characters in Jia's crime films also aspire to improve their social standing and economic conditions, frequently see crime as a shortcut to (or perhaps as the sole feasible way to) achieve this goal, and find themselves at odds with the codes of conduct the criminal world so highly values.

Jia's Turn to Crime

When Jia's ambitious feature *A Touch of Sin* premiered in the main competition of the Cannes Film Festival in 2013 (where it won the prize for best screenplay), several critics expressed their surprise alongside their appreciation. This new work was clearly a larger production than the director's past few films (several of which were documentaries) and signaled a move towards recognisable genre territory, if not exactly a mainstream version of that. Justin Chang, in his review of the film for *Variety*, called *A Touch of Sin* 'unquestionably Jia's most mainstream-friendly work', and noted that Jia had 'abandoned the docu-fiction experimentation of 2008's *24 City* in favor of a relatively robust narrative, replete with the sort of balls-to-the-wall brutality more typically encountered in the work of Quentin Tarantino or Takashi Miike' (2013). Other trade reviews of the film echoed Chang's perspective, with *The Hollywood Reporter*'s David Rooney stating that 'there are certainly bloody genre elements here that are new to Jia's work'(2013). The unexpected genre elements in question firmly belong to the category of the crime film, as the four storylines in this portmanteau film clearly indicate. *A Touch of Sin* is made up of four unrelated segments, each running approximately thirty-five minutes, with the common factor being the prevalence of crime in all segments. Some of the stories begin with a major criminal act and follow the criminals in the aftermath of the incident, while others build up more gradually and culminate in criminal action. But regardless of how individual narrative arcs are constructed, each section of the film tells a story of crime.

All four stories in *A Touch of Sin* are based on real-life crimes, taking place in different corners of China in the 2000s. Crucially, these are not the kind of major events frequently discussed in official media reports, but rather the sort of violent incidents that circulate across social media platforms, often primarily at the local level. Petty crimes and aimless violence, or grassroots corruption and provincial upheaval are not part of the state discourse of constant economic growth, social unity and continued progress. According to Tony Rayns, Jia actually found the real-life stories that he 'recycled' into *A Touch of Sin* on Weibo, a Chinese social media service that functions as a combination of Twitter and Facebook, where he has 'legions of followers' as 'an avid user' (2013: 32). The first story, which actually took place in 2001, is set in a small mining town in the Shanxi province (Jia's home region) where the protagonist kills more than a dozen local authorities, dealers, and business owners after his complaints about corruption and abuse of power are repeatedly ignored. The second story follows a man who commits a series of murders and kills several people across multiple Chinese cities, clearly reminiscent of the real-life crimes committed by a gunman named Zhou Kehua between 2004 and 2012. The third story, starring Jia's wife and frequent collaborator Zhao Tao (who appears in all three films analysed in this study), is about a massage parlor employee who kills two customers after they sexually harass her. The men, ignoring the woman's repeated remarks about not being involved in prostitution, believe that their money entitles them to abuse female employees. Furthermore, this third story, loosely based on events that took place in 2009, includes a second crime plot about a jealous wife who arranges for her husband's young mistress to be threatened and physically abused. Finally, the concluding chapter of the film, the only section where the 'crime' is attributed to a broader understanding of living conditions and industry practices rather than an individual act, is based on a series of suicides in a dormitory for low-wage factory workers, all employees in a large industrial facility in Shenzhen.

These series of real-life incidents are comparable to petty crime stories seen in earlier Jia films like *Pickpocket* (*Xia Wu*, 1998) or *Unknown Pleasures* (*Ren Xiao Yao*, 2002). However, their screen portrayal in *A Touch of Sin* is shaped by a different cinematic sensibility that values stylised imagery and sudden bursts of violence over the elegiac, quiet realism of the independent films Jia made in the late 1990s and the early 2000s. Before the title card of *A Touch of Sin*, with the text appearing over a vivid background of green leaves (revealed to be a particularly lush wallpaper), is shown, we are confronted with a scene of graphic gun violence where a motorcycle rider executes a gang of young criminals who block the road and try to extort money from him. This scene is constructed through a series of lengthy steadicam shots, with the camera circling around the gunman and covering almost 360 degrees. Jia then cuts to a chase, with the gunman going after the last remaining gang member, who tries to run away but fails. The camera follows the gang member as he runs, and the gunman tails him on his motorbike and fires a shot without any expression or sentiment. Jia uses a close up of the gun shot, shows the young man falling down on the road, and we see blood bursting out of a wound on his back. The scene is set in a barren landscape dominated by rocks and sand, with the widescreen photography effectively using a colour palette and iconography associated with the western genre rather than a social-realist drama.[2]

Given the efficiency of the shoot-out, crisp editing and polished cinematography of the sequence and the juxtaposition of western imagery with the Chinese setting, viewers could be forgiven for mistaking this to be a Johnnie To film, particularly one of his Sam Peckinpah-influenced triad films that make use of similar mountain or desert settings. The best-known example of this kind of western-*jianghu* hybrids directed by Johnnie To is *Exiled/Fong Juk* (2006) and the evocation of a famous shoot-out sequence from that film in the opening scene of *A Touch of Sin* is not coincidental. Later in the film, when the gunman in the second story takes an overnight bus ride, the film playing on the television on the bus (as a form of communal on-board entertainment where all the passengers watch the same film on a single screen) is none other than To's *Exiled*. The gunman gets out of his seat and abruptly asks the driver to stop the bus. Since he comes closer to the television screen in order to talk to the driver, we clearly hear the sounds of the guns on the soundtrack, which establishes a strong connection between the opening scene and the To film playing on the screen. In her analysis of *A Touch of Sin*, Shenshen Cai also observes the similarities between the film and Hong Kong triad pictures[3] (even though she does not identify Johnnie To or *Exiled* as one of the influences) when she states that Jia 'creates a criminal knight character ... also found in the 1980s and 1990s Hongkongese movies that adapted traditional concepts of chivalry and brotherhood to stories of contemporary crime and violence' (2015: 70).

Cai's characterisation of the protagonist as a 'criminal knight' is most clearly applicable to Dahai (played by Jiang Wu) in the first story as this character fights single-handedly against a corrupt and oppressive system, using violence as a means to avenge the injustices he and his people have suffered. I do not suggest that social injustice justifies murders, executions, or graphic violence. However, I argue that it is a very significant distinction to note that the crimes in *A Touch of Sin* are committed with a strong sense of purpose, in a search for fairness and integrity, even though the methods of this search are problematic. At this point, it could be useful, for example, to compare and contrast the uses of crime in *Unknown Pleasures* (not a crime film, but an early Jia drama with elements of crime in the narrative) and *A Touch of Sin*. The protagonists of *Unknown Pleasures* try to rob a bank near the end of the film but fail in their attempt. This drastic criminal activity is not motivated by any sense of social responsibility, desperation in the face of corruption, or search for justice in a society in transition. Writing on *Unknown Pleasures*, Matthew Holtmeier notes that the bank robbery is just an attempt to 'reestablish a psychological sense of direction . . . through which they [the two young protagonists] might make sense of their lives and perceive some sort of movement or purposefulness' (2014: 156). Crime in *A Touch of Sin* and Jia's subsequent films, on the other hand, serves a larger, more socioeconomically driven purpose than this personal state of boredom and adolescent ennui. As Yanjie Wang argues, Jia uses crime stories in *A Touch of Sin* in order to 'debunk the neoliberal promise, laying bare the means by which the state power and private capital alienate, exploit, and entrap the poor, especially the rural population and migrant workers' (2015: 160). This close association between growing sociopolitical turmoil and a rise in criminal activities in the financially disadvantaged segment of society forms the unifying thematic element across the four stories in *A Touch of Sin*, and it can be observed in various aspects of the consequent films Jia directed as well.

Crime and Romance in Three Acts

Mountains May Depart, which, like the other two films mentioned in this study, had its world premiere in the main competition of the Cannes Film Festival, can be more accurately described as a romantic drama with some elements of crime rather than a fully-fledged crime film like *A Touch of Sin* or *Ash is Purest White*. But despite the different genre conventions it follows, *Mountains May Depart* employs a similar narrative structure and explores many of the same themes as the other two films. Therefore, I argue that this film should be recognised as an essential connecting chapter between Jia's two major crime films.

Mountains May Depart is divided into three chapters, each indicated by a title card that reveals the time period. The film opens in 1999 as Jinsheng (played by Zhang Yi) and Liangzi (Liang Jingdong) compete for the affections of Shen Tao (Zhao Tao). Liangzi works in the local coal mine while Jinsheng owns a gas station, therefore a socioeconomic divide between the characters is instantly established from the beginning. Jinsheng says he is 'too busy bundling up all the cash' he recently made and shows off his new red car in a bid to impress Tao. He exclaims that the car is 'just right for the new century' (a phrase which is repeated by the entire trio when they sing about 'stepping proudly into the new century') and talks about purchasing the mine for cheap when it 'bottoms out'. Despite her long-term fondness for Liangzi, Tao chooses to marry Jinsheng in the end of the first part. However, these ambitions of upward class mobility are revealed to have a high cost in the second part set in 2014. The couple are separated and their son Daole (pronounced as 'Dollar' as a playful indicator of Jinsheng's relentless efforts to accumulate more capital at any cost) lives with his father, who now uses the English name Peter, in Shanghai. In the futuristic third part set in Australia in 2025, the characters recall how China 'was caught up in a big anti-corruption campaign' in 2014, which retroactively explains that Peter and Daole's immigration to Australia is attributable to Peter's shady business and the illegal ways through which he rapidly expanded his wealth. An older Peter remembers that he immigrated after learning that a business associate named Xing was prosecuted on corruption charges and even remarks that the word 'Xing' sounds too much like the Chinese word for 'criminal'. Multiple guns and bullets are shown on the coffee table in Peter's and Daole's luxurious apartment, further emphasising Peter's connection with the underworld. In his review of the film, Nick Pinkerton highlights this portrayal of Australia as a refuge for Chinese criminals and observes that 'Australia circa 2025 has repealed laws to become a gun nut's paradise' in the film (2018: 72). In another scene where Daole's Chinese teacher Mia (played by Sylvia Chang[4]) helps the father and son to have a meaningful confrontation by translating between Chinese and English, Jia once again uses close ups of multiple guns and even a rifle lying dormant on the table. When Daole says he wants to quit college and move out of his father's apartment, Peter threatens him by picking up a gun and loading it, to which Daole replies 'go and play with your guns', referring to his father's criminal past.

In the conclusion of the film, Jia returns to the Shanxi province in China, where Tao still resides, and reminds the audience of ordinary working-class citizens in provincial China, whose economic fortunes have not improved in such drastic fashion since they kept on living and working according to an older code of law, decency and equity. Instead of directly tackling crime as a major narrative element, *Mountains May Depart* argues that a turn towards crime and illegal activities essentially serves as a shortcut to wealth and more privileged socioeconomic standing for many Chinese citizens from the provinces, who embraced neoliberalism and globalisation with open arms, without pausing a second to weigh the price their peers, friends and former colleagues would need to pay. Jia sets the final part of his film in the future in 2025, but rather than infusing *Mountains May Depart* with genre conventions from an obvious corpus of science fiction or fantasy texts, he chooses to highlight crime and criminality as a tool for confronting the past (corresponding to present-day China at the time of the film's release). The love triangle in the film bypasses the futuristic trappings the setting may suggest, instead giving way to a story about a fragmented society of young people driven to crime in their search for prosperity and the common people they left behind.

Jia employs the same structure in *Ash is Purest White*, which is again divided into three chapters in order to tell the story of a doomed romance spanning approximately twenty years (there is no on-screen text indicating the chapter divisions in this case but jumps in time are noticeable in every aspect of mise-en-scène from set and costume design to aspect ratio, lighting and texture). *Ash* is *Purest White* can be interpreted as a combined reworking of the two earlier films; using the epic scope and romantic undertones of *Mountains May Depart* alongside the overt crime film conventions, graphic violence, and highly polished audiovisual construction observed in *A Touch of Sin*. The protagonist of the film Qiao (played once again by Zhao Tao) is the girlfriend of local mob boss Bin (Liao Fan). Bin's criminal activities are based on petty real-life crimes, not unlike those that inspired the stories in *A Touch of Sin*, since this character, as Jia explains in a letter he wrote upon the US theatrical release of the film, is modelled on a 'big brother' from his childhood neighbourhood (2019). Qiao is shown to be more than simply a romantic interest for Bin as she exerts power over all members of the gang and is an influential figure in the small mining town where the first part of the film, set in 2001, takes place. Early in the film, she is said to 'pack a real punch' and initiates a toast for members of the gang to take an oath of loyalty and righteousness (she herself drinks a shot alongside the men). When Bin is attacked by a group of young gangsters from a rival gang, Qiao fires a warning shot to disperse the violent criminals. Since the gun is not legally owned and firing a gun in public is a criminal act, she is sentenced to several years in prison. This first part of the film is rich in background detail that provides a socioeconomic subtext. It is revealed that the mining town is dealing with financial difficulties since the price of coal has fallen and there are plans to shift the mine from the Shanxi province to the Xinjiang region. Bin notes that relocation and compensation plans do not apply to transportation workers like him and is hesitant about leaving the town as he knows people from his background are likely to be left out of such projects of economic growth and urban development. In Bin, we once again see a character from a financially disadvantaged provincial milieu using crime as a tool to improve his economic situation and social stature in the face of broader societal changes that threaten to leave him behind. He seizes the town as his territory and says that, when the town is rebuilt as a part of a redevelopment project, it will be all theirs for the taking. Qiao, resembling Tao in *Mountains May Depart*, does not agree with her lover or share his ambitions of upward class mobility through crime.

The second part of the film is set in 2006 as Qiao is released from prison. Bin initially refuses to see her, partly because he is no longer the powerful and influential gang leader he used to be (when former acquaintances migrate to urban centres and get rich in the construction business, they have little reverence for a has-been small-time gangster from an impoverished mining town). But Bin and Qiao finally meet after Qiao navigates her way through multiple encounters with crime (her bag is stolen, she impersonates other people to find food and money, survives an attempted sexual assault, and steals the assaulter's motorbike). Bin is burdened by the shame of falling from a position of relative power; he no longer has a place to stay, spends his nights in saunas or karaoke bars, and meets Qiao only in a cheap, damp hotel room. When Bin avoids her questions, Qiao says '*jianghu* guys like you never speak plainly', directly associating him with a certain type of criminal life (and tradition of crime films) that shaped Jia's two previous films. Another clear reference to *jianghu* films occurs in a scene where Bin and several other gangsters watch *Tragic Hero/Ying Hung Ho Hon* (1987), a popular *jianghu* classic starring Chow Yun Fat (a favorite actor of both Johnnie To's and John Woo's), on television, reminiscent of the aforementioned *Exiled* reference in *A Touch of Sin*.

The transition to the final part of the film, set in 2017, occurs with a dream-like sequence where Qiao sees a UFO and is followed by a futuristic bird's-eye view shot of a fast train. Like *Mountains May Depart,* Jia teases the possibility of some science fiction elements in the concluding section of *Ash is Purest White* but opts for a return to the romance and the crime story at the core of his film. Qiao and Bin are reunited, but at this late stage in their lives, Bin's fall from power has hit its low point (he is not able to use his legs anymore) and it is impossible for the couple to recapture the authority and respect they enjoyed during their heyday as gang leaders. Their existence in 2017 is marked by everyday struggles, common financial problems, mundane tasks and daily chores. In an interview with Lux Chen and Cynthia Rowell, Jia explains that this thematic emphasis on everyday life and spaces is a key factor that distinguishes his films from Hong Kong triad films, which form an important visual and narrative reference point. He notes that 'unlike the underworld in Hong Kong gangster films, ours has no extravagant conventions or rituals, but is rooted in everyday life' (2019: 23). Rather than the characteristically fast-paced and stylised shoot-outs in Hong Kong triad films, criminal life in in *Ash is Purest White* is depicted through scenes of mundane activity such as mahjong games, Qiao cooking vegetables, conversations in a tea house, or dancing in a night club. As it is the case in *A Touch of Sin*, physical assault and gun violence in this film also occur only sporadically, as unexpected bursts of graphic violence punctuating important turning points in the lives of the protagonists.

The transnational co-production practices that shaped all three films must also be briefly recognised as an additional factor, which strengthens the connections between Jia's recent cinematic output and diverse crime film traditions around the world. All three of the films analysed in this study are co-productions between China, Japan, and France. Alongside Jia's own production company Xstream Pictures, Office Kitano from Japan and MK2 from France are co-producers in each case. It is worth noting that Office Kitano has also produced many Japanese crime films, most significantly a series of acclaimed Yakuza stories that explore similar themes such as loyalty, code of honour, hierarchy and righteousness. Jia's use of violence in sudden bursts that break an unhurried sequence of mundane events is highly reminiscent of the minimalist Yakuza films Japanese auteur Takeshi Kitano has directed for his own production company.

Furthermore, such transnational connections are reflected in Jia's films on audiovisual and thematic levels beyond the flow of funds and talent across borders. Cecília Mello argues that 'Jia Zhangke's cinematographic project contains, rather congruently, a significant itinerant impulse', and notes that almost all of his films 'reveal a penchant for dislocation, mobility and transience' (2019: 6). This is clearly embodied in Tao, Daole, and Jinsheng's mobility between various corners of China as well as Australia in *Mountains May Depart*, Qiao's constant travels in all three parts of *Ash is Purest White*, the influx of foreign capital or the gunman's lengthy journeys from one city to another in the second segment of *A Touch of Sin*. Jia's formative collaborations with cinematographers Yu Lik-Wai from Hong Kong and Eric Gautier from France or Taiwanese actress Sylvia Chang in these three crime films can also be understood in this transnational context. Such 'itinerant impulses' or themes of mobility, migration, and rootlessness have long been part of the *jianghu* world and Hong Kong triad cinema as well. Writing on Johnnie To's *Exiled*, a major influence on Jia as mentioned above, Valerie Soe states that *Exiled*, like many other crime films from Hong Kong, deals with 'alienation of disenfranchised minorities, the difficulties of hybrid identity, and the continual search for a home and place of belonging' (2019: 473). The thematic emphasis on mobility in Jia's films, with all of his characters drifting from one place to another in their quests for wealth, justice, or romance, serves a similar function. As portrayed in Jia's recent works, a life of crime means a life on the road, in which the criminals are never fully able to realise their ambitions of catching up with the times, climbing the socioeconomic ladder in a rapidly evolving society, or finding a stable home that they can claim as their own.

Conclusion

In this study, I explored the increasing prevalence of crime film elements in Chinese auteur Jia Zhangke's cinema by identifying several points of reference that have influenced his recent output and unpacking the thematic implications of these connections. Jia's sources of inspiration are very diverse, ranging from real-life news items and individuals he interacted with during his youth to the large corpus of Hong Kong triad films, the complex notion of *jianghu* or transnational collaborations with individuals from countries with distinctive crime film traditions (chiefly Japan and France).

In order to understand the significance of these connections for Jia's work on a textual level, it is useful to investigate the filmmaker's long-term thematic preoccupations. Three such themes are particularly prevalent in Jia's crime films. First is his interest in chronicling the transformation of China in the 21st century in the face of rapid urban development and influx of global capital. Second is his commitment to critically demonstrating the destructive impact of these socioeconomic changes on the provincial working-class populations, who are most often left behind in a relentless race towards wealth and economic growth. Third is his preference for telling sprawling stories that cover a long span of time from an intimate perspective that places the experiences of displaced individuals in perpetual motion front and centre.

As demonstrated throughout the study, Jia's films are in dialogue with each other, with each new work expanding and enhancing his previous efforts. In the same vein, the presence of crime in his early films must be recognised in order to highlight how his more recent turn to crime film as a genre, starting with *A Touch of Sin*, moves his oeuvre forward. Crime, associated with an individual sense or boredom, provincial ennui, and youthful lack of purpose in early Jia films, evolves into a tool for socially conscious and pointed resistance against inequality, corruption and exploitation. An equally important function of crime as a prevalent element in Jia's recent films is its portrayal as an instrument for upwards social class mobility, an often-futile attempt to catch up with the changing times. His 2018 film *Ash is Purest White* brings all of these threads in Jia's cinema together and presents them in the form of an elegant crime epic. Since this film represents the culmination of Jia's cinematic output in the past two decades and appears to mark the conclusion of a chapter in his filmmaking journey, it will be interesting to observe where Jia's camera takes him next.

Notes

1. *Jianghu* is an elusive concept, defined in several different ways in various contexts. The two characters literally mean 'river' and 'lake'. Stephen Ching-Kiu Chan cites Ho Ng is describing *Jianghu* as "'A world with 'its own set of laws, its own code of ethics, and its own social structure'' . . . [distinguishing this] unique world from . . . "home," that is the ordinary life outside *jianghu* . . . it is "subject to a social order quite distinct from those of the ordinary world found at home."' (2001: 491). In relation to crime films, *jianghu* often refers to an honourable code of conduct in which all members of a group (a gang, the police force and so on) uphold shared values of loyalty, brotherhood, and righteousness despite the crises and conflicts they face.
2. While I unpack references to westerns and Hong Kong triad films in this study, it must be noted that another key influence on *A Touch of Sin* is the wuxia tradition in Chinese-language cinemas (as indicated by the nod to King Hu's 1971 wuxia masterpiece *A Touch of Zen/Xia Nu* in the film's English title).
3. Cai's reference point is John Woo's *A Better Tomorrow/Ying Hung Boon Sik* (1986) rather than any Johnnie To film.
4. Acclaimed actress and filmmaker Sylvia Chang has appeared in many significant crime films throughout her long career. She collaborated with Johnnie To on multiple occasions, acted in several *jianghu* films, and was part of the popular *Lucky Star* film series about a group of petty criminals who assist the police after being released from prison. Chang's casting in *Mountains May Depart* can be interpreted as yet another nod to the Hong Kong crime film tradition.

Works Cited

Cai, Shenshen. 2015. 'Jia Zhangke and His A Touch of Sin'. *Film International* 13, 2: 67–78.

Chang, Justin. 2013. 'Cannes Film Review: A Touch of Sin'. *Variety*, 16 May 2013. <https://variety.com/2013/film/global/cannes-film-review-a-touch-of-sin-1200482687/> (last accessed 19 February 2022).

Chan, Stephen Ching-kiu. 2001. 'Figures of Hope and the Filmic Imaginary of Jianghu in Contemporary Hong Kong Cinema'. *Cultural Studies* 15.3-4: 486–514.

Chen, Lux, and Cynthia Rowell. 2019. 'Searching for Dignity in the Ocean of People: An Interview with Jia Zhangke'. *Cineaste* 44.2: 22–25.

Gateano, Arianne. 2009. 'Rural Women and Modernity in Globalizing China: Seeing Jia Zhangke's The World'. *Visual Anthropology Review* 25.1: 25–39.

Hjort, Mette. 2009. 'On the Plurality of Cinematic Transnationalism'. In *World Cinemas, Transnational Perspectives*, edited by Natasa Ďurovičová and Kathleen E. Newman, 12–33. New York: Routledge.

Holtmeier, Matthew A. 2014. 'The Wanderings of Jia Zhangke: Pre-Hodological Space and Aimless Youths in Xiao Wu and Unknown Pleasures'. *Journal of Chinese Cinemas* 8.2: 148–159.

Jia, Zhangke, dir. *A Touch of Sin* (*Tian Zhu Ding*). 2013; Kino Lorber, 2014. DVD.

Jia, Zhangke, dir. *Mountains May Depart* (*Shan He Gu Ren*). 2015; Kino Classics, 2016. DVD.

Jia, Zhangke, dir. *Ash is Purest White* (*Jiang Hu Er Nu*). 2018; Cohen Media Group, 2019. DVD.

Jia, Zhangke. 2019. 'Jianghu: How it Started for Me'. <https://www.landmarktheatres.com/ash-is-purest-white-filmmaker-letter> (last accessed 19 February 2022)

Ke Jinde, Kelvin. 2019. 'Politics, Social Order, and Hierarchies in Post-Millennium Hong Kong Cinema'. In *A Companion to the Gangster Film*, 480–496. Edited by George S. Larke-Walsh. Hoboken, NJ: John Wiley & Sons.

Leitch, Thomas. 2002. *Crime Films*. Cambridge: Cambridge University Press.

Mello, Cecília. 2019. *The Cinema of Jia Zhangke: Realism and Memory in Chinese Film*. London: I. B. Tauris.

Pinkerton, Nick. 2018. 'Mountains May Depart'. *Sight & Sound* 28.1: 72–73.

Rafter, Nicole. 2000. *Shots in the Mirror: Crime Film and Society*. Oxford, New York: Oxford University Press.

Rayns, Tony. 2013. 'Heard It Through The Grapevine'. *Film Comment* 49.1: 30–35.

Rooney, David. 2013. 'A Touch of Sin: Cannes Review'. *The Hollywood Reporter*, May 16, 2013. <https://www.hollywoodreporter.com/review/a-touch-sin-cannes-review-524099>

Soe, Valerie. 2019. 'Gangsta Gangsta: Hong Kong Triad Films, 1986–2015'. In *A Companion to the Gangster Film*, 463–479. Edited by George S. Larke-Walsh. Hoboken, NJ: John Wiley & Sons.

Teo, Stephen. 2007. *Director in Action: Johnnie To and the Hong Kong Action Film*. HongKong: Hong Kong University Press.

Wagner, Keith B. 2013. 'Jia Zhangke's Neoliberal China: The Commodification and Dissipation of the Proletarian in The World (Shijie, 2004)'. *Inter-Asia Cultural Studies* 14.3: 361–377.

Wang, Yanjie. 2015. 'Violence, Wuxia, Migrants: Jia Zhangke's Cinematic Discontent in A Touch of Sin'. *Journal of Chinese Cinemas* 9.2: 159–172.

6. TIT FOR TAT: AVENGING WOMEN AND SELF-FASHIONING FEMININITY IN MALAYALAM CINEMA

Rohini Sreekumar and Sony Jalarajan Raj

INTRODUCTION

Crime film is one of the most popular and persuasive genres in the world. With various sub-genres like cop films, court dramas, investigative thrillers and heist films, it generally portrays a crime-oriented plot where interactions between savior protagonists and criminal antagonists define the structural template of the film. Crime narratives usually revolve around the valiance of the traditional 'hero' who displays exhilarating masculine pride either through physical strength or intelligence. The construction of heroic masculinity varies with actors; for example, from Pierce Brosnan to Liam Neeson and Will Smith to Morgan Freeman, implications of masculinity – in terms of physical appearance and intellectual activity – construct multiple versions of masculine pride. In the context of Indian cinema, onscreen masculinity follows similar structures. From the 'Angry Young Man' image of Amitabh Bachchan in the 1970s to the latest gangster films of Bollywood, Indian crime cinema strove to perpetuate the patriarchal ideology ingrained in the heroic image. In other words, when male heroes are given the agency to control the narrative of a crime film, female characters are often portrayed as victims who need saving or glamorous objects that act as distractions to heroic gallantry. However, there have been some meagre attempts to portray women in unconventional gangster roles where femininity is equated with vigor, fervor and muscularity as seen in films like *Bandit Queen* (1994) and *Gulab Gang* (2014). In this rare context, this chapter looks at Malayalam cinema, a regional film industry of India, where a few films in the crime genre have tried to portray women as both victims and avenging survivors, thereby thwarting the idea of machismo as a heroic element in crime thrillers. Here, 'she' is the victim, survivor, avenger and the punisher. The films taken for this study fall under the sub-category of female revenge drama, where heroic elements are not only detached from masculinity but confined to the feminine traits of the protagonist. This study analyses the construction of female action heroes and avenging women in Indian national cinema and identifies and differentiates these female characterisations in the emerging context of new women-orientated (or feminised) versions of crime fiction in Malayalam regional cinema.

BANDIT HEROINES: TOWARDS THE CONSTRUCTION OF A 'MACHO FEMININITY'

Bollywood cinema, since its inception, has predominantly been a male-dominated industry. Earlier Bollywood films concentrated on portraying domesticated and self-restrained ideal women (who can either be mothers or gullible wives). However, by the 2000s, portrays of women shifted to more glamorous and bewitching counterparts almost irrelevant to the narrative of the film. When such portrayals of gender roles in films and other visual media began to create ideal images of femininity and masculinity, the identity of the wife becomes a stereotype of a caretaker of the husband and her ostensibly sacred wifehood must be sustained through torture and oppression.

Self-sacrificing mother/wife roles have been proliferating and reigning onscreen for over a large period in the history of Bollywood cinema. For instance, *Mother India* (1957) – considered as one of the best Indian films – metaphorically represents the nationalised 'mother' identity of post-independence India. The protagonist Radha in *Mother India* had three sons and was pregnant with the fourth when her husband left her due to his insecurities and lack of self-esteem. The story revolves around the loss of her two kids, her lonely fight for life, the sacrifices she made to raise her other two sons amidst advances from a lecherous moneylender, and her obligation and rationality towards the society that forced her to shoot her own son – a selfless act that helps to restore the social order in the village. The posters of this film were so popular that the picture of Radha carrying a heavy bull-plough (played by Nargis, one of the greatest actresses in Indian cinema) resembles the crucifixion of Jesus Christ: an iconic image that incorporated divine suffering into the symbolism of self-sacrificing motherhood.

Later on, to validate this illustration, narratives began to normalise a binary in female characterisation where, on the one hand, the ever-tolerating and sacrificing woman who pawns her life for the family is sanctified, and, on the other, the 'bad girl' who exemplifies qualities that contradict the ideal women imagery begin to be recognised. Hence, instances of strong and active women weaving their independent sociopolitical lives outside the confined family setup were rare in films of this era. During the 1990s and 2000s, 'woman of action' tropes began to find a space in narratives as female characters played the role of glamorous companions of the hero. In films like *Ajnabee* (2001), *Race* (2008), and *Race 2* (2013), women participate in criminal heists and conspiracies along with their male counterparts. However, here are some discernible differences in conceptualising male and female antagonists in such films:

> While male goons are presented as leading the life of a criminal by choice, female counterparts usually associate themselves with crime only for a strong reason such as love . . . safeguarding their existing position. There is always an attempt in the narrative to justify the criminal behavior of a woman through her woeful past in order to encourage audience sympathies with the female antagonist, even if she is a gangster. (Raj et al. 2018: 215)

Nonetheless, as we have demonstrated in an earlier essay on women gang leaders in Indian cinema, these onscreen action women have 'helped to change commonly held beliefs about gender identity in Hindi films with the assistance of realistic plots and aesthetics' (Ibid.: 215).

It is right to say that the spell of the ideal female image has influenced the progression of female characters even in the twenty-first century. The construction of characters is frequently influenced by the dilemma of balancing the binary image of ideal femininity with the trope of the avenging action woman. Hence, associating women with a crime is a process that creates challenging narratives and precarious spaces in the visual medium. Creative artistry in characterising female action leads is limited as their acts need to be more convincingly justified than those of their male counterparts. The gendering of genre seems relevant here; crime films have traditionally been male-oriented and are based on the assumption that violence, gallantry and heroism are associated with masculinity (Gates 2006). The construction of femininity is such that it precludes the ideal female walloping a guy or restoring social order through violence unless and until it is through association with the male characters represented – not least in the Indian context as national movements struggle to deliver justice and equality for women in society.

The image of an ever-sacrificing wife and mother that these films have passionately portrayed shows resistance to ideological change at the national level. Hence, the closest and the most riveting character persona that can be associated with the image of the avenging women is that of the dacoit. Dacoity or banditry was a very common criminal activity in regions in the north of India and was considered as a vigilante response to feudal exploitations that were common in northern villages. Popular dacoit figures like Paan Singh Tomar and Phoolan Devi were inspirations for many Bollywood films. Thus, the past and present of female dacoits become equally relevant with a moral and emotional context often justifying her deeds. Films like *Putlibai* (1972), *Sherni* (1988), *Bandit Queen* (1994) and *Gulab Gang* (2014) can be classified under this genre. There two main characteristic features that define Indian action heroines: (i) they are biographical or inspired characters; (ii) most of them are bandits or underworld goons who have a history to justify their ingress into the criminal world. *PutliBai,* a film released in 1972, chronicles the life of Gauhar Banu, considered as India's first female dacoit who was initially a nautch girl (a dancer who performed at court or for men of the ruling classes). Subsequently, many films featuring female dacoits began to find narrative presence, including *Bandit Queen* (1994) featuring Phoolan Devi, the Chambal dacoit who turned into an activist and politician; *Godmother* (1999), depicting the life of Santokben Jadeja who ran the mafia operations in the late 1980s; and *Haseena Parkar* (2017) portraying the titular character as sister of the unapprehended drug lord and gangster, Dawood Ibrahim.

A common ingredient holding crime films with dacoit heroes together as a category is the evolution of the characters; from their normal domestic lives as teenagers, circumstances push them into banditry. Characters progress from their ordinary lives to savagery and thereby achieve the strength of an avenging hero. While strength is associated with masculinity as in the case of male crime films, these women-oriented films appropriate to this formula and equate femininity with vigor, fervor and muscularity – the desired qualities of a ferocious gang leader. There is a balance between the helplessness of a woman and her revenge against society. Therefore, in these cases, her deeds are not questioned since her acts undermine questions of moralism as she has a past that justifies her present.

This again prompts further scrutiny of acts associated with masculinity that are used to portray intrepid femininity on screen. As Grant explains, classical Hollywood genre systems were built on gendered assumptions that drove production and marketing of films (2007: 80–81). This is particularly clear in the case of action films that mostly address the male audiences, as well as musicals and melodrama that largely cater to a female audience. Thus, notable female revenge dramas of the Malayalam regional film industry work against the grain of conventions of gender globalised through Hollywood cinema and also have the quality of subverting the hitherto definitions of avenging femininity in Indian cinema.

Malayalam Cinema, Female Characters and the Revenge genre

The first state to achieve a nearly one hundred per cent literacy rate in India, Kerala, has been identified as a major locus point for social research from the early 1980s onwards. Though Kerala has upheld matrilineal systems, it was never a matriarchal society, making debates on social development and women's empowerment more complex and intriguing. Matrilineality is traditionally called 'Marumakkathayam' in Kerala, where the property is inherited through the mother or female member of the family. However, women were never directly invested with power in this system. Kerala was one of the first Indian states to provide reservations for women in government services owing to a higher rate of education and employment along with a higher female health index. On the surface, this indicates that the women in Kerala achieved a higher status in social progress. However, in reality, a relatively higher rate of crime against women – dowry, suicides and domestic violence top the list – challenge such claims about the myth of the 'progressive woman'. This obfuscation can be seen in characterisations of female roles in Malayalam cinema.

Gender is a cultural product that has been historically constructed and socially performed in the public sphere. Through the repeated reproduction of performative gender identities that solidify normative structural and semiotic patterns, films try to construct and popularise the notions of normative femininity. These notions are propagated through images of good wives and sacrificial mothers that signify idealised versions of domestic life and household labour. In most cases, their role is questioned and defined through the 'promulgation and enforcement of these rigid female identities' (Menon 2009: 286). As Pillai describes, Malayalam films served as a 'manual for femininity', a kind of reference book on how to be an ideal woman (2015: 9). For instance, in *Kuruppinte Kanakku Pusthakam/Kurup's Ledger* (1990), the titular character Kurup's wife is a lawyer by profession, but her passion leans towards upholding the moral demands and petty chores that her husband wants her to execute for him (a type of submission that she enthusiastically enjoys). This includes her handing over the toothbrush with the right amount of paste and preparing bathing water at a suitable temperature, all according to her husband's exact needs. Their marital love and compassion are strictly materialistic and portrayed through images of a hegemonic husband and docile wife.

Malayalam cinema has always been an intimate and popular entertainment medium in society, and mainstream films demonstrated an affinity towards content with higher social and emotional themes. Since its inception, Malayalam cinema engaged with contemporary social realities to raise questions that sparked public debates; as more and more classic and reformative literary works began to be adapted into the cinematic medium, the space became even more riveting. Therefore, unlike other regional cinemas in India, content related to middle-class life, feudal system, class/caste discrimination, and so on have been prevalent in Malayalam cinema. However, it is hard to say that these changes have made significant differences in the construction of female characters in such films. Female subjectivities are constructed and performed within the realm of the home and even when women started working in films, the female character is judged (or performed) based on the dexterity of her domestic life. Often a dichotomy is placed before the audience to evaluate and validate this, as the director-screenwriter Sanju Surendran notes: 'Women in Malayalam cinema until now were presented through a bipolar construction – either they were saintly caregivers or they were hypersexual, uncontrolled women out to seduce the hero' (as quoted in Najib 2019: n.p.). It is at this complex juncture that gendered revenge films demand more critical analysis. Even though investigative crime and suspense thrillers are very popular genres in the region, it is typically women who are portrayed as victims and for their redemption that male agents evolve as heroes.

In the revenge genre, female characters are agents of violence, often seeking revenge and justice as solutions to their past tragedies. Hollywood films like *Kill Bill* (2003, 2004) and *Inglourious Basterds* (2009) often feature vengeful characters that go on missions to eradicate their enemies. In *Inglourious Basterds*, Tarantino uses an alternate history narrative where a Jewish protagonist destroys Nazi Germany's leadership. For protagonists in films like *I Spit on Your Grave* (1978) and *Revenge* (2017), revenge is an escape from a dangerous situation involving violent men. In the case of Malayalam cinema, which is deeply rooted in social and regional themes, it is hard to envision women as '*Sherni*' or '*Bandit Queen*', as Kerala never had such violent female bandits prominent in either its society or in the region's cherished folklore. The challenge for Malayalam filmmakers was to simultaneously situate the image of the ideal woman within the chaste domesticated domain and associate her with a crime that would not disgrace the stereotypes. This challenge has been energetically accepted by many films that seamlessly combine the masculinity associated with crime genre with the more femininity associated with melodramatic genres.

Avenging Women in Malayalam Cinema

Before further discussion and definition of female vigilantes in Malayalam cinema, an analysis of some select films and their female characters is pertinent as context and background. Hence, four films have been chosen for analysis: *Yavanika* (1982), *Kannezhuthi Pottum Thottu* (1999), *22 Female Kottayam* (2012) and *Puthiya Niyamam* (2016).

Yavanika (Translated as 'Stage Curtain')

During the 1970s–80s, a hybrid cinematic form called 'middle cinema' came into prominence where the conventions of art films met commercial elements, making the films of 'middle cinema' a golden age of Malayalam cinema. One of the most celebrated filmmakers of this period was KG George who experimented with his characters across various genres and is often regarded as a filmmaker who explored female characters and their exposition of femininity in Malayalam cinema. *Yavanika*, directed and scripted by George, is considered his magnum opus. It is a psychological thriller set under the backdrop of a drama theatre and its actors. Ayyappan is a *tabla* artist (a twin drum instrument popular in India) in a theatre group who finds his pleasure in alcohol and seducing women. He is staying with Rohini, who he brought from the village under the pretense of a secure job at the theatre. She is forced into acting due to her poverty-driven circumstances, which Ayyappan exploits for his own benefit. He makes her a mistress against her will, and she silently endures his wickedness fearing the harm he is capable of inflicting on her poor family.

The film begins with the theatre group getting ready to depart for a show at night, only to find that Ayyappan is missing. Rohini tells the troupe owner that she has not seen him since the previous night. After a few days, when their search for Ayyappan ends in vain, they file a complaint to the police. Inspector Jacob is assigned with the job, and he starts his investigation into Ayyappan's disappearance. Ayyappan's character and his life journey evolve through the recollections of other troupe members including Rohini and her pitying co-artist Joseph. As the investigation seems to be going nowhere, his body is recovered from a paddy field, and the probe turns towards the possibility of a homicide. Police identify a keychain from the crime scene that points their suspicion towards Joseph, and, upon interrogation, he admits that he accidentally murdered Ayyappan as a result of an argument that night. However, Jacob has some doubt on Joseph's confession and began to investigate the role of Rohini in this crime by setting a plot to let Joseph return to troupe from police custody only to make Rohini apprehensive about his arrest and interrogation. She enters the stage in the middle of the drama and confesses to the audience that it was not Joseph, but she who murdered Ayyappan. She explains that Ayyappan sold all her ornaments and was trying to lure her sister as well to stay with him, which provoked her to stab him. She sought help from Joseph, who always empathised with her for destroying her life for a womaniser like Ayyappan. Joseph helped her to bury the body in the paddy fields and was even prepared to go to prison for her. Both of them are taken into custody, and the film ends with the troupe members entering the bus and continuing their routine travel and work.

Even though *Yavanika* is an investigative thriller, it is narrated in a melodramatic way, or at least the notion of melodrama is emphasised as the whole narration is interlaced with the stage play of the troupe. Here, the character of Rohini is juxtaposed with the stage character she is performing within the film. In the play, she has the affect of a very bold character willing to speak aloud of her feelings and her affair with a poet against the will of her parents who are trying to marry her off to her cousin, a millionaire. The collocation of both sides of her characters creates a binary that differentiates the 'reel' and 'real' lives of a woman, thus constructing a platform to contest the performativity of femininity on screen. In the play, the character played by Rohini is seen murdered at the hands of her cousin, but in the film, she is determined to avenge herself on the man who ruined her life. Crime films can be narrated either from the perspective of the criminal, victim or the saviour who reimposes social order. George's film is a perfect blend of all these perspectives. Although the film starts with an indication of a crime and the possible involvement of various male characters in the act, the perspective gradually shifts towards the victim who eventually turns out to be the avenger, the murderer and, ultimately, a saviour in a real sense. Rohini's stage character did not act out of vengeance for her chastity despite the fact that her submission was more or less unwilling. Although the film cannot be accurately categorised as only a revenge drama, it serves as point of departure to discuss the role of a strong female protagonist in female-oriented crime investigation thrillers. Moreover, this film acts as an intermediary between the traditional portrayal of women within the domestic and household spheres and the more modern portrayal of women roles of greater social agency.

Kannezhuthi Pottum Thottu (the title of this film, 'Eye-lined and Wearing a Pottu', metonymically refers to Malayalee girls who traditionally wear a coloured dot sticker on their forehead and line their eyes black): *Kannezhuthi Pottum Thottu* can be considered to be the first real female revenge drama in Malayalam cinema. Narrated through the protagonist Bhadra, a formidable and seductive peasant woman, the film was ahead of its time. Bhadra is portrayed as a bold character who seeks revenge against Natesan, a landlord, who killed Bhadra's parents 15 years ago. Bhadra's father Chandrappan who was a worker in Natesan's field had a dispute with him on wages that led Natesan to kill him and bury his body in a swamp. To escape from the seductive eyes of Natesan, her mother took her own life by burning herself near the swamp where her husband was buried. In order to hide this heinous crime, Natesan unleashes a bogus story that Chandrappan ordered the other workers to bury him alive to mend the breach in the embankment. The story circulates and becomes legend with Chandrappan turning out as a martyr rather than a victim. After 15 years, Bhadra manages to get work at Natesan's field and, later, at his house as a helper. She learns that Natesan's son Uthaman is a womaniser like his father. Knowing that her physical power will never help her in killing Natesan, she works out a plan to lure Natesan through feminine wile. At the same time, she also tries to seduce his son Uthaman, which eventually leads to jealousy and hostility between the father and son. To set the climax for her vengeance, she invites both of them to her small hovel in the paddy field. Just as she planned, Uthaman kills his father in the field near the swamp where her father was buried. Uthaman is electrocuted to death by a power cable that came down as a result of heavy rain. She watches everything with rage and satisfaction.

Using men as pawns and staying completely away from having blood on her hands, Bhadra comes out as a winner in her game of vengeance. As opposed to what one sees in *Gulab Gang* and *Bandit Queen*, femininity is not equated with the hypermasculinised power of male heroes to transform the victim into a menacing goon or bandit. She wants revenge just as much as any man, but the way she delivers it lacks the quality of being 'manly'. Her acts are tightly linked to her femininity; the film depicts her as doing things only a woman can do with matchless mental power, dedication and shrewdness instead of engaging in an apotheosis of a feigned machismo. She even openly expresses her love for the local bangle seller Moosakutty while letting him know that she is not ready to marry yet as she has some 'responsibilities' to fulfill. As opposed to Rohini in *Yavanika*, Bhadra has a very shrewd ploy to avenge her enemies. She was clear and meticulous in it. She was so courageous and optimistic in her vendetta that she does not seek help or validation from others. As such, Bhadra personifies 'Bhadrakaali' – the Hindu goddess considered as an epitome of fierceness and strength – and the film employs popular imagery of the goddess that consists of open hair, fiery eyes and red saree. In the final scene, Bhadra appears as *Kaali* with her open hair, round big bindi and red saree, where she is seen fiercely and satisfactorily basking in the final moments of her enemies. The highlight of the film is that it never tries to take Bhadra out of a feminine identity, but instead presents the avenging woman with attributes that strongly bind her to female characteristics that are suppressed in media valorisations of ideal or normative femininity.

22 Female Kottayam (2012) ('22 Female Kottayam') is perhaps the most celebrated, debated and acclaimed female-oriented cinema, not just in Malayalam, but across India. The film was held in high regard by both critics and the public for its exemplification of women's empowerment through a shocking climax. The story recounts the life of a 22-year-old Malayali nurse, Tessa, from Kottayam (a District in Kerala). During her visa procedures for a job in Canada, she gets to meet Cyril Mathew, a travel agency worker, and soon ends up in a romantic relationship with him. Tessa moves out to live with Cyril, and they have a passionate premarital relationship. Things take a turn when Cyrils's boss Hegde rapes her and leaves her severely wounded while Cyril is not at home. Learning about the heinous act, Cyril tries to attack his boss, but Tessa, with innocent credulity, calms him down to not make the situation worse for her. Pretending to ask forgiveness, Hegde visits her again at home only to rape her again in the absence of Cyril. Tessa is then imprisoned for keeping drugs in her bag, a crime she did not commit. In jail, she realises that it was Cyril who set her up for the drug charges. Through her cellmate Zubeida, Tessa learns that Cyril is a known pimp in the city and was cheating her along with his boss Hegde. Zubeida gradually instils in Tessa a criminal mindset that will give her the strength and courage needed to strike back at Cyril and Hegde.

Tessa transforms into a fierce and bold woman with the trenchant goal of taking revenge on her rapists. Getting out of prison, she heads straight to the promiscuous DK (Tessa's roommate's married and non-monogamous lover) who helps her kill Hegde by poisoning him with a cobra. Targeting her next foe, Tessa, posing as an aspiring young model, reaches Cochin where Cyril is running a modelling firm. She manages to lure him in and hooks up with him at his studio. He reveals that he recognised her at first sight and proceeds to beat and abuse her, claiming that she is just like any other 'mere woman' who would sleep with anyone to reach her goals. But Tessa manages to calm him down and soon Cyril starts to enjoy her company while again moving in to exploit her. However, that night, Tessa accomplishes her revenge on Cyril by performing penectomy on him, physically removing his masculine pride. It is this blindsiding climax that make this film stand out as exceptionally disturbing within the category of Malayalam revenge films. It explicitly raises questions about destroying patriarchy and masculinised power.

The same climax and ending scenes also put the film under scrutiny as some critics believed that the film reaffirmed patriarchal norms through these scenes. After all, Tessa was seeking the help of a dissolute man like DK, promising him sexual pleasure in return, which makes her look weak and submissive. While the audience waits for a frail and humiliated Cyril to wake from his sedation, he emerges unabashed from his loss and shuns her by saying that his masculinity does not depend on what she removed, and he is still as capable as any other man. He confidently challenges Tessa to meet her in Canada at which Tessa smiles and escapes. As Gopinath and Raj propose,

> Notions of morality are dismissed, but when she is raped and confronted with sexual trauma, she takes the route that patriarchy expects of a woman: she objectifies her body, exploiting men's sexual interest in order to take revenge on her abusers. (2015: 7)

However, this can also be read through a very different lens. Tessa is a very unconventional heroine and exhibits a type of femininity unfamiliar for the Malayalee audience (or, at least, one not frequently exhibited in cinematic representations). She does not speak with regret about her virginity or her premarital relationships. While she manages to kill Hegde for what he did to her, she wanted to impose a more severe consequence on Cyril for his crimes that he would bear his entire life. She neutralises the power of phallus from the pimp that defines his life by it because the emptiness that this castration delivers is far more lethal than any other punishment.

Puthiya Niyamam ('New Law')

Puthiya Niyamam is yet another woman-oriented revenge drama released in Malayalam with a bigger star cast. It is a rape-and-revenge drama similar to *22 Female Kottayam* but varies in its plot construction and characterisation. Vasuki, a Kathakali artist, lives with her husband Louis, a lawyer and a television film critic, and her school-going daughter. She is raped by her neighbourhood engineering students along with a Tamil man who irons clothes in the community. This incident scars her for life, and the trauma forces her to withdraw from social life and domestic labour. Fearing the impact it might cause on her marital life, she hides this from her family including her loving husband. One day during a dance performance, she meets the new police commissioner, Jeena Bhai, who congratulates her on her performance. Vasuki felt positive and optimistic talking to Jeena so she gets her phone number from Louis's mobile.

Jeena began to advise Vasuki and and encourage her to exact revenge upon her rapists because, according to her, the laws have many loopholes that would help the culprits to escape from punishment. Through her telephonic assistance, Vasuki kills her rapists one by one prudently by setting up each event as an accident or suicide. Once her vengeance has been fulfilled, Jeena tells Vasuki to keep their conversation a secret and that she should never try to contact her again. But it is later revealed to the audience that Louis had already learned what has happened from a neighbouring old man who helplessly witnessed these heinous crimes from his apartment. Through a mobile software that can turn Louis's male voice into a female, he has mimicked Jeena and guided Vasuki to murder her rapists. He realised that this was the only way she could get redemption, and he decided to keep this as a secret from her so that she could feel the contentment of a revenge that leads to a peaceful life. Even though a part of the film is focusing on the vengeful side of Vasuki, a larger light is shed on the forbearance and endurance of Louis who declares in one of the scenes that 'for me, my family is above everything, even the Indian Constitution that I respect'. The gullible Vasuki is protected, guided and redeemed by Louis performing the role of a saviour, thus ultimately attributing all vigilante heroism to the male protagonist.

The next section looks at the shared characteristics of these vigilantes to better understand and define the range of social functions expressed by feminine heroes in the revenge films of Malayalam cinema.

Revenge as Fulfillment: Self-fashioning New Forms of Femininity

Characteristics of a genre are culturally specific, and it is also from within these cultural conditions that gender identities are constructed. The pattern and narratology adopted by a genre are better understood through, as well as inspired by, the cultural and social context within which a genre film is made. Moreover, audience engagement in a film is closely related to the above constructs of genre and gender as the themes and their treatment, narration and even characterisation must be socially relatable as far as the general public is concerned. The embeddedness of genre within gender, and the films' deployment of these interlocking structures, can be illustrated using three main points. Firstly, female protagonists in these films represent a good sample of their population in the society in depictions of careers and home lives shared by women in the audience – for example, a nurse, dancer, daily wage worker, housewife. Hence, they are not bestowed with any super heroic power or masculine flair through which they would exhibit an exceptional audacity. In 22 *Female Kottayam*, for instance, Tessa represents the desires of many nurses in Kerala who aspire to migrate to western countries for better careers and opportunities. According to The World Health Organization Report on the Migration of Nurses, nurses trained in India form a significant portion of internationally educated nurses working overseas, second only to nurses trained in the Philippines (2017). Secondly, the vengeance of female vigilantes is very personal and instinctive. These acts of revenge are not a collective response as in the case of *Gulab Gang* or *Bandit Queen* where the female protagonist unleashes her vendetta to advance justice in society with the help of a large group of followers. Thirdly, all female vengeance films are thematised around rape or female sexual violations in one way or other. Thus, as a result, they can be more directly described as rape-revenge dramas.

According to the National Crime Records Bureau of India, Kerala accounts for 2.8 per cent of the total number of crimes against women in the country. There have been 1945 incidents of rape reported in 2018 alone in Kerala, and in 98.4 per cent of these cases, the assaulter has been known to the victim. Bhadra in *Kannezhuthi Pottum Thottu,* Tessa in *22 Female Kottayam* and Vasuki in *Puthiya Niyamam* also knew their perpetrators. Although these films shape society by deliberately or unintentionally creating new archetypes of heroic femininity, rape-and-revenge dramas with popularity in mainstream cinema directly engage daily crises of gendered violence while also provide a public space for working out a vision empowered femininity that dramatically challenges ideal or normative feminine traits.

In addition to this, these films pose questions about the nature of justice and the judicial system. In most rape cases, victims are guaranteed justice. In 2011, Kerala woke up to reports of a brutal rape and murder of a 23-year-old girl, Soumya, who was commuting from her workplace to her hometown on a local train. The convict, Govindachamy, raped her on the rail track after allegedly throwing her off the moving train. In his trial in the Supreme Court, he was represented by his lawyers who argued that the culprit was a mentally unbalanced vagrant and petty thief to reduce his death penalty to just seven years of imprisonment. The verdict caused disappointment among the public that wanted capital punishment for the convict. A year later, India was hit by yet another rape and murder case that triggered questions about the safety of women in public. The victim died from her injuries days after being brutally raped by six men on a moving bus. As one of the perpetrators was a minor at the time of the crime, he had to serve only three years in the juvenile home as the maximum term possible for a juvenile in India. These miscarriages of justice have slowly led to new anti-rape laws in India.

Heller-Nicholas suggests that rape-revenge films are not cohesive in nature considering the variety of films on this subject matter and the innovative ways in which the genre is treated by filmmakers around the world (2021: 103–104). This, along with the neglect with which it has historically directly dealt with as a grave crime with deep social ramifications, is one reason that some scholars consider these films as a subgenre of horror (as Clover 1993 has positioned it) or as a hybrid to other popular genres like comedy or science fiction. Here, genre acts as a key to understanding and interrogating the meaning of rape within a cultural and social milieu. The intensity with which the 'act' of rape is portrayed often defines the narrative purpose of these films. This is a fundamental reason why, for a large period of time, rape-revenge dramas from many countries were considered as B-grade films as they were perceived to cater to the voyeuristic pleasure of the audience rather than discussing serious questions about crime, gender and sexuality. Due to the strict censorship rules in India, sexually explicit scenes are always suppressed, and the directors of Malayalam cinema show instances in which a rape scene can seem veiled yet also reveal the severity of the torture that the victim goes through. The more focus is put on the emotional state of the victim to make her transformation into a vigilante more engaging. As in the case of real-life events, these films also question a judicial system that must be held responsible for protecting the rights of women and the neglect of the state is put on heart-wrenching display when women are punished in these films. For instance, in *Yavanika*, the ordeals that Rohini had to face living with Ayyappan (who raped her initially) were never taken into account when she was arrested for his murder. Similarly, Tessa in *22 Female Kottayam* was deceived and framed by Cyril, which leads to her arrest for a crime she never committed.

The ongoing construction of femininity in these films is what defines the female revenge drama in Malayalam cinema. Rape and sexual exploitation are not novel themes in cinema; however, earlier Malayalam films delineated female protagonists as sexually chaste – and a denial to this often ends in a woman's onscreen suicide. Rape is considered ignominious, and the weight of this crime is often placed with surprising dexterity back upon on the female protagonist. This sexual chastity is one of the factors that have historically defined ideal or normative femininity in Malayalam cinema previous to the recent popularity of rape-revenge films. Agential roles for female protagonists were very rare (Rajendran 2014), and their sexuality was often contested within their private or domestic spheres in these films. *Yavanika* was released at a period when traditional concepts about moral and sexual purity were being perpetuated in regional and national cinema, and hence, unlike the other three films analysed here, retribution is not met with an optimistic outcome. The female protagonist's decision to cohabitate with the very man who exploited raised questions regarding her morality, and, thus, her retaliation at the end does not completely negate the criminality of the act of murder for the audience.

Femininity in these films cannot be comprehended as a fixed set of traits that collectively define the identity of every woman. However, by negating an approbation of virility of the masculine, the performance of femininity in these films splits into numerous interpretations that make it impossible to accumulate the various versions of femininity into one single manifestation. Evoking the power of masculinity to demonstrate brashness cannot positively redefine femininity in characterisation as either the equivalent or opposite of masculine traits. The act of revenge adopted by women characters in these films ultimately refers to a self-defined and self-sustaining agency that is essential to the construction of a feminine identity formed autonomously from a hegemony of gender normativity instituted by the dominance of the masculine. The orchestration of revenge in an explicitly violent manner onscreen promulgates a self-fashioning of the modern female character. It can be marked as a paradigm shift that overthrows the macho-masculine female bandits to establish an independently conceived trope of a traditional female avenger. The films analysed in this study offer a context where normal women with no extraordinary powers are able to carry out revenge as a form of resistance inevitable for their survival, recovery and regeneration. Therefore, the avenging woman transforms from a monolithic stereotype to a collection of identities that originate from spaces ranging from the households to the public sphere. Her presence is not ephemeral or an anomaly as she is no longer a manifestation of the abject woman that horrifies spectators but a fellow companion who must travel from victimhood to redefine a feminine essence.

Conclusion

Malayalam cinema has long been defined by narratives that popularise gender stereotypes and heteronormative characteristics. It is for this reason that cinema specifically classifies those films that contain a prominent female protagonist or themes as 'women-oriented' – a term used in opposition to mainstream cinematic tradition. The revenge thrillers are only one category of such women-oriented films that seek identify and contest definitions of femininity, but this number will continue to increase as the ethical and political need for such films grows alongside appeals to fulfill guarantees of gender equality in a society where crime against women continues unabated.

Indian cinema's failure to acknowledge or consider domestic/private violence as something that demands a response from the state and the public is evident in its narratives. While popular national cinema stops short of fully empowering women within the domestic sphere, presenting the family as social institution and sacred space where gender constructs are sustained and normalised, female revenge is considered an anomaly that is incapable of challenging the existing notions of normative femininity. Anomalous examples of female revenge thrillers, therefore, detach the woman protagonist from the familial space to attain a masculine dacoit persona: a vigilante that hides behind the mainstream hegemonic power structures. Gopinath and Raj assert that in these films the 'focus is on the individual far away from the institution of family, giving the filmmaker more freedom to create characters without upsetting his own sense of morality' (2015: 7). According to the National Family and Health Survey 2021 (NFHS), spousal violence continues to be a major concern for women, and 10 per cent of married women have experienced some form of physical violence from their husbands. It is also alarming to see that only 24 per cent of women seek help, and a majority have only tried to hide such violence from their immediate relatives. According to an NFHS report previous to this study in Kerala, 65.7 per cent of women and 54.2 per cent of men believed that spousal violence was justifiable if there was sufficient cause such as the neglect of the household or children, disrespect shown to in-laws or suspected infidelity. According to the database of Kerala Police, 11,124 cases were registered by the police as crimes against women in 2021. These are the social conditions through which Malayalam cinema must route expressions of female identity and sexuality as defined within the structure of the family.

Female revenge dramas exploit different narrative possibilities in addressing these issues. There have been novel attempts in Malayalam cinema in recent years that carve out spaces for heroines within the purview of their private and public domains. These films often manage a balanced image of the avenging woman as traditionally family bound and actively independent, thereby maintaining the structure of the family but giving the protagonists new spatial roles through narrative. Dismissing the macho-female vigilantism that has been at the core of female criminal heroes in Bollywood, these women pursue instincts for revenge as a response to impending threats of violence that hinder their existence and thereby redefine femininity as self-fashioned agency. The films discussed in this article exemplify situations where women take revenge on perpetrators without compromising what is represented onscreen as a shifting and adapting ontology of the feminine. Such narrative portrayals of women emphasise reinvention of the self as a quality of female agency, and the evolution of subgenres like rape-and-revenge glimpse a collective processing of a woman's journey from trauma into an empowering self-fashioning of identity. Future of cinematic visualisations of the avenging woman will continue to add new dimensions the multiplicity of feminine gender possibilities to push these beyond the limits of heteronormative binaries.

Works Cited

Butter, Stella. 2019. 'Troubling Justice: Narratives of Revenge'. In *Narrative in Culture*, 165–184. Edited by Astrid Erll and Roy Sommer. Berlin: De Gruyter.

Clover, Carol J. 1993. *Men, Women, and Chain Saws: Gender in the Modern Horror Film*. Princeton, NJ: Princeton University Press.

Connell, R. W. 2005. *Masculinities*. Cambridge: Blackwell Publishers.

Gates, Philips. 2006. *Detecting Men Masculinity and the Hollywood Detective Film*. Albany: State University of New York Press.

Ghosh, Tapan K. 2013. *Bollywood Baddies; Villains, Vamps and Henchmen in Hindi Cinema*. New Delhi: SAGE.

Gopinath, Swapna and Sony Jalarajan Raj. 2015. 'Gender construct as a narrative and text: The female protagonist in new generation Malayalam cinema'. *South Asian Popular Culture* 13.1: 65–75.

Grant, Barry Keith. 2007. *Film Genre: From Iconography to Ideology*. London and New York: Wallflower.

Heller-Nicholas, Alexandra. 2021. *Rape-Revenge Films: A Critical Study*. Jefferson, NC: McFarland.

Kumar, Preeti. 2015. 'Hegemonic Masculinities in Two Comic Films in Malayalam: Meesa Madhavan and Rajamanikyam'. *ArtCultura*, Uberlândia 17.30: 31–42.

Leitch, Thomas. 2002. *Crime Films*. Cambridge: Cambridge University Press.

Menon, Rajiv Kannan. 2009. 'Intimate terrors: changing representations of structural violence against women in Malayali cinema'. *Studies in South Asian Film and Media* 1.2: 285–301

Najib, Rihan. 'Stronger, bolder, louder: The new female leads in Malayalam films'. *Business Line*. 28 June 2019. <https://www.thehindubusinessline.com/blink/cover/the-evolution-of-the-female-lead-in-malayalam-cinema/article28197171.ece/photo/1/> (last accessed 16 February 2022).

Pillai, Meena T. 'Becoming women. Unwrapping Femininity in Malayalam Cinema'. In *Women in Malayalam Cinema: Naturalising Gender Hierarchies*, 3–24. Edited by Meena T. Pillai. New Delhi: Orient Blackswan Publishers.

Rajendran, Aneeta (2014). 'You Are Woman Arguments with Normative Femininities in Recent Malayalam Cinema'. *Economic & Political Weekly* 49.17: 61–69

Raj, Sony, Rohini Sreekumar and Nithin Kalorth. 2018, 'Ruling the Men's Den: Crime, Outrage and Indian Women Gang Leaders'. In *A Companion to the Gangster Film*, 413–429. Edited by George S. Larke-Walsh. Hoboken, NJ: Wiley Blackwell.

Sparks, Richard. 2008. 'Masculinity and Heroism in the Hollywood 'Blockbuster'. In *Crime, Criminal Justice and Masculinities*, 249–262. Edited by Stephen Tomsen. London: Routledge.

World Health Organization. *From brain drain to brain gain: Migration of nursing and midwifery workforce in the state of Kerala* (Report). 2017. <https://www.who.int/workforcealliance/brain-drain-brain-gain/Migration-of-nursing-midwifery-in-Kerala-WHO.pdf?ua=1> (last accessed 16 February 2022).

SECTION II

TRANSGRESSION

Part II
Modes of Transgression vis-à-vis State Repression and Violence

7. COMMUNIST NOIR: THE HUNT FOR HIDDEN TRAITORS, SABOTEURS, SPIES, REVISIONISTS AND DEVIATIONISTS IN ALBANIA'S REVOLUTIONARY VIGILANCE FILMS OF THE 1970S AND 1980S

Jonida Gashi

Part I: Historical Background

On 4 March 1966, the Central Committee (CC) of the Albanian Party of Labor (APL) addressed all communists, workers and military personnel in Albania through an open letter in which it condemned in the harshest terms possible the phenomenon of bureaucratisation in both state and party apparatuses. Describing bureaucratisation as a 'remnant of the past and an expression of the pressure exerted by the class enemy and his ideology on our ranks', the CC also denounced the excessive formality and 'officialism' that characterised the work of state institutions, their separation from the masses, the inflated public administration, the intelligentsia's contempt for physical labour, their tendency to seek personal comfort and personal glory, and so on. The CC's open letter marked the official start of the anti-bureaucratisation campaign in Albania, a campaign that brought about significant changes in the organisation and functioning of the entire justice system, while also leading to a reconfiguration of the relationship between the masses and the law in general. For instance, in the aforementioned open letter the CC calls on the masses not to leave the formulation of laws exclusively in the hands of bureaucrats and technocrats, but rather to become actively involved in this activity 'by expressing their opinions and presenting their criticisms', so that the 'bureaucratic distortions' and 'unnecessary excesses' (the example given in the letter is 'the obsession with anticipating all possible scenarios') that made laws incomprehensible or difficult to understand for the working masses could thereby be avoided (Komiteti Qendror 1966: 1).

On 1 November 1966, almost exactly eight months after the Central Committee's open letter, Enver Hoxha, the First Secretary of the APL, discussed the anti-bureaucratisation campaign and the pursuit of the mass line by the party and state apparatuses at length in his report to the Fifth Party Congress. Hoxha's speech is notable for two reasons as far as the anti-bureaucratisation campaign and the pursuit of the mass line are concerned. The first reason has to do with the fact that in his discussion of bureaucratisation Hoxha singled out the work of the prosecution and the courts (which the CC had refrained from doing in its open letter) and heavily admonished them for their 'severe weaknesses' (Hoxha 1966: 10). The second reason has to do with the fact that Hoxha framed the anti-bureaucratisation campaign and the pursuit of the mass line in terms of the continuation and deepening of class struggle in Albania (which the CC had also refrained from doing). The backdrop was the impending announcement of the Albanian Ideological and Cultural Revolution on the heels of the Chinese Cultural Revolution.[1] In Hoxha's speech, the aims of the anti-bureaucratisation campaign and the pursuit of the mass line on the one hand, and the Ideological and Cultural Revolution on the other, are not merely compatible; they are closely aligned. The anti-bureaucratisation campaign and the pursuit of the mass line are depicted as having first and foremost a preemptive function, which was the elimination of the objective conditions that might lead not only the party but the entire country to slide towards modern revisionism, thus paving the way for the restoration of capitalism. Those conditions would be the creation of a socialist bourgeoisie on the basis of a privileged bureaucratic stratum like in the Soviet Union. The Ideological and Cultural Revolution, on the other hand, is depicted as having first and foremost a proactive function, where the 'full triumph of the proletarian, socialist ideology in the consciousness of the working people' – as one of the main goals of the revolution – was seen as guaranteeing the 'victories of the socialist revolution in the political and economic realms'; and the creation of the 'new man' – as another of the main goals of the revolution – represented the 'decisive factor' in the construction of the true communist society in Albania. This could only be achieved through the waging of the class struggle 'in the people's midst' and 'in every person's consciousness, mind, behavior and attitudes' (Ibid.: 10).

Even though Hoxha went on to instruct in his speech that the class struggle on the ideological and cultural front would *not* focus on the 'kulaks and other elements of the former exploiting classes, the imperialists, or the Titoist and Khrushchevist revisionists', this did not actually mean that the old-fashioned, so to speak, class struggle against such 'elements' had lost and/or was going to lose any of its intensity, quite the contrary (Ibid.: 10). Kadri Hazbiu, the then Minister of Interior Affairs, declared in his discussion of Hoxha's report to the Fifth Party Congress that there had been 'an intensification of enemy activity' against the People's Republic of Albania since the Fourth Party Congress in

1961. He also claimed that the 'modern revisionists' were largely responsible for this, thanks in no small part to their 'vile, subversive intelligence work' involving 'the recruitment and activation of tens of agents from the spy networks of the countries ruled by the revisionists' who had plotted to 'sabotage the economy, weaken our unity and the country's defenses'. Indeed, Hazbiu went so far as to posit 'the revisionist platform has served as the point of departure for every attack undertaken against our socialist order by all of our enemies, inside as well as outside the country' (Hazbiu 1966: 5). Needless to say, the continuation and deepening of the class struggle on not one but two fronts – 'in the people's midst' and 'in every person's consciousness, mind, behavior and attitudes' as well as against the 'kulaks and other elements of the former exploiting classes, the imperialists, or the Titoist and Khrushchevist revisionists' – necessarily required a continuation and deepening of the revolutionary vigilance.

But how were the Central Committee's and especially Enver Hoxha's directives regarding the anti-bureaucratisation campaign and the pursuit of the mass line interpreted and, more importantly, put into practice by the Albanian justice system? Arianit Çela, the newly-appointed Chief Justice of the Supreme Court of the People's Republic of Albania, announced in a speech held in mid-January 1967 that one of the key ways in which the courts were going to wage their war against bureaucratisation and strengthen their ties to the working masses was by asking for their 'opinions, advice and suggestions' in connection with specific court cases (Çela 1967). Noting that 'consultation with the working masses' should be incorporated into the working methodology of the courts, Çela also stressed that it should be carried out 'at all stages of the trial process, as needed', meaning before the trial, during the trial and even after the trial – so as to 'work through the verdict with the collective where the crime was committed, get an opinion on how the verdict was received by the masses, undertake self-criticism and answer for the unjust judgment, the wrong verdict'; and also 'for different purposes', from uncovering new evidence to determining the defendant's character and past, his or her attitudes at the workplace and in society, and so on (13). Lefter Goga, the then Prosecutor General of the People's Republic of Albania, gave a similar speech only a few weeks later, in late February 1967, in front of a gathering of public prosecutors from around the country. Unlike Çela, however, Goga also used his speech to warn against the potential dangers of taking consultation with the working masses too far, effectively instructing his subordinates to not 'become a slave to their opinion, because it can happen that the working masses, for a variety of reasons, are not entirely clear about the case and the specific circumstances in which the crime took place' (Goga 1967: 11). This can be read as an early indication that the participation of the masses in the administration of justice in Albania would remain under the state's and the party's strict control.

Another important way in which the justice system waged its antibureaucratisation campaign and pursued the mass line, which had the added benefit of being very tangible, was through the organisation of what were known as 'on-site trials'. 'On-site trials' were public trials that were held outside of the courts, in cooperatives and factories for instance, as well as in both rural and city centres, in front of an audience. The practice of 'on-site trials' was by no means a new one. They had been held for decades, mainly for educational purposes. The most high profile and the most infamous type of 'on-site trials' that were held in Albania during the communist period were the show trials against traitors, saboteurs, spies, revisionists and deviationists. After the Central Committee's Open Letter and the Fifth Party Congress, the number of 'on-site trials' increased dramatically.[2] The anti-bureaucratisation campaign and the Ideological and Cultural Revolution seem to have ushered in a new era in which the basic model of the communist show trial trickled down to (was adapted for) the lowest instance courts and the pettiest of crimes, violations, and legal disputes. Of course, this presented certain challenges. Sami Baholli, the then deputy Chief Justice of the Supreme Court of the People's Republic of Albania, outlines some of these challenges in an article published nearly one year after the Fifth Party Congress and in the process provides the reader with a basic definition of what a show trial is (Baholli 1967). Baholli begins by warning that 'the on-site trial must not resemble an arena of curiosities where a few idle people go to pass the time', but, rather, must 'sharpen the revolutionary vigilance of the masses' (Ibid.: 8–9). He then stresses the importance of ensuring that 'the public assisting at the trial can hear the proceedings ... through radiophones, and that they have a good view of the judges and the litigants who must be positioned in a conspicuous spot' (Ibid.: 9). Finally, Baholli instructs that during an on-site trial 'it is necessary that the development and the conclusion of the trial are properly anticipated', and that the audience 'must be well known to the court' (Ibid.: 9).

The anti-bureaucratisation campaign and the pursuit of the mass line by and within the Albanian justice system was a complex, drawn-out process that went beyond 'consultation with the working masses' and the organisation of 'on-site trials'. As I have already mentioned, this campaign eventually led to a complete reorganisation of the Albanian justice system and an overhaul of the Albanian legislation (Nova 1982). I have decided to focus on the aspects of 'consultation with the working masses' and the reorganisation of 'on-site trials' for three (interconnected) reasons. Firstly, because of the centrality of 'consultation with the working masses' in the discovery and investigation of crimes in the Albanian revolutionary vigilance films, a genre that emerged in the late 1960s and early 1970s and which is the topic of the second part of this article. Secondly, because as mentioned above, the organisation of 'on-site trials' clearly evokes the practice of the staging of show trials, and the Albanian revolutionary vigilance films owe their aesthetic in part to the newsreels and documentary films based on the proceedings of the communist show trials. Lastly, because taken together 'consultation with the working masses' and the organisation of 'on-site trials', as their borderline feverish discussion in the pages of daily newspapers and specialised publications like *Drejtësia Popullore* throughout 1967 indicates, denote a relationship to the law that both explicitly and implicitly attempt to recapture (some of) the revolutionary origins of socialist law. The earliest partisan trials organised during the Second World War were arguably one of the most exemplary embodiments of that revolutionary spirit and, interestingly for my purposes here, they also provided one origin story (and a specifically national one) for the emergence of the institution of the communist show trial after the war's end.

Part II: The Revolutionary Vigilance Films

It would be difficult to overestimate the impact that the Ideological and Cultural Revolution had on the arts in the People's Republic of Albania. In the case of the cinema, the main theses and contradictions at the heart of the Ideological and Cultural Revolution, such as the gap between the intelligentsia and the working masses; the intelligentsia's tendency to seek personal comfort, personal glory and its contempt for manual labour; the struggle against 'backward habits' (such as religious beliefs and superstitions) and the struggle for the emancipation of women; the importance of critique from below and self-critique and so on, were widely reflected in all manner of films and film genres, from newsreels and documentary films to comedies and dramas. At the same time, the Ideological and Cultural Revolution in conjunction with the anti-bureaucratisation campaign and its emphasis on the participation of the working masses in the administration of justice, created the necessary conditions for the emergence of an entirely new genre of films in Albanian cinema. This group of films – all feature-length fictions – was produced by *Kinostudio 'Shqipëria e Re'* (New Albania Film Studio) mainly during the 1970s and 1980s and became known as the 'revolutionary vigilance films'. They include, in chronological order, *Silent Duel/Duel i Heshtur* released in 1967, *The Trace/ Gjurma* released in 1970, *Cutting the Ties/Fijet që Priten* released in 1976, *The Guest/Mysafiri* released in 1979, *The Old Cartridge/Gëzhoja e vjetër* released in 1980, *An Incident at the Port/Një ndodhi në port* released in 1981, *The Threat/Kërcënimi* released in 1982, *The Trap/Gracka* and *Traces in the Snow/ Gjurmë në Dëborë* which were both released in 1984, *Nothing Is Forgotten/ Asgjë nuk Harrohet* from 1986, *The Investigation Continues/Hetimi Vazhdon* from 1987, *The Mission Across the Sea/Misioni Përtej Detit* from 1989, and *Who Is the Killer?/Kush Është Vrasësi?* which was released in 1989.

As the name suggests, the revolutionary vigilance films centred on the revolutionary vigilance of the masses as a safeguard and a weapon against the dangers posed by both internal and external enemies. Additionally, the revolutionary vigilance films functioned as cautionary tales about the potentially fatal consequences of even the smallest concession towards not only the class enemy but also oneself as well as one's neighbour, colleague, friend, family member and so on. In other words, the revolutionary vigilance films combined, rather dynamically it must be said, the 'old' class struggle against the 'kulaks and other elements of the former exploiting classes, the imperialists, or the Titoist and Khrushchevist revisionists' with the 'new' class struggle on the cultural and ideological front taking place 'in the people's midst' and 'in every person's consciousness, mind, behaviour and attitudes' (Hoxha 1966: 10). In terms of plot, the revolutionary vigilance films stage a *danse macabre* with three figures: the enemy of the people, who primarily takes the form of an internal agent of imperialism/revisionism who has been hiding in plain sight (at the heart of communist society)[3], the ordinary communist who still carries remnants of petit-bourgeois ideology in his consciousness making them liable to being compromised by the enemy of the people, and, finally, the agent of the *Sigurimi i Shtetit*, that is, the secret police. It usually plays out as a race (against time) between the attempts of the enemy of the people to advance and/or finalise a criminal master plan; the attempts of the ordinary communist who has been compromised by the enemy of the people to untangle themselves from the web they have been drawn into before they are themselves branded as a class enemy; and the efforts of the agent of the *Sigurimi i Shtetit* to uncover the identity of the enemy of the people and to liquidate the risk posed by their criminal exploits before it is too late.

Usually, the criminal master plan that the hidden agents of imperialism and revisionism must advance or finalise consists in the appropriation (illegally of course) of state secrets on account of foreign intelligence services and obscure espionage networks, with the aim of preparing/carrying out an act of sabotage targeting Albania's socialist industry (*Gjurma, Fijet që Priten, Mysafiri, Gëzhoja e Vjetër, Një Ndodhi në Port, Hetimi Vazhdon, Kush është Vrasësi?*), and sometimes even the socialist military (*Kërcënimi*) and socialist power as such (*Duel i Heshtur, Gracka, Gjurmë në Dëborë*).[4] Alongside the element of espionage, the element of crime also plays a key role in the production of suspense in the revolutionary vigilance films. I am referring here to the crimes committed by the agents of imperialism and revisionism (predominantly though not exclusively) in order to cover their tracks. Apart from providing key clues that help uncover the acts of sabotage being planned by the enemies of the people, these crimes, which almost always take the form of murder and, more rarely, attempted murder, are also notable for the degree of violence that characterises them: from the extended gun fight to the death between the enemy group led by Sergeant Ramiu and lone sailor Skënder Guri set in the highly claustrophobic interiors and exteriors of a motorboat on choppy seas in Dhimitër Anagnosti's 1967 film *Duel i Heshtur*, which ends with Sergeant Ramiu and another member of his group losing their lives while the third member is spared only in order to be handed over to the authorities (that will certainly sentence him to death at a later point); to the grotesque scene of Dilaver Dilo's murder in Mark Topallaj's 1987 film *Hetimi Vazhdon*, perhaps the darkest of the Albanian revolutionary vigilance films, in which the actual murder takes place off-camera so that what we see on-camera as we hear the victim's skull being cracked open is the blankly inscrutable face of the deeply repulsive leader of the enemy group Niko, while a moment later we see a reflection of the victim and his murderers on a mirror that the victim shatters with his fist as his final gesture while two rats scurry out from behind the reflection.

In the postsocialist period, the revolutionary vigilance films have often been referred to as detective films but the label is an ill-fitting one (Lako 2004). Firstly, because it obscures the centrality of the component of espionage in the revolutionary vigilance films. Secondly, because it does not fully capture the dark undertones that characterise the revolutionary vigilance films. Thirdly, because the revolutionary vigilance films do not actually privilege the viewpoint of the detective, or the agent of the *Sigurimi i Shetit*, favouring instead an approach where the perspective of law enforcement and that of the criminal underworld are intertwined. *Fijet që Priten* is an interesting example here, since we can virtually cut the film in two: During the first half of the film, its narrative is dominated by the viewpoint of enemies of the people Sami Ameni and Marko Rovina; whereas during the second half of the film, the narrative is dominated by Besa's viewpoint – who becomes embroiled in Sami Ameni and Marko Rovina's devious plans due to an oversight at work, and that of Gjergji – who is the agent of the *Sigurimi i Shtetit* charged with investigating Sami Ameni and Marko Rovina's questionable behaviour. Finally, because in contradistinction to the figure of the classic detective, the agent of the *Sigurimi i Shtetit* is not endowed with an especially distinctive intellect, intuition and/or perceptiveness, attributes that would grant him a unique insight into crime. This does not actually mean that the revolutionary vigilance films are devoid of moments where such attributes are displayed, quite the contrary, such moments exist and they often play a key role in driving the narrative. The difference is that in the revolutionary vigilance films these moments tend to be spread out among a variety of characters, including what are essentially extras, which means that in these movies the figure of the detective, or the agent of the *Sigurimi i Shtetit*, is not a privileged character in this respect. This was, of course, completely intentional, which critics at the time did not fail to take note of. For instance, this is how one reviewer of *Fijet që Priten* described everyone who participated in resolving the criminal conspiracy at the heart of this film *apart from the detective*:

> They, by analyzing with political maturity and revolutionary vigilance certain facts and behaviours that at first sight seem unimportant . . . are

able to uncover the hand of the enemy, to identify and punish him in time. (Mandili 1976: 13)

'They' are: Marko Rovina's coworkers who manage to notice the very subtle shifts in his behaviour first when Marko Rovina spots the ring on Sami Ameni's finger inside the 'Shqipëria Sot' [*Albania Today*] exhibition hall and, a few nights later, when the headlights of a passing car briefly interrupt their meeting, startling and frightening them both; the sympathetic foreign tourist who picks up on the fact that Sami Ameni seems to understands Albanian; the Albanian translator who becomes suspicious upon discovering that his watch is suddenly ten minutes behind; the waiter who tricks Sami Ameni into showing him the identifying scar above Sami Ameni's eyebrow; and, finally, the child who causes Sami Ameni to say precisely the words needed to unlock the old professor's memory, whose testimony confirms Sami Ameni's identity as an Albanian Nazi collaborator pretending to be a foreign businessman on a touristic trip. On this point, it is important to note that in addition to not being endowed with an especially distinctive intellect, intuition and/or perceptiveness that would grant him a unique insight into crime, he (the agent of the *Sigurimi i Shtetit* is typically a male) is not endowed with any attributes that might make him stand out period.

In 'Why Stalinist Cinema Had No Detective Films, or How Three Becomes Two in *Engineer Kochin's Mistake*', Julie A. Cassiday argues that Stalinist cinema failed to successfully launch its own version of the Hollywood detective film in the 1930s not for lack of trying or other lofty (read: ideological) reasons but, rather, because such an undertaking entailed the elimination of a component that she considers to be the chief attraction (for audiences) of the detective genre, both in literature and in film (Cassiday 2014). That component is, in Cassiday's words, 'the opportunity to open up, enter into, enjoy, and perpetuate the place of the third' (62). Cassiday's point of departure in her analysis of thirdness in the Stalinist detective film is Jacques Lacan's reading of the detective genre's obsession with triangulated relationships in his 'Seminar on "The Purloined Letter"'. It posits that the detective genre's obsession with triangulated relationships repeats the same basic pattern, an 'intersubjective triad' wherein the first position is occupied by the Law, the second position is occupied by its subject (transgressor), and the third position is occupied by the detective. Furthermore, it causes the first and second positions in the intersubjective triad to be locked in an 'imaginary relationship of coercive mirroring' between them, an impasse that is only resolved by the detective when he finally solves the crime. By exposing the culprit(s) at the end of the film, the detective allows the audience to both enjoy their transgressive desire and get away with it, which produces the specific pleasure associated with the detective genre. The detective's position outside of the dyadic relationship between the Law and its subject is conveyed in myriad ways, most typically through the detective's portrayal as a 'para-authority' with asocial, sometimes asexual and all manner of (other) eccentric tendencies. In the Stalinist detective film, on the other hand, the detective represents an amalgam of the first and third positions in the Lacanian schema, so that the element of thirdness paradoxically serves to intensify identification with the first position, namely that of the Law or, in this case, Stalin. Ultimately, however, the Stalinist detective film undercuts the detective's ability to occupy both positions simultaneously, revealing the Socialist Realist detective's thirdness to be merely a 'simulacrum' and his identification with the first position to be unsustainable. This causes the detective, as well as all the other characters that populate the Stalinist detective film and, by implication, the audience too, to fall into the second position in the Lacanian schema. The implications of this forced identification with the second position, which has the effect of removing the enjoyment associated with transgression, are compounded by the fact that in the Stalinist detective film the second position is not synonymous with transgression but, rather with 'essentialized criminality' as Cassiday puts it. It is thus that the Stalinist detective film 'obliterates the third position of the detective and coerces our perverse enjoyment not of transgression, but of obedience' (Ibid.: 59).

There are many similarities between the Stalinist detective film as outlined by Cassiday and the Albanian revolutionary vigilance films, including – but not limited to – the association of marital betrayal with treason, the association of promiscuous women with enemies of the people, the tendency for the detective to be an officer of the secret police as opposed to the ordinary police, the tendency for the detective to be an amalgam of the first and third positions in the Lacanian schema, the symptomatic proliferation of purloined letters and so on. Apart from this, the comparison to Stalinist cinema is useful also because, by the late 1960s and early 1970s, Albania was the last remaining Stalinist outpost in Eastern Europe.[5] While this does not mean that we can make simplistic comparisons between Soviet Russia in the 1930s and Albania at the height of the Ideological and Cultural Revolution in the late 1960s and early 1970s, or their respective cinematic outputs for that matter, Cassiday's article nevertheless raises an important question, namely, how come and why exactly did the Albanian revolutionary vigilance films manage to sit well with both authorities and audiences alike?[6] Especially since, more often than not, the detective in the Albanian revolutionary vigilance films suffers a similar fate to the NKVD investigator in *Engineer Kochin's Mistake* (1939), the Stalinist detective film that Cassiday discusses in her article. Namely, while the agent of the *Sigurimi i Shtetit* is ultimately always successful in solving the mystery at the heart of the film (the minor of the enigmas in any case, since the big conspiracy remains shrouded in mystery), he is also put in his place so to speak. For instance, approximately halfway through *Fijet që Priten* young investigator Gjergji is shown struggling under the weight of the responsibilities that come with being an agent of the *Sigurimi i Shtetit* and pathetically longing for the days when he was a manual labourer. Similarly, two-thirds of the way through *The Old Cartridge* veteran investigator Thanas is shown feeling humiliated by his inability to crack the case as quickly as the party expects him to. Cassiday's analysis also suggests a path towards one (potential) answer to this question, namely, by looking closely at the pattern of the connections formed between the agent of the *Sigurimi i Shtetit*, the ordinary communist with petit-bourgeois remnants in his or her consciousness, the enemy of the people and, finally, the vigilant masses. What emerges from such an analysis is that, unlike in the Stalinist detective film where it is a case of 'how three becomes two', in the Albanian revolutionary vigilance film it is more a case of how three becomes four.

This is because the figure of the vigilant masses and the role it plays in the revolutionary vigilance films shatters the triadic structure that underpins classic detective fiction – which is why the revolutionary vigilance films for the most part managed to sit well with the authorities, while at the same time salvaging the place of the third and which is arguably why the revolutionary vigilance films managed to sit well with audiences too. It should be noted that, in the Albanian revolutionary vigilance films, the vigilant masses are depicted as a rather heterogeneous bunch, including workers (obviously) as well as peasants, students as well as young children, civil servants as well as members of the so-called intelligentsia, and so on. There is, nevertheless, a hierarchy here, with the workers positioned at the top. This is clearly illustrated in one of the earliest revolutionary vigilance films, Kristaq Dhamo's *Gjurma* from 1970. The mystery at the heart of this film revolves around the suspected suicide of a well-known surgeon from the capital in an isolated, remote sawmill via a gunshot to the head, supposedly following a failed attempt to cross the border illegally. While the surgeon's long-time colleagues and even his closest friend as well as his wife are quick to accept this version of events, the workers at the sawmill where the surgeon was stationed are adamant that the good doctor could not have possibly killed himself. This pushes the lead investigator into the surgeon's death to look for clues pointing to another version of events, and, indeed, at the end of the film it is revealed that the surgeon was murdered in a struggle to prevent the real would-be fugitive – who, predictably, turns out to be a hidden agent of revisionism – from crossing the border illegally. Similarly, while the vigilant masses stand above all the other figures that populate the Albanian revolutionary vigilance films, since the revolutionary vigilance itself may be compared to an all-seeing eye under whose gaze everyone – the class enemy as much as the agent of the *Sigurimi i Shtetit* – find themselves equally exposed, they are nevertheless more closely affiliated with the agent of the *Sigurimi i Shtetit*. Herein lies the explanation, or one of the explanations, as to why the Albanian revolutionary vigilance films managed to sit well with both the authorities and audiences alike.

Much like the NKVD investigator in *Engineer Kochin's Mistake*, the agent of the *Sigurimi i Shtetit* in the Albanian revolutionary vigilance films is an amalgam of the Law and the third. That said, his affiliation with thirdness is possibly even weaker than that of Officer Lartsev in *Engineer Kochin's Mistake*. This is because, as was already mentioned, what relatively little thirdness there is to go around in the Albanian revolutionary vigilance films is divided between the agent of the *Sigurimi i Shtetit* and the vigilant masses. Conversely, while the Stalinist detective's identification with the Law ultimately proves impossible to maintain, as evidenced by Officer Lartsev's symbolic castration and suicide at the end of *Engineer Kochin's Mistake*, the identification of the vigilant masses with the Law in the Albanian revolutionary vigilance films does not.

As is probably apparent by now, the revolutionary vigilance films focused on the kinds of crimes and criminals that were the subject of the Albanian communist show trials. In fact, the revolutionary vigilance films, by showing the audience the criminal exploits of the culprits as well as the hunt for the culprits – through images that is, and moving images at that – effectively showed them what the communist show trials could not show directly but had to convey by other means and through other effects. In Albanian, the communist show trials were widely known as *gjyqe të popullit* (the people's trials). According to renowned socialist jurist Koço Nova, the origin of the term *gjyq i popullit* harks back to the ad hoc proto-military trials conducted by the first partisan detachments beginning in 1942 – during the occupation, in other words, long before there was a socialist legal system in place in Albania and, indeed, before the National Liberation Army as such existed even (Nova 1982). The term was ostensibly coined by the participants in these trials and reflected the informal, open debate form that characterised their proceedings, with the guilt (or innocence) of the defendant/s and their punishment also being determined collectively by all the participants. While the 'romantic procedural democratization' of the first partisan trials had all but disappeared by the war's end as Nova points out, the designation of the postwar show trials as *gjyqe të popullit* was clearly intended to establish a link between the two that, most likely (since Nova does not state this explicitly), centred precisely on the element of audience participation in the trial proceedings, even if only or chiefly as a spectacle (in the case of the postwar show trials) (Ibid.: 99). In fact, the show trials that were organised in Albania (and elsewhere in Eastern Europe) in the aftermath of the Second World War were largely based on the model that was developed in the Soviet Union in the 1920s and that reached its zenith during the infamous Moscow Trials of 1936–1938. The element of audience participation had been a key concern for Soviet organisers and theorists of the show trial, so that Nova's account of the origin of the term *gjyq i popullit* – whether it is true or false – is in line with what was considered to be one the defining characteristics of the phenomenon, even though it implicitly attempts to put a nationalist spin on it.[7]

The most interesting thing about the Albanian case for my purposes here, however, is that the practice of organising and staging show trials in the Stalinist vein continued largely unchanged until the 1980s (Idrizi 2001).[8]

Even though the connection between the Albanian revolutionary vigilance films and the Albanian communist show trials is quite clear, the former still feel compelled to announce their connection to the latter, or the importance of that connection, by including an obligatory reference to the countless, terrifying *gjyqe të popullit* taking place in Albania. The reference is typically made by the internal class enemy (who is hiding at the heart of 'healthy' socialist society) to the external agent of imperialism/revisionism (who has been sent from abroad to reactivate him or her) and its obvious function is to convey the former's dread of facing such a trial him- or herself. Another interpretation is that this announcement is, instead (or also), directed at the audience of the revolutionary vigilance films. From this point of view, it is no coincidence that the Albanian revolutionary vigilance films share the distinctly noirlike aesthetic and style of the newsreels and documentary films based on the proceedings of the Albanian communist show trials. Beginning with the installation of communist rule in Albania in 1944 and until the regime's twilight years in the 1980s, the hunt for hidden traitors, saboteurs, spies, revisionists, deviationists and so on, was based on a kind of noir scenario. Similarly, the proceedings of the Albanian communist show trials followed a kind of noir script, which is reflected in the documentary films and newsreels based on the proceedings of these trials, all of which were, extraordinarily, staged inside movie theatres. The filmmakers behind these newsreels and documentary films exploited the inherent properties of black and white film as well as the architecture and darkness of the movie theatre to create a highly theatrical, claustrophobic and doom-laden atmosphere perfectly matching the events taking place on (and off) the stage, where extraordinary accusations were matched by equally incredible confessions (Gashi 2018). Additionally, the *mise-en-abîme* produced when footage of the proceedings of a trial unfolding inside a movie theatre and in front of a live audience was screened inside a similar movie theatre in front of a similar audience, vividly identified the cinematic audience of the newsreels and documentary films of the communist show trials with the actual audience of said trials. Thus, the obligatory mention of the *gjyqe të popullit* taking place in Albania in the revolutionary vigilance films, alongside their noir-like aesthetic and style forces a double identification: between the audience of the revolutionary vigilance films and the vigilant masses depicted in the revolutionary vigilance films within the boundaries of the filmic text, and between the audience of the revolutionary vigilance films and the audience of the newsreels and documentary films of the communist show trials outside of the boundaries of the filmic text. This is the other key reason why the Albanian revolutionary vigilance films managed to sit well with both audiences and the authorities. Audiences were invited to derive from this genre, which I am tempted to call 'communist noir', a specific kind of pleasure that they were, moreover, already familiar with.

NOTES

1. The 'official' start of the Albanian Ideological and Cultural Revolution is usually placed in February 1967, whereas that of China's Great Proletarian Cultural Revolution in May 1966. In 'China and Albania: the Cultural Revolution and Cold War Relations', Ylber Marku (2017) offers an overview of Chinese-Albanian relations at the outset of China's Great Proletarian Cultural Revolution. In 'Mao and the Albanians', Elidor Mëhilli (2014) offers an overview of Chinese-Albanian relations throughout the Cold War. Another useful reference is 'The Albanian Cultural Revolution' by Nicholas Pano (1974), which represents a historical account of the Albanian Cultural and Ideological Revolution as it was unfolding.
2. Throughout 1967, the *Shkëmbim Eksperience* (Exchange of Experience) section of *Drejtësia Popullore*, the publication of the General Prosecution Office and the Supreme Court, is filled with reports by prosecutors and judges (and not only) stationed all around the country attesting to the fact that the number and quality of 'on-site trials' organised in their jurisdiction has increased dramatically ever since the Fifth Party Congress.
3. Generally speaking, in the revolutionary vigilance films, the internal agent of imperialism and revisionism is portrayed as having lied dormant for a long time and is reactivated by an external agent (or agents) who usually outranks him or her in the intelligence organisation or espionage network of which they are both part.
4. The films *Asgjë nuk Harrohet* and *Misioni Përtej Detit* are exceptions to the rule. Both of them focus on the desperate attempts of Albanian Nazi collaborators to evade justice for the crimes they committed during WWII.
5. For a discussion of the factors, both internal (national) and external (transnational) that helped shape and later cement the Albanian Party of Labor's Stalinist line in the second half of the 1950s, albeit an account that intentionally downplays the weight of ideological positions as such, see 'Defying De-Stalinization' by Elidor Mëhilli (2011).
6. At the time when the first revolutionary films were produced, the film industry in Albania was still quite new and its cinematic output quite modest. The fact that these films continued being produced at more or less regular intervals (especially in the 1980s) until the end of the communist period in 1991, in itself indicates that they agreed with both the authorities as well as audiences. On a more anecdotal note, in his memoir *Të Pathënat* [*The Unspoken*], director Muharrem Fejzo (2015: 178–9) recounts the enthusiastic reception of his film *Fijet që Priten* by audiences in 1976, noting that in one of the more extreme cases movie-going crowds had tried to barge into the cinema by kicking down the doors while in another case they had attempted to prevent the celluloid reels from being transported to another venue.
7. Interestingly, avant-garde and amateur theatre, and in a different way the cinema too, played an important role in shaping audience participation (and not only) in the Soviet show trials of the 1920s and 1930s. This topic is tackled from different

angles, which are nevertheless interconnected, by Lynn Mally (2000) in *Revolutionary Acts: Amateur Theater and the Soviet State 1917–1938*; Julie A. Cassiday (2000) in *The Enemy on Trial: Early Soviet Courts on Stage and Screen*; and Elizabeth A. Wood (2005) in *Performing Justice: Agitation Trials in Early Soviet Russia*.
8. Idrizi goes so far as to compare Hoxha's last purge of the APL's ranks in the early 1980s (Hoxha died in the spring of 1985) to Stalin's Great Terror. While this particular argument is not entirely convincing, Idrizi's suggestion that we approach the Stalinist character of Hoxha's rule, and of the Albanian Party of Labor in general, through a study of its purge practices and techniques is intriguing.

Works Cited

Baholli, Sami. 1967. 'Të Kuptohet Gjërë dhe të Zbatohet Drejt Vija e Masave në Gjykim.' [*The Mass Line Must Be Broadly Understood and Applied Correctly.*] *Drejtësia Popullore* 5 (September–October): 3–12.

Cassiday, Julie A. 2014. 'Why Stalinist Cinema Had No Detective Films, or How Three Becomes Two in *Engineer Kochin's Mistake*.' *Quarterly Review of Film and Video* 31.1: 56–73.

Cassiday, Julie A. 2000. *The Enemy on Trial: Early Soviet Courts on Stage and Screen*. De Kalb, IL: Northern Illinois University Press.

Çela, Arianit. 1967. 'Të Ngrejmë Nivelin e Punës së Gjykatave në Lartësinë e Detyrave që Shtroi Kongresi i V-të i PPSh.' [*Let Us Raise the Performance of the Courts to the Level of the Tasks Assigned by the 5th Congress of the APL.*] *Drejtësia Popullore* 1 (January–February): 3–20.

Fejzo, Muharrem. 2015. *Të Pathënat*. [*The Unspoken.*] Tiranë: Botimet Toena.

Gashi, Jonida. 2018. 'Cinema on Trial: The Films of the Albanian Communist Show Trials.' *Visual Past* 5: 99–114. http://www.visualpast.de/archive/pdf/vp2018_0099.pdf.

Goga, Lefter. 1967. 'Të Ngrejmë Nivelin e Punës të Prokurorive në Lartësinë e Detyrave që Shtroi Kongresi i V-të i PPSh.' ['*Let Us Raise the Performance of the Public Prosecutors' Offices to the Level of the Tasks Assigned by the 5th Congress of the APL.*'] *Drejtësia Popullore* 2 (March–April): 3–16.

Hazbiu, Kadri. 1966. 'Diskutime mbi Raportin e Shokut Enver Hoxha: Nga Diskutimi i Shokut Kadri Hazbiu.' ['*Discussions on Comrade Enver Hoxha's Report: From Comrade Kadri Hazbiu's Discussion.*'] *Bashkimi*, 5 November 1966.

Hoxha, Enver. 1966. 'Kongresi i 5-të i Partisë: Raporti i Shokut Enver Hoxha.' ['*The 5th Party Congress: Comrade Enver Hoxha's Report.*'] *Bashkimi*, November 2, 1966.

Idrizi, Idrit. 2021. 'Enver Hoxha's Last Purge: Inside the Ruling Circle of Communist Albania (1981–1983).' *East European Politics and Societies*: https://doi.org/10.1177/08883254211036184.

Komiteti Qendror. 1966. 'Letër e Hapur e Komitetit Qendror të PPSh.' [*'Open Letter of the Central Committee of the APL.'*] *Bashkimi*, 6 March 1966.

Lako, Natasha, ed. 2004. *Filmografi e Filmit Shqiptar 1953–2003 – Vëllimi I: Filmi Artistik*. [*Filmography of Albanian Film 1953–2003 – Volume I: Fiction Films.*] Tiranë: Botimet Toena.

Mally, Lynn. 2000. *Revolutionary Acts: Amateur Theater and the Soviet State 1917–1938*. Ithaca, NY: Cornell University Press.
Mandili, Jorgo. 1976. 'Një Film me Vlera Edukative.' [*'A Film with Educational Values.'*] *Drita*, 27 June 1976.
Marku, Ylber. 2017. 'China and Albania: the Cultural Revolution and Cold War Relations.' *Cold War History* 17.4: 367–383. doi: 10.1080/14682745.2017.1307179.
Mëhilli, Elidor. 2014. 'Mao and the Albanians.' In *Mao's Little Red Book: A Global History*, edited by Alexander C. Cook, 165–184. Cambridge: Cambridge University Press.
Mëhilli, Elidor. 2011. 'Defying De-Stalinization.' *Journal of Cold War Studies* 13.4 (Fall): 4–56.
Nova, Koço. 1982. *Zhvillimi i Organizimit Gjyqësor në Shqipëri*. [*Development of the Organisation of the Judiciary in Albania*.] Tiranë: Universiteti i Tiranës.
Pano, Nicholas. 1974. 'The Albanian Cultural Revolution.' *Problems of Communism* 23, 4 (July–August): 44–57.
Wood, Elizabeth A. 2005. *Performing Justice: Agitation Trials in Early Soviet Russia*. Ithaca and London: Cornell University Press.

8. THE CASE OF THE SPANISH *GIALLI*: CRIME FICTION AND THE OPENNESS OF SPAIN IN THE 1970S

Fernando Gabriel Pagnoni Berns

Giallo (Italian for 'yellow') cinema was a cycle of films made in Italy beginning in the late 1960s and through the 1970s.[1] The term derives from the yellow covers of the paperback mystery novels the Italian publishing house Mondadori sold cheaply after 1929. The paperbacks were so popular that the in 'Italian usage the term can apply to any crime fiction' (Dyer 2015: 204), including crime cinema. The Italian cycle of crime films known as *giallo* (or *gialli*, in plural) was one of the most stylistic corpora of films ever made. Filled with strident colours, black-gloved killers, red herrings, confusing plots, jazz soundtracks, art-house sensibilities, beautiful women, very long titles and spectacular murders, the cycle tapped into vernacular social and cultural anxieties of the era. The corpus 'represents the encroaching hegemony of modernity on the private' (Koven 2006: 58) when Italy became modern and cosmopolitan almost overnight.

As Mikel Koven argues, the *giallo* is a vernacular cycle, deeply embedded within the social fabric of its time and geography. Paradoxically, it triggered a transnational trend. Furthermore, the italian *giallo* itself was a product of cross-fertilisation. As Austin Fisher explains, the *giallo* plugs into a 'rich vein of transcultural borrowing in Italy, through which foreign narrative models offer a filer for the familiar locale' (2017: 260). The *giallo* derived heavily from the German *krimi* films based, in turn, on crime novels wrote by British author Edgar Wallace (Koven 2006: 5). 'The Italian *giallo* mixed the *krimi* with the police procedural and added a twist of its own; an almost fetishistic attention to the murderer and the killings' (Fisher 2017: 260). The Italian cycle ended in the earlier 1980s, not before serving as inspiration to one of America's most renowned cycles: 'the *giallo* might usefully be seen as the missing link between the protoserial killer narratives of Frederic Brown and Cornell Woolrich and the American slasher' (Hunt 2000: 330).

There is a resurgence of interest on the Italian *giallo* cycle, with new studies such as Alexia Kannas' *Giallo!: Genre, Modernity, and Detection in Italian Horror Cinema* and Alexandra Heller-Nicholas' *The Giallo Canvas: Art, Excess and Horror Cinema* published in 2020 and 2021, respectively. Still understudied, however, is the Spanish *gialli*, a cycle of films made in Spain through the 'tardofranquismo' (late Francoist period, roughly from 1960 to 1975). Spanish films such as *A Dragonfly for Each Corpse/Una Libélula para cada Muerto* (Leon Klimovsky, 1974), *The Corruption of Chris Miller/La Corrupción de Chris Miller* (Juan Antonio Bardem, 1973), *The Glass Ceiling/El Techo de Cristal* (Eloy de la Iglesia, 1971) or *The Fish with the Golden Eyes/El Pez de los Ojos de Oro* (Pedro Luis Ramírez, 1974) recuperate the narratives and tropes of Italian *giallo* for Spanish audiences. What remains opens to investigation are the reasons behind this transnational flux of crime film fiction.

In this chapter, I will argue that Francoist Spain was a fitting geography to embrace the narratives of the Italian cycle. Spain at the earlier 1970s was experiencing new processes of modernity after decades of social and cultural stagnation. The so-called Spanish Miracle 'that refers to the economic resurgence of Spain in the latter half of the Franco dictatorship' (Nichols 214: 168) mirrored the economic miracle framing Italy in earlier years, as Spain opened itself to the world and modernity in an attempt to draw in tourism and money. The *giallo* mold fitted especially well into the particular context of 'a culture and society driven by the archly conservative worldview of the Franco dictatorship' (Willis 2017: 104). My purpose in this chapter is to address not the regimes of coproduction between Italy and Spain but to acknowledge how anxieties about modernity and openness to the world informed the *giallo* cycle and had an impact on both, Spain and Italy, thus favouring a transnational flux of narratives.[2]

European Economic Miracles: Dreading/Desiring Openness

Two circumstances have linked Italy and Spain in the 1960s: 1) an economic 'miracle' that pushed forward a process of modernisation which 2) put both countries on the map as potential touristic destinations. The Italian economic miracle of the postwar period refers to the striking (in terms of quality and speed) reconstruction of Italy after the years of Second World War and the fascist regime of Benito Mussolini. This period, encompassing 1958–1963, was possible in part thanks to the contribution of funds from the Marshall Aid programme, which supported Italian economic policies. Italy made good use of these funds, especially making investments in the most underdeveloped region, the southern area of the country (Sorlin 1996: 115), thus changing the landscapes forever when industrialisation brought urbanisation to a (mostly) agricultural country. Further, the Italian miracle was part of a global 'golden age' of capitalism, 'which created a new world market for consumer goods and forced Italians into a modern, industrial world' (Foot 2003, 138). Establishing the cultural presence of Italy on the global scene, Italy's national cinema contributed to the country's international fame: Italian cinema 'was extraordinarily robust, and the art films that defined the Italian cinema internationally were only a part of its flourishing and robust film industry' (Restivo 2002: 8–9). The neorealist movement of filmmaking was embraced in film festivals and the art house circuit, and accepted by general audiences as well, thus attracting attention to Italy as a geography of vital importance for art and tourism.

As a consequence of this economic and cultural boom, Italy became a renowned destiny for global tourism. The country was literally 'transformed by highways and tourism' (Hendrix 2003: 35), and the invasion of hundreds of visitors from the entire globe brought to Italy new anxieties concerning the rapidly changing social, cultural and geographical landscapes. Even if the changes were for good, many Italians, arguably, were anxious about what the future of their country was within this highly fluid landscape.

Gialli reflected these social and cultural changes: Koven suggests that the relationship between *gialli* and modernity is one based on 'ambivalence'. 'Modernity is not condemned in these [*giallo*] films, but neither is it praised' (2006: 16). The changes within Italian culture can be seen through the cycle 'as something to be discussed and debated – issues pertaining to identity, sexuality, increasing levels of violence, women's control over their own lives and bodies, history, the state – all abstract ideas, which are all portrayed situationally as human stories in the *giallo* film' (Ibid.: 16). Answering the new social and cultural anxieties brought by the changing landscapes, the *gialli* were filled with visual and narrative elements that signified 'modernity'. The stories of Italian *giallo* take place in locations directly related to travelling and tourism and highly recognisable train stations and airports are displayed through the narratives. Gary Needham argues that 'the obsession with travel and tourism not only ... mark ... the newly emerging European jet-set ... but [are also] representative of Italian cinema's selling of its own 'Italian-ness' through tourist hotspots ... as well as countless deaths in or around famous squares, fountains and monuments' (2003: 136). The display of touristic locations has a dual function: on the one hand, these locations add a cosmopolitan, modern layer to the story and, on another, they function as an index of the attractive geographies that Italy had to offer to viewers worldwide (thus increasing real tourism). Still, the ambivalence mentioned by Koven manifests itself as tourists are repeatedly named as suspects in the murders or become amateur detectives (2006: 46) as in Dario Argento's *The Bird with the Crystal Plumage/L'Uccello dalle Piume di Cristallo* (1970) or *Tenebrae* (1982). As Koven describes, 'this is one of the areas in which the genre articulates its ambivalence toward modernity: specifically through juxtaposition of luscious travelogue visual footage with diegetic horror and tragedy' (Ibid.: 51). In brief, as Italy became part of the cosmopolitan world this new openness to the exterior brought 'suspicious' ideas involving moral 'decadence', including sexual freedom or ideologies associated with 1960s and 1970s countercultures and feminists into a still conservative mindset. As Koven notes, the 'Otherness' of the killer is marked not only by a 'foreign' character, but 'as being from outside the hegemonic society' (Ibid.: 56) as well.

Like Italy, Spain underwent processes of anxiety-ridden shifts to modernity. Unlike Italy, however, Spain's modernisation took place under the strong hold of dictatorship, a military government that preferred, up until the 1960s, to keep the national culture supressed under obscurantism and autarchic politics.

Francoist Spain can be divided, broadly speaking, into three main stages taking place after the Civil War (1936–1939) that devastated the country and provoked the collapse of the democratic Spanish Republic and the enthroning of a military dictatorship led by General Francisco Franco. The first stage was fascism, right up until the end of World War II. Those were years in which Franco tried to graft onto Spain the fascist governments of Adolf Hitler or Benito Mussolini, even if the dictator 'never fully adopted the entire core fascist revolutionary ideology' (Payne 1999: 326). Oppression took on a predominantly violent form in the cities and towns, as any form of resistance or sympathy towards communists or leftist ideology met with imprisonment without a proper trial, as well as physical disappearances and executions. After the fall of the fascist regimes in Europe, Spain was under an autarchic economy and international isolation until 1959. Finally, and after the complete failure of this autarchic stage, Spain embraced 'modernity', dominated by a sense of what historian Antonio Cazorla-Sánchez denominates 'peace and progress' which lasted until Franco's death in 1975 (2010: 149).

This third political and historical stage was characterised by social peace as Spaniards had become mostly habituated to Franco's dictatorship. While it was relatively unknown or unacknowledged, Spain was beginning a process of disintegration due political stagnation and Franco's old age. An economic boom from 1962 to 1972 gave birth to a consumerist society which ran parallel to political apathy. This created the conditions for the climate of 'peace and progress' that Cazorla-Sánchez describes.

Indeed, Spaniards were enjoying, as late as the 1960s, becoming consumers for the first time in their lives. Economic prosperity not only allowed many citizens to buy luxurious things such as cars, TV sets and apartments (Buchanan

2007: 91), but the economic conditions also skyrocketed Franco's popularity (Cazorla-Sánchez 2010: 150). There were three main keys to this consumer revolution. From 1964 until the severe recession that marked the end of the economic miracle in 1974, the average annual increase of private consumption was 5.7 per cent. The second element was that the increase in income lagged behind that of productivity until the early 1970s. The third key was that many members of the working class struggled out of poverty by starting to work while very young and without having completed their education. 'Literally every consumer good in a humble house was paid for by years of education missed' (Cazorla-Sánchez 2010: 151). In terms of capitalist modernity, Spain was quickly catching up with other European states.

Amidst this climate of consumerism, Spain was 'sold' abroad as a picturesque, affable and carefree country; the slogan 'España es diferente' (Spain is different), devised by the Franco regime in the 1960s, was promoted to attract European and international tourism, offering the country as a mixture of medieval cities and modern, cosmopolitan life. Imagery was built around sea, sand, flamenco, bullfighting and the ease of modern travel associated with European cosmopolitanism (Barke 2002: 82). Franco feared all things foreign (preferring keeping Spain isolated from the democratic ideas sweeping Europe after World War II), but his government desperately needed the flux of money that came with tourism. Grudgingly, Franco's dictatorship opened Spain to the world, including a relaxation, even if slight, of the laws of censorship in cinema and television (Mir 2002). This relaxation opened the path to a new wave of horror/crime cinema (Pulido 2012). Before the *giallo* cycle, Spain's only engagement with genre cinema was in the 1950s, when the country saw the surge of a corpus of vernacular *noir* films that were predominantly B-movies, 'cheap and unpretentious, with no star names, produced mainly in Barcelona and Madrid (Jordan and Morgan-Tamosunas 1998: 88). To some, these *noir* films can be read as attempts of critique of the Francoist regime (Kinder 1993: 60); any reference to moral corruption within the Spanish institutions, however, was muted in the majority of the films (Jordan and Morgan-Tamosunas 1998: 87). Unlike these *noir* examples, the Spanish *giallo* cycle addressed urgent issues of its time, the more problematic being the modernity that was both helping and threatening Spain in the new era of openness.

Examining the Spanish Giallo: Fearing the Different

When Spain became modern in the 1960s, the number of routes, highways, bridges, rails and roads increased to facilitate travelling between provinces and as part of a broader effort to improve Spain's pro-European, international tourist reputation. As Sasha Pack observes, this improvement on 'roads, municipal services, hotels, and restaurants to meet international standards' also implied 'a tolerance and even an embrace of foreign attitudes and behaviours' (Pack 2007: 56–57). This 'welcoming', however, was framed by the same sense of ambivalence that Koven noted in Italian *gialli* regarding modernity.

It is common in Spanish *gialli* to begin the stories on the road, emphasising the sense of mobility and travelogue. *Maniac Mansion/La Mansion de la Niebla* (Francisco Lara Polop, 1972), a film set in an old, dark mansion with *giallo* elements (people being murdered one by one in an isolated, closed space) is split into two parts. The beginning of the film takes place on the road and the film later introduces viewers to a variety of people holed up at an abandoned mansion. The lengthy sequence after the initial credits involves a man driving a car through a Spanish suburban road (the backdrop a beautiful landscape filled with vegetation and mountains) and a young man on a motorcycle trying to pass him. The film's first minutes narrates the battle of wheels between the two men, as each one tries to leave the other one behind. Since audiences do not know who these young men are yet, the sequence is basically a travelogue. The men's clothes – expensive sunglasses, shirt, jacket, tie and coat – the car, the motorcycle (both framed in close shots), the road and the pretty landscape present an imagery that visualises the 'Spain is different' slogan of the 1970s; a cosmopolitan social class mobilised within the striking Spanish natural landscapes.

Films beginning with travelogues were a common practice in Spanish *gialli*. *The Killer is One of 13/El Asesino está entre los 13* (Javier Aguirre, 1974), a film revolving around upper-class guests gathered around a widow, Lisa Mandel (Patty Shepard), takes place in an isolated mansion under mysterious circumstances where the guests are murdered one by one. Through this narrative, the film stages issues of modernity and mobility. The arriving of upper-class guests at the isolated house in the film's first minutes aptly devised to depict roads – lined with beautiful natural landscapes – modern cars and expensive clothing – ascarves, sunglasses, coats, and hats. In one instance of dialogue marking the social mobility of the consumerist society of the 1970s, characters mention that Jorge (Alberto Fernández), is 'newly rich', and likes to drive 'very expensive cars'.

While roads and cars very directly symbolise the aspirations for mobility in the 'Spain is different' slogan, there is a subtle irony in ghastly crimes occurring in idyllic landscapes that the Spanish government hoped would become tourist attractions. *El Pez de los Ojos de Oro* begins with a murder taking place in a paradisiacal beach where a young girl sunbathes before being killed. In *The Bell from Hell/La Campana del Infierno* (Claudio Guerin, 1973) the title credits run over a lengthy sequence of Juan (Renaud Verley), the film's hero, travelling by motorcycle through the pastoral roads of La Coruña, Galicia, with the camera panning through touristic hotspots and ancient buildings in the picturesque landscape of the mountains. *The Blue Eyes of the Broken Doll/Los Ojos Azules de la Muñeca Rota* (Carlos Aured, 1973), a rural *giallo* also later released under the English title *House of Psychotic Women*, begins with Gilles (Jacinto Molina), the film's lead, walking aimless through the Spanish roads. *A Candle for the Devil/Una Vela para el Diablo* (Eugenio Martin, 1973) begins in an airport but later cuts to touristic life in Grazalema, a beautiful small Spanish village. Like the Italian *gialli*, the Spanish films opened the country cinematically to the world through brief travelogues – the beauty of which often conflicts with the violence of narrative but effectively conveys the marvels that tourists will encounter in Spain.

Together with transnational mobility, however, came foreign ideas of democracy and progressive ideologies that clashed sharply with Franco 'abhorrence of anything approaching a liberal ideology' (O'Byrne 2014: 40). This ideological clash was politically charged, and the films transformed the conflict into acts of criminality that also engage the obscurantism that Franco favoured in earlier years. *Una Vela para el Diablo* emphasises the colliding of points of view brought by the opening of Spain to foreign tourism in the 1960s. Two sisters, Marta (Aurora Batista) and Veronica (Esperanza Roy), running a small hotel in rural Spain start killing female tourists whose morals do not meet their strict religious standards. The tourists visiting the house wear miniskirts and revealing blouses, scandalising not only the two sisters but also all the people in the village where the hotel is located. The murders of *Una Vela para el Diablo* are triggered by events signaling the belatedness with which modernity came to Spain, thus favouring the existence of conservative geographies that were easily threatened by any sense of newness. The sisters may be the deranged killers, but the village feels uneasiness before the young female tourists who travel through the world alone, wear skimpy clothes and ask for American Coca Cola in the bars. The film's hints at the hypocrisy involved in this contradiction, both social and personal: regarding the latter, the killer sisters are portraits of sexual repression. While Aurora bitterly remembers how her husband-to-be abandoned her at the altar for a younger woman, the mild-mannered Esperanza, easily dominated by her older sibling, carries on a secret love affair with a young handyman. In turn, social hypocrisy is represented by the disgust clearly depicted in the villagers, who are scandalised by the modernity brought by tourists but are more than happy to accept their American dollars.

Similarly, in a depiction of foreign touristic youth as the carrier of a potentially poisonous disease of modernity, Ramírez's *El Pez de Ojos de Oro* presents a scene that parallels the cultural clash depicted in *Una Vela para el Diablo*. Ramírez's film deals with Gilles, who finds job with Claude (Diana Lorys) a young woman with an orthopedic hand who offers him employment as a handyman in her rural home. Claude lives along with her two sisters, red-haired nymphomaniac Nicole (Eva Leon) and Ivette (Maria Perschy) who is wheelchair-bound. After Gilles' arrival, a series of brutal murders start, all the victims being blue-eyed blonde girls whose eyes are pulled out during the killings.

In one scene that evolves autonomously from the main narrative (as it does not advance the story or add any clue), three young female tourists hitchhiking through the country visit the little village's bar: the girls wear either denim shorts or tight jeans and their blouses are knotted midriffs. They pay no attention to the older men at the bar, the latter looking at the young women with a mix of revulsion and sexual arousal. When one of the girls bend over the bar counter to ask for their Coca Colas, the camera frames her from a low angle, and, from behind, her buttocks show through her shorts. Arguably, the scene has been filmed for titillation; still, it emphasises hypocrisy as the men are horrified by the group of girls but simultaneously visually consuming them through their gaze. The scene has no further development in the film as nobody within the group is a future victim or killer (none of the girls show up again in the narrative). Much like corresponding scenes in *Una Vela para el Diablo*, this anomalous scene illustrates how the shock of openness to progressive ideology in Spain was attended by the construction of an otherness around the figure of the tourist.

Youth, communism, anarchism and feminism crystallised into ambiguous forms of criminality that remained open-ended and deliberately diffuse to interpretation. At the same time, the Spanish *gialli* constituted an ideal tool for probing the nature of social deviances, presenting aberrations from ideological norms viewers as criminal. Depicting bad deeds done by the representatives of the counterculture, the films also legitimate surveillance of foreign ideas within the country. As Roberta Salper argues, while United States and some European countries, such as UK or Italy, were experiencing the counterculture movements of the 1960s, 'Spain was still frozen in the past', with only the leftist students at universities actively laying 'the groundwork for a democratic Spain' (Salper 2014: 10). As such, Franco could count on the media sustaining his rule (essentially, this included all media, as censorship intervened all aspects of communication at the time) and media outlets started a campaign to discredit young, left-wing, members of the counterculture that were characterised as enemies of the moral and the family values sustaining Spain. The traditionalist newspaper *Pueblo*, for example, published a brief note of repudiation on the counterculture simply titled 'Hippie' in its 18 September 1967 issue that ended with 'tu cara pecosa y despeinada, orlada de claveles, es la más exacta representación de la decadencia de Occidente' ('your freckled, dishevelled face, trimmed with carnations, is the most accurate representation of the decline of the West') and then continued with the exhortation: 'abróchate la camisa y ponte a trabajar' ('fasten up your shirt and get a job'). A small editorial titled 'Jòvenes melenudos' ('Young long-haired men') in the conservative newspaper *Mataro* warned about 'ciertos elementos' ('certain elements') that live in other countries that would now, with Spain's openness, try to set root in new geographies. It stated that these 'elements' were composed of 'jóvenes descarados y mal educados para los que están de más las leyes más esenciales de la urbanidad y cortesía' ('a group of shameless and poorly educated young people for whom the most essential laws of civility and courtesy do not exist') and who 'no respetan nada ni a nadie, ya que para ellos todo es igual con tal de hacer su capricho y voluntad' ('do not respect anything or anyone, since everything is possible in order to do their whim and will'). Fortunately, the editorial continues, Spain did not have 'hippies' and, therefore, it is the obligation of civil society to keep surveillance on any 'subversive' elements from outside walking the streets. Basically, the newspapers followed Franco's prejudices and were led to 'view as criminal [. . .] anything that appeared to attack the basic principles of the *Movimiento* [Francoist movement]' (Tusell 2007: 213).

Spanish *gialli* tapped into cultural anxieties regarding 'shameless youth' effectively by turning any countercultural agent into a criminal. In *El Assesino está entre los 13*, the only guest belonging to the counterculture (Jack Taylor) not only paints for the sake of art (as he mentions) but also makes reproductions of masterpieces which he then later sells as authentic pieces. His despising of all things bourgeois codes him as 'countercultural'; his real 'job', passing off fake paintings as genuine, makes him a criminal. In *La Campana del Infierno*, Juan, an insane inmate of an asylum who is released and returns home for vengeance on his aunt (Viveca Lindfors) and her three daughters who had him declared crazy in order to take his inheritance, is depicted as a hippie. Before being declared insane, Juan wants to travel the world and experience 'free sex' without materialistic worries on his mind. Because of this perspective, his aunt imprisons him in an asylum so he cannot spend the family's money. Even if Juan is the film's main victim, his plans for vengence involve raping and butchering all his cousins and killing his aunt after directing a swarm of wasps to attack her. In *The Corruption of Chris Miller/La Corrupción de Chris Miller* (Juan Antonio Bardem, 1973), the young man who arrives and enters the lives of Ruth (Jean Seberg) and her stepdaughter Chris (Marisol) is coded as both a hippie and a killer. Both Ruth and Chris live in an isolated mansion in the countryside, waiting for the same man: Ruth's husband and Chris's father, who left them behind to start a new life. Ruth wants to get even with him for what he has done to her, and to do this, she uses Chris, his daughter. As part of her plan, Ruth wants to morally and mentally corrupt Chris. Barney (Barry Stokes) comes to the mansion looking for work and, once there, seduces both women. Meanwhile, a black-clad serial killer roams about the countryside, killing with a scythe. At the film's climax, Ruth and Chris stab Barney to death, as they both suspect he is the killer. However, as the killer is revealed to be a maniac roaming the countryside, the suspicions of both women appear to be completely based on simple prejudice. Long-haired and homeless, Barney is the prototypical anti-establishment hippie. Even if Barney is not the killer assaulting the village, the film's opening insinuates that the young man is, indeed, the killer of his lover, a rich woman who was determined to end the romantic affair.

If his involvement this in murder is left in ambiguity, Barney's sexual relationship with both Ruth and Chris is revealed to be a ruse instigated by the young man to uncover up where the women are hiding their money. Barney may not be a murderer, but he is depicted as morally corrupt in taking advantage of the vulnerability of women with his good looks.

Through the 1960s and 1970s, the fascist regime found in the movement of anti-authoritarian youth uniting in universities a cause for worry. While the working and the upper class suffered from political apathy, the leftist intellectual youth kept anti-Franco sentiments alive (Valencia-García 2018). These groups became the target of a process of coding into criminality in depictions that treated them as inherently anti-social. Both *Murder by Music/Las Trompetas del Apocalipsis* (Julio Buchs, 1969) and *Una Libélula para Cada Muerto* emphasised the depiction of the counterculture as inextricably associated with underground criminality. *Una Libélula para Cada Muerto* deals with Paolo Scaporelli (Jacinto Molina), a police inspector assigned by his chief to investigate the case of the 'dragonfly' killing series that have been committed by a murderer in the city of Milan (a geographical dislocation selected to avoid domestic censorship). The killer puts a dragonfly on the corpses of his victims (these include pimps, sex workers, drug addicts, and other social pariahs) and calls himself a 'cleaner' of the streets. The detective on the case, Inspector Scaporelli, in fact, agrees with the killer's ideology, as he feels the city has been slowly corrupted by modern ways. Since the inspector is the film's hero, the story invites viewers to share this ideological point of view. Police brutality, for example, is not criticised through the film, and Scaporelli is never chastised for beating suspects. In the film's opening, a young man (long-haired and wearing imported mod fashion) walks alone the empty streets at night is approached by an older man. The scene hints that two related activities are forms of social degeneracy: homosexuality and drugs. The young man retires to his apartment, where he injects heroin into his veins and becomes the victim of an axe murder. His apartment, like those of all the killer's victims, has psychedelic paintings hanging at the walls, indicating that the deviant people living there (which the audience presumes includes transvestites and homosexuals from the mise en scène) belong to the counterculture. In a key scene, the inspector fights for his life against a gang of long-haired hippies, all of them sporting swastikas on their arms. It is worth mentioning that there is no other reference Nazism in the story and the scene operates to conflate counterculture with extreme (and passé) ideologies.

More direct in the linkage between hippie subculture and criminality is *Las Trompetas del Apocalipsis*, a story describing a piece of esoteric music that, heard after the consumption of psychedelic mushrooms, is able to produce such a profoundly distressing malaise in the listener that the desperate individual will kill themselves after listening to it. An anonymous person, meanwhile, is willing to steal, and even kill, for the sheet music to the song. Much of the film has a gloomy view of the city: dingy bars play swinging psychedelic music where long-haired hippies not only dance but also plan criminal acts. The hippy collective is also directly linked to the underground activity of gangs quite literally as some hippies live in tunnels under the streets. In contrast with the hippies, the film's hero, Richard Milford (Brett Halsey), works with the marines and the military. Wearing a dark suit and a tidy haircut, Milford marks a sharp difference with characters appearing as 'degenerate'. In the narrative, women in the hippie groups are more interested in getting romantically involved with Milford than with their counterculture boyfriends, accentuating appeals for normality and normativity made by the film. The disc jockey of the dingy bar where the hippies socialise together is a classical music fan and, at one point in the film, confesses that he dons a long-hair wig to pass unnoticed amidst the 'dingy degenerates' that dance to the rhythm of psychedelic pop. As in *Una Libélula para Cada Muerto*, the film's hero expresses a strong disgust of the hippie lifestyle. *Las Trompetas del Apocalipsis* closes with the inspector stating, after examining the psychedelic mushrooms in the disc jockey's room (revealed at the end as the criminal tracing the sheet music), that the people of the counterculture will always find a way to 'violate the laws of normalcy'.

These films were released in a context in which the counterculture collective was not only represented in Spanish media as criminal, but also as a group that consistently advocated for the violation of one simple norm: gender identification that separates all things female from male. The cover of the Spanish newspaper *Alba* from 16 to 31 May 1968, is illustrated with a cartoon labelled 'Modas Modernas' ('Modern Fashions') that exemplifies the philosophy that spilled over from the conservative apparatus of Franco's regime: in the vignette two mature and slightly angry men point to a young couple walking with their backs at them. Both youngsters wear pants and long hair. One of the mature men comments, '¿Será chico o chica?' ('Is he a boy or a girl?') to which the other responds 'No sé; por los pantalones parece chica, pero por la melena diría que es chico' ('I don't know; she seems to be a girl because of her pants, but I would say he is a boy because of his long hair'). The attempt at humour demonstrates the wider anxieties caused by the counterculture and the release of stereotypes that it entailed in Spain. Both *Una Libélula para Cada Muerto* and *El Asesino está entre los 13* address the fact that the killer could be both, a woman or a man, as the only clues about the murderer's identity identifies them as wearing gender neutral clothes. In *Una Libélula para Cada Muerto*, Inspector Scaporelli mentions that the damage practised upon the victims by the killer could be done, with enough leverage, by a woman, thus reiterating the gender confusion. Furthermore, the film's real killer is revealed, at the climax, as one of Scaporelli's friends, a man who works at a night club as a transvestite. Curiously, the film had never mentioned this fact before, thus suggesting that crossdressing is just another layer of a more general moral decadence within which the inspector must identify the sexual deviance that signifies true criminality. In the climax of *Los Ojos Azules de la Muñeca Rota*, gender confusion abounds, as the killer is first revealed as one of the sisters, another twist is added when a male doctor is discovered as the real responsible of the murders. Gender non-normativity was one of the most dreaded enemies of the Franco regime. The dictatorship was sustained in part on a Christian Catholic vision of family values, which prompted the Church to agree with the politics of the dictator. Furthermore, confusions regarding the killer's gender identity were one of the main tropes of the Italian *gialli* in which they frequently figured as a metaphor for sexual freedom and female empowerment (Koven 2006: 56). Fears about freedom from gender stereotypes – associated in turn with feminist collectives and anti-authoritarian youth culture – were mobilised in Spanish *gialli* in parallel to establishment condemnations of gender fluidity and counterculture, However, the irony in these representations is that they also envisioned alternative forms of cosmopolitan culture onscreen in order to make conservative statements about the need for more morality and order.

Conclusions

Not all the tropes that the Spanish *giallo* borrowed from its Italian cousin were related with anxieties regarding modernity. Some narratives point exclusively to terms of a transnational fluidity trying to capitalise on foreign success. As such, Spanish *gialli*, like the Italian, told stories about killers obliged to murder due to infantile traumas: in *El Pez de los Ojos de Oro*, the killer executes his murders after seeing, as an adult, a young woman being butchered at the beach. The scene awakened dormant, repressed anxieties regarding the murder of his mother that was carried out before his eyes when he was a small child. The killer of *Una Libélula para cada Muerto* kills because they are pushed by the evocation of a youth spent with parents that were, according to the film's dialogue, 'trash'. Other films aimed for success in the domestic market by simply sampling from the formal logic established by Dario Argento with his 'animal trilogy' – *Four Flies on Grey Velvet /4 Mosche di Velluto Grigio* (1971), *The Cat with Nine tails/Il Gatto a Nove Code* (1971) and *L'Uccello dale Piume di Cristallo* – of creating long titles in which the animals described are revealed as red herrings, thus the construction of titles like *El Pez de los Ojos de Oro*, *Una Libélula para cada Muerto*, and *El Asesino está entre los Trece* or *Los Ojos Azules de la Muñeca Rota*.

The transnational flux was, however, mostly predicated on political and economic parallels shared by both Italy and Spain, which favoured a good reception of *giallo* narratives. The countries were rapidly transforming into cosmopolitan geographies where traditional philosophy sharply clashed with a need for foreign money. People were invited to visit and even live in Italy and Spain, but their ideologies were feared. The traditionalism that had long persisted in Italy and Spain was under threat, and, thus, the *gialli* were created to navigate cultural fears about the loss of vernacular traditionalism.

The Spanish *giallo* survived until Franco's death, a time which, paradoxically, signified the end of the horror and crime film cycles. With Francoism now a historical wound that would require a long process of healing, Spanish cinema undertook the job of analysing and unpacking the last decades of history. There was no longer a dedication towards the production of genre cinema and the state's money and assistance would be channelled to directors with more serious intentions: narrating the horrors of the Francoist dictatorship. The black-clad serial killer vanished from the Spanish cinema, and the *giallo* cycle in both Italy and Spain became defunct at the beginning of 1980s. Spain, healthy enough economically and with freedom of speech for the first time in almost four decades, was ready to talk about the criminality of Franco and his regime, turning its back on narratives of crime in commercial cinema (Kinder 1997: 247).

Rather than being purely vehicles for escapism, the crime films of Spain in the 1970s were anxiety-ridden stories revolving around an evolving society. As Nicole Rafter argues, 'crime films raise anxieties and instil fear, but they usually conclude by sending experts to our rescue' (2000: 61). Here, the experts coincide in their diagnosis: Spain needed to carefully watch over those who come to visit the country, as their dollars might be stained by an intoxicating modernity linked to criminality. And, as it was widely known in the Spanish 1970s, the Francoist regime only allowed 'peace and progress'.

Notes

1. According scholarship, the right term to describe the *giallo* cycle is that of *filone* ('vein' in Italian), meaning, a 'generic cycle' presenting tropes, images and themes 'which can be copied while public interest lasts, then abandoned for the next fashion.' (Ramos Arenas 2013: 90).
2. See Willis' essay 'Violence, Style' for an excellent study on the dimensions of coproduction between the two countries.

Works Cited

Barke, Michael. 2002. 'Inside and Outside Writings on Spain: Their Relationship to Spain Tourism.' In *Literature and Tourism: Essays in the Reading and Writing of Tourism*. Edited by Mike Robinson and Hans-Christian Andersen, 80–104. London: Thomson.

Buchanan, Tom. 2007. 'How "Different" Was Spain? The Later Franco Regime in International Context.' In *Spain Transformed: The Late Franco Dictatorship, 1959–75*, ed. Nigel Townson, 85–96. New York: Palgrave Macmillan, 2007.

Cazorla Sánchez. 2010. *Fear and Progress: Ordinary Lives in Franco's Spain, 1939–1975*. Malden, MA: Wiley-Blackwell.

Mir Curcó, Conxita. 2002. *Vivir es Sobrevivir: Justicia, Orden y Marginación en la Cataluña Rural de Postguerra*. Lleida: Milenio.
Dyer, Richard. 2015. *Lethal Repetition: Serial Killing in European Cinema*. London: BFI.
Fisher, Austin. 2017. 'Italian Popular Film Genres.' In *A Companion to Italian Cinema*, edited by Frank Burke, 250–266. Malden, MA: Wiley Blackwell.
Foot, John. 2003. *Modern Italy*. New York: Palgrave Macmillan.
Heller-Nicholas, Alexandra. 2021. *The Giallo Canvas: Art, Excess and Horror Cinema*. Jefferson, NC: McFarland.
Hendrix, John. 2003. *History and Culture in Italy*. Lanham, MD: University Press of America.
'Hippie.' *Pueblo*. 18 September 1967.
Hunt, Leon. 2000. 'A (Sadistic) Night at the Opera: Notes on the Italian Horror Film.' In *The Horror Reader*. Edited by Ken Gelder, 324–335. London: Routledge.
Jordan, Barry and Rikki Morgan-Tamosunas. 1998. *Contemporary Spanish Cinema*. Manchester: Manchester University Press.
'Jóvenes melenudos.' *Mataro*. 7 May, 1966.
Kannas, Alexia. 2020. *Giallo!: Genre, Modernity, and Detection in Italian Horror Cinema*. Albany: State University of New York Press.
Kinder, Marsha. 1993. *Blood Cinema: The Reconstruction of National Identity in Spain*. Los Angeles: University of California Press.
Kinder, Marsha. 1997. *Refiguring Spain: Cinema, Media, Representation*. Durham, NC: Duke University Press.
Koven, Mikel. 2006. *La Dolce Morte: Vernacular Cinema and the Italian Giallo Film*. Jefferson, NC: McFarland.
Needham, Gary. 2003. 'Playing with Genre: Defining the Italian Giallo.' In *Fear Without Frontiers: Horror Cinema across the Globe*. Edited by Steven Jay Schneider, 135–144. Godalming: FAB Press.
Nichols, William. 2014. 'Geography of Capital: Torremolinos, Modernity, and the Art of Consumption in Spanish Film.' In *Toward a Multicultural Configuration of Spain: Local Cities, Global Spaces*. Edited by Ana Corbalán and Ellen Mayock, 165–176. Madison: Fairleigh Dickinson University Press.
O'Byrne, Patricia. 2014. *Post-war Spanish Women Novelists and the Recuperation of Historical Memory*. Woodbridge: Tamesis.
Pack, Sasha. 2007. 'Tourism and Political Change in Franco's Spain.' In *Spain Transformed: The Late Franco Dictatorship, 1959–75*. Edited by Nigel Townson, 47–67. New York: Palgrave Macmillan.
Payne, Stanley. 1999. *Fascism in Spain, 1923–1977*. Madison: The University of Wisconsin Press.
Pulido, Javier. 2012. *La Década de Oro del Cine de Terror Español (1967–1976)*. Madrid, T&B Editores.
Rafter, Nicole. 2000. *Shots in the Mirrors: Crime Films and Society*. Oxford: Oxford University Press.
Ramos Arenas, Fernando. 2013. 'Towards a Generic Understanding of the *Giallo*: Crime-Horror Hybrids in Italian Cinema of the 1970s.' In *Genre Hybridisation: Global Cinematic Flow*. Edited by Ivo Ritzer and Peter W. Schulze, 81–94. Marburg: Schüren.

Restivo, Angelo. 2002. *The Cinema of Economic Miracles: Visuality and Modernization in the Italian Art Film*. Durham, NC: Duke University Press.
Salper, Roberta. 2014. *Domestic Subversive: A Feminist's take on the Left, 1960–1976*. Tucson, Arizona: Anaphora Literary Press.
Sorlin, Pierre. 1996. *Italian National Cinema: 1896–1996*. London: Routledge.
Tusell, Javier. 2007. *Spain: From Dictatorship to Democracy. 1939 to the Present*, trans. Rosemary Clark. Malden, MA: Blackwell.
Valencia-García, Louie. 2018. *Antiauthoritarian Youth Culture in Francoist Spain: Clashing with Fascism*. New York: Bloomsbury.
Willis, Andy. 2017. 'Violence, Style and Politics: The Influence of the Giallo in Spanish Cinema of the 1970s.' In *Global Genres, Local Films: The Transnational Dimension of Spanish Cinema*. Edited by Elena Oliete-Aldea, Beatriz Oria, Juan A. Tarancón, 103–114. New York: Bloomsbury.

9. THE SHORT ARM OF THE LAW: THE POST-DICTATORSHIP CRIME FILM AS A BAROMETER FOR JUSTICE IN CONTEMPORARY ARGENTINA

Jennifer Alpert

'The truth, that which is so desired and so feared, that which gets silenced, sometimes because of evil, others because of pain, or simply because time extended a veil of fatal concealment, and the more it hides, the stronger it is. Because it can be silenced, forgotten, but even then it clamors in its own way to be noticed. Although sometimes, life shows that nobody can be completely happy except at the cost of a certain ignorance'[1]

Dr Pablo Rouviot, *Los padecientes*

On 13 January 2006, many Argentineans were glued to their televisions watching intently while the events of what would be known as the 'heist of the century' unfolded in real time. As part of a meticulously planned theft, a band of robbers simulated a holdup gone awry in a bank's lobby while their accomplices accessed safety deposit boxes through an underground tunnel, escaping with approximately nineteen million US dollars. Left behind was a one-sentence note that read: 'In a neighborhood of deep pockets, without weapons or grudges, it's just money and not loved ones.' Since then, the thieves have been hailed as heroes, and their heist's painstaking planning has achieved mythical proportions. The unusual background of its mastermind (born in a well-to-do family, no criminal background, and a partial university education), along with the group's ability to trick the entire police force, have made them celebrities. Some media outlets have even dubbed them modern day Robin Hoods referencing their note, which seems to allude to economic inequality but without offering redistribution of wealth beyond the thieves' pockets.

Media coverage and subsequent retellings of the event elevated it to the country's most famous and celebrated heist. As a *Clarín* newspaper article titled 'Río Bank: the Robbery that Turned into Legend' claims, 'Books, songs, countless publications on social networks and on the web turned the episode into a milestone, which is now reinforced by the reissue of *Sin armas ni ladrones* (*Without Weapons or Thieves*), the investigative book that Rodolfo Palacios dedicated to this event, the publication of *El ladrón del siglo* (*The Thief of the Century*), the memories of Luis Mario Vitette, one of the protagonists, and the brand new film directed by Ariel Winograd, *El robo del siglo* (*The Robbery of the Century*)' (Aguirre 2020). These narratives of differing degrees of fictionalization have cemented the heist's legendary status in the national imaginary. More importantly, the theft's sustained notoriety evidences a national population fascinated with crime.

Alongside critically acclaimed films crafted within the *Nuevo cine argentino* (New Argentine Cinema) independent movement that began in the 1990s, successful and lucrative *policiales* (crime films) have contributed to Argentina's renewed respected status in the international cinema landscape. Crime films such as *Ashes of Paradise/Cenizas del paraíso* (Marcelo Piñeyro, 1997), *Nine Queens/Nueve reinas* (Fabián Bielinsky, 2000), *Burnt Money/Plata quemada*, Marcelo Piñeyro, 2000), *The Aura/El aura*, Fabián Bielinsky, 2005), *The Secret in their Eyes/El secreto de sus ojos* (Juan José Campanella, 2009), *Betibú* (Miguel Cohan, 2014), and *The Clan/El clan* (Pablo Trapero, 2015) among others have transited national and foreign screens. All of the aforementioned movies have played at international festivals, including Venice, Toronto, La Habana, Telluride, Sundance, San Sebastián, London, Bogotá, and Miami. The genre currently yields some of the country's highest grossing movies, among them *El secreto de sus ojos*, which netted Argentina its second Academy Award, *El clan*, which in the first four days following its Argentinean release broke records with more than half a million spectators (*Télam* 2015), and *El robo del siglo*, a comedic *policial* which surpassed two million local viewers after just eight weeks in theatres (*La Nación* 2020).

These films' widespread success has led critics to state that their commercial aesthetic eschews national specificity in favor of global appeal,[2] particularly as economic constraints have led many filmmakers to seek transnational funding and collaborations; yet, other scholars disagree.[3] Dolores Tierney has noted that despite engaging with aesthetic global trends or with popular genre templates more commonly found in Hollywood filmmaking; receiving script development support from US-based institutions such as the Sundance Institute or US- or partially US-owned companies such as Disney, Miramax, Patagonik; whole or fractional funding from transnational or multinational corporations and benefiting from their marketing and global distribution, films do not forego their ability to remain 'connected to significant issues of national and continental specificity' (2018: 1–2). Similarly, Luisela Alvaray claims that 'interaction and alliances between foreign and local film companies . . . do not necessarily impede addressing national and regional issues through their cinematic endeavours' (2012: 72). Crime films present stories that, while appealing to foreign audiences, are also distinctly national: through genre conventions, aesthetics, and narrative choices, they reveal a crucial aspect of the country's history.[4]

Argentina's enduring interest in criminal narratives brings to light the country's complex relationship with justice and the law. Although the nation established a democratic organisation after its independence in 1816, it has faced six military insurrections and subsequent despotic regimes in the 20th century.[5] Of these, the last dictatorship (1976–1983) was the most brutal. The scars of this period can still be felt today, as it left a legacy of thirty thousand *desaparecidos*, the Spanish term for those kidnapped, tortured, and murdered at the hands of the autocratic state.[6] During the aftermath of this horrific period and despite promises to enact justice for the victims of human rights abuses, the democratic regimes that began rebuilding the country responded to these crimes in a manner that favored impunity, granting amnesty to many military perpetrators. As a result, few were adequately punished for the atrocities they committed. Today, people continue to demand justice through means such as public protests, legal action, and the press.

In a country where the military, the police, and the legal system are consistently regarded with distrust and skepticism, attitudes towards failed justice have figured prominently in various socio-cultural spheres. One of those has been the screen, where fictional films have depicted the consequences of state violence and genocide and have investigated the meaning of crime and the limits of the law in the contemporary national landscape. In this context, *policiales* have served as a barometer for the state of justice in the post-dictatorship era. Since democracy's return, films that depict different types of crime have offered indicators of shifting popular demands and anxieties regarding the promises that democratic governments have failed to deliver. These narratives most often do not directly represent the crimes that the state perpetrated during the dictatorship. Beginning in the early to mid-1990s, films such as *Lost for Lost/Perdido por perdido* (Alberto Lecchi, 1993), *Wild Horses/Caballos salvajes* (Marcelo Piñeyro, 1995), the aforementioned *Nueve reinas*, and *At the End of the Tunnel/Al final del túnel* (Rodrigo Grande, 2016) shift from earlier and more overt depictions of the dictatorship to displaced or veiled representations that justify retribution outside the law as a moral form of justice within a context in which legal institutions have failed. More recently, under renewed calls to sentence human rights abusers, *policiales* like *The Suffering/Los padecientes* (Nicolás

Tuozzo, 2017), *Black Snow/Nieve negra* (Martín Hodara, 2017), *Dark Buildings/Las grietas de Jara* (Nicolás Gil Lavedra, 2018), *Lost/Perdida* (Alejandro Montiel, 2018), *Accused/Acusada* (Gonzalo Tobal, 2018), *Blood Will Tell/La misma sangre* (Miguel Cohan, 2019), and *Intuition/La corazonada* (Alejandro Montiel, 2020) investigate the role of complicity in helping perpetrators get away with murder. These films seem to signal another turning point in cinema's representation of crime and justice as we approach the half-century mark since the day that inaugurated the latest military dictatorship. *Policiales*, thus, act as symptoms of a society that continues to question and reckon with its role in the failures of a broken legal system. Justice has remained a consistent theme in the cinema of the post-dictatorship era; however, the narrative and aesthetic codes surrounding it have not remained fixed. From *policiales* centred around the figure of the *justiciero* (justice seeker) to films that confront complicity, the genre has mediated the national trauma of genocide and has condemned the short arm of the law. The shift in the *policial*'s conventions accompanies and accommodates a changing historical context and redefines the role of its social actors while offering new ways of imagining and addressing the country's past and its bearing on the present.

When Crime Begins to Pay: The *Policial* Genre's Transformation during the Redemocratisation Era

The *policial* genre has enjoyed a storied trajectory since its arrival to the country's screen. Its popularity in local cinemas dates back to the 1930s, a time of rampant corruption and illegitimate governments often referred to as the *Década Infame* (Infamous Decade). During this period, films such as *The Flight/La fuga* (Luis Saslavsky, 1937) and *Outside the Law/Fuera de la ley* (Manuel Romero, 1937) drove audiences to the theatre. These early representatives of the genre consolidated the efforts of a few earlier films centred on criminal exploits and their consequences – for example, *Monte Criollo* (Arturo S. Mom, 1935) and *Porteño Shadows/Sombras porteñas* (Daniel Tinayre, 1936) – that did not receive the same critical and popular acclaim. Since these antecedents, which told stories of characters embroiled in a life of crime, the genre has continued to shift. According to Mabel Tassara, during its golden age in Argentina (1947–1952), the *policial* begins to exhibit recognisable conventions (1994). Most notably, 'a characteristic of many Argentinean *policiales* before the '60s is that the story is usually told from the perspective of the law' since, with noted exceptions, 'the narration compels the spectator to adopt the vision of the law, or that of *honest* characters' (Tassara 1994: 156). Despite what Tassara notes as a consistent subsequent decline in crime genre productions (with exceptions, as in 1961), *policial* films have experienced a revival in the post-dictatorship era. One of the crime film's most salient features has been its adaptability, particularly 'a comfortable insertion into the local context' (Ibid.: 154). In its resurgence, the *policial*'s conventions have been reformulated to reflect upon a different context and social conditions.[7]

After this early period, the *policial*'s revival has yielded some of the most socially aware films within popular culture as the last military dictatorship represented a significant turning point for crime genres. Emilio Bernini argues that since 1976, when the latest military dictatorship usurps power, 'the genre's politics become notoriously sensible to this new juncture of the state's criminal imposition. Indeed, how does one film the world of crime when the State itself is a terrorist institution?' (2016: 189). The *policial*'s adaptability to its socio-political context and its potential for critique represent a means to articulating cinema's relationship with shifting anxieties surrounding accountability, morality and crime. According to Elena Goity and David Oubiña, 'only after the decade of the 1960s' and particularly beginning with Adolfo Aristarain's films in the late 1970s and early 1980s, 'the optic regarding the protagonists changes and the statute of the law becomes problematized' (1994: 210–211). Aristarain's *The Lion's Share/La parte del león* (1978), *Time for Revenge/Tiempo de revancha* (1981), and *Last Days of the Victim/Ultimos días de la víctima* (1982) were released during the years of strict censorship that accompanied the military regime; yet, this crime trilogy encompasses politically engaged films that uncover 'the perversion of a whole system: . . . the break in values defines society as a whole and implicates the offenders as much as the figures of the law' (Ibid.: 210). These three films' social critique sets the stage for the *policial* in the era of redemocratisation, when films begin explicitly portraying and condemning the horrors of Argentina's history of state violence.

When democracy returns and censorship restrictions are abolished, the *policial* begins to contend with the country's traumatic and embarrassing past. Films of the immediate post-dictatorship period focus on telling stories which expose state violence and abuse in poignant images that cement the need for democracy. As Ana Laura Lusnich argues, films in the first decade after the end of the dictatorship tend to 'encourage the reestablishing of the democracy lost in 1976', among other objectives (Lusnich and Kriger 1994: 83). Throughout the 1980s, *policiales* portray the traumas that remained latent in the post-dictatorship social climate, including state terrorism, corruption, and the pursuit of truth and justice. In this way, *policiales* add a visual dimension to the horrors that had been executed privately and that remained hidden, but which survivors had presented through testimony. These films set the stage for another genre reformulation, which takes place after the first post-dictatorship president completes his mandate. During this time, the genre takes on concerns that question the morality of a legal system that has begun to show its failures.

The *policial*'s moral guidelines become a useful tool for addressing the country's failures during and after the period of redemocratisation. The sentencing handed down at the close of the emblematic trial against the military high commanders in 1985 did not provide closure, relief, or vindication for the *desaparecidos*, their families, or the nation. The promise of justice was quickly undone in the following years with measures of impunity, including Presidents Raúl Alfonsín's amnesty laws and Carlos Saúl Menem's pardons for the perpetrators.[8] In this context, the early 1990s usher in a new era for the *policial*. The genre explores further distrust and disdain for official institutions, constructing allegorical fictional worlds in which the line between morality and crime becomes effaced and characters seek justice by their own means.

Juan Carlos Desanzo's *At the Edge of the Law/Al filo de la ley* (1992) serves as a transitional film since it carries the vestiges of the cinema of the 1980s in its storyline. *Al filo de la ley* depicts security officer and former policeman Rodolfo Rivas attempting to avenge his hotel's robbery in what appears to be justice intent on punishing criminals characteristic of the previous decade. Yet, it also bridges the concerns of the 1990s in which protagonists engage in actions that have traditionally been considered criminal but in the name of justice, reformulating the ethics of transiting outside the law. However, this apparent change in moral compass is not gratuitous: the partnership between criminality and justice emerges during a time in which ex-policeman Rivas and thief Raúl Fontana team up to rescue their love interest from corrupt authorities embroiled in a crime ring. When Mónica, a Latin American incarnation of the Hollywood *femme fatale*, escapes and warns Rivas and Fontana that they are being set up, she arrives in a green Ford Falcon presumably seized from her captors. The appearance of this car in the film, recognisable in Argentina as the military's preferred vehicle for their covert operations, links the criminal organisation to the dictatorship (and vice versa). In the end, Rivas, Fontana, and Mónica become partners and establish roots as hoteliers in Miami. The final scene reproduces the opening shots but with strategic changes: Mónica dons a white dress in lieu of the black one she wears at the beginning and performs at the bar where she was once employed but now presumably co-owns. As the audience watches her intently, it is now former thief Fontana who apprehends the same pickpocket that Rivas had captured as the hotel's security guard during the opening sequence. Both men reassure the bar goers that there is no cause for concern, after which Mónica utters the last words of the film: 'Law and order have been restored.' The law and order that Mónica identifies are not those of the government, but are instead executed outside the accepted national channels, which her utterance in a foreign language seems to reinforce.[9] This circular ending signals the closely forged relationship between crime and retribution, which in the 1990s becomes normalised on screen: circumventing the ineffective law is the only possible way to achieve justice.

Finding resolution outside of the law becomes a crucial element in a cluster of stories that question the ostensible criminality of this strategy if the ends justify the means. Unlike films that feature the military prominently to chronicle the authoritarian past, this group of *policiales* offers allegorical images of the current state of the redemocratised nation and addresses the past through stories that display the consequences of the dictatorship, without directly focusing their narratives on the military's wrongdoings. Among these are the 1993 film *Perdido por perdido*, which portrays revenge as the only way out of violent extortion: the protagonist must break free from the mafia after they provide a short-term lifeline when he is caught in dire financial circumstances, which in turn are a consequence of the country's neoliberal economic crisis. A robbery in the 1995 movie *Caballos salvajes* becomes a way to recover what was previously stolen from an honest man, serving as a form of individual justice against a corrupt institution. Similarly, in the 2000 release *Nueve Reinas*, Valeria and her boyfriend Juan decide to con her brother Marcos to recover inheritance money that he has appropriated, bypassing a court system that has failed to provide a fair and timely resolution. These case studies are among many that feature characters who sustain a social injury and for which retribution becomes the means to survival. Their individual pursuits of justice drive the narrative of these *policiales* forward, enacting what Goity and Oubiña identify in films of the 1980s and early 1990s as *justicia por mano propia* (justice by one's own hand) as they fight against corrupt systems that make illegitimate use of power or the law (1994: 216). These characters then become *justicieros* (justice seekers) who look to settle the score and achieve restitution for what was once taken from them or their loved ones. Their quests for justice take place outside the ineffective or corrupt reach of the law through which they present a new world order that turns these characters from victims to actors or, rather, justice-seeking heroes with agency. Through their actions, the genre proposes a grassroots solution that offers an alternative to legal justice on screen, and through which the concepts of morality and crime become redefined.

In the Name of Justice: The Avenger in the *Policial* Film

The *policial* embodies its newly defined morality in the pivotal figure of the avenger or *justiciero* (justice seeker). This character does not simply engage in a 'marathon of revenge' or the logic of an 'eye for an eye' that characterises earlier films (Goity and Oubiña 1994: 212). Through their quests, characters enact resistance to corrupt systems of power that operate underground and that they have to escape, dismantle, or expose in the name of personal survival. The *justiciero* must circumvent the official channels not only because they are ineffective, but also because they are often compromised – as they were during the last dictatorship – and are frequently the source of (or help sustain) a social injury.

These characters are vicarious conduits for the justice that remains unrealised in their contemporary context, and argue that it can (and should) be served.

Through the *justiciero*, the *policial* redefines the relationship between morality and traditional notions of crime. This figure is often both a criminal and a justice seeker, much like José in the opening sequence of *Caballos Salvajes*. José has lost everything: his adult son was murdered, his wife dies of grief, and a bank steals his life savings when it files for bankruptcy and reemerges under a new name. With the plan to reclaim what is his, he walks into the newly reconstituted bank and threatens to kill himself if the institution does not return the money they embezzled, which he needs to save a group of horses he raised after rescuing them from the slaughterhouse. José is the quintessential *justiciero*, and his actions are legitimised in the name of settling the score. His actions are both illegal and heroic, a duality inherited from a long-known figure of the Argentinean lore that inhabited older forms of popular culture.

Before appearing in post-dictatorship *policiales*, the *justiciero* makes his appearance in Argentinean culture under the name Juan Moreira, a historical figure that challenged the corrupt social order throughout his adult life. As Josefina Ludmer claims, Moreira 'incarnates violence in its pure state, directly aimed at oppression: its victims are the enemies of the people. He articulates "crime" with law, economy, and state power, and he makes the crossing required of a popular avenger: *the passage from legality to illegality because of an injustice*' (1999: 233). Wronged by the village grocer who refused to pay back a loan and the town sheriff who desired Moreira's wife, this gaucho outlaw became an icon in his quest for revenge. Putting an end to the merchant's life in a duel and also singlehandedly killing the sheriff and his two acolytes while resisting arrest, Moreira became known for his fighting skill and prowess. After his death in 1874 at the hands of the state, writer Eduardo Gutiérrez immortalised him in a serial dime novel published in the paper *La Patria Argentina* between 1879 and 1880. His fame extended well into the 20th century after becoming the subject of furor among the literate masses at the end of the 19th century. According to Ludmer, Moreira's story has been dramatised widely since his initial literary emergence, including in theatre and cinema. On screen, he is notably central in the eponymous biopic *Juan Moreira* (Leonardo Favio, 1973) and in a classroom scene as the literature teacher and his students reenact Moreira's death in the emblematic *The Official Story/La historia oficial* (Luis Puenzo, 1985), which tells the story of a history teacher who slowly realises her adopted daughter might be a child of *desaparecidos*. Moreira, celebrated in the action of criminally rebelling against a repressive state apparatus that imposed a series of injustices upon him, lives on in cinema under other names as the spirit of righteousness when legal channels are otherwise compromised. Like this iconic character, the post-dictatorship *justiciero* seeks restitution, sometimes in ways that make audiences question where the lines between good and evil and legality and illegality are drawn, and how far these boundaries have migrated in the post-dictatorship era.

In this journey, the justice seeker lays bare the historically ineffectual and corrupt cooptation of the legal system, which at times operates as an enduring surrogate for the repressive state apparatus. The *policial*'s central attention to this figure is the focal point to secure elusive justice in alternative ways. Usually male, the justice seeker appears embodied in an outsider, a recluse, or a detective who is able to shed light upon the plot's (and the nation's) mystery or untangle levels of corruption that remain hidden under legitimate surface appearances. Films such as *El secreto de sus ojos*, and *Cenizas del paraíso* are concerned with the legal process and the inability of achieving justice through traditional channels. Like the former, in *Caballos salvajes* justice can only be served by an anarchist outlaw's own hand, earning him the name *indomable* (indomitable). Other films such as *Nueve reinas* and *Al final del túnel* follow along these lines by engaging with the moral quandary of stealing from thieves. These films reembody Juan Moreira under different names in every achievement of justice through behaviour that is only criminal because it resides outside the law. It is, in every other way, a morally 'just crime' (Page 2009: 83). Moreira's reincarnation gives justice a name, and a face that emerges from the ranks of the oppressed. His prominence under the many identities of *justiciero* characters during the post-dictatorship era signals that, in this time of rupture, justice must be a grassroots effort. Built at the hands of civilians, it becomes a demand for a future in which the government must serve its people instead of persecuting them.

In the process of seeking to address an injustice lodged in the past, the *justiciero* not only solves a crime or avenges a wrong but restores social bonds and emotional attachments. Importantly, these are not only romantic couplings or reconstituted families that serve to bring closure to the narrative, but instead signal a strategy of countering processes of atomisation characteristic of the latest military rule. In the process, the crime or investigation allows the characters to work through an unresolved trauma, either by elucidating a mystery or by exacting revenge and achieving justice. In *El secreto de sus ojos*, retired court clerk Benjamín Espósito's attempt to write a book about a previous murder case and his discovery of a makeshift prison where the widower keeps his wife's pardoned murderer leads to the closure he needs to romantically reunite with an old flame, Judge Irene Menéndez Hastings. As a widower, Ricardo Morales can only impose the life sentence he was promised through his own personal action when the corrupt government sets the convicted murderer free to employ him as a paramilitary agent. It is also the journey in the road movie hybrid *Caballos salvajes* and the constitution of the two main characters as modern-day Robin Hoods that identify José and Pedro as *justicieros*. While avenging the injustice José has suffered, they also temporarily alleviate others:

they feed Ana, a houseless victim of wealth inequality driven by desperation and share the excess spoils of José's robbery with working class inhabitants of a small rural town as an act of repudiation against the capitalist machine. In the process, Pedro morphs from a young and conceited corporate banker who puts stock in an upwardly mobile lifestyle to a righteous fugitive, achieving a successful coupling with Ana that effectively ends their shared loneliness. The fictional bonds constituted in these films offer a vicarious way to repair the deeply damaged fabric of society, as the fibers of citizenry are stronger when woven through interpersonal relationships.

These relationships are central to the 2016 film *Al final del túnel*, which depicts a crime committed for reasons other than personal restitution: foiling a heist to preempt thieves is not a matter of personal survival but a moral obligation, an act of retribution for someone else's sake, someone that the gang leader has violently abused. The protagonist, Joaquín, has been rendered paraplegic after a car accident in which he loses his wife and his daughter. The camera tightly frames him constantly on the move, pulling himself with his arms through claustrophobic tunnels to preempt a group of bank robbers by stealing their bounty in order to achieve justice for his new love interest and her daughter. In the process, the protagonist discovers the thieves' alliance with the corrupt police chief. For a nation in danger of feeling immobilised in the aftermath of genocide and sustained state violence, Joaquín models a way to overcome trauma and demand justice for the greater good. The film mobilises the renewed historical discourse of finding truth and justice for the victims of state terror in its suggestion that it is not just personal needs that drive protagonists to act against corruption.

Al final del túnel presents an example of how the individual pursuits geared towards survival that typify films of the 1990s and 2000s now become reckonings in the service of fulfilling a moral obligation towards others. These *policiales* show how the need for individual survival shifts to the collective interest, effectively dissolving on screen the atomisation that characterised the dictatorship's practices of forced disappearance. The justice that the screen enacts provides a measure with which to mediate the shifting anxieties surrounding accountability, as time passes and perpetrators of (immoral, unjust) crimes only experience suitable punishment in the world of fiction.

Paying the Consequences: Concerns over Culpability and *Policiales* of Complicity

Alongside the *policiales* that thirst for and serve justice on screen, the country's culture of impunity had seemingly begun changing. In 2002, Argentina's Congress sanctioned and promulgated National Law n° 25,633, which instituted observance of a Day of Memory for Truth and Justice on 24 March, the anniversary of the last military coup. This legislation inaugurated an era during which renewed popular calls for investigations and trials propelled governmental policies aimed at protecting human rights. In 2004, President Néstor Kirchner declared the creation of the Space of Memory and Human Rights ex ESMA, a museum that now occupies the site of one of the dictatorship's largest clandestine detention, torture, and extermination centres. During this public act, he repudiated military rule, pledged to seek justice, and apologised on behalf of the state for 'the shame of having been silent during 20 years of democracy to so many atrocities' (Kirchner 2004). Between 2005 and 2010, legislators declared Alfonsín's and Menem's governmental actions of impunity unconstitutional, and charges against known perpetrators have either been initiated for the first time or reinstituted. Additionally, in 2013 the National Ministry of Human Rights established the *Registro Unificado de Víctimas del Terrorismo de Estado* (RUVTE, Unified Registry of Victims of State Terrorism).[10] The promotion of discourses aimed at securing the 'fundamental rights of Memory, Truth, and Justice' (RUVTE 2015: 2) – including the 2015 publication of what RUVTE's website calls an 'exhaustive research and compilation report' (RUVTE 2015: 1) – seemed to show promise of the government's steps towards combatting impunity.

However, these new measures have not proven satisfactory so far. The institutional hurdles of the legal system have presented a stark contrast with the promised results that the democratic governments in power since have failed to deliver. In 2016, RUVTE revealed that its findings only accounted for 6348 *desaparecidos* and 952 victims of murder without forced disappearance when it responded to an information request, grossly underreporting the 30,000 that human rights organisations have historically documented (De Vedia, 2016).[11] This official count further reignited national controversies concerning the mishandlings of the popularly elected regimes that have been in power since the dictatorship's demise. According to the National Public Prosecutors Ministry, as of March of 2019, there are 611 human rights abuses cases related to the last military dictatorship on file. Of those, 40 per cent are still in the discovery phase, while just 2 per cent are in trial and only 36 per cent have been sentenced. Many of the legal cases may still be open in 2025 – almost half a century since the military's last takeover – given that the average time to finish transiting through the judicial system currently tops five years. More alarmingly, 46 per cent of the 3161 people accused are currently free while 22 per cent have died, and only 36 per cent remain detained. Of the latter, 65 per cent are under house arrest (Ministerio Público Fiscal 2019), a disproportionate figure compared to only 0.73 per cent of those sentenced to home confinement for any kind of crime in the national general incarcerated population (Dirección Nacional 2018: 7). These figures only reinforce the sense amongst Argentineans that justice is still a distant, if not improbable goal today.

In this context of impunity where hope is in short supply, contemporary crime films show signs of shifting preoccupations relating to the topic of justice and collective accountability. In 2017, a new wave of *policiales* seemingly emerges to investigate the role of complicity in helping perpetrators get away with murder, thematising and expanding the responsibility of the silence for which President Kirchner had apologised more than a decade earlier. In films where the sun rarely makes an appearance and fragmented flashback reconstructions offer restricted and unreliable perspectives that mirror the structure of traumatic memories, the *policial* questions the role of those who look the other way in order to foreground their culpability in the crimes of the past. Dark settings and sharp, stark shadows that shroud characters and objects depicted on screen do more than present a bleak picture of society. They also help to conceal the horrors of the past that can only be brought to light through the eyes of a character that will (sometimes only reluctantly) serve as a detective or a witness – or both. The act of seeing and discovering does not absolve the characters but rather implicates them, serving to expose secrets that cast doubt on the meaning of culpability and complicity.

As an early, transitional exponent of this new era, the 2017 film *Los padecientes* merges the figure of the *justiciero* (who enacts a crime of retribution as survival and moral impulse), the darker aesthetic of contemporary *policial* films, and thematic concerns over culpability, accountability, and actions that lead to the concealment of a crime. The search for truth drives this narrative: the famous psychoanalyst Dr Pablo Rouviot becomes a reluctant detective after being recruited to serve as an expert in judicial proceedings. This case involves an affluent young man who has confessed to his father's murder, while his older sister seeks to establish his legal immunity due to mental illness. With his professional oath to always seek the truth guiding him, Dr Rouviot embarks in an investigation that endangers his life and that of those around him as he uncovers the dark secrets lurking behind the murder. The late entrepreneur Roberto Vanussi was the head of an underage prostitution and human trafficking ring that did not spare his own offspring. His oldest daughter Paula, a victim of her father's sexual whims, is the one who hires Rouviot and later confesses to the murder in an explanatory flashback. Her brother Javier also claims to be guilty, and both confessions are in service of protecting their youngest sister Camila, who the film reveals as the murderer in one of the final scenes. Her motivation is witnessing her father violently beating her brother and sexually abusing her sister, shown in a graphic flashback during which a cut from that brutal scene to Camila watching immersed in shadows creates a correspondence that establishes her as another victim. The murder takes place immediately after, as the patriarch enjoys a drink and runs his hands over Camila's newly developed teenage body. As he asks her to come closer and lasciviously embraces her, she slits his neck, therefore avoiding her older sister's fate. The story is told in a series of flashbacks intertwined through editing, with interactions that at times resemble talk-therapy sessions. Throughout, Dr Rouviot investigates the cost of covering up a crime to protect what the film characterises a justifiable kind of murder: one in the service of survival, self-preservation, and the common good.

The Vanussi clan's outward appearance as a perfect family harbours secrets of violent patriarchal abuse, incest, human trafficking, and underage prostitution, traumas that within the confines of their opulent gated mansion mirror the remorseless covert operations of abduction, clandestine internment, torture, and murder in which the military engaged during the last dictatorship. *Los padecientes* constantly repeats the transition from the particular to the general, which enables a reading of the film as another mediation of the national traumas of the past. Vanussi's repugnant behaviour recalls the violent abuses the state perpetrated towards its people, whose individual stories aggregated the whole of a painful collective history that left few untouched. The opening credits show the actors' names transform from handwritten cursive to typeface letters, signaling a transition from the personal to the impersonal or rather, from the individual to the general. Similarly, in a scene in which Dr Rouviot has a consensual sexual encounter with a nurse from Javier's residential institution, she offers him access to the suspect's clinical history. Upon this proposal, the camera dollies out from the intimacy of Rouviot's bed to the unmistakable cityscape of Buenos Aires at night. This camera movement reiterates that this story of unique individuals (the Vanussis) is one of many and stands in for that of the city as a whole, one of the epicentres of military repression during the last autocratic government. This aesthetic device confirms in visual terms the mantra that many characters repeat throughout the film: 'things are not always what they seem', referencing the deep-seated trauma that the abused offspring (and the nation) harbour under the surface. Similarly, Camila explains life at the Vanussi household and their mother's attempts to protect them through a flashback that verbally and visually compares her joy among darkness to the Holocaust film *Life is Beautiful/La vita è bella* (Roberto Benigni, 1998), creating a correspondence between these experiences of trauma and recalling through one more narrative strategy the country's history of genocide.

Los padecientes is centred on the act of locating the truth that lies beneath surface appearances, echoing the demands of a multitude of human rights groups and families and friends of the *desaparecidos*. This is apparent in the monologue through which Dr Rouviot sets the stage to tell Camila's story: at the moment she stands on a stage about to play a violin concerto with a full orchestra in front of a large audience. Rouviot's voiceover establishes the stakes of the narrative, the film, and, to an extent, Argentina's search for closure as he declares: 'The truth beats silently. It hides the darkest corners of the mind, forgotten in old judicial records, hidden in the confusing oracular opinions, simply prey to repression or ignorance as if it were one of those animals that hibernate for a long time without manifesting itself but that even in that state remain alive.' This thematic focus reminds us of the country's plight, asking itself how to unearth the truth and how to assign guilt when authorities have failed.

The noir-like aesthetic of the film, its dark spaces, and pronounced shadows prefigure the unfathomable, painful secrets that its narrative uncovers in an unsettling fantasy that tricks us into believing that perhaps justice can be served. The film begins with a shot of a black screen that allows glimpses of a hand playing the violin at the centre of the frame in an image that progressively sharpens, revealing shot by shot more complete information, as the film's flashbacks will later replicate. Similarly, in a subsequent shot, the camera tracks from shadows to the light, letting us see Camila's face in the process before leaving the screen in darkness. This camera device anticipates her journey, though not unambiguously: as she watches her sister's abuse and kills her father, she is dressed in white as a sign of purity, but while standing in front of the concert's audience and now free from the threat of sexual violence, she is dressed in black, no longer pure yet swathed in light and celebrated through roaring applause. She is a virtuous teenager who has been forced to kill to serve justice, a secret held only by the trinity that the camera highlights with close-ups and eyeline matches at the end of the film: as Camila plays, Dr Rouviot and Paula share a knowing look and a smile. In sharing this secret, the audience is implicated, though not necessarily accused of guilt. Camila's concert serves as an excuse to revisit her (and hi)story, told in a flashback composed of memories that offer us the opportunity to discover a shocking, morally repugnant truth alongside the protagonist. In the end, his search for the veridical facts becomes irrelevant to the legal process, as he declares the confessed killer not imputable for his actions despite knowing he was not guilty. Rouviot's decision puts forth the balance between what is criminal and what is moral, deciding that concealing the truth will save this family from further pain. His cover-up is a sign of justice, the one that courts would never be able to deliver through their slow, ineffective operation. We are privy to the truth and witnesses to justice, and the circular structure that begins and ends with Camila's concert represents a rhetorical device that foregrounds the shift in notions of complicity in post-dictatorship Argentina, as the country further delves into the historical traumas of the past.

Another film released in the same year shares thematic preoccupations that examine culpability in relation to murder and impunity, but this time the former allows the perpetrator to continue and conceal his incestuous relationship. *Nieve negra* begins with a flashback of a child turning around upon hearing his name, and in later flashbacks we see him immediately fall after getting shot while his blood spreads on the white snow. Despite the belief that Juan's death was a hunting accident, the dead child's father spends his years physically punishing his older son Salvador, whose innocence we discover towards the end of the film. Thirty years later, the middle brother Marcos travels from his new home in Spain to dispose of his father's ashes and discuss the inheritance with Salvador, who has become a hostile recluse in the family's remote cabin in Patagonia. Marcos' Spanish wife Laura serves as the audience's eyes as she slowly discovers the tensions between the brothers (and their sister, who is hospitalised in a psychiatric institution) and endeavors to find out the truth. As Salvador becomes more and more aggressive towards Marcos, Laura shoots him in what she thinks is self-defense, and Marcos helps to cover up his murder. It is not until he goes to the police station to provide a statement that we realise, through Laura's perspective, the unspeakable family secret trapped in one of her sister in law's notebooks: she was having an incestual relationship with her brother Marcos, who decides to silence their younger sibling Juan after he discovers them. Upon this realisation, Laura decides to alter and outwardly misinterpret the evidence against her husband for financial gain, as Salvador's death has made the couple the sole heirs of the family estate. Organised around a series of flashbacks that fixate on and progressively reveal the horrors of this family's traumatic past like a repressed memory, the film gradually unveils the immoral and murderous designs of a man who not only got away with murder but also found someone else to take the blame and is now replicating this pattern in his new family through his wife, who is pregnant with his child. Unearthing this trauma does not serve to cleanse him (or her) but rather to make us complicit, as we are the only ones who can access what Laura knows and has decided to conceal.

In a remote, desolate location, a cloak of white snow hides an unfathomable evil in which we now participate through Laura's eyes and actions, covering up a truth that remains buried with the family's casualties in the depths of the Patagonia landscape. The location is significant: *Nieve negra* incorporates the stunning natural scenery of a region usually associated with a safe haven for perpetrators of human rights abuses. This is one of the places where World War II Nazis hid from their deserved punishment and, in many cases, lived the rest of their years fraudulently as upstanding members of their community. The film visually highlights the region's copious white snow through shots that privilege the landscape, which becomes a fitting backdrop for a story about deception (of both characters and audiences).

As is also the case in *Los padecientes*, *Nieve negra*'s dysfunctional family serves as a stand-in for the nation. In this case, one member suffers the consequences of the other's actions, while the rest remain quiet and even cover over the perverse atrocities they discover. The film tells us that, without speaking up, we too are complicit with those who have gotten away with murder. This nefarious tale of incest, fratricide, and trauma that remains buried as deep as the bodies under the white innocent snow contrasts with the optimism of *justiciero policiales* made between the early 1990s and the mid 2010s, which often offer resolutions that restore a degree of justice in the end. *Nieve negra* presents symptoms of the lack of hope that injustice has yielded as more and more perpetrators – in a genocidal rather than individual scale – get away with murder. The continued emergence of films that investigate culpability and the hopelessness of a reigning impunity seems to indicate another turning point in the journey towards the *policial*'s elaboration of this lingering historical trauma.

Subsequent works have thematised the meaning of culpability through narratives that question whether witnesses who did not prevent deaths have a degree of guilt. Films such as *Acusada* and *La misma sangre*, released in 2018 and 2019 respectively, feature protagonists who leave others to die. In *Acusada*, Dolores finds her best friend Camila – who had recently betrayed her by leaking a personal sex tape – stabbed and bleeding in her living room, but, after seeing her finger and eyes move, she walks away. In *La misma sangre*, the patriarch of the family watches as his wife, who intended to divorce him, is choked to death when her necklace becomes tangled in the powerful movements of her industrial baking mixer. Similarly, in *Las grietas de Jara*, architect Pablo Simó helps his supervisors bury the body of a neighbour who they claim died accidentally while trying to stop the foundation from being poured in their high-rise development. The neighbour, Nelson Jara, extorted the architecture studio after discovering they were skirting building codes, which he claimed caused a crack in his wall. The film begins when a mysterious woman appears looking for Jara, who has vanished. Throughout the film, we uncover the truth of Jara's whereabouts, and in the end his death is retold from the perspective of one of the two supervisors, a female architect with whom Simó shares a physical attraction. Simó eventually realises that the accident may not have been such, and that helping to bury the body under the foundation has made him an accessory to murder. The film *Perdida* also probes the degree of culpability that resides in inaction, as a teenage Pipa leaves her best friend Cornelia behind at a bar during a class trip to Patagonia. Their tour guide presumably grants the group of teenage friends access to alcohol, and, when they are heavily inebriated, he takes them back to their inn. This is when Cornelia disappears and becomes the victim of sex trafficking. We later learn that he kidnaps her because she witnesses him raping one of her teenage friends. Pipa attempts to find her for years and even becomes a police detective as an adult to save other young girls from succumbing to the same fate. Cornelia's resurgence as a leader in a prostitution ring, and the later uncovering of Pipa's police chief's involvement, lead to a confrontation in which the two women meet again. This prompts Cornelia to explain that her disappearance was akin to a death, in no small part because she was left behind. Though these narratives follow similar thematic patterns, their structural and visual elements offer further meditations of how the genre's conventions provide an apt tool for measuring the role of ignorance in guilt and how the *policial*'s shifts mediate and explore the shortcomings of justice in contemporary Argentina.

These films are often situated in the present, after the original event or crime has transpired, and the trauma of that past is reconstructed through limited perspectives or flashbacks that progressively lead us to an understanding of the truth. These flashbacks often open the film, as in *Nieve negra*, or begin appearing on screen shortly after, as in *Los Padecientes*, *Las grietas de Jara*, and *Acusada*. In *Perdida* and *La misma sangre*, the films begin in the past and quickly fast forward to the present, identifying the initial history as an unresolved trauma that will reappear on screen through retellings, remembrances, drawings, or other devices that serve as emblems of the past. These memories are crucial to the audience's reconstruction of the crime. Each flashback presents more information, as if allowing us to remove a veil inch by inch with each of its repetitions, while also foregrounding the factual unreliability embedded in personal perspectives. *Nieve negra*'s initial flashback is perhaps the most poignant. The opening scene, which depicts a boy hearing his name and turning around, sets up a mystery to be resolved throughout the course of the film. In the next flashback, we see the brothers and their father wielding rifles, hunting for food, and we later observe drops of blood falling on the snow. As more information becomes available in these flashbacks, we see the child, Juan, turn around upon hearing his name and immediately falling to the ground after being shot. The mystery of the shooter's identity is soon to be erroneously resolved as the father punishes the older brother who is crouched next to the body. In the end, we discover through Laura's perspective that the missing part of that flashback is her husband shooting his brother. The camera is placed behind Juan as his name is called, and he turns around staring straight at the audience, offering us the perspective of the killer. We discover the murderer's identity through the eyes of his wife, who also kills (this time, her husband's older brother) but remains silent about the identity of both murderers, thereby placing us in a position of complicity. In a similar manner, *Acusada* allows us access to the protagonist's perspective, as Dolores continuously remembers the day her friend Camila was murdered. Her first flashback is brief and shows a bird flying through a party's leftovers. As Dolores routinely declares her innocence, the recurring flashback becomes more complete, and her testimony during court hearings paints a clearer picture through which we see the bird as only part of a messy apartment. As she awaits her verdict, Dolores' memories and retellings expand to include Camila's bloodied body slumbered on a couch, still alive and labouriously trying to ask for help. These serve as examples of how the *policial* engages in a structural stylistic exploration of a traumatic past that relied on the country's complicity, whether deliberate or involuntary. The progressive access to information that the flashbacks present mirrors the way many Argentineans discovered the military's human rights abuses, in a gradual yet painful process of recollection after the return to democracy. In its mediation of the traumas of history, this new incarnation of the *policial* does not seem to offer comfort, but instead asserts that silence involves culpability and that limited information or even ignorance – willful or otherwise – does not completely absolve bystanders and those who did not stop atrocities from happening.

These films examine culpability in different ways through visual cues that foreground their point of view when it comes to complicity. In its opening scenes, *Las grietas de Jara* places Pablo Simó behind or in front of structures that look like jail cells: the architecture studio's façade composed of vertical bars, the subway banister at each side of the staircase that leads to the street (also flanked by a tall iron fence), the tight entrance of his apartment with French doors in the background, and his balcony's rail guard. Throughout the film, the character appears further imprisoned, only freeing himself after confessing his role as an accessory to murder to his soon-to-be ex-wife. The sense of confinement that permeates *Las grietas de Jara* also figures prominently in other *policiales* through camera angles that represent the characters as captive. In tight shots and close-ups that create claustrophobic images, the camera does not often remain still. Instead, it dollies or zooms in to further heighten the pressure it inflicts on the characters. As these shots close in, they intensify the audiences' emotional response to suggest and cement complicity with the crimes in question. In *Acusada*, the camera circles vertiginously around Dolores and her father as she confronts her role in Camila's death, highlighting the unsettling personal negotiation involved in determining her guilt. These circular movements only stop when she confesses that she 'left her there to die'. In its frequent movements that eschew static shots, the camera privileges the instability that this dynamism conveys to indicate the precarity and unreliability of each story as it develops. Like these shots, our perspectives constantly shift in these *policiales* as we continue watching each film untangle its mystery and reveal the truth.

The emphasis on characters' perspectives present in the *policial*'s structure through flashbacks, memories, and retellings also establishes seeing and witnessing as central to determining complicity and guilt. In *Los padecientes*, Dr Rouviot uses psychoanalytic clinical approaches to uncover a horrific secret hidden under layers of trauma. He is an expert witness, the last relic of an era that believes in truth but must conceal it for moral justice to be possible. *Nieve negra* buries this hope for justice twice: first with Juan's body, a witness himself who paid the ultimate price for discovering his siblings' incestuous relationship, and second, as it turns out, the character who serves as our eyes into an accomplice after discovering her husband's culpability. The last scene of the film, during which she manipulates this truth into a narrative that absolves her husband to better suit her purposes, ends with her looking straight into the camera. Her direct look implicates us, presenting a disturbing corollary for inhabiting her perspective. Similarly, in *Las grietas de Jara*, architect Pablo Simó builds with his memories a structure through which we can understand the story of a disappearance, but as we discover his involvement in a purported accident, he realises his role as an accessory to murder. *Acusada*, which hinges on the failure to act after seeing, presents a close-up of the protagonist's eyes as its first shot. This opening clearly establishes the film's central preoccupation: where does guilt lie when one can prevent death from taking place but does not? *Perdida* follows a different path that highlights the dangers of imprecise testimony, which enabled the human trafficking ring's success. In this story about a disappearance, the camera depicts a young Pipa as she watches from inside an inn as the search for her friend continues in Patagonia's snowy terrain. In the next shot fourteen years later and now an adult in Buenos Aires, the camera shows Pipa waiting in her car swathed in rain, looking in the opposite direction than the preceding shot. She then conducts a successful raid, not in a group as in the previous search but alone. Her trauma has led her to individual action: her search for Cornelia has turned her into a police detective focused on dismantling human trafficking rings. Pipa is not absolved when she finds Cornelia at the end of the film: the latter is now a woman hardened through years of slavery and sex trade and goes by Nadine, a replacement for the person who symbolically died long ago when her friends abandoned her. Through these characters' eyes and the perspective these films offer, spectators become the ultimate witnesses. Sometimes audiences are implicated, sometimes they serve as observers, but they are always asked to understand the moral perils of silence as the films offer reflections on complicity and responsibility.

The *policial* of complicity presents guilt as permeating the characters and their society and, as a result, no longer identifies urban space as the primary scene of the crime. Earlier films characterised the city as a dangerous locale from which only bucolic spaces can provide a respite. For example, as Joanna Page argues, *Nueve reinas* 'intends to shock the viewer into the unsettling recognition that the apparent normality of city life conceals depths of unseen criminality', which 'do not take place in some criminal underworld but in the common public spaces of the city' (2009: 92). The *justiciero* films – among them *Perdido por perdido*, *Nueve reinas*, *Caballos salvajes*, and *El secreto de sus ojos* – uncover the city as a threatening space where the horrors of state brutality hide under the surfaces of usual and quotidian locations. Through their narrative and aesthetic presentation, these images revealed the hidden realities of large urban areas like Buenos Aires, which acted as the epicentre of systematic repression. However, the *policial* of complicity no longer serves to reveal underground truths regarding torture and murder as exclusive to the city, but instead extends this unsettling condition to the rural spaces that have traditionally represented the promise of an escape or a hiding place. In this way, the *policial* more accurately reflects the widespread incidence of crimes against humanity perpetrated during the last dictatorship, while placing emphasis on the people who commit these crimes rather than the spaces in which they occur.

The Future of the *Policial* and the State of Justice in Argentina Today

As these works depict it, the future does not seem bright. The cinematography, rife with chiaroscuro lighting, dark and shadowy indoor spaces, and the lack of sun outdoors, creates a sense of gloom that previous *policiales* had already adopted when portraying the city as a perilous, crime-ridden battleground. However, this darkness also extends to bucolic spaces, which some characters – like Dolores in *Acusada*, or Elías in *La misma sangre* – visit in search of respite from their downwardly spiraling lives and emotions, only to be forced to come to grips with their culpability. It is only on seldom occasions that the sun makes an appearance in *policiales* that investigate complicity. For example, *La misma sangre* only shows the sun at the beginning of the film, when it establishes the farm as a family heirloom, and at the end, when Elías dies following a confrontation during which he kills his wife's lover. He has gone from witnessing – and willfully failing to prevent – his wife's death and grappling with culpability to murdering her lover; sunshine appears on the day of his death and his funeral as a celebration of his demise. But his death does not settle the film's concern with culpability. In his final hours, as Elías tries to hide the body of the man he just shot, he collapses near the same place his father passed away. As a result, he is impaled with a wooden stake. He dies after his daughter – who has rushed to the farm and proceeds to question him about her mother's death – takes a step to walk away. In an effort to prevent her from leaving, he falls off his resting place, which causes the wooden stake to dislodge from his body and open the flow of blood. In this turn of events, the film seems to suggest that a single step can distinguish a witness from a murderer: Elías' step towards his wife as she is being strangled by the mixer, his step towards her lover as he fires a shotgun, his daughter's step away from him as he lays on the couch in critical condition, and her final act of walking away as he takes his last breaths while bleeding on the floor. The film does not leave room for hope. A shot from above that shows Elías' motionless body and his blood slowly spreading on the floor provides a full picture, suggesting that his culpability is now something he has deeded to his daughter as she walks away leaving him to die. In addition, during the funeral, we see her son holding the fang keychain that Elías inherited from his father, who, in turn, inherited it upon his other son's untimely death. The presence of this family heirloom indicates that this history of death and tragedy will continue being passed down from generation to generation. *Nieve negra* presents a similar concern, as Marcos' wife also conceals culpability just like her husband. Her pregnancy seems to suggest that murder, complicity, and culpability will continue to be passed down the lineage of Marcos' new family. *Las grietas de Jara* also presents a future in which history will repeat itself. The final shot depicts Pablo Simó chiseling a crack in the wall to presumably attempt to extort the contractors erecting the building next to his new apartment, as Jara did before his burial under a concrete foundation. The circularity of these endings presents the argument that impunity is so deeply embedded in the nation that history is bound to repeat itself, from one generation to the next.

However, not all films offer a definitively fateful view. *Acusada* seems to present an ambivalent future despite the dark, blue-toned lighting throughout the film: it is only at the end that the sun shines, on the day of Dolores' not guilty verdict, and as family and friends celebrate her exoneration. The last scene shows her discovering a puma (that once seemed to be only the figment of a neighbour's imagination) looming on the roof of a house. The puma's unlikely existence introduces a hopeful element into a story that, despite featuring redemption through the court system, does not completely absolve the protagonist as she continues to question her role in her friend's death. Despite her legal acquittal, there is no clear resolution of the question of Dolores' complicity. The film's last shot shows her symbolically imprisoned behind a window inside of her house as the camera tracks back to progressively reveal many other houses that form Buenos Aires' unmistakable skyline. This camera movement signals that this story is one of many, and under the roofs we can see in this broad, high angle perspective of the city we can find many others who, although not legally liable, might nonetheless carry a degree of guilt for past murders. In such open, unsettling endings, the *policial* shifts from solely assigning guilt to examining the forces that allow for immoral crime and impunity to continue.

As Argentina struggles to sentence human rights abusers almost four decades after the end of the last dictatorship, cinema remains a crucial tool for elaborating this national trauma. The *policial*'s capacity to mediate concerns and anxieties over culpability, complicity, and justice in a discrete amount of screen time stands in contradistinction to lengthy and ineffective trials that have largely failed to provide adequate punishment for these horrific abuses (if such a thing as adequate punishment exists). Like a constant reminder of this brutal, unresolved past that counters the military's project of erasure, the screen acts as a site that reenacts and reconfigures a wound that remains open. Each of these films examines this wound and takes a step towards closing it.

The nation's grief continues to unfold as it comes to terms with its own history, its past, and the different factions and actions that made the dictatorship possible. The emergence, persistence, success, and trajectory of the crime genre after the country's most recent return to democracy indicates that it continues to be an apt vehicle to explore, investigate and mediate anxieties over the state of justice in Argentina. In the immediate aftermath, it was certain who the perpetrators were and the *policial* depicted them with unabashed violence, but after it became clear that impunity would prevail, cinema (and crime films in particular) demonstrated a preoccupation with how to achieve justice when legal channels had failed. As President Néstor Kirchner acknowledged his shame over the government's many years of silence, a new realization emerged: the majority had stayed silent. Or as Jara puts it as he attempts extortion in *Las grietas de Jara*, 'Little fish, instead of defending their own, always end up defending the bigger fish' one way or another. This silence and its implied complicity have become a new source of inquiry in the process of grappling with Argentina's history.

While scholarship has traditionally centred on documenting the stories and testimonies of activists, in recent years new historiographies have investigated the roles of legitimating actors in the dictatorship's success, including the large (and understudied) middle class sectors. In *Consent of the Damned: Ordinary Argentinians in the Dirty War*, David Sheinin claims that 'as human rights organizations chronicled emerging data on abuses after March 1976, the military began a process of legitimizing its own human rights gray zone ... by appealing directly and indirectly to a public that, if not openly supportive of the dictatorship, tended in its majority to be ambivalent in many regards and in some cases sympathetic to the military's objectives' (2012: 6). In addition, Sebastián Carassai argues that 'the majority of the middle classes ... kept their distance from the type of commitment and mode of participation that characterised the activists. This distance, however, did not necessarily imply a lack of interest in politics. Those who formed this middle-class silent majority may not have been the protagonists of history but they were no mere spectators' (2014: 3–4). Similarly, crime films in this new era seem to say that a mere observer may not necessarily be only a witness. Actress, human rights activist, and mother and grandmother of *desaparecidos*, Nya Quesada, remembers that during the dictatorship 'people were totally frightened. It was horrible. That is why people did not protest, because they were paralysed by fear. If everybody had protested, things might have been different' (quoted in Arditti 1999: 81). Through the conventions of the *policial* of complicity, Argentina confronts a reckoning that insists that its people's silence must be reevaluated.

Cinema allows us an inside look at what could be the latest turn in the country's quest for justice: as Argentina's eyes turn inwards, it is the whole nation that is on trial. Without this realisation, upon which *policiales* shine a spotlight, there is the danger that this history of repression and state violence will not evolve as the country's grief and genre's aesthetic codes have. Instead, the peril is that this history might be repeated again and again. Future films hold the clues to articulating whether the *policial* of complicity will gain further critical mass or serve as another transitional turning point towards further explorations of the nation's shameful historical past. Cinema's voice begs to be heard, exculpating the *policial* from the complicity of silence that has been so prevalent. The genre reminds us, through its shifts since the end of the dictatorship, that justice in Argentina is yet to be served. In a country that has responded to mass murder with impunity, there is the sinking feeling that the nation's fascination with crime films will continue for decades to come.

Notes

1. Unless noted, all translations are the author's.
2. Discussing the work of director Juan José Campanella, who has enjoyed great commercial success in both the US and Argentina in film and television, Jens Andermann argues that his films, 'as transnational ventures, also counteract in their own production model the affective nationalism they preach. They actively solicit the favours of a global audience by their typified representations of the national . . . and by inserting the experience of social crisis into plot structures that maintain an orthodox adherence to rules of genre' (Andermann 2012, 43). Similarly, while discussing a visually spectacular crane shot in *El secreto de sus ojos* (another Campanella film), Matt Losada argues that this shot 'is the closest Argentine cinema has come to fulfilling the Hollywood metaphor that touts a film as a 'rollercoaster ride.' . . . Since a vast portion of film viewings today are of 'rollercoaster' films, does this mean that the cinema conceives of itself as an equivalent of an amusement-park ride? If so, how could it possibly deal with the present legacy of past trauma? Could it do anything *but* exploit it as a titillating spectacle, while suppressing any aspects that might complicate its enjoyment as such?' (Losada 2010). These are just two examples of a debate that places genre cinema and its commercial aesthetic in direct opposition with the *Nuevo cine argentino* and values the latter over the former in terms of its ability to speak to and about national concerns.
3. For a nuanced definition of this term, see Hjort, Mette. 2010. 'On the Plurality of Cinematic Transnationalism.' In *World Cinemas, Transnational Perspectives*, edited by Natasa Ďurovičová and Kathleen Newman, 12–33. New York: Routledge. For more on transnationalism in the cinemas of Latin America, see Dolores Tierney, *New Transnationalisms in Contemporary Latin American Cinemas* (2018) and Tamara Falicov, *Latin American Film Industries* (2019).
4. In the essay 'Crime and Capitalism in Genre Cinema', Joanna Page (2009) explores questions of genre and how international conventions become appropriated in cinemas of the periphery in service of national stories, showing how 'crime remains a powerful tool in articulating the conflict between national and international economic interests and in imagining the relationship between the individual and the capitalist state in a globalised world' (82).
5. During the authoritarian periods that began in the years 1930, 1943, 1955, 1962, 1966 and 1976, those in power ignored, suspended, or temporarily changed the law to conform to their agenda.
6. Although figures regarding the number of *desaparecidos* during the last military dictatorship range according to different sources, this is historically the most commonly accepted number, eliciting consensus among human rights organisations, press outlets, and a large portion of the country's civilians. It is important to note that the practice of forced disappearances began in 1973 but became more widespread after the military dictatorship ousted President Isabel Martínez de Perón and seized power in 1976. The sheer magnitude of disappearances has established these practices of genocidal repression as the trademark of the autocratic regime that illegitimately governed the country from 1976 to 1983.

7. Crime films have a long history of revealing or manifesting society's anxieties (and sometimes, enacting corrective action for social conflicts). In *Crime Films: Investigating the Scene* (in which this category functions as an umbrella term for many genres and subgenres), Kirsten Moana Thompson (2007) argues that in Britain and the United States, 'until 1970 many crime films foregrounded some social problem – such as prison brutality, police corruption or urban crime – but also offered the solace of that problem's resolution ... Crime films also raise issues about the relationship between the public sphere and the actions (and privacy) of the individual, and at different historical moments have shaped attitudes to different social practices' (3–4). In the Argentinean context, Ana Laura Lusnich (2011) argues in her analysis of the crime film *Nueve reinas* that the country's 'sociohistorical context informs and shapes many of the films produced in the late 1990s' (118). Similarly, in an article devoted to the same film, Gabriela Copertari (2005) argues that 'the demand for justice staged in the film's plot synecdochically represents the broader social demand for justice existing in Argentine society as a response to the deception or disillusionment produced by 'the promise of globalization' (280). There is a wealth of literature on this topic, particularly as there are many subsets of the crime film.
8. These measures included the 1986 and 1987 laws of *punto final* (full stop) and *obediencia debida* (due obedience) that President Raúl Alfonsín (1983–1989) instituted, which allowed many lower rank perpetrators to escape punishment. In 1989 and 1990, his successor President Carlos Saúl Menem (1989–1999) enacted his infamous *indultos*, which granted pardons to many commanders who had perpetrated human rights abuses during the dictatorship. Menem also put into practice neoliberal economic policies that can be understood as a continuation of the political agenda of the dictatorship. During this period, the judicial institutions fail to deliver justice and what is legal no longer results synonymous with what is moral. More importantly, these measures of impunity exemplify that the legal system does not seem to offer a pathway towards justice.
9. Although the characters and the hotel are located in Miami, both songs Mónica performs and some of the dialogue in this location are in Spanish, so the use of the final words in English is notable.
10. RUVTE was created as part of the Secretariat for Human Rights and Cultural Pluralism, a programme formalised in 2014.
11. The report acknowledges that the numbers to which it arrives are not definitive, as cases reported to other organisms (such as the Justice Department) and those that remain unreported 'make it impossible to account for this universe in a complete manner' (RUVTE 2015, 1). Nonetheless, RUVTE's numbers appear as an affront to the magnitude of state terrorism that history has recorded.

Works Cited

Aguirre, Osvaldo. 2020. 'Banco Río: el robo que se convirtió en leyenda'. *Clarín*, January 17, 2020. <https://www.clarin.com/revista-enie/ideas/robo-convirtio-leyenda_0_lEK7mYia.html>

Alvaray, Luisela. 2012. 'Are We Global Yet? New Challenges to Defining Latin American Cinema', *Studies in Hispanic Cinemas* 8.1 (January): 69–85. https://doi.org/10.1386/shci.8.1.69_1.

Andermann, Jens. 2012. *New Argentine Cinema*. London and New York: I. B. Tauris.

Arditti, Rita. 1999. *Searching for Life: The Grandmothers of the Plaza De Mayo and the Disappeared Children of Argentina*. Berkeley: University of California Press.

Bernini, Emilio. 2016. 'Políticas del policial en el cine argentino'. In *Crimen y pesquisa, el género policial en la Argentina (1870–2015): literatura, cine, televisión, historieta y testimonio*, edited by Román Setton and Gerardo Pignatiello, 185–191. Buenos Aires: Título.

Burucúa, Constanza. 2009. *Confronting the 'Dirty War' in Argentine Cinema, 1983–1992: Memory and Gender in Historical Representations*. Woodbridge: Tamesis.

Carassai, Sebastián. 2014. *The Silent Majority: Middle Classes, Politics, Violence and Memory in the Seventies*. Durham, NC: Duke University Press.

Copertari, Gabriela. 2005. 'Nine Queens: A Dark Day Of Simulation And Justice'. *Journal of Latin American Cultural Studies* 14.3: 279–293. https://doi.org/10.1080/13569320500382534.

De Vedia, Mariano. 2016. 'Los 7010 desaparecidos, un registro de Cristina'. *La Nación*, November 9, 2016. https://www.lanacion.com.ar/politica/los-7010-desaparecidos-un-registro-de-cristina-nid1954498.

Dirección Nacional de Política Criminal en Materia de Justicia y Legislación Penal. 2018. 'Informe Ejecutivo SNEEP 2018'. <https://www.argentina.gob.ar/sites/default/files/informe_ejecutivo_sneep_2018.pdf> (last accessed 22 June 2020).

Falicov, Tamara. 2019. *Latin American Film Industries*. London and New York: Bloomsbury.

Goity, Elena, and David Oubiña. 1994. 'El policial argentino'. In *Cine argentino en democracia, 1983–1993*, edited by Claudio España and Gabriela Fabbro, 209–229. Buenos Aires: Fondo Nacional de las Artes.

Hjort, Mette. 2010. 'On the Plurality of Cinematic Transnationalism'. In *World Cinemas, Transnational Perspectives*, edited by Natasa Ďurovičová and Kathleen Newman, 12–33. New York: Routledge.

Kirchner, Néstor. 2004. 'Palabras del Presidente de la Nación, Doctor Néstor Kirchner, en el acto de firma del convenio de la creación del Museo de la Memoria y para la promoción y defensa de los derechos humanos'. *Casa Rosada, Presidencia de la Nación*, 24 March 2004. www.casarosada.gob.ar/informacion/archivo/24549-blank-79665064.

La Nación. 2020. 'El robo del siglo llegó a los 2 millones de tickets'. *La Nación*, March 10, 2020. https://www.lanacion.com.ar/espectaculos/el-robo-del-siglo-llego-a-los-2-millones-de-tickets-nid2341544.

Losada, Matt. 2010. 'The Secret in Their Eyes: Historical Memory, Production Models and the Foreign Film Oscar'. *Cineaste* 36.1 (Winter). https://www.cineaste.com/winter2010/the-secret-in-their-eyes-historical-memory-production-models-and-the-foreign-film-oscar-web-exclusive.

Ludmer, Josefina. 1999. *El cuerpo del delito: un manual*. Buenos Aires: Editorial Perfil.

Lusnich, Ana Laura, and Clara Kriger. 1994. 'El cine y la historia'. In *Cine argentino en democracia, 1983–1993*, edited by Claudio España and Gabriela Fabbro, 82–103. Buenos Aires: Fondo Nacional de las Artes.

Lusnich, Ana Laura. 2011. 'Electoral Normality, Social Abnormality: the *Nueve Reinas/Nine Queens* Paradigm and Reformulated Argentine Cinema, 1989–2001'. In *New Trends in Argentine and Brazilian Cinema*. Edited by Cacilda M. Rêgo and Carolina Rocha, 117–129. Bristol: Intellect.

Ministerio Público Fiscal. 2019. 'Estado actual del proceso de juzgamiento de crímenes contra la humanidad'. Procuración General de la Nación República Argentina, 15 March 2019. www.fiscales.gob.ar/wp-content/uploads/2019/03/Lesa-Infografia.pdf.

Page, Joanna. 2009. *Crisis and Capitalism in Contemporary Argentine Cinema*. Durham, NC: Duke University Press.

RUVTE. 2015. 'Palabras preliminaries'. *Informe de Investigación RUVTE-ILID*, November 2015. https://www.argentina.gob.ar/sites/default/files/1._palabras_preliminares-investigacion_ruvte-ilid.pdf.

Sheinin, David. 2012. *Consent of the Damned: Ordinary Argentinians in the Dirty War*. Gainesville: University Press of Florida.

Tassara, Mabel. 1994. 'El policial: la escritura y los estilos'. In *Cine Argentino: La Otra Historia*, edited by Sergio Wolf, 147–167. Buenos Aires: Ediciones Letra Buena.

Télam. 2015. 'Récord histórico de taquilla para 'El Clan' en sus primeros cuatro días'. *Télam*, 7 August 2015. <https://www.telam.com.ar/notas/201508/116680-cine-argentino-record-taquilla-el-clan.html>

Thompson, Kirsten Moana. 2007. *Crime Films: Investigating the Scene*. London and New York: Wallflower.

Tierney, Dolores. 2018. *New Transnationalisms in Contemporary Latin American Cinemas*. Edinburgh: Edinburgh University Press.

SECTION III

TRANSVALUATION

10. FRANCHISING THE FEMALE HERO: TRANSLATING THE NEW WOMAN IN VICTORIN JASSET'S *PROTÉA* (1913), FRANCE'S FIRST FEMALE SPY FILM

Sarah Delahousse

In 1913, unforeseen circumstances forced Éclair and its most notable director, Victorin Jasset, to change course in their crime film repertoire to maintain profitability as a company. The company enjoyed great success in France and the US with Jasset's adaptations of Léon Sazie's popular *Zigomar* crime novels over the past two years until Sazie broke his contract after the third film, *Zigomar, Eel Skin/Zigomar, Peau d'Anguille* (1913), was released. Francis Lacassin claims that Sazie resented that the film bore little resemblance to his novels (1993: 81) while Jacques Deslandes explains that Sazie was infuriated over an elephant burglar scene, which lead to him to break his contract with Éclair, and that Jasset wanted to retain control over his work (1976: 283–284). In either case, Éclair lost the rights to its most bankable series, and the company sought to preserve its position within a competitive global market. Jasset subsequently wrote and directed *Protéa* (1913), which featured a groundbreaking character in French cinema – a female spy – whose qualities were informed by American female adventure heroines that circulated in Europe at the time. In addition to being entirely new to French audiences, the character's combination of feminine charm and dangerous, clandestine actions were, according to Deslandes, appealing to domestic audiences (1976: 284–285). The film's success in France encouraged Éclair to release it in the US where it was well-received and enjoyed prolonged circulation well into 1914 in part because of the vigorous promotion of the film's qualities as a female adventure film while downplaying its French affiliation, which indicates a concerted effort to better appeal to American tastes.

What is also significant is the film's handling of its female character in relation to its symbolic coalescence between the New Woman and the redefinition of France's role in imperial, pre-war politics. The film's popularity stemmed from the protagonist's athleticism and use of disguise that mirrored the actions of those popular American female adventure heroines who are also notable for their representation of women confronting modern society outside the home in which they face peril but use their wits and sometimes technology to overcome the danger they confront in thrilling scenarios that appealed to male and female audiences. It is, thus, the application of the American female adventure heroine's qualities that enabled Protéa to be accepted by French audiences who were more skeptical of a New Woman figure because – like her American counterparts – her actions and role as a pre-Mata Hari female spy were entertaining but safely unrealistic so that she did not overtly challenge contemporary patriarchal hegemonic views on women. Furthermore, Jasset's choice of casting a woman as a brave spy from the fictional country of Messenia who takes on an assignment to steal a treaty from the rival nations, Celtia and Slavonia, that holds significant and possibly threatening implications for her country powerfully assigns her in the role of the marginalised Other who gains agency and is allowed to exist because she embodies positive physical attributes and motivations for breaking traditions that addressed pre-war apprehension over a woman's position in modern society. The film also draws from the growing concerns over the escalating conflict in the Balkans by subtly repositioning France's image as a benevolent imperial influence in Europe[1] and embodying this image in its heroine.

The provenance of the female spy film genre in France, thus, marks a significant moment when an early transnational cultural exchange led to both a challenge to aesthetic traditions and a navigation of cultural expectations regarding gender without fully destabilising them for its domestic audience. It also provided Éclair with a means to assert itself economically and politically abroad. The results of this cultural exchange, I argue, reveal a cautious recognition of the New Woman that laid the groundwork for future French female spy films and allowed Éclair to maintain economic viability abroad by modelling American narrative and marketing practices.

Jasset, Zigomar and Josette Andriot

In tackling this project, Jasset was a logical choice. He enjoyed notable success with his adaptions of the Nick Carter dime novels[2] that circulated in the United States for nearly twenty years prior to their distribution in France by A. Eichler, Printer-Publisher in 1907 where they quickly gained popularity (Deslandes 1976: 263; Lacassin 1993: 61,63). According to Richard Abel, these films differed from previous French melodramas because they drew from low priced American popular literature that focused on the same fictional detective (1998: 195). Abel adds that the French Nick Carter diverges from his American counterpart in which he used his disguises and investigative abilities to alleviate his middle-class clients' anxieties instead of relying on his athleticism and white superiority to solve a case (Ibid.: 197–198). Moreover, Jasset openly admired the American company, Vitagraph, and its films' ability to create an illusion of everyday life with scenes that were made to appear natural in terms of their *mise en scène* and of their actors' calmer, less presentational actions and expressions that were authenticated by their audience (1911: 26–27). Jasset, according to Abel, applied this method to the first *Zigomar* film in which he combined the film's sensational violence with more realistic décor and backdrops that helped make the film a success (1998: 359).[3] Actress Josette Andriot's casting in the *Zigomar* films as Zigomar's nefarious assistant, Rosario, and in *Protéa* further contributes to Jasset's incorporation of verisimilar elements because, according to Lacassin, her past experience as a swimmer, equestrian and gymnast enabled her to perform difficult stunts on camera that other French actresses of the period were incapable of accomplishing (1993: 87).

The Politics of the French New Woman

What is remarkable about *Protéa* is that it exists despite the pervasive and often negative view in France regarding the New Woman in the early twentieth century. According to Debra L. Silverman, particular social movements in the 1880s and 1890s gave rise to both the New Woman and the reactions against her perceived threat to middle class values and stability. A small number of middle-class feminists, which included philanthropists and wives of politicians or educators, sought a 'broadly based solidarity among women of different classes' where wealthy women could teach and assist poor and other vulnerable lower-class women better childcare methods, and they wanted to change the law so that married women could obtain more control over their household finances (Silverman 1989: 65). Andrea Mansker adds that militant feminists called for voting rights and access to birth control as part of their larger demand for greater 'civic participation' (2011: 13–14). Furthermore, middle class women gained wider access to high school and university education as a result of the advocacy of politician Camille Sée, which was, ironically, intended to divert women from the church in favor of preparing them to be wives and mothers who served the Third Republic but not to encourage them to pursue traditionally masculine careers such as law, education, or medicine. However, according to Silverman, many unmarried middle-class women chose to pursue these careers, which 'fueled the symbolic power of the *femme nouvelle*' (1989: 64). Silverman also explains that the declining birth rate in France caused alarm because Germany – which was a significant industrial and military rival – enjoyed a rate that doubled France's, and the prospect of the country losing its military strength further painted the New Woman as a menace against not only in French culture but its political stability.

Furthermore, the expanding capitalist economy that emerged after the Third Republic's establishment in 1877 raised concerns regarding bourgeois stability because it enabled middle class women to become consumers. The female consumer – both working and domestic – was a conflicted force in pre-war France because she was, according to Lisa Tiersten, a part of significant political debates over civic culture and economic growth that 'questioned the ideals of liberal individualism that were enshrined in the market' (2001: 16). She was a new and important force in the modern economy, but conservative politicians were mistrustful of the female shopper because she frequented department stores unaccompanied. These stores were, theoretically speaking, open to all social classes, and they allowed women to freely shop for self-gratification that critics believed made these women 'neither fit nor willing to serve as mothers' (Ibid.: 16–17). Furthermore, Tiersten notes that critics were concerned that the modern marketing techniques department stores employed using printed ads on public streets to attract female shoppers encouraged them to be, in reference to Walter Benjamin's levels of urban spectatorship, gawkers – or *badauds* – instead of observant *flâneurs* who act selfishly and immorally in which they took pleasure in obtaining unlimited goods for themselves and in being admired by strangers for their appearance in these stores, which further disconnected them from guiding moral forces such as priests and husbands.

Another contributing factor to the negative perception of the New Woman in France was that she fit into a larger concern over maintaining masculine honour and a masculine definition of citizenship. Mansker explains that '[m]any believed that French manhood was imperiled during these decades by the perceived psychological and social effects of rapid urbanization, the introduction of universal male suffrage, militant trade unionism in the 1890s, nationalist and anarchist challenges to the Republic, and by the increased visibility of middle-class "new women" who supposedly chose work and independence over marriage and motherhood' (2011: 5–6). Coupled with the aftermath of the Franco-Prussian War and the declining birthrate, there was a concern over France losing its political, economic, and military influence in addition to the moral degeneration of its population – certainly the middle class – that was inevitably linked with the family and the man's ability to maintain it through his and his wife's behaviour. Mansker further explains that the French believed that a man's honour was defined by moral behaviour and virtue in relation to family, work and adherence to the law. His honour was also determined by his wife's fidelity to her marriage vows and to child-rearing. Thus, the wife was expected to exhibit self-control in avoiding sexual temptations or any behaviour that was perceived as inappropriate for a female citizen. In other words, citizenship for a man was based on moral character and upholding civic duties whereas nurturing and maternal qualities defined a woman's citizenship. A woman who did not marry, did not have children or who took on masculine behavior 'threatened conventional family values' that was, by extension, a threat to democracy because she contributed to the political and moral degeneration of her society by not adhering to the male honour code (Ibid.: 30).

The concern over the social decline resulting from socio-economic modernisation extended to working class women as well. This concern was a well-established topic within nineteenth century social criticism that, according to Ann-Louise Shapiro, focused on the belief that 'the conditions of urban life exacerbated women's inherent or inherited weaknesses' (1996: 20–21). Two types of working women defined this concept. If she were born in the city, she worked as a 'seamstress, milliner, hairdresser, clerk florist or laundress', married a man who could provide for her, and she would leave the workforce once she had children (Ibid.: 21). A woman who migrated to the city, leaving her family behind, was often employed as a 'domestic or industrial worker' but fell into prostitution because she could not handle living in poverty and surviving in an urban setting (Ibid.: 21). There was also the concern that working women were more susceptible to corruption because they were no longer supervised by their families and were not restrained from the 'false glamour of clubs, cafés, spectacles and public dances' and from the advances of wealthy men who could fulfill these desires (Ibid.: 21). This belief echoes the patriarchal expectations of middle-class women in which working class women did not contribute to personal as well as social decline if they followed acceptable female behaviour and employment options, certainly if they were inherently familiar with urban life. However, this ideology also implies that women who came from more rural backgrounds exhibited less self-control in terms of recognising appropriate behaviour and her proper position in society because 'the conditions of urban life exacerbated women's inherent or inherited weaknesses' (Ibid.: 20–21). Thus, the working woman represented an additional perceived threat to French society because she was linked with criminality.

American Influences: The American Cowboy Girl and the Female Detective

At first glance, Protéa immediately aligns with the American serial queen heroines that were popular during the 1910s because she flirts with danger, uses disguises and performs shunts that enable her – like these heroines – to vacillate, as Ben Singer explains, 'between contradictory extremes of female prowess and distress, empowerment and imperilment' by confronting the perils of modern society through unconventional gender roles and the threat of victimisation that signaled both the fantasy of female empowerment and the limits of such empowerment in order to appeal to male and female spectators (2001: 222). This interest stemmed from these heroines' balance between '"masculine" qualities, competencies, and privileges' with '"feminine" glamour, charm, and dependence on male chivalry' that celebrated the 'pleasures and perils of a young woman's interaction with a public sphere traditionally restricted to men' that was authentic and entertaining to a broad audience (224–225). Singer also states that these films enjoyed popularity with male and female audiences because of the novelty behind these heroines' stunts and other masculine actions. Jennifer Bean adds that these actresses' stamina along with the perceived realism of and the improvised nature of their stunts questioned commonly accepted social norms and beliefs in mainstream America regarding what a female body could perform in comparison with male strength and ability in order to assign a new and more complex mode of female subjectivity in these films (2002: 407–408).

However, these particular adventure heroines were not introduced in France until 1915 after these films enjoyed prolonged success in the US (Canjels 2008: 216). It was the precursor to the serial queens – the cowboy girl – that embodied the assertive yet safely unrealistic qualities inherent in the American female adventure genre that likely informed Jasset because they displayed a mitigated representation of the modern woman and an idealised depiction of the American West that appealed to American and French audiences.[4] Cowboy girl films reflected the popular interest in the West that was fueled by the circulation of 'juvenile series for girls such as *The Ranch Girls,* which began publication in 1911, and the commanding presence of women in Buffalo Bill's Wild West and especially the Miller Brothers' 101 Ranch Wild West' shows that featured female sharpshooters (Abel 2006: 118). More importantly, American films had been exported to Europe since 1910 with westerns being the most popular because, as Abel surmises, Europeans were long familiar with representations of the American West 'from the exhibitions of George Catlin in the 1840s to the initial tour of Buffalo Bill's Wild West in the late 1880s and early 1890s' (Ibid.: 105). Furthermore, Lacassin notes that Buffalo Bill dime novels were translated and circulated in France starting in 1907 (1993: 63). The popularity of this genre in France and the consistent circulation of films by companies such as Bison and Kalem that produced many westerns undoubtedly exposed French audiences to a heroine who was not culturally familiar to them.

Moreover, the cowboy girl enjoyed popularity abroad because she was 'a vigorously active heroine, a "Western species" of what the Europeans perceived as a distinctly *American* New Woman' (Abel 2006: 119). In these films, this heroine defended herself, navigated her environment, protected a loved one or outwitted a male enemy by relying on her ability to use a firearm, disguised her identity or utilised her physical or intellectual strength. Certainly, these films presented romanticised depictions of the American frontier, but they, along with Civil War films, according to Laura Horak, 'helped forge the symbolic boundaries of the American nation and the virile character of its citizens' where frontier space allowed young women to 'embody the most prized traits of a powerful, masculine, American identity . . . [C]owboy girls display what were understood to be distinctly "frontier" attributes, such as athleticism, horsemanship, and outdoor skills' (2016: 57). Horak also explains that these physical attributes relate to the popular interest in children and adults taking part in outdoor activities locally or out West as an antidote to the 'disastrous effects of urbanization and industrialization' that threatened 'the health of the white American "race"' (59). Cowboy girl heroines, especially those who cross-dressed, could exist because, while they traversed social boundaries, their actions upheld rather than wholly challenged positive American masculine constructs and racial and national ideals. Their transgressions were also temporary because they would return to their feminine appearance or heteronormative roles by the film's conclusion.

Another American female adventure heroine, the female detective figure, also contributed to *Protéa*'s acceptability. As previously discussed, French social critics were concerned over the growing number of female consumers because they shopped unaccompanied and were perceived as being vulnerable to immoral behaviour due to their pleasure in buying goods and to them being openly observed performing this action. A female protagonist taking on detective-like qualities enabled her to resist this criticism while satisfying patriarchal conventions. As Walter Benjamin asserts, the detective is a consequence of the modern urban experience because the detective combines the *flâneur*'s detached observation with the *badaud*'s ability to disappear into a crowd in order to uncover a crime since, in the uncontrolled urban space, anyone could potentially be a suspect and, more importantly, '[n]o matter what trail the *flâneur* may follow, every one of them will lead him to a crime' (1973: 40–41). However, as Anke Gleber contends, this theory applied only to men because the experiences walking on city streets gave them gendered bourgeois authority over what they saw and interpreted along with enjoying the unrestricted freedom to take such initiatives. She also argues that Benjamin failed to acknowledge that women also strolled the urban streets, but their experience on the streets was accessed through a male chaperone or by dressing in men's clothing because they could not circulate alone without fear of scrutiny or attack. Furthermore, women who idly observed the crowd in the same manner as a *flâneur* were viewed as prostitutes, and, in contrast to Tiersten, Gleber explains that they could not stroll through the city as a casual observer or active consumer unless they circulated in a controlled space such as a department store (1999: 174).[5] The early 20th century cinematic female detective figure, thus, offered a justification for female *flânerie* to exist because these characters performed masculine actions to restore social order without disguising the fact that she was observing the crowd. The detective role also provided a female protagonist with a purpose behind her gaze and circulation in the urban space that deflected inevitable suspicion of her venturing out in modern society.

Furthermore, this persona simultaneously adhered to Western European patriarchal expectations to ensure mainstream acceptance. Joan Warthling Roberts explains that '[d]etective fiction had "justified" the masculine activities of the female detective by a handful of different strategies: (1) that she employed her skills only to clear the name of a loved one; (2) by making her the assistant of a male relative; (3) by reuniting her with a male love interest at the end of the adventure; or (4) by suggesting that her crime-fighting career is over with the solution of this . . . case' (as cited in Gates 2011: 24). Moreover, Philippa Gates notes that, like the serial queen heroines, 'the female detective of the 1910s and 1920s embodied female power through her display of heroic action but was also subjected to victimization' (2011: 27). This character was certainly progressive in representing the growing number of women who were working and consuming outside the home while contributing to the reclassification of beliefs surrounding who circulated and used the modern space. Yet, her actions predictably risked her safety while her motivations for investigating had to be limited to exonerating a relative or male love interest, eventually returning to traditional domestic roles with the implication of future matrimony, or to being relegated to doing the legwork for a male detective such as her father. In this way, she did not overtly challenge but, instead, worked within the confines of patriarchal cultural hegemony to appeal to male and female audiences.

Protéa and its Marketing

Protéa's opening montage establishes its female protagonist's broad appeal and acceptability. The first half features brief clips of Protéa (Josette Andriot) disguised as a demure society woman waving a fan, a scantily clad lion tamer bending a whip and a male military officer holding a sword. On one hand, this sequence risks contradicting this character's motivations because it is reminiscent of the familiar opening of Louis Feuillade's *Fantômas* (1913–1914) films, the first of which debuted earlier that year, and a painted image featuring a black masquerade mask and the film's title appearing between each costume change further references that popular antagonist. On the other hand, unlike the smooth lap dissolves that are characteristic of *Fantômas*' opening sequences, the title card interrupts the montage's flow that demystifies the costume changes and reminds the spectator that it is always a female performing these roles. This title card also signals her identity as a clandestine spy, and her adoption of different class and gender roles conveys more entertaining rather than threatening qualities because of the sheer novelty of a female spy in French cinema whereas Fantômas' ability to seamlessly transition between age and class communicates a more realistic threat. Furthermore, the subsequent montage of Protéa's male assistant, the Eel (Lucien Bataille), as a military officer, chauffeur and then a tramp through lap dissolves reduces her threatening qualities in which they rhyme each other's movements, thus justifying her fluid use of male and female personas. However, his wild contortions at the beginning, the dark minimalist background and his jumping offscreen at the end of his segment contrast with her calm demeanour and depiction within a brightly lit and more feminised setting, thus establishing that she has the moral authority and control over the mission rather than him in order to justify their roles as equal cohorts rather than depicting her as a subordinate.

Furthermore, Protéa's experience in navigating dangerous situations provides the balance needed to neutralise her socially inappropriate behaviour as a spy along with displaying French interpretations of the familiar character traits evident in the American female adventure genre. The Messenian chief of police, Baron Nyborg (Charles Krauss), selects her because he believes that she, as a famous adventuress, is the only person who can steal the treaty. Protéa's actions as a spy also invert the American ideals and investigative motivations embodied in the American cowboy girl and the female detective figure in which they are validated through her patriotic duty to protect her country to neutralise the French concern over the New Woman's lack of interest in marriage and procreation. Protéa also differentiates from these American female adventure heroines in that some of her actions in her attempts to obtain the treaty lead to – at times – aggression against less threatening characters in her quest to obtain the treaty. For instance, she, masquerading as an old woman, facilitates a costume change by holding up the Celtian minister's personal assistant at gunpoint, taking him behind a curtain and then emerging having exchanged her costume for his. Holding the gun inches from his head, she compels the assistant to sit in a chair with his face downcast as she walks backward with the gun still pointing in his direction until she decides to run back to the Eel who is in the minister's office. In a later scene, they follow the Albanian ambassador and his wife into an empty room as they leave the minister's ball early where they blindfold the defenseless couple from behind, steal their attire and leave them bound and gagged on the floor. The character, thus, takes on a harsher persona that French audiences would accept but avoids criticism due to her sense of duty in protecting her country's interests. In addition to Protéa's disguises and assertiveness, the film's climax powerfully mirrors the strength and peril emblematic of American female adventure films while highlighting divergent cultural reactions to Andriot's performance. While being pursued by Celtian agents, she must cross a bridge on a motorcycle to reach Messenia and hand over the treaty to Baron Nyborg to complete her mission. The agents manage to reach the bridge first, light it on fire and wait for her arrival. Instead of stopping or faltering in panic, she speeds forward and successfully jumps over the bridge to safety (Fig. 10.1). This stunt was

Figure 10.1 Protéa's Climactic Scene in a World Special Films Corporation advertisement, *Moving Picture World*, 22 November 1913, 905.

an element of a female adventure film that American audiences would anticipate and take pleasure in observing the actress' accomplishment. However, according to Lacassin, this scene was even more surprising and thrilling to French audiences because the mere sight of a woman performing such an act was 'at that time an unimaginable act for a woman' to accomplish (1993: 85). Protéa, thus, proved authentic to mass audiences in both countries as a result of her actions' perceived realism and the fact that they did not fully supplant patriarchal norms due to their implausibility outside of fictional scenarios.

Another feature that diminishes Protéa's threat to cultural gender codes and the film from enduring the typical xenophobic criticism that befell French productions of the period in the US is the overt signaling of the main characters' disguises and costumes changes. In addition to not fully upending gender conventions, *Protéa*'s blatant signaling of when the primary characters are in costume or are making a costume change avoids this association with social disorder and, thus, from being marked as foreign and in bad taste. For example, in an early scene, the establishing intertitle explains that the ambassador of Slavonia receives a note warning that Protéa will be travelling to Celtia on the Orient Express and that he sends his secretary, the Count of Varallo, to delay her arrival and to alert the authorities. The following scene depicts a medium shot of Protéa dressed in middle class attire wearing a hat and glasses, pretending to read a newspaper with her face in full view of the camera. The Eel, wearing a suit in the centre frame, turns to her to inform her that Varallo is heading for their seating compartment. However, the Count fails to recognise them and sits down upon entering. The characters' on-screen costume changes also demystify the characters' presence. While masquerading as the Celtian minister's personal assistant,

Protéa – with a forged note by the Eel in hand – attempts to obtain the treaty from the minister's secretary in his office. However, her ruse is uncovered, and she manages to escape apprehension by breaking the minister's guards' grasp on her arms, running out the door and then jumping into an armoire that is strategically placed by Messenian spies led by the Eel who are dressed as workpeople. Two spies block the armoire's door long enough for Protéa to emerge as a working-class servant carrying a basket. She feigns confusion as the minister and his men burst into the hallway and then run past her as they run out the front door. Instead of raising anxiety over the characters' actions, their disguises serve as an entertaining device that elevates the film's suspense and shifts their positions between being in control and facing the threat of victimisation that legitimises their attempts to steal the treaty. Furthermore, these overt costume changes become a source of novelty in which the audience anticipates them and waits to discover what the characters' new appearances will be.

Protéa's most significant disguise, a black bodysuit, further demonstrates her appeal with French and American audiences. After infiltrating the Celtian Foreign Minister's office posing as a couple waiting for an appointment, she and the Eel sneak into two nearby closets where they change into the suits and later search his office after dark. Unlike the form-fitting silk bodysuit that Musidora later donned in Feuillade's *Les Vampires* (1915) as Irma Vep, Andriot's was made of cotton, which was a material that, according to Vicki Callahan, 'emphasizes the athletic dimension of [her] activities' (2005: 87). Thus, the interest is placed on her athleticism rather than any erotic aspects of her body, making the character less sensationalised and threatening as a result. She also imitates the Eel's slinking gestures as they crawl out from underneath two desks in the room and search for the treaty, and his presence, thus, counteracts her inappropriate actions by diminishing the gender dismantling connotations her movements would convey if she were acting alone. The film also resists from completely disrupting heteronormative codes governing female behaviour and identification in which Protéa's face remains fully visible throughout the office scene unlike Irma Vep who commenced that famous cat burglary scene wearing her bodysuit with her face fully concealed until the criminal, Moreno, unmasks her. The film, thus, reminds the audience of her femininity and disassociates Protéa with willful criminal behaviour that would otherwise render her socially disruptive and unacceptable.

This theme carries over into the film's American marketing as well because surviving promotional materials strongly indicate a concerted effort to publicise the film within the American female adventure genre. For instance, an advertisement in the 8 November 1913 edition of *The Moving Picture World* (Fig. 10.2) identified Protéa as a 'woman spy' but follows this detail with the adjectives 'unique', 'daring' and 'spectacular' in order to associate Protéa's occupation with thrills (Protéa Advertisement 1913c: 641). Furthermore, an 11 October review

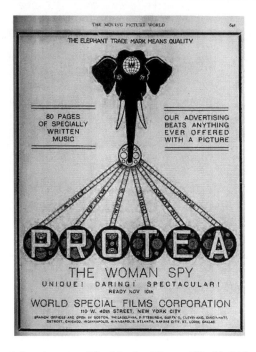

Figure 10.2 Protéa Advertisement, *The Moving Picture World*, 8 November 1913, 641.

in *The Moving Picture World* identified Protéa as an 'adventuress', explained Protéa's motivations for becoming a spy and described the costume changes as treating the audience to 'a succession of changes of costume, rapid and startling, until one begins to wonder what can possibly be next' ('Protea' 1913c: 137). The focus on the thrilling aspects of the character's disguises with an explanation behind them detracts from the review's subtitle indication that the film would be released by Éclair. It also detailed the notable stunts that Protéa and the Eel performed with some of their disguises, even claiming that Josette Andriot spent six months in the hospital after performing the climactic scene where she jumps her motorcycle over the burning bridge ('Protea' 1913c: 137). By framing these costume changes within the context of the characters' – particularly Andriot's – daring athleticism, the review portrays Protéa within an acceptable context that aligns her with American adventure heroines and that solidifies her as a stabilising figure who protects her vulnerable country's interests rather than using her disguises for social disruption. Similar language and emphasis on the film's costumes and stunts later appeared in publicity materials in the 8 January 1914 edition of *The Wichita Daily Times* (Wichita Falls, Texas) and in the 14 July 1914 *Chillicothe Constitution* (Chillicothe, Missouri), which demonstrates that this was a successful strategy to undertake.

Furthermore, *Protéa* benefited from being distributed by an American company, the World Special Films Corporation, and from being accepted by critics prior to its release. It initially had no American distributor as evidenced by a 4 October, 1913 advertisement in *The Motion Picture News* noting Éclair's US office address. However, according to *The New York Clipper*, World Special Films Corporation bought the distribution rights soon after ('Film Fancies' 1913: 10), which demonstrates both rapid interest in the film's potential and Éclair following the period practice of hiring an American company to distribute international productions on a wider scale. This potential is also informed by reviews of the film before its 11 November release. *The Motion Picture News* noted that '. . . the acting is the cleverest, all the staging details are carefully watched and the photography, the regular high-class work that made famous the name of "Eclair" [sic]' ('Protea' 1913a: 21). *The Moving Picture World*'s review of the film defended its action sequences and frequent costume changes in the last paragraph by stating that the film 'depends entirely upon photographic tricks, but they are so well done that one's admiration is at once aroused and interest is kept at so high a tension that the succession of incidents do not become tiresome. To this must be added consideration for the good photography and splendid settings' ('Protea' 1913c: 137). *The New York Dramatic Mirror* was somewhat more blatant when it expressed *Protéa*'s success in avoiding the problems with a 'lack of action and the pitfall of lurid sensationalism' that plague multi-reel films because it 'teems with action, yet the excitement is of a healthy sort that does not repel' ('Protea' 1913b: 32). A weapon that American trade presses used against French films dating back to 1908, according to Abel, was to denounce them as being overly realistic and, thus, morally suspect, which fed into the public's growing xenophobia stemming from the largest influx of immigrants in 1907 (1999: 119, 121). Pathé, for instance, sought to combat this criticism by producing *films d'art* and marketing them as higher quality than American ones with little success. However, for American films, Abel explains that realism was acceptable if the narrative and mise en scène were 'fused' with photographic quality 'into an aesthetic privileging "authenticity" in representing not just life but *American life*' (1999: 137). Praising a film, especially an American one, for its artistic qualities such as its photography and realism marked it as respectable for American audiences to patronise. Thus, this attention to *Protéa* along with its action sequences being commended for their quality and for not being offensive presented the veiled suggestion that it was deemed appropriate to be shown to a mass American audience because it aligned with the American female action genre and more effectively catered to American tastes.

As a result, the film was popular with American audiences. *The Motion Picture News* ran an advertisement that featured a letter that was reputedly written by the exhibitor at the Jewel Theatre, Mrs E. L. Tyler, claiming that it was the 'best show that ever played in Flint [Michigan]' (Protéa Advertisement 1913b: 41). A list of multi-state branch offices appeared below, indicating the film's large distribution. A 1914 advertisement announced that *Protéa* would be playing for one day only at the Majestic Theater in Wichita Falls, Texas on Friday, 9 January (Protéa Advertisement 1914a, 3), which indicates that it was that week's special feature that was intended to attract a large audience. The film was in such demand that, according to the *Motion Picture News*, authorities confiscated duped prints in Philadelphia and New Orleans ('"Pirated Film" Seized' and Untitled Article 1914: 24, 29). *Protéa* notably appeared as a double feature with the first episode of Edison's popular female adventure series, *Dolly of the Dailies* (1914), starring Mary Fuller in Emmetsburg, Iowa (Protéa Advertisement 1914b: 8). A brief article that appeared on the front page of *The Chillicothe Constitution* in Missouri announced that tickets were sold in advance for a one night, Friday showing on 17 July ('The Story of Protea' 1914: 1), which demonstrates the film's continued demand. Furthermore, the film's popularity encouraged Éclair to release the first non-Jasset directed sequel, *Protéa II* (1914). It was included in a World Film Corporation[6] advertisement that appeared in the 11 July, 1914 *The Moving Picture World* well ahead of its 14 September release. There is also evidence that the sequel experienced reasonable circulation. For instance, *The Victoria Daily Advocate* in Texas featured an advertisement for a Thursday, 1 October 1914 showing that included a picture of Protéa standing on a balcony wearing a black bodysuit looking at a would-be male attacker lying prostrate on the ground with his arms raised in her direction (Protéa II Advertisement 1914: 5), which signals that the newspaper was promoting the familiarity of the character's most memorable costume from the previous film. *Protéa II* later played on 20 October at The Ark Theatre in Logansport, Indiana ('At Our Ark Today' 1914: 10) and on 22 October and Friday, 23 October at The Lyric in Piqua, Ohio ('Protea II' 1914: 8). However, surviving newspaper materials and notices in the trade press grow scant by early 1915, thus signaling waning American interest in the character.

Protéa's Legacy

Regardless of how long it circulated in the US, *Protéa* serves as an important early product of transnational influence and circulation that relied on an acceptable image of the New Woman for profitability. It also enabled Éclair to retain a stake in both markets by anticipating what an audience would view as authentic in an aesthetic and commercial sense. More importantly, the film's success rests largely on its title character's translation of the athletic and thrilling qualities inherent in the American female adventure heroine. What is perhaps the film's most enduring legacy is its impact on French cinema. While interest in the character waned in the US, Éclair released four sequels in France until 1919 when Andriot left Éclair and the company folded (Lacassin 1993: 87). This franchise, furthermore, established the female spy genre in France and enabled later films such as Luc Besson's *La Femme Nikita/Nikita* (1990) to exist and even, in the latter film's case, make a similar impact abroad. The source of this enduring and adaptable representation of the modern woman, thus, traces back to Protéa's balance of charm and cunning in the name of duty that challenges gender expectations without completely overstepping them.

Notes

1. Immigration from the now-former colonies did not occur in significant numbers until after World War II and was not of great concern at the time.
2. *The Doctor's Rescue/Nick Carter: Le Guet-Apens* (1908) and *Nick Carter: The Suicides Club/Nick Carter: Le Club des suicides* (1909).
3. Abel surmises that *Zigomar* was popular in the US because the newness of the special feature and the American audience's unfamiliarity with the novels contributed to its success. However, I argue that his reference to W. Stephen Bush's 28 October, 1911 article in *The Moving Picture World* praising *Zigomar* and other multi-reel melodramas' quality suggests that the film's realism also contributed to its success. See *Americanizing the Movies and 'Movie-Mad' Audiences*, 191–192.
4. Abel explains that Civil War films were produced by a select number of companies in the early 1910s and that those films were exclusively marketed in the United States. They were not, consequently, circulated in France for Jasset to have been aware of the Civil War girl spy. See *Americanizing the Movies and 'Movie-Mad' Audiences*, 143.
5. Gleber focuses on Weimar Germany in her study on early 20th century European *flânerie*.
6. The World Special Films Corporation reformed as the World Film Corporation earlier that year. See 'World Film Anniversary.' *Moving Picture World*, 20 February 1915, 1153.

Works Cited

Abel, Richard. 2006. *Americanizing the Movies and 'Movie-Mad' Audiences: 1910–1914*. Berkeley: University of California Press.
Abel, Richard. 1998. *The Ciné Goes to Town: French Cinema 1896–1914*. 1998. Berkeley: University of California Press, 1998.
Abel, Richard. 1999. *The Red Rooster Scare: Making Cinema American, 1900–1910*. 1999. Berkeley: University of California Press.
'At Our Ark Today.' *The Journal-Tribune* (Logansport, Indiana), 20 October 1914, 10.
Bean, Jennifer. 2002. 'Technologies of Early Stardom and the Extraordinary Body.' In *A Feminist Reader in Early Cinema*. Edited by Jennifer M. Bean and Diane Negra, 404–443. Durham, NC: Duke University Press.
Benjamin, Walter. 1973. 'The Paris of the Second Empire in Baudelaire.' *Charles Baudelaire: A Lyric Poet in the Era of High Capitalism*, 9–102. Translated by Harry Zohn. London: NLB.

Callahan, Vicki. 2005. *Zones of Anxiety: Movement, Musidora and the Crime Serials of Louis Feuillade*. Detroit: Wayne State University Press.
Canjels, Rudmer. 2008. 'Localizing Serials: Translating Daily Life in *Les Mystères de New-York*.' In *Early Cinema and the 'National*.' Edited by Richard Abel, Giorgio Bertellini and Rob King, 215–225. New Barnet: John Libbey.
Deslandes, Jacques. 1976. 'Victorin-Hippolyte Jasset.' In *Anthologies du Cinéma*, Tome 9, 243–97. Paris: Avant-Scène du Cinéma.
'Film Fancies.' *The New York Clipper* (New York, NY), 25 October 1913, 10.
Gates, Philippa. 2011. *Detecting Women: Gender and the Hollywood Detective Film*. Albany: State University of New York Press.
Gleber, Anke. 1999. *The Art of Taking a Walk: Flanerie, Literature, and Film in Weimar Culture*. Princeton: Princeton University Press.
Horak, Laura. 2016. *Girls will be Boys: Cross-Dressed Women, Lesbians, and American Cinema*. New Brunswick, NJ: Rutgers University Press.
Jasset, Victorin. 'Étude sur le mise-en-scène en cinématographie.' *Cinéma-Journal*, 25–27, 25 November 1911.
Lacassin, Francis. 1993. 'The Éclair Company and European Popular Literature from 1908 to 1919.' *Griffithiana* (May) 47: 61–87.
Mansker, Andrea. 2011. *Sex, Honor and Citizenship in Third Republic France*. London: Palgrave Macmillan.
'"Pirated Film" Seized.' *The Motion Picture News*, 28 February 1914, 24.
'Protea.' *The Motion Picture News*, 4 October 1913a, 21.
'Protea.' *The New York Dramatic Mirror* (New York, NY), 15 October 1913b, 32.
'Protea.' *The Moving Picture World*, 11 October 1913c, 137.
'Protea II.' *The Piqua Daily Call* (Piqua, OH), 21 October 1914, 6.
Protéa Advertisement. *The Motion Picture News*, 4 October 1913a, 4.
Protéa Advertisement. *The Motion Picture News*, 6 December 1913b, 41.
Protéa Advertisement. *The Moving Picture World*, 8 November 1913c, 641.
Protéa Advertisement. *The Wichita Daily Times* (Wichita Falls, TX), 8 January 1914a, 3.
Protéa Advertisement. *The Emmetsburg Democrat* (Emmetsburg, Iowa), 29 April 1914b, 8.
Protéa II Advertisement. *The Victoria Daily Advocate* (Victoria, TX), 29 September 1914, 5.
Shapiro, Ann-Louise. 1996. *Breaking the Codes: Female Criminality in Fin-de-Siècle Paris*. Berkeley: University of California Press.
Silverman, Debra. 1989. *Art Nouveau in Fin-de-Siècle*. Berkeley: University of California Press.
Singer, Ben. 2001. *Melodrama and Modernity: Early Sensational Cinema and Its Contexts*. New York: Columbia University Press.
'The Story of Protea.' *The Chillicothe Constitution* (Chillicothe, MO), 14 July 1914, 1.
Tiersten, Lisa. 2001. *Marianne in the Market: Envisioning Consumer Society in Fin-de-Siècle Paris*. Berkeley: University of California Press.
Untitled Pirated Protea Article. *The Motion Picture News*, 28 February 1914, 29.
World Film Corporation Advertisement. *The Moving Picture World*, 11 July 1914, 166–167.

11. *SHIRKERS* (2018) LOST AND FOUND? TRACING TRANSSENSORIAL TRAUMA IN A TRUE-CRIME ROAD MOVIE

Jiaying Sim

Sandi Tan's *Shirkers* (2018) opens with the soft pulsating tones of vibraphones as the scribbled credit titles 'A Netflix Original Documentary' appear in white penmanship over a black screen. The gentle reverb of the ethereal soundtrack, 'Waking Up', is interrupted abruptly by the click of a film roll as scattered light streaks flash across the screen. An establishing shot of a swan gliding across a lake in a park is rolled in reverse as the scene appears as negative-image, while the lilting soundtrack transitions into a shrill mix of static white noise, scratches and sonorous vocals. The audience next observes the same image of a swan gliding in reverse across a lake before the scene cuts to a closeup of a brown leather suitcase on lush green grass. Here, the camera pans slowly and clumsily to a hand gently clutching the handle of the suitcase. The camera traces up the hand towards the face of a young bespectacled Sandi Tan lying on the grass with her eyes closed (See Fig. 11.1). Sounds of crackling static noise pepper the scene before the off-screen voice of Sandi finds their way to the audience:

> When I was 18, a long time ago now, I had the idea that you found freedom by building worlds inside your head. That you had to go backwards in order to go forwards. That little kids had the answers to everything.

A montage sequence follows: a wide shot of S (young Sandi Tan) sitting on the edge of a bed, moving game pieces on a whimsically-designed board game that is propped on the same leather suitcase in the earlier scene; close-ups of

199

Figure 11.1 Sandi Tan lying on the grass in *Shirkers* (2018).

Figure 11.2 Close-up of boardgame in *Shirkers* (2018).

the board game that features tiny figurines standing in the middle of a bullseye target amidst other quirky hand-drawn artworks of a piano, a scooter, a dog, just to name a few (See Fig. 11.2); a reverse-footage of vehicles driving through a tunnel; a static shot of S and a small boy standing by a shop front with mannequins on display before walking away. The opening sequence returns to a medium close-up of young Sandi Tan lying on the patch of grass with earplugs in her ears and a vintage camera slung across her neck. The monologue continues, 'When I was 18, I had so many ideas I hardly slept at all'.

Beginning of the Road: Shirkers as Global Cultural Product

Sketched together with a series of dissonant images and a haunting soundtrack, the opening moments of *Shirkers* hint at one of the core tropes of the road movie genre: a travel narrative surrounding a main protagonist who rebels against social conventions by (day) dreaming of ways to escape their everyday existence. *Shirkers* is a documentary that attempts to paint a full picture about the unique events leading up to a feature-length road movie of the same name 'Shirkers' (from here on known as 'Shirkers 1992'). In 1992 Singapore, a group of three 18-year-old Singaporean girls – Jasmine Ng, Sophie Siddique, and Sandi Tan herself – banded together to write, fund, and produce a film about a teenage killer named S who goes around Singapore saving children's souls. Jasmine Ng was the editor, Sophie Siddique was the producer, and Sandi Tan was the screenwriter and lead actress. The director of 'Shirkers 1992' was a man named Georges Cardona, the young filmmakers' film teacher at a film class they attended at the Substation.[1] 'Shirkers 1992', like most road movies, features a hodgepodge of quirky characters from different social groups and classes that range from a giant dog named Cherish to others such as Cecilia the nurse, her daughter Monster who has epileptic episodes but loves to dance and a commuter on the bus named Montano Bob, as well as a 'visibility inspector'. All of whom contribute toward alternative narratives of counterculture about how these characters wander around a city with different or no agendas. The road movie usually invokes audience intrigue through the sudden inclusion of unexpected plot twists that come in the form of a crime committed on the journey or simply through the developing criminal relationships between main characters in the film. Similarly, *Shirkers*'s premise is pegged largely to Cardona disappearing with 70 cans of 16mm film reels of 'Shirkers 1992' shortly after filming wrapped. For two decades, the cast and crew who were part of the production process of 'Shirkers 1992' found themselves with no film to show for at the end of the shooting process. That is until Cardona's sudden death in 2011, which led to his widow returning all 70 cans of unprocessed films in near-pristine condition to Sandi Tan. Audio recordings from the 1992 shoot were lost over the years. It is from within this phantom space between 'Shirkers 1992' and *Shirkers* that this chapter begins, where the theft of the original film reels becomes crucial to the way we make sense of the film's meaning.

The metafictional and transmedia contexts surrounding the premise of *Shirkers*, hence, produce a film about a film, a film within a film, but also a film that deliberately escapes itself through its collaborative and disjunctive 'sense-making' screen experience that is akin to the processes of a crime scene investigation and criminal profiling. Rather than orientate or situate the audience in a fixed place and time, the opening moments of the film set Singapore up as an ambivalent space of both collaboration and contestation. Even though *Shirkers* first presents itself as a platform for the debut of 'Shirkers 1992' and the exposé behind the reels that were missing for over 20 years, audience satisfaction of knowing the true story – or the complete story – is consistently interrupted. Already fragmented found footages of 'Shirkers 1992' are interspersed and intercut with behind-the-scene footages; interviews with the original cast and crew; other paratexts such as audition flyers; official letters written by Sophia Siddique to Kodak; glimpses of the original screenplay and production schedules; intertextual references to novels like *Catcher in the* "Rye"; film magazines like *Film Comment*; and allusions to the French New Wave such as Jean-Luc Godard's *Breathless* (1960), American independent films such as Steven Soderbergh's *Sex, Lies and Videotape* (1989), and Swedish films such as Ingmar Bergman's *The Seventh Seal* (1957). The global network of films and cultural products alluded to could be traced as the genealogy of films that influenced Sandi Tan while growing up that found themselves into the cultural narrative surrounding 'Shirkers 1992'. Certainly, the film evokes a position as a global cultural product with its intertextual references and influences. However, it will be too reductive to classify *Shirkers 1992* as a by-product of Euro-American cinematic influence.

In spite of its global references, the film was shot and made in Singapore with a cast and crew made up of local talents and personnel. At the time of filming in June 1992, Tan was studying at the University of Kent, England, Ng was in New York, Siddique was in Los Angeles, and Cardona was in Singapore. The mobility of these young adults suggested that they embodied the flow of talent and cultural exchanges through their physical movement to and from Singapore. This inherent mobility that the film encompasses gestures towards Neil Archer's argument in *The Road Movie: In Search of Meaning* that the road movie 'as a global genre, cannot be so easily tied down to a particular place or national context', where 'the global imaginary of the road movie as part of their form and function' (Archer 2016: 9). The road, thus, takes centre stage where the audience soon learns that *Shirkers* is not limited by either literal or figurative national borders, but 'the crossing of these borders, and the national and cultural contexts they contain, becomes the very point of the road movie in the era of globalisation' (Archer 2016: 9). Furthermore, Arjun Appadurai helps us to make sense of the film's contesting sites of power dynamics that move beyond representational modes of signification. Appadurai explains in *Disjuncture and Difference in the Global Cultural Economy* that '[t]he new global cultural economy has to be seen as a complex, overlapping, disjunctive order, which cannot any longer be understood in terms of existing center-periphery models (even those which might account for multiple-centers and peripheries)' (Appadurai 1990: 260). Cultural products involve various social practices and economic processes that can no longer be considered a phenomenon exclusive to certain localities but the movement of persons, ideas, and money. Instead, these global processes are multifaceted and may be disconnected. The significance lies in thinking about global cultural products as fragmented processes, rather than as unified, finished products that may stem from any point(s) of origin.

In the same vein, *Shirkers* can be read less as completed 'things' that are embedded with sets of inherent qualities or defining characteristics, and more as 'complex, overlapping, fractal shapes [that] constitute not a simple, stable (even if large scale) system' (Appadurai 1996: 46). Global cultural products are fluid processes that require tracing and tracking, however chaotic and unsystematic these flows may be. Appadurai argues that different movements that include people, science and technology, money and investments, media images, and ideas produce imagined landscapes of global flows between geographical and national spaces. Similarly, this paper makes a case that cinema as a medium enables us to turn to the material, physical and spatial movements of persons, resources and ideas to evoke immaterial affective-scapes and sensoria-scapes of film meanings. *Shirkers* offers a roadmap that the audience may move through to (re)trace these filmic sensoria that are created through deeply transnational and complex film experiences and cinematic processes. Instead of straightforward answers and a clearer understanding of the possible reasons why George Cardona might have stolen the cans of film reels and preserved them over the span of two decades till his death, the film raises more questions: What becomes of the filmmaking process when there is no product to show for at the end of all the affective and physical labour? How does one account for or file a claim against the theft of intellectual property? To whom does a film belong to? Who has the authority to possess the film? This chapter 'thus' addresses the conflicting 'microanalytics of power' of narratives that is located within documentary filmmaking (Jenkins and Carpentier 2013: 267). It contends that *Shirkers* is a true-crime documentary that masks itself as a road-movie, vice versa, to invoke audience participation in piecing together of a coherent narrative behind the stolen films. Through the film's narrative, which foregrounds every stage of filmmaking from pre-production, production to post-production and distribution, collaborative and transsensorial 'sense-making' is emphasised. In *Media and Crime*, Yvonne Jewkes further suggests that the crime film is equally capable of encompassing other genres such as 'the Western, the gangster films' because of its focus on 'good' versus 'bad', 'outlaws' versus heroes, all of which can be found in the storytelling methods in *Shirkers* (Jewkes 2004: 17). By interweaving generic conventions of the road-movie as a performative tool, the film curates a landscape of transnational sensoria that transgresses time, place, cinematic form and medium. The audience, in their participation, is directed away from any initial fixation with the explanation or justification of the crime surrounding the theft of 'Shirkers 1992'. In fact, *Shirkers* posits that the only way to 'make-sense' of traumatic events is not to understand the perpetrator, or their intentions or motivations, but to recognise and acknowledge the patterns that point toward psychopathic abusive dynamics. Particularly, *Shirkers* experiments with the transnational and transmedia forms of audiovisual expressions to reveal the aftermath of survivors who have been targets of criminal psychopathy as filtered through the twists and turns of a road movie. At the end of the film, the shifting subjectivities of the narrative take the audience through a transsensorial experience that blurs the dichotomy of perpetrator/victim, stolen and theft. Rather than to obsess over 'whodunnits', the cinematic experience gestures toward the meandering narratives of film meaning that may be gleaned through the circulation, exhibition and distribution of the film.

On the Road with a True-crime Documentary

As a 'Netflix original documentary', *Shirkers* sits comfortably amidst Netflix's steady increase in global film and television productions since 2013. Tanya Horeck explains in *Justice on Demand: True Crime in the Digital Streaming Era* that Netflix true-crime originals are one of the most commercialised and marketable genres; its increased popularity is related to the high quality productions that make use of fiction-like stylistic techniques (dramatic soundtracks, plot twists, unpredictable revelations) to build audience engagement and reimagine the docudrama crime film (Horeck 2019: 17). The ease of access to the crime film genre through Subscription Video on Demand (SVOD) platforms also aligns with the rise of audience's ability to engage with the film through convergent media techniques even after the film ends its run time. Furthermore, Horeck argues that the true-crime documentary form, especially with subject matter surrounding gruesome murders or other violent acts, brings to the fore a 'graphic revelation of the affective stakes involved in cinematic retrospection and the mediated reenactment of the past through home video footage' (Ibid.: 17). Even as a documentary, *Shirkers* exhibits tropes of the road movie genre such as the desire to escape and an inability to settle by staying on the road. While *Shirkers* does not feature any gruesome murders or physical scenes of violence often associated with true crime documentaries, the film is haunted by an affective undertone that may be described as a whimsical suspense and air of uncertainty. In *Affect Poetics of the New Hollywood: Suspense, Paranoia, and Melancholy*, Hauke Lehmann contends:

> Suspense is not based on spectator engagement, but is rather the very thing which generates this engagement in the first place; it itself represents

a particular way of affectively involving the spectator in the film's events as a specific mode of cinematic expressivity. (2019: 48–49)

This degree of suspense is not subjective or a measure of how engaged the audience is. Instead, suspense is tied to the specificity of the cinematic medium that enables audience engagement in the first place. As seen in the opening sequence of *Shirkers,* different post-production techniques of filmmaking such as film editing, colour grading of the image, adjustments of playback speeds, and sound design showcase the potential of the cinematic form to create suspense. Sensorially, the film affects the audience before they are able to make sense of the premise, genre or intention of the film. In fact, this formalistic quality is evocative of David Laderman's assertion in *Driving Visions Exploring the Road Movie* that road movies as a cinematic genre critique conservative ideas of social norms and problematise hegemonic definitions of home and conventional cinematic techniques in the following ways:

> cinematically, innovative traveling camera work, montage, and soundtrack; narratively, in terms of an open-ended, rambling plot structure; thematically, in terms of frustrated, often desperate characters lighting out for something better, someplace else. (2010: 2)

One of the most evident ways in which *Shirkers* creates suspense is through its destabilising opening scenes and the haphazard ways in which the film narrative develops. Presented almost as case files of an unsolved crime, the audience quickly takes on an active investigative role where they continually backtrack and reconstruct the events surrounding the stolen film, even – or especially – as Sandi Tan steers the open-ended, rambling plot structure in a voice-over that dictates the trajectory and pace of *Shirkers* at every turn of events, producing detours throughout the film. However, Tan's tone of voice is not one that is lackadaisical, but it is both measured while detached in declarations such as, 'In the Summer of 1992, my friends and I shot a road movie on the streets of Singapore that was to become a kind of urban legend'. The use of the word 'summer' to connote time in relation to Singapore's warm and tropical all-year weather is jarring and unusual insofar as it displaces the audience and the film from being fully located within the geographical location and setting of Singapore as well as the country's understanding of and reference to time of the year. Tan's subjectivity conjures a sense of otherness, alienation, and a deliberate gazing-in at Singapore from a detached distance since nobody from Singapore would ever denote the time of year with seasons.

Narratively, we are told that the stolen film was shot in 1992 but over the years only existed as a widely circulated rumour and urban myth. Cinematically, the audience is presented with contradictory series of found footage from 'Shirkers 1992' that have been processed and re-produced in a myriad of stylistic reimagings. This urban legend of a film that was 'shot' but never quite produced, thus, acts as the starting and focal point for *Shirkers,* the driving force of suspense which invites the audience to regard the processes of filmmaking rather than the product of filmmaking. *Shirkers*, as a self-reflexive and self-referential documentary film, invites the audience into the film knowing for a fact that they will be in for a ride.

Travelling Circus: Tracing Evidence within/across Border

The question remains to be addressed: for what purpose does the road serve? The following section addresses the different ways in which the 'road' may be understood to make sense of the criminal suspect Georges Cardona, his motivations, as well as the various relations of power. In *The Global Road Movie* (2019), Timothy Corrigan and José Duarte attribute the popularity and continued interest in the road movie genre as a cinematic concept that exercises a 'powerful grasp upon the narrative imagination' (2019: 22). Particularly, 'their incisive and flexible explorations of the human identities of rebels without causes, wanderers away from home, lost souls seeking new lives and road warriors escaping oppressions' (Corrigan and Duarte 2019: 7). Similarly, the specific type of journey *Shirkers* unpacks for its audience refers not only to the physical traversing across and between countries, but also to the movement through past, present and future times, as well as the blurring of boundaries across mediums of gameplay, film, photography and imagination.

For Corrigan and Duartre, the road movie challenges oppressive sociocultural structures within and without which the protagonist navigates and forges new individual pathways. This motif is swiftly recognisable in the plot of 'Shirkers 1992', where teenager S journeys through Singapore searching for cultural currency amidst a claustrophobic sociopolitical landscape that stifles the individual's creativity. *Shirkers* addresses the relationship between the state and the arts in Singapore in the late 1980s where the movement of film products across borders was not as widespread as today because of the embargo placed on imported film and television content. For example, to watch David Lynch's *Blue Velvet,* Sandi Tan engaged the help of her cousin Vicki who was living in Florida, USA. Between them, a 'clandestine video-taping syndicate' distribution circuit transpired. These personal paths of exchanges made possible by individuals who are based in different parts of the world became a powerful way to escape censorship of international films.

However, here I focus more on the symbolism of the road in *Shirkers* through cinematic and non-cinematic spaces that help to reconstruct audience understanding of the events surrounding the stolen reels. It is revealed to the audience that prior to the actual filming of 'Shirkers 1992', a transnational exchange of ideas took place amongst the key persons behind the film. Tan, upon realising that she 'had left her tribe in Singapore' to study in Kent, UK, began writing letters to Jasmine who was in Los Angeles at the time. Faxes were also sent to Georges, to which he did not write back. Instead, he sent occasional voice recordings that the audience gets to hear at various junctures in *Shirkers*. The snippets of voice recording, thus, create an affective audio space where the audience bears witness to the voice of the perpetrator, and this sets the audience up for a cinematic form of criminal profiling. The preoccupation with criminal profiling and 'true crime' investigative processes have piqued audience interest since the 16th Century (Bruzzi 2013). *Shirkers* reveals the historical development of this genre, which has shifted from what Bill Nichols argues as a single or truthful representation of criminal events to what can better be understood today as a turn to affective realism of multiple subjectivities as embodied through the trope of a moving suspect. Rather than privileging the voice of the filmmaker over that of other subjects, the audience literally hears the other voices in the reconstruction of the events leading up to the theft of 'Shirkers 1992'. The amalgamation of different types of audio files that range from voice-over, tape recordings, to face-to-face interviews with the other cast and crew of 'Shirkers 1992' open the audience up to different 'witnesses' to the crime.[3]

This mode of cinematic retelling is reminiscent of Trish FitzSimmons' conception of the 'braided' documentary voice, which follows new media theories on the convergence of different levels of power within productions of documentary (2009: 138). Tan's role as narrator and filmmaker problematises Bill Nichols' seminal theorisation that the voice in documentaries conveys 'a sense of a text's social point of view' (2001: 18). For Nichols, the voiceover functions metaphorically as a mouthpiece for the filmmaker's single and coherent point of view and perspective. Matthew Sorrento writes in 'Documenting Crime' that the crime documentary film is a genre that is fraught with contradictions since 'crime documentary' suggests the 'practice of recording the phenomena of crime in various media, though principally in prose' (2016: 246). The term has also synonymously been adopted alongside the 'true crime' that present evidence of crime but in a realist form that may encompass nonfiction prose, television broadcasts, short subject documentary film (Ibid.: 246). Sorrento contends that fictional crime films hardly attempt to reveal the truth but are mediated through narrative styles.

Similarly, the audience is periodically teased with the possibility of learning the 'true' story behind the missing films only to have that information persistently deferred and convoluted. Even the journey that the stolen cans of films took is cause for suspicion. The stolen cans of film reels followed Cardona as he shifted residence in multiple locations: moving from Singapore to Perth to Seattle, and eventually back to Singapore after his death. Throughout the years, the

Figure 11.3 Film reels preserved in an air-conditioned room in *Shirkers* (2018).

stolen reels were kept in air-conditioned rooms 24 hours a day, an act which requires commitment and dedication to the films' preservation and conditions (Fig. 11.3). Underlying these multiple sets of evidence and perspectives that are presented in front of the audience is the question that haunts the film: *why did Georges Cardona steal the films?* The audience is, thus, compelled to take on the active role of an investigator in the process of uncovering the reasons for the theft. The evidence presented in the film points towards a suspect who loved film for its materiality, keeping film reels in its unprocessed, undistributed form, almost to the point of obsession. Yet, his uncharacteristic behaviour only leads to audience's confusion or difficulty in profiling criminal intent.

Criminal Profiling: Who is Georges Cardona?

Evidently, *Shirkers* is not afraid to stylise the documentary form as seen in its opening sequence where Sandi Tan, in 'true-crime' documentary fashion, takes on the primary voice of the storyteller (documentarian) who pieces together a narrative out of evidential materials surrounding the lost and found of 'Shirkers 1992'. The aesthetic curation of *Shirkers* evokes a haunting and enigmatic mystery surrounding the character of Georges Cardona. The moving car or the road function as leitmotifs that mark Cardona and his haunting presence throughout the film, but the road is also never leads the audience to him. The elusive nature and enigmatic personality of Cardona continues to permeate the film. Even a road trip that Sandi Tan takes with Cardona's widow at the time of filming to New Orleans where Cardona used to live did not seem to yield additional insights to him as a person or his motivations behind the stolen films. The audience goes on a seemingly fruitless trip along neighbourhoods that Cardona may or may not have grown up in appear like a form of distraction rather than a revelatory journey. Tan reveals that it is 'so Georges' to have her chase after him the way she did across America. The film then implies that the search for Cardona can only be gleaned through the persons and bodies with whom he crossed paths with who had been the target of his sociopathic behaviour.

Citing Stella Bruzzi, such true-crime documentaries are characterised as 'emotion driven, sensual and – in that it sometimes asks its spectator to respond to it spontaneously on a gut, almost physical level – primal in its appeal' (2007: 248). As seen in *Shirkers,* the retrospective home investigation is enabled through filmmaking processes that reconstruct criminal personalities and events leading up to the crime. We learn that criminal profiling within the field of 'forensic semiotics' draws links between dysfunctional behaviours to one's mind and language (Danesi 2013: 99). Here, the audience takes on the role of a crime reconstructionist, which is not surprising considering the relationship between crime and film genres. Yvonne Jewkers argues in *Media and Crime* that 'striking parallels can be found between the efforts of criminologists and media theorists to understand and "unpack" the relationships between crime, deviance and criminal justice on the one hand, and media and popular culture on the other' (2011: 3) Furthermore, as W. Jerry Chisum and Brent E. Turvey explain in *Crime Reconstruction,* 'there is no limitation as to what may represent trace evidence in particular cases. Nearly anything in the physical world can become evidence when a crime occurs' (2006: 9). The sensorial and affective screen experience enables one to regard at the immaterial evidence that might have been missed otherwise.

Through the film's narrative twists and turns, ambiguities and contradictions that arise from Tan's accounts in relation to other eyewitness experiences, doubt and suspicions are instilled in the audience towards the unreliable narrator, Sandi Tan. In fact, Tan is one of the many reasons why Cardona's criminal intent remains unclear and ambivalent. As an auto-documentary, *Shirkers* instils doubt in the audience about the reliability of Sandi Tan's single perspective who is both a narrator and victim of the events that had transpired around the disappearance of the film. Tan's unreliability compels the audience to consider all the other leads presented through the documentary format and critically engage with these different factions of the events. Berny Tan similarly ascertains that Sandi Tan 'consciously destabilises the fixed 'truth', maintaining this state of flux that excavates that 'wider landscape' for the viewer's contemplation of the narrative' (Tan 2019). However, this inconsistency in subjectivity then allows Cardona to fall under closer scrutiny. This is reminiscent of the tradition adopted by the crime genre, where focus remains on 'the criminal's point of view and fascination with the criminal's psychology' (Leitch 2002: 12). Particularly, the form of crime genres tends to be fraught with symbols, chaos, and mess, as the goal of the film is to ensure the audience 'co-experience the anguish and the insecurity which are the true emotions' as evoked through the crime genre (Ibid.: 34).

One such area of contention lies in the representation of Georges Cardona, the culprit behind the stolen films. Cardona is first introduced by Sandi Tan as 'a man of unplaceable age and origin', someone 'who was like no other adult [she] knew in Singapore'. In one of the interviews, Siddique describes her first impression of Cardona as someone who 'projected himself as an American filmmaker who was there [the Substation] to teach us, impressionable 18, 19 year olds about film production in Singapore'. With his 'very metallic, almost icy blue' eyes, Siddique describes Cardona's disposition as one that appeared distant and cold, but when he 'spoke in very calm measured tones', he 'had this ability that when he spoke to you, you felt that you were his sole focus'. Cardona is said to have brought the girls into 'the inner circle' where he would drive them around Singapore in his car after classes 'looking for ideas'. Interviews were intercut with archival home videos of the Substation film class having gatherings as well as grainy footage of them on the road in Singapore, 'looking for wild dogs'. The audience, thus, bears witness to Cardona in class and his interactions with the girls through the old footage, giving us a glimpse of him personally and directly. Tan explains the nature of Cardona's relationship with the girls as such: 'When film class ended at nine or ten at night, we would drive around the island (Singapore) with Georges. We kept him out late at night even though we knew he had a wife and a baby waiting for him at home'. Old video footage of Jasmine sipping a packet of drink at the back of the car, while the girls giggle over the adventures on the road evoke the sense where the road/ Cardona became a source of creativity, comfort, and even joy to these young girls. In *The Archive Effect: Found Footage and the Audiovisual Experience of History*, Jamie Baron argues that homemade documents 'produce a specific kind of archive effect based on a particular experience of intentional disparity' (2013: 82). Even as the home-made documents enable a 'voyeuristic peek' into other persons' private lives, the film resists giving the audience complete insights to how Cardona used to be. The audiovisual capture evokes a spectral encounter with him, rather than a closer look at his personality.

This true-crime documentary style of filmmaking, thus, presents Cardona as a prime suspect in the case. While Cardona appeared to be an influential mentor and close adult-figure to the young filmmakers, the film emphasised a predatory characteristic to Cardona where 'he picked [them] but he let [them] feel like [they] picked him'. Sandi Tan's accounts describe him as someone who liked to sit and watch the light change, and 'he talked about movies the way [Sandi] wanted to talk about movies'. Despite Cardona's identity and person appearing more as caricature, his influence on Sandi Tan is emphasised confessionally and directly: his love for the French New Wave soon became the interest of Sandi's. In fact, after a road trip Sandi Tan and Cardona took alone in Easter 1992, Tan developed the script for 'Shirkers 1992' and deemed Cardona her 'best friend', where Cardona responded in a letter claiming he was in tears and that Sandi was a 'fucking genius'. As the director of 'Shirkers 1992', however, Cardona appeared to be out of his depth on many occasions and missing from much of the filmmaking process. In fact, 'the only time Georges Cardona was seen' during pre-production casting was when he was caught on video walking across the room. Yet, firsthand accounts argue that Cardona had an uncanny ability to insert himself into situations and positioning himself as a crucial person of authority to the film. On one occasion, Siddique had secured an important meeting with one of the key figures of Kodak Singapore through her letters only to have the meeting hijacked by Cardona at the last instance. It was also through these letters that the young filmmakers managed to secure sponsored film and equipment for 'Shirkers 1992' to begin production. When it came to auditions, Ng designed the audition posters, where the young ladies interviewed and cast all the actors and actresses in the film.

The true-crime documentary was not short of ambiguous drama that affected the audience's ability to completely absolve Tan as a key accomplice. The adoration that Tan had for Cardona surely was not translated to the rest of the crew, where she too confessed that there were two camps: Cardona and Sandi who wanted to go ahead with the film in a short span of two and a half months, as compared to the rest who felt it was wiser to wait a year before beginning production. However, the unreliability of Sandi Tan as a narrator points to her misjudgment of the events, situations, and relationships, as well as herself. These clues make it even more difficult for the audience to piece together the narrative behind the stolen films. In fact, Ng reads off her old production notes at one point of the interview, 'Everything is bloody uncertain. Mister C (Cardona) has no idea what he is doing. He has no idea how he's gonna get the money. He claims he has a production manager who worked on Apocalypse Now' at the request of Tan. Ng then directly addresses Sandi Tan who was off-screen, 'How can we continue with this when I was pointing all these things out? You weren't paying attention to these process reports'. Tan went from being a filmmaker behind the screen to a person of interest that was related to 'Shirkers 1992'. Yet, through the act of directing, Tan is able to divert the attention away from herself. Similarly, Sandi seemed to misread her positions and stance on things that had happened in the past as well. For instance, Ng exclaims that Sandi had an obsession with Bergman only to have Tan reject this claim from off-screen that she did not and that she hated Bergman. This is one of the many ways in which the film disrupts the audience's ability to take the information conveyed at face value. The audience is made to reconsider the authenticity of the facts that were conveyed about the past and Cardona through Tan's accounts. Regardless of the conflicting accounts of their impression of Cardona, the indication 20 years later that Cardona was a 40-year-old who targeted and seemingly primed young girls is hard to ignore.

'Trauma-bonding' through the Crime Film

On the one hand, Angela J. Aguayo illustrates the phenomenon of participatory sleuthing in relation to a new era of true crime in *Documentary Resistance* where 'the relationship between documentary and participatory sleuthing has emerged as one of the most interesting phenomena in media and popular culture' (2019: 77). In this case, Cardona embodies the exploitative nature of filmmaking through his presentation in the film as psychopathic. While the nature of the crime is not cold-blooded murder but the theft of 70 cans of films and their subsequent return 20 years later, the method of investigative and true-crime docu-filmmaking remains the same. The point is not to suggest that some of the accounts may be more indicative of the truth than others or that memory may already be mediated by the act of remembering and retelling. The focus here is less on verifying the details and legitimacy behind the evidence but to address the undisputed patterns that emerge through the accounts. The cinematic medium enables a visualising and retracing of events that otherwise would have been deeply complex and incoherent in any other form.

On the other hand, such affective response to true-crime drama in the form of public sleuthing or collective empathy that relates to 'wider social, political, and ideological messages that such films are attempting to impart' (Horeck 2019: 23). The trauma produced is not only one that is purely personal but may also deeply national and cinematic because it symbolises the gap that was left behind when the film was stolen away from the historical canon of Singapore film history. The format uncovers a deeply exploitable and exploitative quality to the cinematic form that produces affect primarily based on the medium's specificity and stylistic potentials. Yet, it is not the intention of this chapter to ascertain the authenticity of Sandi Tan as narrative. Rather, *Shirkers* exposes Tan's lack of self-awareness and underlying manipulation when the fissures and gaps are presented on screen. Thomas Elsaesser may assert, following trauma theorist Cathy Caruth, that digital technologies may 'fake' or simulate the past, where 'the screen image is thereby dislocated from any authentic or original experience' (2014: 484). However, I contend that these ambiguities reflect the nature of trauma as fragmented and reiterate the experience as convoluted and perplexing, especially in context of encounters with psychopathic personalities who deliberately seek to manipulate and gaslight targets through misinformation and lies. Amresh Sihna and Terence McSweeney argue in *Millennial Cinema* that 'memory take 'form' through various discourses of trauma' where 'film, given its visceral and kinetic properties of narrative, visual and sound has the potency to reflect on the nature of trauma with considerable force' (2012: 9). This cinematic quality of trauma is reflected in the 'recurring motif in the cinema across a diverse variety of genres exploiting the disruption and gaps afforded by memory trauma narratives' (Sihna and McSweeney 2012: 9). As aforementioned, *Shirkers* experiments with various film genres and differing cinematic film styles to consider the traumatic and sudden disappearance of 'Shirkers 1992'. However, in the process, the audience experiences viscerally the post-traumatic realities of those who have become survivors of encounters with Georges Cardona.

According to Robert D. Hare in *Without Conscience: The Disturbing World of the Psychopaths Among Us* (2011) where he attends to various cases of psychopathy and the traits these criminals tend to embody, he describes the psychopath as 'social predators who charm, manipulate, and ruthlessly plow their way through life, leaving a broad trail of broken hearts, shattered expectations and empty wallets' (2011: xi). Rather than to suggest that trauma exists only after verification of criminality, *Shirkers* acknowledges that trauma lingers as sensoria that permeates beyond logical explanation or criminal psychology. Through the cinematic form's, the intangible and presumably random patterns of psychopathic abuse are made palpable and material. This final section attends to Cardona's behavioural patterns and the interpersonal relationships he formed with other persons that reveal his serial psychopathy insofar as he performed repetitive cycles of manipulation. Hare notes that these 'scams rested almost completely on appearances' where the perpetrator 'makes his living by using charm, deceit, and manipulation to gain the confidence of his victims' (Ibid.: 103). The film emphasised Cardona's disposition that was both charming and reassuring, which enabled the easy disarming of his victims. These victims include Cardona's ex-wife, a film producer Stephen Tyler, and the cast and crew of 'Shirkers 1992', all of whom attested to Cardona's ability to con them of either money, time, hope, and ideas. Tan and Cardona's ex-wife's road trip to Cardona's childhood neighbourhood revealed little about Cardona's formative years. Instead, the audience learns that his ex-wife lost $167000 on a Film Center that he claimed he was going to set up with her money. As she drives Tan around the neighbourhood searching in vain for said Film Center, she exclaims with a tone of factual resignation, 'I must have been totally . . . Maybe I was brainwashed who knows?'. Prior to this, Cardona too had managed to convince his ex-wife to pay for a vineyard in Perth where they had lived after moving away from Singapore. In terms of monetary deceit, Cardona had also managed to convince Sophia and Sandi in the final two weeks filming for 'Shirkers 1992' that production would have to be shut down unless they had $10000. As a result, Cardona drove the young ladies from one Automatic Teller Machines (ATM) to another across Singapore to withdraw money from their savings account. The young filmmakers eventually emptied out their bank accounts for the production to carry on.

Hare is also quick to remind readers that the predatory impulse of such psychopaths 'are not confined to simply making money; these qualities pervade their dealings with everyone and everything, including family, friends, and the justice system' (2011: 104). *Shirkers* reveals the string of victims that Cardona had targeted beyond his closest intimate partner, his ex-wife. One other person includes Grace Dane Mazur, a novelist who Cardona exchanged letters with over the years, in the same way he sent voice recordings and faxes to Tan. Cardona had asked Mazur if she would like to collaborate on a movie project with him. The proposed project would be a film noir set in New Orleans, with the working title 'Night Decoy'. The proposed collaborative process would entail Mazur travelling from Cambridge, England where she was at that time to New Orleans where Cardona was at, 'and he would talk to [her], [she] would record it and [she] would go home and make a film script out of it'. Mazur describes Georges' character as 'a constant feeling *of* Peeping Tom-ism to Georges', where he 'could get from [women] what he wanted and what he wanted wasn't always sex'. Instead, Georges managed to convince Mazur 'to work on his dreams for probably four or five years instead of writing [Mazur's] stuff'. Mirroring the sentiments of Cardona's wife, Mazur expressed disbelief, and how 'it's always been a mystery', where she had 'become [Cardona's] intern'. Other witness accounts include filmmaker Stephen Tyler who describe Cardona as having 'this really uncanny way of helping you feel like you could achieve your dream project but then when you got closer to achieving your dream project, he felt the need to sabotage it'. The interviewees who had been in close contact with Cardona throughout his life reflect a recurring pattern where he would charm his victims only to torment them either for his own pleasure or because he is able to.

It becomes evident to the audience of *Shirkers* that the missing film reels of 'Shirkers 1992' were one of many pieces of collateral damage that Cardona's psychopathic tendencies and manipulation caused through the years. Cardona is presented on screen on multiple occasions in the driver seat of his car looking right into the camera placed at the back of the car only to have the image flicker on and off before the scene switches. Here, the film associates Cardona's personality with gaslighting techniques through intertextual cinematic references. The Gaslight Effect is an allusion to the 1944 film of the same name *Gaslight* by George Cukor where Paula a young singer (Ingrid Bergman) marries Gregory, a charismatic, mysterious older man (Charles Boyer) only to be driven insane slowly over a long period of time to win her inheritance. Gregory projects Paula to be ill and weak by continually rearranging household items but denying and accusing her of doing so while manipulating their gas light at home. With time, Paula too starts to believe she has gone mad. The allusion to this concept is recognisable in a few contexts of Cardona's behaviour, where it is often difficult

SHIRKERS LOST AND FOUND?

to ascertain the truth behind his actions or words and where he derived pleasure in psychologically tormenting others. Siddique and Ng explain that it was almost a sadistic 'fun [pleasure] for him to dick [them] around like that'. Siddique recounts a particularly emotional shoot day at the bowling alley where she had asked Georges how were the takes only to have him pop open the film and reply, 'The camera jammed on the first take'. They had shot nothing. Ng related another traumatic incident when in 1993, a year after the film reels disappeared, Cardona had sent boxes of tapes to the young filmmakers. They had planned a watch party since no one had ever seen a single frame of footage from the production of 'Shirkers 1992'. Cardona had sent the young filmmakers boxes after boxes of empty tapes. 'Shirkers was gone', and 'We couldn't believe how ridiculous the situation was, so surreal and so unimaginable'. The effects that these cruel 'pranks' or 'tauntings' left on Siddique was that 'a part of [her] spirit that died' while Ng's energy had been sapped out' completely. If the film manages to demonstrate the emotional and affective trauma and abuse survivors experience in relation to a psychopathic person, it is most epitomised in the responses from the three female filmmakers towards the end of the documentary, where Ng emphasised the deeply toxic and dysfunctional relationship that characterised the production process.

Being probed to the point where she was almost egged on by Sandi, Ng exclaims exasperatedly, 'How many times can I keep telling you that it was extremely annoying and it was extremely disappointing and that it was the relationship that drained and not the production itself that exhausted us', to which Sandi replies with a satisfied 'Thank you'. Ng is shown looking perplexed on screen. Similarly, Siddique describes what could best be read as a shared experience of trauma among the three women, 'This 23-year battle is a double-edge sword for me because you [Sandi], Jasmine and I are bonded in a way that I don't share a bond with anyone else'. The trauma-bond thus creates an 'instant sort of visceral and emotional connection', not solely through the experience of grief towards a lost film. Rather, the loss is only tangible because it is now juxtaposed to what had been found after. These traces that had now been exposed now remind the women how they had been forcefully and violently estranged and removed from the product of their labour for more than 20 years. With little to no protection or legal support to turn to for their lost art work and no material product to concretise the emotional and affective labour that went into the making of 'Shirkers 1992', there was an inevitable lack of closure in relation to the filmmaking process.

While Sandi Tan was asked to write a memoir about 'Shirkers 1992', she denied it as 'Shirkers 1992' could not simply be referenced or explained and would require the material traces in order to make sense to the readers. It was not possible to write about a film that was lost without a trace. The only medium that that may re-produce the sensoria lost through the violent theft of 'Shirkers 1992' is the specificity of cinema that includes the entire line of production from pre-production, production to post. Having any part of the assembly line removed from the filmmaking process will render the film 'missing'. In fact, it is also the appropriate medium that can do more than redeem and make up for lost time. This is seen in the juxtaposition of the theft of both film and soundtrack: Cardona had similarly stolen the original soundtrack of 'Shirkers 1992' from music producer Ben Harrison. Tan explains, 'For more than 20 years, Ben talked about the soundtrack that Georges stole from him. Finally one day I [Sandi] said why don't you just play it for me?'. The film ends with Harrison performing 'Shirkers 1992's soundtrack, cementing the importance of cinematic specificity that is unlike that of music. Harrison could rearrange, and by extension, perform the track for the audience by picking up his electric guitar, tuning the strings and strumming the melody alongside his cellist accompaniment. However, 'Shirkers 1992' could not have been re-made or simply revisited in the same way if not for the fact that the footage had been returned.

Shirkers presents us with a 'transsensorial' approach that considers how cinema thinks across, beyond, and through the sensory, sensible, and that which pertains the senses when it comes to crime and trauma. Sandi Tan repeats in *Shirkers*, 'I wanted to make a road movie for the longest time', but it was only in making *Shirkers* that sought to retrace the making, losing, and finding of 'Shirkers 1992' that Tan was able to make a road movie. *Shirkers*, thus, performs the realities of surviving with the experience of trauma, as Tan admits, 'Making this film, I've come to realise that Georges' ghost will never truly leave me. And I've learned to think that's okay'. Similarly, the importance of regarding processes and specificities of cinema – from pre-production, production, post-production – affect the way we understand how films produce meanings in rhizomatic and open-ended ways. These affective pathways may inevitably carry the traces of trauma that remain enmeshed in lived experiences, something that might not be completely disappear after the emotional violence has been enacted. However, not only is that 'okay', but that could be the most empowering way of reclaiming the lost and found narratives that would have otherwise been silenced completely.

Notes

1. The Substation is Singapore's first independent contemporary arts centre. It was founded in 1990 by Kuo Pao Kun. The space focuses on curating and organising art programmes, exhibitions, and other events to support the diversity of local arts and culture in Singapore.
2. The literary influence for the main protagonist of 'Shirkers 1992'.
3. These voices of the cast and crew such as Philip Cheah who is a Singaporean film critic, Foo Fung Liang, the sound producer and person in charge of storyboarding, and other production assistants on set in 1992.

Works Cited

Aguayo, Angela. 2019. *Documentary Resistance*. New York: Oxford University Press.
Archer, Neil. 2016. *The Road Movie*. London: Wallflower Press.
Baron, Jaimie. 2013. *The Archive Effect: Found Footage and the Audiovisual Experience of History*. London: Routledge.
Branigan, Edward, and Warren Buckland, eds. 2014. *The Routledge Encyclopedia of Film Theory*. London: Routledge.
Bruzzi, Stella. 2002. *New Documentary*. London: Routledge.
Chisum, W. Jerry and Brent E. Turvey. 2012. *Crime Reconstruction*. London: Academic Press.
Danesi, Marcel. 2014. *Signs of Crime*. Berlin: De Gruyter Mouton.
Duarte, José and Timothy Corrigan, eds. 2019. *The Global Road Movie*. Bristol: Intellect Books.
Farrant, Finola. 2018. *Crime, Prisons and Viscous Culture*. Basingstoke: Palgrave Macmillan.
FitzSimons, Trish, 2009. 'Braided Channels: A Genealogy of the Voice of Documentary'. *Studies in Documentary Film* 3.2: 131–146, doi: 10.1386/sdf.3.2.131/1
Hare, Robert D. 2012. *Without Conscience*. New York: Guilford Publications.
Horeck, Tanya. 2014. '"A film that will rock you to your core": Emotion and affect in *Dear Zachary* and the real crime documentary'. *Crime, Media, Culture* 10.2: 151–167. http://dx.doi.org.ezproxy1.lib.asu.edu/10.1177/1741659014540293
Horeck, Tanya. 2019. *Justice on Demand: True Crime in the Digital Streaming Era*. Detroit, MI: Wayne State University Press.
Jenkins, Henry. 2016. *Convergence Culture: Where Old and New Media Collide*. New York: New York University Press.
Jewkes, Yvonne, and Travis Linnemann. 2014. *Media and Crime in the US*. 3rd ed. London: SAGE.
Laderman, David. 2010. *Driving Visions*. Austin, TX: University of Texas Press.
Lehmann, Hauke. 2019. *Affect Poetics of the New Hollywood*. Translated by James Lattimer. Berlin: De Gruyter.
Leitch, Thomas. 2002. *Crime Films*. Cambridge: Cambridge University Press.
Nichols, Bill. 2001. *Introduction To Documentary, Third Edition*. Bloomington: Indiana University Press.
Sinha, Amresh, and Terence McSweeney, eds. 2012. *Millennial Cinema*. New York: Wallflower Press.
Sorrento, Matthew. 2016. 'Documenting Crime: Genre, Verity, and Filmmaker as Avenger'. In *Framing Law and Crime: An Interdisciplinary Anthology*. Edited by Caroline Joan 'Kay' Picart, Michael Hviid Jacobsen, and Cecil Greek, pp. 243–267. Lanham, MD: Fairleigh Dickinson University Press.
Tan, Berny. 2019. 'Go Backwards To Go Forwards: Memory (Re)Construction in *Shirkers*', *Berny Tan Online*, accessed 10 July, 2020. <https://bernytan.com/writing>
Tan, Sandi, dir. Shirkers. 2018. Singapore: Netflix. Online.

12. GATED CRIMES: NEOLIBERAL SPACES AND THE PLEASURES OF PARANOIA IN *LAS VIUDAS DE LOS JUEVES* (2009) AND *BETIBÚ* (2014)

Jonathan Risner

While all nations possess their own distinct spatial dynamics and discourses, Argentina is perhaps unique among Latin American countries for the enduring discursive binary of city and country that emerged from a foundational text by its seventh president, Domingo Faustino Sarmiento. Taking cues from James Fennimore Cooper (Sommer 1991: 52–82), Sarmiento's political tract *Facundo*, which was published in 1845, often serves as ground zero for the spatial imaginary of Argentina. Sarmiento's rural–urban dichotomy often is denoted in shorthand as *civilización y barbarie* – civilisation and barbarism – which encompasses the characterization of urban zones by Western European progress pitted against the rural pampas and, to paraphrase Sarmiento, its immense emptiness and peril owing to gauchos, indigenous savages, and other marauders not yet brought under the thumb of modernisation. While Sarmiento's spatial binary historically extends its national cinema, critics of Argentine film over the past ten years have examined previously overlooked cinematic presentations of rural and urban confines from the past and, most significantly here, detected the emergence of national spaces that expand a narrow city-country spatial imaginary to include depictions of *villas*, or unregulated slums, and *countries*, which is an Argentine term for a kind of gated community. In her study of architecture in post-1990s Argentine cinema, Amanda Holmes asserts, 'Architecture has become a political signifier of contemporary socio-economic conditions' (2018: 2). Given that seven films since 2006 have been set, entirely or partially, in *countries* at a time when Argentina has been in the throes of neoliberal policy,[1] the gated community becomes uniquely associated with Argentine film and, as a cinematic space, intimates some spatial transformations of Argentina.

The *country* has been imagined cinematically through the elastic templates of a multiplicity of genres, including comedies, dramas, art-house cinema, documentaries, and, most importantly here, crime films.[2] And while I will allude to a range of Argentine films set in *countries*, I focus on two recent crime films in which gated communities figure prominently – *Thursday Night Widows/ Las viudas de los jueves* (Marcelo Piñeyro, 2009)[3] and *Betibú* (Miguel Cohan, 2014). The two films and their adherence to select generic facets of crime cinema present an opportunity to examine the intertwining of cinematic narrativisations of neoliberalism in Argentina within the space of the gated community. Given neoliberalism's unstinting emphasis on individualism and the constriction on the state's role in an economy vis-à-vis free market forces,[4] the gated community becomes an emblematic social space wrought by neoliberalism in Argentina. The two crime films are wedded to neoliberalism through setting, and, by indulging in and altering an aesthetics of the crime genre, the films suggest that paranoia is a fundamental and deterritorialised psychological structure of neoliberalism that can be produced and consumed nationally and transnationally. Likewise, fundamental tenets of paranoia – namely, narrative and the substitution of threats – suggest a kind of paranoid spectatorship that is maintained by a transnational flow of genre cinema that includes crime cinema.

Gated Communities as a National Cinematic Space

Albeit distinct within particular films and their respective generic orientation, the emergence of gated communities as a national cinematic space in Argentina accompanies a larger cultural discourse reflected in marketing materials publicising *countries*, novels set in *countries*, and journalistic ethnographies and sociological studies in which *countries* are examined. In the 1990s, paper and virtual advertisements for gated communities began to appear on real estate company websites and in the real estate sections of national and local newspapers, such as *Clarín*. The marketing campaigns of *countries* have been characterised for the popularization of *la vida verde* ('the green life'), which denotes the idea of a gated community affording to its residents idyllic and open settings distinct from that of larger cities (Castelo 2007: 16). Though the construction of gated communities has intensified in Argentina, *countries* date back at least to 1930 with the founding of the first gated community, Tortugas ('Countries: De los barrios'). Other gated communities would soon follow, and, originally, *countries* were occupied exclusively on the weekends and served as vacation spots for brief sojourns away from a larger city, such as Buenos Aires, Córdoba, or Rosario. A profound transformation would begin to unfold at the end of the 1970s during the last dictatorship with the initial imposition of neoliberal policies in Argentina and which would be ramped up during the 1990s. According to sociologist Maristella Svampa, at the end of the 1970s, families headed by young professionals – 'los yuppies' – began to arrive and took up permanent residence in *countries* (2001: 56). In lieu of having two homes – one in the city and another outside the city for weekend getaways – individuals, couples, and families increasingly elected to occupy a single home in a gated zone. *Countries* became de facto bedroom communities as residents would commute from a *country* to larger metropolitan areas for work. Starting in the 1990s during the presidency of Carlos Menem, Argentina witnessed an incredibly rapid growth of gated communities that accompanied the accelerated imposition of neoliberal policies at a pace that scholars often allude to as a means of distinguishing neoliberalism in Argentina from neoliberalism elsewhere (Chronopoulos 2008: 174–175). Alejandro Grimson and Gabriel Kessler have characterised neoliberalism in Argentina in the 1990s by a 'defence of free trade, privatization, and the deregulation of market and workplace' (Grimson and Kessler 2005: 70). When events in other national markets made for a volatile global market, such as the Mexican peso crisis of 1995, the Argentine economy was ill-equipped to deal with massive increases in foreign debt and increased poverty levels (Ibid.: 71).

Countries were one development that captures how neoliberalism affected space. An online special dossier published by *Clarín* provides a comprehensive 70-year overview of the development of *countries* and evidences the plurality of gated communities in Argentina whose commonality is restricted access: *clubes de campo* ('country clubs'), *clubes de chacras* ('farm clubs'), *countries*, and *megaemprendimientos* ('planned communities'). Nevertheless, during the 1990s a particular style of gated community, the *country*, most associated with the upper classes in any number of nations, emerged and can be characterised by fortification and security (walls, private security, check point entrances, surveillance cameras); amenities such as clubhouses, sports leagues, shops and private schools within the gated communities; and bylaws that are often at loggerheads with those of a city, province, and/or nation. *Viudas* and *Betibú* are set in *countries* in close proximity to Buenos Aires, and in a point that I will return to below, what facilitates and exacerbates the spatial and social fragmentation typically associated with neoliberalism in and around Buenos Aires is the boom in freeway construction abetted by private capital that enabled commuters to avoid, or at least minimise, contact with those persons belonging to lower socioeconomic classes.

Argentine films set in *countries* generally reiterate cinematically the notion of *la vida verde* pitched by marketing materials. With the exception of Martel's short film *La ciudad que huye*, in *Los Marziano*, *Betibú*, *Viudas* and *Una semana solos*, one sees open and manicured green spaces, including ponds with cattails, golf courses, purposefully configured trees, and pools. The films exhibit a deliberate landscape architecture characterised by careful planning; in other words, there is nothing accidental about the greenscapes. Such spaces appear unprecedented in Argentine cinema prior to the release of *Cara de queso* in 2006, the first film that features a Jewish *country* occupied by families during the summer.[5] Prior to films set in *countries*, there are scores of well-known Argentine productions, or co-productions, set partially or entirely in open spaces in which longshots of natural landscapes contrast with the urbanscapes of the city of Buenos Aires, a setting that tends to dominate the country's cinema; for example, the open plains of Buenos Aires province in *Juan Moreira* (Leonardo Favio, 1973) and the contrasting Patagonian expanses of deserts in *Historias mínimas / Intimate Stories* (Carlos Sorín, 2002) and forests in *El aura / The Aura* (Fabián Bielinsky, 2005). At variance with the productions that precede it, the *country* film, a genre that can be coined by virtue of its setting, presents a space that is entirely manufactured by human intervention as a product of landscape architecture while still being a natural setting. As noted above, the Argentine films, including *Viudas* and *Betibú*, are set in actual *countries*.

In addition to mimicking or spoofing marketing materials, Argentine *country* films imbibe those motifs of gated communities and their residents that have acquired traction through sheer repetition in book-length journalistic exposés, sociological studies, novels set in gated communities, as well as sensationalised newspaper accounts of murders committed in a *country*, such as *El caso de García Belsunce* ('The case of García Belsunce').[6] Those motifs include the importance of status among many residents; the tensions and resentment of excessive regulations within a country; delinquency of unattended children enabled by the absence of or inattentiveness of parents; the othering of those not residing in a country, which can include domestic servants who often are of a lower class and/or Paraguayan or Bolivian; and the changing relationship between residents of the country and a big city.[7] While all of those motifs are most evident in *Viudas*, in both it and *Betibú*, the gated community is presented as a space incorporated into the narrative template of the crime genre.

Neoliberalism through a Transnational Crime Template

Betibú and *Viudas* are screen adaptations of crime novels written by Claudia Piñeiro, an Argentine novelist whose works have regularly appeared on bestseller lists in Argentina. In the case of the film *Betibú*, Pedro Chazarreta, a resident of the fictitious gated community, *La Maravillosa* is murdered. A newspaper, *La Tribuna*, which is undergoing restructuring having been bought by a Spanish media conglomerate, hires novelist, Nurit Iscar. Nurit, whose nickname is Betibú, is to live in the *country* and write a series of columns about the crime. Aided by two journalists at *La Tribuna*, Mariano and Brena,

Nurit uncovers a series of interconnected murders that relate to a rape that happened decades ago. However, Nurit and her accomplices apparently have uncovered too much about a shadowy criminal network, *La Organización*. At the film's end, operatives associated with *La Organización* pull strings to ensure the group's status remains secret, and a motorcycle pulls up to a jazz club presumably to eliminate Nurit, Mariano, and Brena. *Viudas* is set in December of 2001, a historical moment during which mass protests against the government's policies reached a fevered pitch. *Viudas* refers to wives who figuratively become widows when their husbands congregate each Thursday for a night of drinking and playing cards. The wives literally become widows by the film's end when all of their husbands, with the exception of one, commit suicide by electrocuting themselves in a luxurious pool spurred by a twisted logic of escape and fragile masculinity undergirded by neoliberal thinking in which death is conceived as a business transaction.[8]

Although the crime film as a genre often eludes concise definitions, *Viudas* and *Betibú* conform with select formalistic and narrative tenets of the crime film or subgenres associated with it, such as film noir. Thomas Leitch, for instance, has argued, 'Many crime films adopt visual conventions of film noir' (2002: 11). And while the films hardly qualify as paradigmatic examples of film noir, *Viudas* and *Betibú* possess moments characterised by high-contrast and low-key lighting and night-time exterior shots (Ibid.: 11). Kirsten Moana Thompson's comments regarding narrative in crime films are also helpful here to understand how the two Argentine films are crime films: 'A preliminary working definition might be that a crime film foregrounds the commission of a crime, and/or emphasises its investigation, prosecution, prevention, and/or punishment' (2007: 2). *Viudas* and *Betibú* adhere to and depart from Thompson's definition. Claustrophobic framing and point-of-view shots from the perspective of those examining a crime formally imply the act of investigation. Moreover, the narratives begin en media res with flashbacks and flashforwards and are initiated with a murder. In *Betibú*, the murder at the film's start soon leads to an investigation by journalists who double as detectives. In *Viudas*, the bodies of the husbands are foregrounded at the beginning of the film as a kind of ruse; what ostensibly is a crime is a suicide pact, and the remainder of the movie is an exploration of how they arrived at that point.

Space is a fundamental characteristic of crime cinema with the city most commonly presented as a threatening milieu. However, select critics have invoked crime cinema and its capacity to portray the restructuring and transformations of entire urban environments, namely a city's deterioration.[9] For instance, building on Edward Dimendberg's observations on film noir productions from the United States during the 1940s,[10] Jennifer Fay unpacks film noir's ability to capture urban transformations and how particular films released primarily during the 1940s and 1950s suggest the psychological disappointment that accompanies what ostensibly and originally appeared to be improvements to infrastructure:

> Film noir's aesthetic world turns urban history into the narratives and affects of a reduced human habitat, where the new and presumably more durable residential arrangements, whether in the form of suburban sprawl, nuclearism's survival architecture, or urban public housing, lead to an even more diminished, psychically negating, but also criminally intriguing form of living. (2018: 100)

Albeit concerned with US crime films, Fay's remarks on the spatial relationship between the crime film, economic change, and psychology are instructive for how *Viudas* and *Betibú* chart the effects of the spatial transformations wrought by neoliberalism specific to Argentina. Grimson and Kessler's assessment on the effects of neoliberalism in Argentina capture the crux of what often transpires spatially:

> As free market capital accumulation plays across a variegated geographical terrain of resource endowments, cultural histories, communications possibilities, labour quantities, and qualities . . ., it produces an intensification of uneven geographical development in standards of living and life prospects. Rich regions grew richer leaving poor regions poorer. (2005: 178)

Spatially, and in very broad terms, neoliberalism, first, can be characterised by discontinuity. Private neighbourhoods, or 'homogeneous, highly segregated and protected areas' are separated from the lower classes, who may have formerly occupied the same space (Janoschka and Borsdorf 2006: 96). While there is a kind of uniformity within a gated community itself, the larger spatial entity clashes with its surroundings creating what Mike Davis and Daniel Monk have called a 'geography of exclusion' (2007: ix) when describing gated communities. *Viudas* highlights this exclusion in several shots, such as the one below after the camera is elevated above a wall to make visible a slum that resides immediately on the other side of a *country* (Fig. 12.1). Below, I will return to the psychological conditions of *countries* proposed by *Viudas* and *Betibú*. However, both films, as well as most other *country* films, generally operate as broad moralistic condemnations. Matt Losada rightfully detected *Los Marziano* as an instance of cruel optimism (2018: 137),[11] and Gisela Heffes sees films and novels set in *countries* as illustrating a kind of corruption that pervades *countries* and corrodes all relations between neighbours and families (2013: 323).

The spatial transformations induced by economic policies do not rest exclusively with new conglomerations of large houses, and select crime genre films have possessed the capacity to narrativise those transformations that can be

Figure 12.1 Still from *Las viudas de los jueves* (2009) contrasting the interior of a *country* with a neighbourhood of a lesser economic class. The differences between the two spaces underscores a discontinuous landscape that sometimes characterises the spatial effects of neoliberalism.

initiated with the construction of highways. While focusing on a sprawling Los Angeles and its transformations beginning in the 1920s due to 'suburbanization and decentralization' (2004: 168–169), Dimendberg traces the dynamics of centrifugal spaces in US noir films from the 1940s. As films produced during the first two decades of the 21st century in Argentina, *Viudas* and *Betibú* cinematically portray the ongoing dispersal of Buenos Aires, one of Latin America's megacities whose city proper and surrounding areas contain roughly a third of the nation's population. This population dispersal is abetted by highway construction. In the aforementioned virtual overview about *countries* in *Clarín*, a subsection entitled 'Los corredores que pisan fuerte' ('The passages that tread heavily') describes how the development of *countries* of various kinds expanded exponentially during the last decade to the southeast of Greater Buenos Aires (Gioberchio n.d.). Improvements to already existing routes and the construction of new roadways – Highway 2, routes 58 and 52, and the Ricchieri and Buenos Aires-La Plata highways – were crucial factors that enabled the expansion of *countries* that were more affordable than those to the north of Buenos Aires that emerged in the 1990s (Gioberchio n.d.). The capital city's centrifugal push to the south balanced a previous large wave of expansion of gated communities that happened in the north with the expansion of the Pan-American highway.

In *Viudas*, the role of highways in the creation of spatial discontinuity is depicted when characters leave the walled neighbourhood to go to work, or at least pretend to go to work. Martín loses his job but cannot muster the courage to tell his wife. In turn, he must keep up the appearance of working and goes to a small diner off the highway daily where he stresses about paying bills. And though Martín is beyond the confines of the *country*, he remains an arm's length from Buenos Aires. Otherwise, the city is depicted as a perilous and anarchic space in which protests against governmental policies unfold in spectacular fashion at a distance through a television. In the still below from *Viudas*, Ronnie views the protests unfolding through a television in his bedroom (Fig. 12.2). Such images dominated the national airwaves in December of 2001 when protests deposed two presidents within a month after a years-long economic depression and a governmental measure that limited citizens' ability to withdraw money from banks. Luisela Alvaray has pointed out the shortcomings of conceiving genre cinema not produced in the United States as the simplistic insertion of local, regional, or national cultural elements into a genre template (2013: 69). If Dimendberg underscores highway construction as an influential factor in US crime films, highways may appear to operate as a syntactical trait or variation in the framework for the crime genre that has become resoundingly transnational. But in *Viudas*, these are Argentine highways, and the historical and socioeconomic contexts must be appreciated rather than construed as a repetition of Los Angeles.

Figure 12.2 Image from *Las viudas de los jueves* in which Ronnie watches news footage of looting on the television as protests against the Argentine government unfold. Though Ronnie and others are largely insulated from the political and economic turmoil, the film's timing of December 2001 follows that of the actual unrest in Argentina.

The two Argentine crime films' adherence to genre conventions make them accessible and even attractive to production companies and genre communities in different national markets. And while both have become available on select streaming services with a near-global reach, such as iTunes, YouTube, Google Play, *Viudas* and *Betibú* forces one to consider those markets that are prioritised in the film's transnational circulation, namely Spanish-language markets. *Viudas* received production support from several private companies in Argentina (Haddock, Tornasol, Castafiore), the television channel Telefe, and the government's national film agency INCAA (Instituto Nacional de Cine y Artes Audiovisuales). In addition to Programa Ibermedia, a film fund maintained by multiple Latin American countries, Spain, and Portugal to facilitate co-productions, various film entities associated with the Spanish government, including the ICAA (Instituto de la Cinematografía y de las Artes Audiovisuales), also lent support. *Betibú*, received support from Argentine entities – Haddock, Tornasol, Telefe, and INCAA – as well as the Spanish government. Production support aside, while box office figures are hard to come by, it is important to note the particular markets in which *Viudas* and *Betibú* are distributed. *Viudas* received theatrical distribution across multiple Spanish-language markets: Argentina; Bolivia; Chile; Colombia; Mexico; Paraguay; Spain; and Uruguay ('Las viudas'). *Betibú* was distributed theatrically in Argentina and Spain ('Betibú). Crucial historical and sociocultural differences notwithstanding, both films reiterate how Spain and most Latin American markets can operate as a single block and enable for a single Spanish-language market to appeal to viewers in other markets. Commenting from the vantage point of the Spanish film industry, Marvin D'Lugo and Gerard Dapena rightfully point out:

> The Spanish film industry's awareness of its limited domestic audience . . . is counterbalanced by the colonial dispersion of Spanish-speaking peoples and resulting exchange of cultural products: what amounts to a transnational Hispanic market. This potential audience can be termed a Hispanic "transnation": a deterritorialized population formed through migration and built on the recognition of common linguistic, cultural, and social bonds. (2013: 15–16)

Though *Viudas* and *Betibú* possess the capacity to appeal to viewers in a multitude of markets by virtue of being crime film, both nevertheless appeal first to Spanish-language markets.

Paranoia as Transnational Framework for Spectatorship

Genre cinema is repetition. As Rick Altman writes, 'Most aesthetic theories of genre take as their starting point the issues of repetition and variation, similarity and difference, and the extent to which the elements repeated and varied are simple or complex' (1999: 195). Formal elements and highways aside, the repetitive emotive structures of the crime genre broach how such structures enable a crime film's transnational reach during the age of neoliberalism. Linda Williams' notion of 'body genres' provides a starting point way to consider the emotional and repetitive dimensions of film genres. As is well-known in film studies, in a 1991 essay Williams expanded Carol Clover's notion of 'body [film] genres' to include melodrama alongside pornography and horror. For Williams, the three genres relate to each other for their respective systems of excess, each of which, at least for Williams, hinge on a feminine body being rendered a spectacle for its audience.[12] Williams leaves open the possibility of other genres operating on a spectator's bodies; for instance, she alludes to physical clown comedies. Yet, Williams zeroes in on horror, pornography, and melodrama and sees them as 'low' genres since a hypothetical spectator 'is caught up in an almost involuntary mimicry of the emotion or the sensation of the body on the screen along with the fact that the body displayed is female' (1991: 4). So, if a woman cries in a melodrama, the spectator cries; if a woman screams in a horror film, the spectator screams; if someone orgasms in a pornographic film, the spectator experiences a sexually charged ecstasy.

While Williams' essay is rightfully considered trailblazing for its consideration of bodily reactions and gendered receptions, the presumption of those reactions is reductive. One need not look hard in a theatre for a horror viewer laughing at some moment of gore that otherwise repulses another moviegoer, or a viewer yawning at a joke that falls flat in a comedy while others chuckle. Instead of presupposing a spectator's reaction vis-à-vis a crime film, I prefer to consider its emotive template or tentative instructions for a spectator; that is, how one is supposed to feel vis-à-vis a character's plight irrespective of whether or not the spectator plays along in a game of imitation of what appears on screen. In the case of crime cinema in general, a primary emotion that is held out to a spectator is a vicarious paranoia when a character is pursued and confronted by threats. The unique merits of *Viudas* and *Betibú* come through in their capacity to narrativise and make comprehensible the relationship between space and paranoia and how neoliberalism can foment conditions – exacerbating economic inequality, eroding a larger collective with an unbridled celebration of individualism – to the point of altering space.

While immediately acknowledging its limitations, Freeman and Freeman offer a rudimentary initial definition of paranoia: 'Paranoia is the unrealistic belief that other people want to harm us' (2008: 23). The characters' paranoia in *Viudas* and *Betibú* is stoked by the fear of multiple forces impinging upon them until a threat materialises. In the case of *Viudas*, characters fret over crime, the wayward nature of their children, the need to maintain appearances, and the realities of a precarious economy in the throes of crisis. In *Betibú*, the journalists worry over being discovered by anonymous criminals or being tracked down. Freeman and Freeman allude to 'fear figures' and how those figures change according to geography and historical moment. With regards to the late twentieth-century presumably in the United States or Britain: 'By the 1980s it's the Mafia or the Russians. Today it's MI5, the government, or Al-Qaeda' (Ibid.: 25). Brian Massumi's notion of 'iterative series' of 'threat-events' (2010, 86) to describe the Bush administration's pre-emptive logic during the Global War on Terror further unpacks Freeman and Freeman's idea of 'fear figures:'

> 9–11 belongs to an iterative series of allied events whose boundaries are indefinite. . . . The terrorist series includes torpedoing buildings with airplanes, air missile attacks, subway bombs, suicide car attacks, road-side bombs, liquid explosives disguised as toiletries, tennis-shoe bombs, 'dirty' bombs (never actually observed), anthrax in the mail, other unnamed bioterrorist weapons, booby-trapped mailboxes, Coke cans rigged to explode, bottles in public places . . . The list is long and ever-extending. (2010: 86–87)

Viudas and *Betibú* possess their own chain of 'threat events' that anticipate, maintain, or make manifest a paranoid chain that links one scene to the next at a moment in which neoliberalism abounds in Argentina during the films' production.

Paranoia, in turn, seems to be a psychological structure that can be maintained with the substitution of threats if one threat wanes or is neutralised regardless if the threats are ever real or not. In *The Sublime Object of Ideology* and elsewhere, Žižek alludes to a joke that Lacan makes about a jealous husband who suspects he is being cuckolded by his wife. For Žižek, the veracity of the affair is moot; the psychological structure is the same:

> even if all the facts he quotes in support of his jealousy are true, even if his wife really is sleeping around with other men, this does not change one bit the fact that his jealousy is a pathological, paranoid construction. (2008: 49)

And so it is in *Viudas* and *Betibú*; the veracity of threats is insignificant. The paradox is that even for those residing within the walls of a gated community, a threat arises. Recalling Losada's contention that *countries* proffer an instance of cruel optimism, the space of the gated community ushers the characters to a form of self-imposed doom over the trajectory of the narrative.

The cinematic aesthetics of the crime film double for an aesthetics of paranoia in *Viudas* and *Betibú* through formal elements mentioned above: high-contrast and low-key lighting, ominous music, and claustrophobic framing.

In 'On Landscape in Narrative Cinema', Martin Lefebvre borrows from Victor Freeburg's five categories to describe how landscapes in films becomes subservient to narrative. Neutral, informative, sympathetic, participating, and formative: the five categories compose a scale that convey the external and internal conditions of a character (2011: 64). In the case of spaces of the gated community in *Viudas* and *Betibú*, a space that at first appears purely informative – providing information about the characters' socioeconomic status – the setting of the *country* conveys 'tone or mood' ('sympathetic'), shapes a character ('participating'), and, finally, 'seeks to express the character's interior state of mind' (Lefebvre Ibid.: 64–65).

The space of the *country* in *Viudas* and *Betibú* suggests that the characters' paranoia expressed through formal elements presents itself as a fear of a breach in one's space that exceeds the body. That is, the *country* is an extension of its residents' psychical being. In his essay 'Paranoiac Space', Victor Burgin examines the incapacity of paranoiacs to conceive of themselves as a bounded individual:

> Paranoiacs do not clearly differentiate themselves from other people and things. Their speech does not coincide with their identity, they as speak as if they were an other [sic], or simply an object in a world of objects. They have lost the illusory but necessary sense of transcendence which would allow to position themselves at the center [sic] of their own space. (1991: 26)

Burgin continues: 'In psychosis boundaries fail, frontiers are breached. In psychotic space an external object – a whole, a part, or an attribute of a person or thing – may be experienced as if it had invaded the subject' (Ibid.: 26). The walls of the *countries* serve as a kind of prosthetic shield for the self for the residents which eventually becomes useless. If the city presented threats in other crime films, the *country* presents its own set of threats that emerge from within the space.

Paranoia, I argue, is very much a neoliberal emotion, and the gated community is a paradigmatic neoliberal space signalling that emotion manifests and at work. In *The Architecture of Neoliberalism*, Douglas Spencer contends that architects and architectural theorists 'have posited the human subject as [a] kind of post-enlightenment being – environmentally adaptive and driven by affect rather than rationality' (2016: 4). In the case of the two Argentine crime films that affect is paranoia, which I would deem an emotion, a point to which I will return below. Gated communities evidence the crystallisation – or better, the visibilisation – of paranoia through a spatial practice. Argentina has a long tradition of crime films, and the *country* as the site of the murder or suicide in *Betibú* and *Las viudas* suggests the motif of trouble in paradise. However, to wield the crime genre – a paranoid genre – to narrativise neoliberalism in contemporary Argentina and to set that crime in a gated community reinforces neoliberalism's ties with paranoia.

Another primary tenet of paranoia opens the analysis of two specific Argentine crime films to a broader examination of the transnational circulation of genre films in general: narrative. In Freud's study of Daniel Schreber's memoirs, in which Freud infamously concluded that paranoia stems from homosexual panic, Freud characterises Schreber's paranoia as a narrative system that organises and fits all occurrences and anomalies within Schreber's paranoid system. According to Freud, 'Patient is full of ideas of pathological origin, which have formed themselves into a complete system' (1963: 90). In Freud's view, Schreber is constantly trying to find ways in which anomalous events fit into his elaborate system in which God transforms Schreber into a woman, and Schreber will birth a new race to save humankind. In Freud's estimation, narrative constitutes a fundamental characteristic of paranoia.

However, some qualification about the relationship between narrative and paranoia is needed. In short, all narratives willy-nilly are not paranoid. Rather, to interject some nuance, a narrative becomes paranoid in two basic ways and can do so to varying degrees. First, as touched on above, a paranoid narrative can be characterised by the presence of a threat or multiple threats. Second, the disparity among the threads that make for the narrative and the veracity of those threads can render a narrative paranoid. In other words, one should not dismiss a narrative outright simply for its complexity. Recalling that journalists often become a proxy for the detective figure, there are plenty of valid news stories covering abstruse political and/or economic machinations (for example, Ponzi schemes, money laundering, political deals) that require meticulous sleuthing to illuminate the eventual convergence of multiple threads. Albeit fiction, *Betibú* offers one such narrative in which unlikely hunches and complications materialise. The character, Gato, serves as a source of hidden knowledge for Brena. Gato is surrounded by electronics to gather information in his home, and his house and clothes suggest he belongs to a low economic class. And though Brena accepts Gato's information in exchange for money, Gato is dismissed and ignored when he broaches *La Organización*, as if the secret network exceeds an explanatory narrative. The ostensible lack of truth upholding a thread in Gato's ideas pushes his paranoid narrative into the realm of conspiracy theory for other characters.

As touched on above, Argentina has a tradition of crime films that continues in the present. In addition to *Betibú* and *Viudas*, one can add a number of national productions, or co-productions, that are crime films and that have figured among the highest-grossing films domestically: *The Secret in Their Eyes/ El secreto de sus ojos* (Juan José Campanella, 2009), *Thesis on a Homicide/ Tesis sobre un homicidio* (Hernán Goldfrid, 2013), *7th Floor/Séptimo* (Patxi

Amezcua, 2013), *Death in Buenos Aires/Muerte en Buenos Aires* (Natalia Meta, 2014), *El Ángel* (Luis Ortega, 2018). One might conjecture that the sustained popularity of crime films in Argentina upholds cinematically Bruno Bosteels' argument that left-wing conspiracy theories regarding the country's political and economic collapse under neoliberalism operated as a mode of 'filling the void in consciousness' started by the spontaneous mobilisation of people in December 2001 against the government (2012: 278–279). The aforementioned Argentine crime films are hardly exercises in leftist politics. Yet, the crime films – and not just those set in gated communities – metonymise a kind of suspicion or paranoia of hidden power structures in Argentina, to which there is some measurement of truth.

The modest circulation of *Viudas* and *Betibú* reiterates the transnational circulation and appeal of crime films. Crime films are, of course, one among many paranoid genres that have become highly exportable and circulate over borders. If a baseline for paranoia is a threat conceived in narrative form, a legion of other genre films could double as a paranoid genre films: horror, escape films, thrillers, science-fiction, and action films. Threats are a crucial part of all such genres with each possessing their own templates for paranoid aesthetics that vary according to mise en scène, screen violence, sound, villains, and settings. Many critics, including myself, have weighed in on how neoliberalism has affected cinema from Latin America, such as the reduction of governmental funding for film production (Sandberg 2018: 6–7), the emergence of the romantic comedy as an affective strategy for reconciling class differences in Mexico (Sánchez Prado 2014), superficial treatments of societal dynamics such as sexual identity (Venkatesh 2016: 4), and the financialisation of the mise en scène through product placement (Risner 2017).[13]

Moving beyond these contentions, I argue here that the transnational exportation and importation of paranoid genre films – again, crime films, action films, horror films, and thrillers – peaks with neoliberalism and creates a circulation of paranoid aesthetics that emerge from and appeal to different national audiences. In turn, the circulation of paranoid genre films creates a loop of paranoid aesthetics among markets. Streaming services have exercised a considerable influence on the production of genre films or genre series, and, although US cinema dominates on platforms such as Netflix and Amazon Prime, those same platforms have enabled the circulation of paranoid genre films and series coming from different foreign markets, one of which is Argentina. In a *Wire Magazine* article entitled 'Genre, Genre Everywhere: the Netflix Effect Spreads', Peter Rubin describes how the success of Netflix's *Black Mirror* and *Altered Carbon* have inspired other streaming services, such as Prime and Hulu, to make genre series, many of which depending on their genre, possess their own paranoid aesthetics and threats that drive the narrative. It is no secret that genre series and films are much more bankable than, say, experimental cinema, and the offerings of transnational online streaming platforms include comedies, dramas, documentaries, and action films. To be sure, the transnational circulation of paranoid genres and genre cinema, which include crime films, is nothing new. However, the quantity and breadth of that circulation and the multiplicity of directionality are unprecedented. To be more concrete, US commercial cinema has long dominated domestic and international box offices. Streaming platforms, however, facilitate the movement of non-US films into other markets, including the United States.

This circulation of paranoid genre films makes for what I call paranoid spectatorship. Paranoid spectatorship is characterised by a penchant for paranoid genres but is not necessarily limited to those genres. The preference for genre cinema, including its formal properties and emotive template, is maintained by a circulation of genre cinema emerging from transnational nodes of production and abetted by digital viewing platforms that provide nearly unlimited access to cinema at transnational nodes of consumption. As described above, paranoia is a psychological structure that is maintained by the substitution of threats, which have multiplied with the ubiquity of technology and which are organised into narrative. Akin to paranoia, genres are defined by emotive structures that have become clichéd – that is, marketable and profitable – with repetition over decades. If emotions are the 'socio-linguistic fixing of the quality of an experience' (Massumi 1995: 88), affects are '. . . unqualified . . . not ownable or recognizable, and . . . thus resistant to critique' (Ibid.: 88). Transcribed onto cinema, the consumption of genre cinema resembles an emotion and is the 'fixing' of cinematic formulas that have been captured and honed by production studios and consumed among multiple markets. Prima facie, genre cinema appears to be the cinematic analogue of a paranoid structure. Yet, here, it is a spectatorial structure that favours narrative and whose emotive template can be attended to and maintained by a near-endless circulation and substitution of genre cinema and series primarily through online streaming platforms. However, I would argue that, if genre films conform to and offer a viewer a familiar emotive template, genre films still hold out a possibility for an emergence of affect that is lesser than, say, an experimental film. Albeit never guaranteed, affect can arise in a genre film with syntactic variations of that genre, such as the insertion of a gated community as a threatening landscape in a crime film as in the case of *Viudas* and *Betibú*. To set a crime film in a gated community holds out the possibility one may feel differently about neoliberalism and its spatial transformations.

A paranoid spectatorship rests with an ever-expanding catalogue of genre cinema – including paranoid genre cinema and series – which enables the practice of binge watching. In his study of the cognitive psychological effects of binge watching, Zachary Snider points to his own paranoid positioning after having successively watched seasons of the show *Damages*, and he alludes to psychological research about problems with trust that accompany bouts of binge watching. Paranoia and a paranoid spectatorship, however, need not be a negative thing per se. Studies of conspiracy theories have pointed to the pleasures of paranoia that accompanies having all the pieces of a puzzle fitting together to explain an obscure problem. In short, paranoia underscores the pleasures of interpretation, something with which all critics, academic or otherwise, can identify. Mark Fenster's comments on conspiracy theories are instructive for illustrating this point:

> More troubling still, the narrative faces the nearly impossible burden of finding an ending. A conclusion would call a halt to interpretation – conspiracy theory's key practice and source of pleasure – by suggesting either that the conspiracy has won or that it did not represent the existential threat it seemed to promise. (2008: 14)

Genre cinema, including crime cinema from Argentina and elsewhere, proffers the pleasure of spectatorial interpretation, and streaming cinema provides the potential for that pleasure to continue ad infinitum.

NOTES

1. *Cara de queso*/*Cheese Head* (Ariel Winograd, 2006), *La ciudad que huye*/'The City that Flees' (Lucrecia Martel, 2006), *Una semana solos*/*A Week Alone* (Celina Murga, 2007), *Las viudas de los jueves* (Marcelo Piñeyro, 2009), *Los Marziano*/'The Marzianos' (Ana Katz, 2011), *Betibú* (Miguel Cohan, 2014), and *Historia del miedo*/*History of Fear* (Benjamín Naishtat, 2014). Though a Spanish film with substantial parts filmed in Buenos Aires, *Pájaros muertos*/'Dead Birds' (Guillermo Sempere and Jorge Sempere, 2008) could also be included among those movies set in gated communities. In the case that Argentine films have distribution in an English-language market, I have included the title in italics. Otherwise, I have translated the titles into English and enclosed those titles in quotation marks. It is worth noting that the quantity of recent Argentine films set in gated communities runs risk of exhausting a genre that coagulates along the question of space or setting.
2. Albeit less frequent, gated communities appear in films set in gated communities in other Latin American settings, especially Mexico City. For example, a gated community in Mexico City is featured extensively in Rodrigo Plá's *La zona*/*The Zone* (2007), and, in Alfonso Cuarón's *Y tu mamá también* (2001), Diego Luna's character Tenoch lives in a private neighbourhood in Mexico City.
3. Subsequently, I will refer to *Las viudas de los jueves* simply as *Viudas*.
4. While here I will discuss the emergence of *countries* as a consequence of neoliberalism particular to Argentina, other fundamental tenets of the ideology include the primary role of the market to determine governmental policies and the minimalization of state intervention to correct unfortunate consequences of the market. More concretely, neoliberalism has resulted in the shrinking of the welfare state and the privatization of national industries in numerous countries.

5. Discrimination against Jewish families moving into countries in Argentina was unfortunately common in sociological and journalistic accounts of countries written during the 1990s and early 2000s. See, for example, Castelo and Svampa.
6. 'El caso de García Belsunce' refers to the murder of Argentine sociologist María Marta García Belsunce in October of 2002, which garnered immense mediatic and popular attention. García Belsunce was a resident of a gated community called Carmel located in Pilar, a town north of Buenos Aires, and her corpse was discovered in a bathroom of her home. With the original autopsy, authorities concluded that García Belsunce's injuries indicated she had slipped in a tub, hit her head on the faucet, and drowned. A second autopsy brought to light that those examiners conducting the initial autopsy somehow missed the five bullets that were lodged in her head. Under ambiguous evidence, Carlos Carrascosa was convicted for García Belsunce's murder but later absolved.
7. In several studies of gated communities, parents are often originally from large cities who have relocated to a *country*. In turn, a large city can become a place to which one commutes primarily for work or leisure. As parents, those adults sometimes express exasperation at how their children possess a different relationship to a big city and are often frightened by it (Castelo 2007, 86–89).
8. Such an interpretation of death recalls Wendy Brown's characterisation of neoliberalism as 'the financialization of everything and the increasing dominance of finance capital over productive capital in the dynamics of the economy and everyday life' (2015, 28). The depiction of masculine angst in *Viudas* appears in other contemporary Argentine commercial films. In her study of masculinity in contemporary Argentine commercial cinema, Carolina Rocha argues that 'the cinematic representation of middle-class masculinities in crisis is related to the inception of neoliberalism in Argentina' (2012, 2). For Rocha, a middle-class Argentine masculinity is pegged to the State and, as precarious conditions ensued with the imposition of neoliberal policies and the shrinking role of the State, 'unemployment, lack of prestige, and the inability to achieve glory made Argentine men feel emasculated' (2012, 12). In *Viudas*, emasculation happens not owing necessarily to the contraction of the State, but rather a life bereft of solidarity within families and among friends.
9. See, for example, Holmes.
10. Like Thomas Leitch, among other critics, I consider film noir to be a subgenre of crime films (1).
11. Cruel optimism is a concept coined by Lauren Berlant, and, while I am oversimplifying, cruel optimism refers to 'a relation of attachment to compromised conditions of possibility . . . the condition of maintaining an attachment to a problematic object in advance of its loss' (2006, 21).
12. With excess, or a system of excess, Williams alludes to the repetitive aesthetics of spectacle that are typical of a genre, such as a dance number in a musical.
13. The essays in *Contemporary Latin American Cinema: Resisting Neoliberalism?* (eds. Claudia Sandberg, Carolina Rocha) provides an excellent overview of neoliberalism's effects on Latin American cinema and touches on subjects ranging from film festivals, distribution, and content.

Works Cited

Altman, Rick. 1999. *Film/Genre*. London: British Film Institute.
Alvaray, Luisela. 2013. 'Hybridity and Genre in Transnational Latin American Cinemas.' *Transnational Cinemas* 4.1: 67–87.
Berlant, Lauren. 2006. 'Cruel Optimism.' *Differences* 17.3: 20–36.
'Betibú.' *IMDb*. June 6, 2020. https://www.imdb.com/title/tt3022898/.
Bosteels, Bruno. 2012. *Marx and Freud in Latin America: Politics, Psychoanalysis, and Religion in Times of Terror*. New York: Verso.
Brown, Wendy. 2015. *Undoing the Demos: Neoliberalism's Stealth Revolution*, Cambridge, MA: MIT Press.
Burgin, Victor. 1991. 'Paranoiac Space.' *Visual Anthropology Review* 52.7: 22–30.
Castelo, Carla. 2007. *Vidas perfectas. Los countries por dentro*. Buenos Aires: Sudamericana.
Chronopoulos, Themis. 2008. 'Neoliberalism in the Southern Cone.' *Latin American Perspectives*, 35.6: 174–178.
Cohan, Miguel, dir. *Betibú*, 2014; Spain: Cameo, 2015. DVD.
'Countries: De los barrios cerrados a los megaemprendimientos.' *Clarín*. Accessed May 30, 2020. http://70aniversario.clarin.com/countries/#como-fueron-variando-las-urbanizaciones
Davis, Mike and Daniel Monk. 2007. Introduction to *Evil Paradises: Dreamworlds of Neoliberalism*, ix–xvi. Edited by Mike Davis and Daniel Monk. New York: New Press.
Dimendberg, Edward. 2004. *Film Noir and the Spaces of Modernity*. Cambridge, MA: Harvard University Press.
D'Lugo, Marvin and Gerald Dapena. 2013. Introduction to 'Transnational Frameworks' in *A Companion to Spanish Cinema*, 38–40. Edited by Jo Labanyi and Tatiana Pavlović. Malden, MA: Wiley-Blackwell.
Fay, Jennifer. 2018. *Inhospitable World: Cinema in the Time of the Anthropocene*. Oxford: Oxford University Press.
Fenster, Mark. 2008. *Conspiracy Theories: Secrecy and Power in American Culture*. Minneapolis: University of Minnesota Press.
Freeman, Daniel and Jason Freeman. 2008. *Paranoia: The 21st-Century Fear*. Oxford: Oxford University Press.
Freud, Sigmund. 1963. *Three Case Histories*. New York: Collier Books.
Gioberchio, Graciela. n.d. 'Los corredores que pisan fuerte.' *Clarín*. <http://70aniversario.clarin.com/countries/#como-fueron-variando-las-urbanizaciones> (last accessed 5 July 2020).
Grimson, Alejandro, and Gabriel Kessler. 2005. *On Argentina and the Southern Cone: Neoliberalism and National Imaginations*. New York: Routledge.
Heffes, Giselle. 2013. *Políticas de la destrucción / Poéticas de la preservación. Apuntes para una lectura (eco)crítica del medio ambiente en América Latina*, Rosario: Beatriz Viterbo.
Holmes, Amanda. 2017. *Politics of Architecture in Contemporary Argentine Cinema*. Cham: Palgrave Macmillan.
Holmes, Nathan. 2018. *Welcome to Fear City: Crime Film, Crisis, and the Urban Imagination*, Albany: State University of New York Press.

Janoschka, Michael and Axel Borsdorf. 2006. 'Condominios fechados and barrios privados: The Rise of Private Residential Neighbourhoods in Latin America.' In *Private Cities: Global and Local Perspectives*, 89–104. Edited by George Glasze, Chris Webster, and Klaus Frantz, New York: Routledge.
'Las viudas.' *IMDb*. June 9, 2020. https://www.imdb.com/title/tt1386741/?ref_=fn_al_tt_1. Lefebvre, Martin. 2011. 'On Landscape in Narrative Cinema.' *Canadian Journal of Film Studies* 20.1: 61–78.
Leitch, Thomas. 2002. *Crime Films*. Cambridge: Cambridge University Press.
Losada, Matt. 2018. *The Projected Nation: Argentine Cinema and the Social Margins*. Albany: State University of New York Press.
Massumi, Brian. 1995. 'The Autonomy of Affect.' *Cultural Critique* 31: 83–109.
Massumi, Brian. 2010. 'The Future Birth of the Affective Fact: The Political Ontology of Threat.' In *Digital and Other Virtualities*, 79–92. Edited by Anthony Bryant and Griselda Pollock. New York: Bloomsbury.
Piñeyro, Marcelo, dir. *Las viudas de los jueves*. 2009; Argentina: Tornasol Films, 2010. DVD.
Risner, Jonathan. 2016. 'How I Learned to Stop Worrying and Grudgingly Accept Product Placement: Nicolás López, Chilewood and a Criteria for a Neoliberal Cinema.' *Journal of Latin American Cultural Studies* 25.4: 597–612.
Rocha, Carolina. 2012. *Masculinities in Contemporary Argentine Popular Cinema*. New York: Palgrave Macmillan.
Rubin, Peter. 2018. 'Genre, Genre Everywhere: the Netflix Effect Spreads.' *Wired Magazine*. 25 July. <https://www.wired.com/story/hulu-netflix-amazon-sci-fi-streaming/>
Sánchez Prado, Ignacio. 2014. 'Regimes of Affect: Love and Class in Mexican Neoliberal Cinema.' *Journal of Popular Romance Studies* 4.1: 1–19.
Sandberg, Claudia. 2018. 'Contemporary Latin American Cinema and Resistance to Neoliberalism: Mapping the Field.' In *Contemporary Latin American Cinema: Resisting Neoliberalism?*, 1–23. Edited by Claudia Sandberg and Carolina Rocha. Cham: Palgrave Macmillan.
Snider, Zachary. 2016. 'The Cognitive Psychological Effects of Binge-Watching.' In *The Netflix Effect: Technology and Entertainment in the 21st Century*, 117–128. Edited by Kevin McDonald and Daniel Smith-Rowsey. New York: Bloomsbury.
Sommer, Doris. 1991. *Foundational Fictions: The National Romances of Latin America*. Berkeley: University of California Press.
Spencer, Douglas. 2016. *The Architecture of Neoliberalism: How Contemporary Architecture Became an Instrument of Control and Compliance*. New York: Bloomsbury Academic.
Svampa, Maristella. 2001. *Los que ganaron. La vida en los countries y barrios privados*. Buenos Aires: Editorial Biblos.
Thompson, Kristen Moana. 2007. *Crime Films: Investigating the Scene*, London: Wallflower.
Venkatesh, Vinodh. 2016. *New Maricón Cinema: Outing Latin American Film*. Austin: University of Texas Press.
Williams, Linda. 1991. 'Film Bodies: Gender, Genre, and Excess.' *Film Quarterly* Summer: 2–13.
Žižek, Slavoj. 2008. *The Sublime Object of Ideology*. New York: Verso.

13. ENSEMBLE OF EXPERTS: *RELENTLESS* AS 'NIGERIAN NOIR'

Connor Ryan

Before we see anything, we hear the ripping cough of an electric generator as it leaps into action. In a flash, the iconic National Arts Theatre stands illuminated against the night sky left pitch black by a chronic power outage. The generator's whir dissolves into the zipping two-stroke engine of an *okada* motorcycle taxi, anticipating the visual dissolve that, moments after, provides the image. Its driver, lit by the headlights, opens up the throttle and weaves away through dense Lagos traffic. The sound of laboured breathing bridges the series of shots before we see its source; a man walks toward the camera with the limp body of a woman in his arms. The identity of these characters is withheld while the disjunctive editing skips across time and space, in effect, refusing to ground viewers. These shots comprise the opening sequence of Andy Amadi Okoroafor's *Relentless* (2010). We struggle to gain our bearings, and in this specific sense, the sequence makes full use of the darkness that regularly engulfs Lagos given its faltering electrical grid, while the soundtrack lends the aura of a bustling city.

Relentless stands out as an example of growing diversification in Nollywood, and the rise of a so-called New Nollywood that seeks to break into the vetting institutions and distribution circuits of 'global' cinema, to meet what industry insiders imagine to be 'global standards'.[1] Some New Nollywood filmmakers, in a strategy meant to garner recognition, have consciously adopted longstanding genre conventions as a token of cinematic expertise and fluency that this chapter examines as a practice of transnationalism. Notably, this chapter adopts a transnational framework to denote the scale of industry practices that operate 'above the level of the national but below the level of the global' (Durovicova and Newman 2010), while it also deploys the term 'global' to capture the way that word has come to broadly connote 'the social relations that selectively constitute global society' and *crucially*, 'the statuses and ranks that it comprises' (Ferguson 2006). This distinction has bearing, also, on matters of representation as the evolution of New Nollywood genre films in turn modulates the representation of Lagos, presenting a city with a reputation for insecurity and crime through the lens of transnational genre frameworks that can generate global legibility (Subirós 2001, Agbola 1997). This chapter will discuss how *Relentless* remakes the cityscape of Lagos into a noir dystopia, stylised after other noir and neo-noir cityscapes around the world, and thereby *produces* Lagos *as* such a place. Even as the film draws upon the transnational circulation of genre to create its intertextual urban assemblage – that is, to render Lagos 'noir' – *Relentless* also adopts film noir's signature skepticism and dissatisfaction with the modern world, a widely shared structure of feeling that accounts, in part, for the genre's broad appeal.

In keeping with noir's affinity for gritty urban settings, Okoroafor makes inventive use of the city's chronic power outages, congested traffic, and generalised condition of scarcity to offer Lagos up not as a shining metropolis, but rather a crossroads of globalisation's malcontents. However, I argue that this transnational intertextuality reveals less about contemporary Lagos than it betrays about structural shifts within the Lagos-based screen media industry, and the intense competition among media professionals, who take up transnational genres in order to differentiate their work from hundreds of other releases made in local genres. The attentive mobilisation of noir and neo-noir visual styles, character types, narrative scenarios, and affective registers serves to signal – to audiences and other industry members – the filmmaker's cinematic expertise, especially in an industry where shifts in training, technology and taste place such knowledge and skills in high demand.

Ensemble of Expertise

It is crucial that representations of crime in Lagos are understood against the backdrop of structural changes in the screen media industry, rather than social or historical circumstances within city. In 2007, Nollywood witnessed a distribution crisis that laid bare the constraints of the industry's characteristic informality in finance, labour and distribution. Since then, Lagos-based production and distribution networks have undergone structural transformation, most notably with the development of new distribution venues, revenue streams, and production norms (Ezepue 2020, Haynes 2018, Jedlowski 2017, Miller 2016, Adejunmobi 2011). One upshot has been the appearance each year of handfuls of top-of-the-line films characterised by larger budgets, higher production values, 90-minute runtimes, and windowed releases in regional multiplex cinemas and on video streaming services – but *not* in local video markets, notably. The term New Nollywood has come to refer to those within the industry working in this mode. At the same time, mainstream Nollywood continues to successfully combine small sums of capital, personal relationships between producers, talent and distributors, and marketplace networks of informal commerce, and I would strongly emphasise that these video films remain the vast majority of what is viewed by regional audiences. However, alongside the mainstream filmmakers have appeared various newcomers with film school training, access to formal finance, a studious familiarity with the stylistic trends of cinema elsewhere, and quite a different vision for Nigerian screen media. In fact, Ezinne Ezepue asks aloud whether these structural transformations should be welcomed as processes of 'professionalization', or regarded as effectively the incipient 'gentrification' of the industry (Ezepue 2020, 2).

One trend among this new group of films has been an increased focus on Lagos, which is often depict as the centre of the nation's rising middle class. Some New Nollywood films showcase commodities, technologies and lifestyles oriented around the experience of connectivity, mobility, and contemporaneity with global consumer culture, while an expanded repertoire of film styles now includes transnationally recognisable genres such as romantic comedies, psychological thrillers, police procedurals, and films noir. Andy Amadi Okoroafor's crime film *Relentless* represents an early example of the performance of cinematic expertise through studious observation of transnational genre conventions. Viewed as a production practice, I contend that *Relentless*'s 'noir' genre aesthetic illustrates the efforts of Lagos-based media professionals to distinguish their work from the countless releases in Nollywood's over-saturated video film market, especially as formal training, sophisticated technique, and extroverted taste increasingly become the markers with which some filmmakers position themselves alongside but apart from mainstream Nollywood. In other words, a filmmaker can employ genre to demonstrate expertise, where expertise consists of deep familiarity with and the skills to adapt transnational genres.

This approach connects the interpretation of genre films to the film industries and the media professionals that produce them. The trends in New Nollywood outlined above point to the formation, within Nigerian screen media, of what Aihwa Ong calls an 'ecology of expertise' wherein the entrepreneurial ethos of neoliberalism drives the formation of transnational networks of 'professionals' who are courted by governments and corporate management intent upon accruing advantage within the so-called knowledge economy. Ong sources her 'ecological' vocabulary from the business sphere's own euphemistic jargon, but quite rightly anchors its meaning in the critical theory of Gilles Deleuze and Felix Guattari, and specifically tethers it to the notion of assemblage, or 'a contingent ensemble of diverse practices and things that', in Ong's gloss, 'is divided along the axes of territoriality and deterritorialization' (Ong 2005: 338). With Singapore's information technology industry as case study, Ong describes corporate and government initiatives to attract expert professionals, but more importantly to foster an *ecology* of expertise, or the 'ecological conditions of intense mobility and interactivity' thought to engender creativity (Ibid.: 339). This mode of neoliberal governance, or management, 'depends on novel combinations of mobile knowledge and actors connected to diverse sites and labors' (Ibid.: 339), and effectively aims to harness the kinetic creativity of professional labour assemblages to generate advantage and value. Given that screen media industries are increasingly organised around flexible assemblages of finance, infrastructure and human resources, wherein mobility, interactivity and specialisation are believed to drive creativity (Curtin and Sanson 2016), we might speak more pointedly of an ecology of media expertise.

Of course, the production practices recognised as signs of expertise in each industry are historically and materially contingent, as much as they also depend on the discursive 'boundary-work' with which media professionals in specific industries assert 'the criteria of legitimate membership and professional standards' (Ganti 2012: 9). Tejaswini Ganti argues, for instance, that some Hindi filmmakers adopt 'sentiments of disdain' to disparagingly characterise the production and aesthetic norms of the wider industry and 'practices of distinction' that signal their unique departure from convention (Ibid.: 10). Such practices of distinction, which include strict adherence – without improvisation – to a bound script, selective casting, and the conspicuous use of technology not prevalent in the industry, perhaps matter most within screen media industries where relatively low barriers for participation – in terms of finance, technology, and training – create high levels of output and therefore tremendous competition between releases, and indeed, Nollywood is such a place.

In terms of training, two national institutions stand out: the Nigerian Television Authority (NTA) and the Nigerian Film Institute (NFI). Historically speaking, the NTA has been much more influential in talent development, as the first generation of Nollywood screenwriters, producers and directors, whose work inaugurated the video film 'boom' of the 1990s, by and large cut their teeth in television production (Haynes 2016, Adesanya 1999). This fact, alongside the prevalence, on local channels, of inexpensively licensed foreign soap operas and telenovelas, partially explains the garrulous performances, elastic storylines, and melodramatic mode of Nollywood video films, several qualities among a longer list of perceived shortcomings that critics invoke to distance Nollywood from comparison to 'cinema' and the aesthetic, intellectual, and political seriousness the term is thought to connote. However, in the past decade, several NFI alumni, including Yinka Edward, Kenneth Gyang, and Daniel Oriahi, have brought more markedly 'cinematic' visual and narrative technique to their filmmaking. Moreover, the New York Film Academy has hosted workshops in Lagos, and also trained a number of New Nollywood figures, the most successful of which is surely Kunle Afolayan. Others, such as Emamode Edosio, Abba Makama and Dare Olaitan schooled at film programmes in universities in the United States. Fortunately, the films released by this new generation demonstrate a wide array of visual and narrative styles, which unsettles easy conclusions about the overbearing influence of formal training on local film aesthetics. More importantly, the filmmakers named above are, by and large, based in Lagos where such expertise can insert itself into the city's wider media milieu of facilities, equipment, and technicians, as well as corporate distributors, such as EbonyLifeTV, FilmOne, IrokoTV, and Netflix.

Although not a film school graduate, Okoroafor's experience prior to the release of *Relentless* centred around the visual arts and design, including work in print media, editing and releasing the biannual *Clam Magazine* through his creative studio by the same name. His profile at the magazine foregrounds his work in Paris as a photographer and art director of music videos, an exhibition of his photography and video art in Germany, and his selection as a TED Fellow, among other accomplishments. More to the point, the publication's website describes *Clam Magazine* as 'a venue to think about images, develop images, and also to make a living from doing images', and adds: 'We are passionate about images.' In fact, the repeated claim to specialisation in images represents a remarkably consistent through line for Okoroafor's public discussions of his work, as when he quips in interview with *Pan-African Space Station*: 'In my passport is written "Art Director." I'm a creative director, an art director, a filmmaker. I tell people "I do images."' Such invocations of expertise with images represents an example of the boundary-work through which Okoroafor distinguishes himself from other filmmakers producing in Nigeria, as when he explains to the host of *I of Africa* that, 'I don't go directing a Nollywood film, I don't know how to do that. So, I do images: I direct images, I curate images, I exhibit images, I manufacture images.' Perhaps mindful of the large extent to which dialogue drives action in mainstream video films, Okoroafor describes his production practice as centred on image, which not only lends his film the distinction of difference, but also that of prestige, since attention to cinematic image implies expertise in countless other technical dimensions of cinematography that are presumed – incorrectly – to be scarce in Nollywood. It follows that the visual conventions of film noir, with its widely recognised iconography, would appeal to Okoroafor, whose astute observance of genre in *Relentless* represents a performance of cinematic expertise.

New Nollywood and its City

In recent years, the growth of video film production in cities like Accra, Abidjan, Dar es Salaam, Kano, Kinshasa and Lagos has presented one of the most dramatic changes to the way such cities are represented on screen. For instance, historically, Lagos drew together the transnational flows of commodities and technologies that made possible Nollywood's rise in the early 1990s, and for its part, Nollywood engendered a new aesthetic sphere of images and stories about the city where the collective imagination could grapple with life in Lagos (Haynes 2007, Adesokan 2004, Okome 2003, Oha 2001). Today this relationship remains true for the majority of the industry and the mainstream video films it produces about Lagos, but New Nollywood filmmakers are pursuing an aesthetic shift in visual, narrative and genre conventions. For instance, the depiction of Lagos in recent romantic comedies tends to focus upon lifestyle brands, luxury items, technology, travel and other trappings of elite participation in global consumer culture, while the adaptation of transnational film genres, such as the romantic comedy, itself exemplifies that very same participation. As a result, the representational city that emerges in these films corresponds with the image that the Lagos elite hold of themselves. Curiously, although Okoroafor's *Relentless* was one of the first in this new generation of films, it refuses to embrace the same vision of Lagos as a city of promise in a world of opportunity and dwells instead on the promises left unfulfilled by globalisation.

Marked by crime, crooked politics, and the looming shadow of past wars, the Lagos of Okoroafor's *Relentless* offers plenty of reasons for cynicism and discontent. The narrative centres on Obi, the head of a private security company, and Honey, a sex worker living at the margins of society, two characters connected by little else than the experience of losing a loved one, as we later learn. When their lives collide by chance, Obi's attempt to find Honey's disappeared friend, Stella, serves to exorcise the haunting memory of the death, years prior, of his lover Blessing, who he had failed to protect. Each character's efforts to uncover the truth of what befell Stella lead deeper into the Lagos underground, the dangers of which do not daunt Honey, but test whether Obi can assure her safety. Meanwhile, Obi's security firm is contracted to protect Anaki, an infamous politician campaigning for Governor of Lagos, whose rise to power connects obliquely to Obi's own deceased lover, and who increasingly appears implicated in the disappearance of Stella. The narrative's conclusion hinges on whether Anaki will grab power in the election, whether Obi will exact revenge and thereby break his oath to protect, and whether Honey can discover how – and *if* – Stella disappeared from Lagos.

The opening sequence plunges the viewer into the dangers and darkness of the city streets at night, and presents us with that ominous image of Obi holding Honey's limp body in his arms. The montage leaves the temporal sequence of events ambiguous. We do not know what brings the two main characters out into the night, whether it is Honey's dead body in Obi's arms, much less whether this is the beginning or the end of the narrative. Before the sequence can establish its bearings spatially and psychologically, a flashback leaps unexpectedly in time and space to Sierra Leone where Obi, a Nigerian soldier deployed with the UN peacekeeping force during the civil war there, discovers the woman he loves, Blessing, attacked in a raid that has left her mortally wounded. Dismayed at his failure to keep her safe, and by extension to fulfill his mission to protect civilians, Obi breaks down emotionally. With a trembling hand, Obi points the barrel of his gun toward the camera and fires, killing Blessing in an act that, although intended as mercy, underscores the gruesome contradictions with which the film wishes to grapple.

In one sense, the film's conscription of noir techniques to depict Lagos should come as no surprise, given the genre's transnational pedigree. In his influential essay, 'Global Noir', for instance, David Desser traces the transnational circulation of the genre from so-called 'historical' noir to the rise of neo-noir in the 1990s, noting the transnational intertextuality the genre has enjoyed along the way (Dresser 2003: 525). We can infer from Dresser's account that the production, circulation and consumption of film noir has historically taken place in multiple sites and across national borders. Moreover, this 'rich culture of exchange and translation' that surrounds the genre has made film noir, as Jennifer Fay and Justus Nieland assert, 'one of globalizations most eloquent critics and one its very best examples' (Fay and Nieland 2010: xiv). From this perspective we might say that *Relentless* adds to the genre's transnational appeal while drawing from its particular idiom of cynicism and anxiety, which especially suits film noir to express the misgivings of globalisation's discontents.

Following the opening sequence, the narrative returns to Lagos where Obi has tried to put the war behind him and build a new life. In a double of his role as peacekeeper, he has opened a private security firm named 'Blessing Security', an allusion to the deep longing that orients Obi's character, as well as a reminder of the inevitability of loss that marks the film. Moving forward, the thrust of the narrative is organised around a job, one as lucrative as it is suspicious. Alhaji Anaki, a powerful political leader, contracts Obi's firm to guard his party's mysterious candidate, about whom they must ask no questions. 'So, do we take this job?' Obi's business partner inquires, aware of the risk they run becoming involved with dangerous politicians. Although Anaki cloaks himself in secrecy, rumours abound that the general-turned-politician acquired his wealth and power by siphoning money from the peacekeeping mission in Sierra Leone. 'That man ruined our reputation in Sierra Leone', as one friend informs Obi. 'While we were busy dying in the field, he was busy making his money.' The narrative draws its tension from the mutual mistrust between Anaki and Obi, who is determined to discover and reveal the political boss's criminal entanglements. When he uncovers evidence of Anaki's involvement in ritual murder for political gain, he resolves to investigate and bring down a man well outside the reach of the law.

The dark vision of Lagos goes beyond the common popular skepticism for government and the law that one finds elsewhere in Nollywood. In fact, different shades of Nollywood dramas, including crime dramas, typically indulge in an 'aesthetic of outrage' that aims to reveal private scandal to the public in a manner that recasts abuses of power, crime or other malfeasance as moral infractions (Larkin 2008). By contrast, *Relentless* largely does away with clear moral codes in order to embrace the pessimistic notion that no clear moral code can guide one through Lagos and that to redress wrongdoing comes at a price, sometimes an immoral one. And yet, fascinatingly, this emulation of noir conventions reflects, as I state above, shifts in training, technology, and taste within the industry, rather than the social or historical circumstances of Lagos today.

Anaki's presence at the security firm's offices draws the curiosity of Honey, a sex worker in search of her disappeared companion, Stella, who vanished from an event hosted by powerful political and military officials. The only evidence damning enough to incriminate Anaki is Honey's own testimony, which forces Obi to decide if he can gamble Stella's safety, and ultimately her life. Obi is more willing to press his security agent Bola to submit testimony to the police, but as he objects when the police ask for Honey's statement: 'If I bring that girl here to make a statement, I'm only signing her death sentence, and I can't do that.' To which the inspector responds, 'What about Bola? He is a lesser being, so you can sacrifice him?' The police inspector's powerlessness to take action against Anaki is not merely as an example of the weakness of the State, but rather reveals the undecidable dilemma of justice in the city. The element of individual struggle in the face of dysfunctional civil institutions fits mainstream Nollywood crime dramas, but in those films individual action not only *can* bring about justice; often it is the *only* reliable recourse. By contrast, *Relenteless* offers no such guarantee. To seek protection under the law, one inevitably exposes oneself to unpredictable consequences.

Amidst the film's ubiquitous skepticism for individual self-determination or agency in the face of a larger societal malaise, an unexpected sympathy develops between Obi and Honey, who have both experienced loss, isolation and a disconnect with life in the megacity. Each character's search comes to take on existential proportions. Obi's fight to expose Anaki and Honey's unwavering determination to find Stella converge when they discover evidence suggesting Stella was Anaki's victim. Obi redoubles his efforts exposing himself to more danger in order to protect Honey from Anaki's retribution and to assuage his deep-seated guilt for his past failure to protect Blessing. The narrative tone remains invariably somber throughout and never permits Obi to make himself vulnerable by articulating his desire for Honey, even to himself, while Honey remains enthralled, almost compulsively, by the morbid fate of her friend.

These various searches do not merely organise the crisscrossing paths of the film's subplots. The motif of the search also functions as a symptom of the profound rootlessness Obi, Honey and other characters experience in the megacity. The symptom registers at the visual level in the abundant shots of street traffic and the high frequency of kinetic following shots, both of which give the film a sense of being always in motion. As a result, the spaces at the foreground of the city are interstitial or connective spaces, not sedentary, iconic, or centripetal locations that might lend some sense of grounding and spatial orientation. Images of streets and alleys, as well as Lagos's extensive network of bridges and freeways, provide the backdrop for the film's many transitional shots, which appear in nearly equal proportion to scenes that move the narrative forward. The liberal use of dissolves to edit together the various images of urban transit during transitional sequences lends itself to a fluid, or even wishy-washy, sense of spatial orientation. In some edits, as many as three images overlap and blur the boundaries of movement and action. The black shadows of the city at night serves as the shared background that subtends the flickering streetlights, the lens flares from headlights, and the actions of characters shot in low-key lighting. Although the cinematography in these transitional sequences works to isolate characters and allude to their individual psychic struggles, it also empties public space of the innumerable street-level activities that keep people busy and the city bustling even after sundown. In this sense, such transitions stitch together an ambitious, but fragmented, storyline that enhances the rootlessness – and restlessness – integral to the film's diegesis. Whether removed from or thrust directly into the bustle of people, movement, and commerce in the streets of Lagos, the film carefully establishes a parallel between narrative structure and spatial structure, between narration and movement in the city.

In fact, many of the film's narrative threads follow similar narrative organisation that reverses typical linearity. While the narrative moves ahead only by looking back, as we learn more about the various characters' backstories, their inevitable end becomes clear. The narrative follows a pattern of concealment and revelation, whereby the story is animated by the drive to dispel the initial mystery that clouds all social relationships. As Obi warns Honey once the two grow more intimate, 'The less I know the better. I just might judge you.' In other words, the plot seeks to satisfy both the obligation to reveal wrongdoings and the desire to forge honest emotional connections, although on both fronts the city throws up its obstacles.

Although *Relentless* remains continually in transit, these movements pull the characters in many directions at once spatially, temporally, and psychologically. While Honey speaks of securing enough money to one day get out of Lagos – to go anywhere but Lagos really – Obi is drawn far north to Kaduna

State in search of his mother's gravesite. The fact that the North appears at all in the film is unusual, especially given the relative silence in mainstream Nollywood surrounding the divide – linguistic, cultural, religious, ethnic, political – between North and South. As the narrative travels briefly to the country's far North, the camera captures the dramatic openness and brightness of space in the countryside. Obi kneels at his mother's grave as an aunt traces with a gesture the boundary of Obi's inherited land – from one nondescript palm tree to another and back. Our eye follows the gesture outward into empty space where boundaries of the family's land, which double for the boundaries delineating a place of autochthony, social belonging, and familial history, remain illegible to the camera. Moreover, Obi himself seems to have lost the ability to read the terrain. The rural landscape expresses no familiarity or belonging, leaving us with the sense that home has lost its meaning for Obi, that his uprooting after years of war and life in Lagos has become totalising. He returns to the city and resumes his wanderings alongside Honey, each in search of a person lost to violence, a person who represents and promises to fulfill their longing for stability and domestic happiness. The counterpart to Obi and Honey's errancy is stability, of which the film offers plenty, even if only as flashbacks and fantasies about past lives, fleeting trips to the family village, or dreams of elsewhere. In other words, the extent to which dysfunction, injustice, and loss thoroughly encompass Lagos depends, paradoxically, on the peace and happiness for which Obi, Honey and others long, but which they will never attain because it is located *elsewhere*, physically and metaphysically speaking. The good life is imagined as somehow always elsewhere.

This incessant displacement resembles, furthermore, the film's displacement of the intimate sentiments and private psychic conflicts of its characters, such that the city comes to embody outwardly the inner discontent of its inhabitants. In this pessimistic social world, the inability to properly mourn, the losses that fester, do not simply reproduce the hardboiled stoicism or rugged individualism of historical American noir. Instead, it seems more compelling to imagine the heightened sentimentalism, and at times the overwrought performance of emotion, as Okoroafor's borrowing from the dominant conventions of mainstream Nollywood dramas. In other words, the projection onto the cityscape of various strong emotional states associated with loss and grief represents one manifestation of the local translation of a transnational film genre.

Geopolitical Imaginary of a Nollywood Film Noir

The distinctly transnational intertextuality of New Nollywood presents a key characteristic that distinguishes these from the many genres and cycles that have long sustained Nollywood and, therefore, have a particular genealogy all their own. Some of the industry's earliest blockbusters, for example, included crime films set in Lagos. The earliest video films depicted Lagos through an admixture of urban legend lifted from newspapers and the local rumour mill and melodramatic style adopted from television and imported soap operas. In crime films of this period, the dark and anxious mise en scène resulted from location shooting in Lagos and, as an aesthetic feature, could be understood as almost a direct reflection of the way the city's darkness impinged upon daily life. As Jonathan Haynes insightfully notes, the city imposes itself on the images Nollywood produces as much as the reverse is also true (Haynes 2007: 133). None of these early films, however, adopted the conventions and iconographic visual style that makes Okoroafor's *Relentless* distinctively noir and, by extension, a display of genre and cinematographic expertise.

Previous cycles of crime films drew their urgency from highly localised events, sometimes even sourcing stories from newspaper headlines or popular rumors. These cycles continue to trade in immediacy because it is stories of proximate experience that resonate with audiences for whom the meaning and appeal of the narrative will be immediately recognisable (Adejunmobi 2010). By contrast, *Relentless* wields noir stylistics in a reflexive manner that seems intended to distance the film from the cycles of local crime films as much as to draw it closer to the film noir of transnational circulation. This is not to say that the film's character types and local experiences would be unrecognisable to Nigerian audiences, but primarily this mobilisation of genre permits a film to stand out in an oversaturated market where a filmmaker must have some strategy in place to differentiate his film from the deluge of new titles. On the other hand, the film's noir vocabulary allows it to speak to audiences abroad who are perhaps already primed to feel weary of an African city as large and storied as Lagos. In this sense, we might say *Relentless* supports an extroverted geopolitical imaginary, especially insofar as the film imagines Lagos within a larger constellation of geopolitical references outside itself.

Allusions throughout the film to major regional events serve something like historical landmarks even as they help mark out the film's geopolitical imaginary, which coalesces around events like Nigeria's deeply fraught civil war, its military involvement in Liberia, the MEND insurgency in the nation's oil-producing Niger Delta region, as well as Sani Abacha's execution of author and environmental activist Ken Saro-Wiwa, a tragedy that left Nigeria an international pariah and lead to its expulsion from the Commonwealth of Nations. As mentioned above, Nigeria's peacekeeping role during the Sierra Leonean civil war provides the founding trauma upon which Obi's character is constructed, while intermittent flashbacks to his time with Blessing in Freetown provide a spatial and temporal counterpoint and frame for the narrative events in Lagos.

Conversely, the generalised sense of disquiet that settles over Lagos finds its point of condensation in the space of the port. In a broader sense, what I call the film's geopolitical imaginary, or how the film imagines the city's place within the world, turns on the port. This is fitting enough given Lagos's distinctive location on the lagoon after which it is named, its historic significance as a colonial entrepot connecting the hinterland and metropole, and its contemporary role as one of West Africa's largest ports, the point through which commodities from around the world pass before unloading, repackaging and distribution, often by petty traders, to marketplaces within the wider region (Diawara 1998). Its historical role as the crossroads of regional transnational trade has indelibly shaped Lagos's identity and its imagined relationship to the world at large. As Onookome Okome writes, '[Lagos] is anxious about its own status in the global tide of goods and services and other kinds of exchange, and its citizens are insecure and anxious of their position within it' (Okome 2003: 71). Okoroafor condenses this apprehensive environment into the architectural symbolism of Apapa Port, across the lagoon from downtown Lagos, as the physical site of the countless abstract processes that comprise globalisation. In this sense, the symbolism offers the pleasurable fantasy of control and comprehension through this localised condensation of the dispersed, worldwide circulation of goods and wealth.

In a cinematographic phrasing reminiscent of the opening sequence, we hear the foghorn of cargo vessel before we see the ship entering the port. The camera dissolve into a blurry shot of the port's floodlights and then slowly pulls the focus until a clear image appears, simulating the protagonist's bleary-eyed gaze as he looks out across the lagoon. Obi casts a look across the lagoon and the camera supplies the visuals of cranes dipping to collect cargo as shipping vessels glide across the frame casting reflections off the dark water. With this activity droning on in the background, Obi confronts Anaki about suspicious blood stains he discovers at the 'shrine' where the politician and candidate are known to conduct ritual sacrifices. 'What is this?' Obi demands, holding out a fistful of blood-soaked sand. 'Security . . .' Anaki retorts, pausing a beat, 'is your business young man. The rest is beyond you, understand?' Here, Okoroafor's decision at this point to incorporate a so-called blood money ritual in the narrative and to locate the 'shrine' at which it occurs along the shore within an earshot of the port generates associations between the incessant activity of the port, the ceaseless 'flows' of globalisation, and a popular expression of misgivings about ill-founded wealth and power.[2] However, the creative decision also illustrates a disconnect with mainstream video film representations of occult rituals, which are staged almost invariably outside public view, within a secret chamber of some large mansion, for instance, or in room ostentatiously adorned with red, black and white markings, the colours that signify occult practice in mainstream Nollywood's own cinematic iconography. The suggestion of human sacrifice slips between these different generic registers, implying another local translation of noir conventions. And suitably so, since stories of human sacrifice that circulate in Lagos, including Nollywood retellings of such stories, are appealing because they provide explanations to phenomenon like globalisation.

The spectacle of the sacrifice is withheld, but the notion itself articulates the economy of power at work here and speaks to the asymmetrical costs and benefits that globalisation has demanded of and provided to the city's elites and its poorest citizens. However, the allusion to money ritual rumours is here more compelling understood as an intertextual reference to Nollywood, a nod to the mainstream's sensationalism, and *not* a direct example of that sensational popular discourse itself. This demands a second-order interpretation of the film's intertextual genre coordinates, in order to avoid overstating a first-order connection to actual popular anxieties. Nonetheless, on these terms the text remains available for close interpretation. The ritual trope in *Relentless* calls to mind a comparison between various values: the value of political power, financial value, and inherent human value. If we extend the reading further, the sacrifice of a human body, with references to the blood spilt in the sand, evoke the imagery of corporeality and the body's activities or labour. The physical connotations of human labour and of accumulation derived from obvious forms of labour all stand in contrast to the abstract financial and commodity flows transpiring at the port. To press even deeper into the symbolism possible here, we might recall the original 'flow' of capitalism that embedded Lagos within *the* constitutive transnational network of Atlantic modernity, namely the trans-Atlantic slave trade.

After he learns of Honey's death, Obi returns to the port to inspect yet again the site of the murder, perhaps hoping still for some shred of evidence to tip the scales against Anaki. The camera pans across the lagoon at night while the foghorns of immense cargo ships sound and the magnesium/sulfuric burn of floodlights illuminates the unloading of shipping containers, and the incessant flow of commodities into the region through this point seems to always, in the background, to carry on slowly but steadily. Obi meets a friend and fellow veteran who, on request, produces a gun from his car's dashboard, and as the two look out over the lagoon the camera again scans the horizon of cranes, floodlights, stacked shipping containers, fuel silos, and razor-wire fencing, an anxious visual landscape of globalisation.

Some Nollywood dramas redirect popular anxieties about 'flounder[ing] in the whirlpool of global tides' into displaced symptoms, such as urban legends, narrative intervention by supernatural forces, or rumours concerning so-called blood money rituals (Okome 2003: 74). By contrast, *Relentless* stokes rather than redirects popular anxieties and even mobilises the Nollywood trope of the blood money ritual, a particularly local, vernacular expression of misgivings about the production and accumulation of wealth, only to adapt it to satisfy the noir play with violence and crime, trust and betrayal, individual struggle within a generalised condition of vulnerability (Fay and Nieland 2010: 127–131).

Conclusion

Debates on genre sometimes centre around identifying, demarcating, and curating what belongs within a particular genre, which can promote the notion of genre as a regulating frame, a controlling category that helps make sense of otherwise arbitrary comparisons of cinema around the world. Another approach supposes that, on the contrary, genre grows as it circulates globally and that genre cycles always entail a repetition with additions. But from this perspective, we might ask what remains constant as genre circulation and changes. We must continually be reminded that the vast majority of Nollywood's production and distribution continues to thrive on the combination of small capital investments, short windows of production and distribution, the informal commercial networks of local marketplaces, and personal relationships of trust. The outsized attention that New Nollywood enjoys speaks more to the efficacy of corporate distributors' marketing and promotions than the actual share of the Nigerian audience with access and preference for these films; it should not be mistaken to represent the mainstream of the Nigerian screen media industry. With this in mind, I tend to agree with Fay and Nieland, who contend that the isomorphic element, the true point of comparison we can trace across national boundaries and historical periods, is the relationship to local conditions that noir supports (2010: xii). However, the 'local' that *Relentless* and other New Nollywood crime films speak to is not the historical circumstances of Lagos today, but rather specific transformations of the Lagos-based screen media industry that respond to new technologies of production and distribution, a widened range of tastes among Nollywood's evolving audiences, the growing importance of formal training for media professionals, and the boundary-work required to distinguish a filmmaker's work from the wider industry. Genre as a production practice represents one such form of boundary work, specifically a performance of aesthetic and specifically 'cinematic' expertise.

Notes

1. While the focus of this chapter is genre as a transnational practice, I employ the term global here, and elsewhere, as the term most often adopted by the filmmakers, producers, and distributors that I speak with in Lagos. In this usage the term does not simply denote a geographic scale, but more connotes an aspired to status within the world.
2. For a brilliant discussion of stories of supernatural phenomenon, such as blood money rituals, and their connection to the impact of neoliberal capitalism on everyday life in Africa, see Jean Comaroff and John Comaroff. 2000. 'Millennial Capitalism: First Thoughts on a Second Coming', *Public Culture* 12.2 (Spring): 291–343.

Works Cited

Adejunmobi, Moradewun. 2001. 'Nollywood, Globalization, and Regional Media Corporations in Africa.' *Popular Communication* 9.2: 67–78.

Adejunmobi, Moradewun. 2010. 'Charting Nollywood's Appeal Locally and Globally.' *African Literature Today* 28: 106–121.

Adesokan, Akin. 2004. 'Loud in Lagos: Nollywood Videos.' *Wasafiri* 19: 45–49.

Agbola, Tunde. 1997. *The Architecture of Fear: Urban Design and Construction Response to Urban Violence in Lagos, Nigeria*. Ibadan: French Institute for Research in Africa.

Comaroff, Jean and John L. Comaroff. 2000. 'Millennial Capitalism: First Thoughts on a Second Coming.' *Public Culture* 12.2: 291–343.

Curtin, Michael. 2003. 'Media Capital: Toward the Study of Spatial Flows.' *International Journal of Cultural Studies* 6.2: 202–228.

Curtin, Michael. 2003. 'Comparing Media Capitals: Hong Kong and Mumbai.' 2010. *Global Media and Communication* 6.3: 263–270.

Curtin, Michael and Kevin Sanson, eds. 2016. *Precarious Creativity: Global Media, Local Labor*. Berkeley: University of California Press.

Desser, David, 2012. 'Global Noir: Genre Film in the age of Transnationalism.' In *Film Genre Reader IV*, ed. Barry Keith Grant, 628–648. Austin: University of Texas Press.

Diarwara, Manthia. 1998. 'Toward a Regional Imaginary in Africa.' In *The Cultures of Globalization*. Edited by Fredric Jameson and Masao Miyoshi, 103–124. Durham, NC: Duke University Press.

Durovicova, Natasha and Kathleen Newman, eds. 2010. *World Cinemas, Transnational Perspectives*. New York: Routledge on behalf of American Film Institute.

Ezepue, Ezinne M. 2020. 'The New Nollywood: Professionalization or Gentrification of a Cultural Industry.' *SAGE Open* (July–September): 1–10.

Fay, Jennifer and Justus Nieland. 2010. *Film Noir: Hard-boiled Modernity and the Cultures of Globalization*. New York: Routledge.

Ferguson, James. 2006. *Global Shadows: Africa in the Neoliberal World Order*. Durham, NC: Duke University Press.

Ganti, Tejaswini. 2012. 'Sentiments of Disdain and Practices of Distinction: Boundary-Work, Subjectivity and Value in the Hindi Film Industry.' *Anthropological Quarterly* 85.1: 5–44.

Haynes, Jonathan. 2007. 'Nollywood in Lagos, Lagos in Nollywood Films.' *Africa Today* 54.2: 130–150.

Haynes, Jonathan. 2016. *Nollywood: The Creation of Nigerian Film Genres*. Chicago: University of Chicago Press.

Haynes, Jonathan. 2018. 'Keeping Up: The Corporatization of Nollywood's Economy and Paradigms for Studying African Screen Media.' *Africa Today* 64.4: 2–29.

Jedlowski, Alessandro. 2017. 'African Media and the Corporate Takeover: Video Film Circulation in the Age of Neoliberal Transformations.' *African Affairs* 116.465: 671–691.

Larkin, Brian. 2008. *Signal and Noise: Media, Infrastructure, and Urban Culture in Nigeria*. Durham, NC: Duke University Press.

Miller, Jade. *Nollywood Central*. London: Palgrave on behalf of British Film Institute, 2016.

Oha, Obododimma. 2001. 'The Visual Rhetoric of the Ambivalent City in Nigerian Video Films.' In *Cinema and the City*. Edited by Mark Shiel and Tony Fitzmaurice, 195–205. Oxford: Blackwell.

Okome, Onookome. 1997. 'Loud in Lagos.' *Glendora: African Quarterly of the Arts* 2.1: 75–83.

Okome, Onookome. 2003. 'Writing the Anxious City: Images of Lagos in Nigerian Home Video Films.' *Black Renaissance* 5.2 (Summer): 65–75.

Okoroafor, Andy Amadi, dir. *Relentless*. 2010. Nigeria/Germany/France: Clam Films.

Ong, Aihwa. 2005. 'Ecologies of Expertise: Assembling Flows, Managing Citizenship.' In *Global Assemblages: Technology, Politics, and Ethics as Anthropological Problems*. Edited by Aihwa Ong and Stephen Collier, 337–353. Oxford: Blackwell.

Robinson, Jennifer. 2010. 'Living in Dystopia: Past, Present, and Future in Contemporary African Cities.' In *Noir Urbanisms: Dystopic Images of the Modern City*, 218–240. Edited by Gyan Prakash. Princeton: Princeton University Press.

Simone, AbdouMaliq. 2010. *City Life from Jakarta to Dakar: Movement at the Crossroads*. New York: Routledge.

Simone, AbdouMaliq. 2004. *For the City Yet to Come: Changing African Life in Four Cities*. Durham, NC: Duke University Press.

Subirós, Pep. 2001. 'Lagos: Surviving Hell.' In *Africas: the Artist and the City*, 34–45. Edited by Pep Subirós. Barcelona: Centre de Cultura Contemporánia de Barcelona

POSTSCRIPT
DESIRES FOR TRANSIT AND MOBILE
GENEALOGIES OF POPULAR CINEMA

Aleksander Sedzielarz and Sarah Delahousse

The studies in *Transnational Crime Cinema* demonstrate that crime films are a primary discursive site in which cinema reflects upon the role of cinema in social transformation: moments in which film becomes an agent active in social, political and economic structures. Chapters in this volume spotlight crime as cinema's channeling of, and challenge to, the established orders of morality that lie beyond the terms of visual representation. With a plurality of aesthetic, stylistic and narrative markers, crime in cinema appears through a matrix of evolving genres, and genre appears in crime films as a key register in cinema's engagement with the processes of its own social discursivity – making this engagement marked and legible. Contributors to this collection each analyse productions of local and national cinema industries across the world in which crime is the feature attraction to bring into view the transnationality of political and economic processes that shape contemporary social realities. These studies, thus, extend beyond a treatment of crime films that merely maps genre or genre cycles. Taking genealogical approaches to the study of popular genre cinema they open the transformations of social and historical discourse to closer examination. Such an approach combines the analysis of ideological and commodity forms established within (but also at times rupturing) globalised capital that Jonathan Risner identifies in this volume as the 'emotive' and 'affective' (a formulation that contrasts shifting sites of consciousness in body, language and experience with the unconscious or semi-conscious registers of affect).

Establishing sightlines on key cinematic works in which these discourses become active sites in the interrogation of the limits of national ideology and the national imaginary, the conceptual framework of this volume anchors critical concepts of transnationalism in bodily/inscriptive terms, in political terms and in economic terms. The chapters in this collection constitute genealogies of transnational bodies: rendered onscreen (and the bodies of the audience that encounter onscreen bodies in moments of crisis) in, or resisting, processes of linguistic and social inscription (especially as gender is absorbed into conventions of genre); in moments of conscription within economic structures; and in processes that weld politics to individual and collective affect. Studying crime films within a transnational frame exposes discourses on power and domination often subsumed within the normative and prescriptive bounds of the national. While anchored in this tripartite framework of the bodily-linguistic symbolic (transcriptive), the political (transgressive) and the economic (transvalorization), the critical aims of each chapter share in a common vision that the 'trans' in transnational always invokes opposing essentialist responses and, above all, that the transitive prefix is processural. This is to say that the transnational is as much an ongoing site of transit that can be traced through effective history as a desire that propels cultural production – a desire of a mass audience that reflects and inflects the political economy.

Song Hwee Lim inquiries into whether transnationalism is merely 'fashionable academic jargon' or whether it can serve as a dynamic through which film scholars can better understand the prismatic nature of concepts of 'nation, class, gender, sexuality and ethnicity' (2007: 40–41). As Lim discovers in comparing the 'trans' in 'transnational and transgender', 'the prefix "trans," while indexing a crossing of boundaries, can in effect fix the boundaries even more firmly and in an essentialist manner' (Ibid.: 46). Moreover, as Lim describes, the examination of processes of deterritorialisation in critical transnationalism is accompanied by an imperative inquiry into 'what motivates people to cross borders, to become the Other, to want to go beyond and challenge the very definition of boundaries?' (Ibid.: 47) While transnationalism posits an ongoing tension between the national and the popular that often reentrenches nationalisms, this tension also activates popular desires for transformation (and for cinema audiences to experience, feel or witness transformation beyond the limitations of the national).

Just as the 'Introduction' of our book cites the affinity between crime and melodrama, several other supergeneric modes of cinema circulate internationally much like crime films. These include, but are by no means limited to, westerns, horror, and pornography. As of late, westerns have been the focus the fervent enthusiasm of critics attempting to forge new analysis of the transnational (besides the studies mentioned below, notable titles include Stephen Teo's *Eastern Westerns: Film and Genre Outside and Inside Hollywood* and *The*

Post-2000 Film Western: Contexts, Transnationality, Hybridity). It is our hope that *Transnational Crime Cinema* will be the first instance of future investigations into transnationalism through a range of filmic modes that encompass popular genres. In *Transnationalism and Imperialism: Endurance of the Global Western Films* – a study that initiates an innovative direction in analysis of genre and empire – Mayer and Roche state that 'at the heart of a transnational approach to film lies the question of Western imperialism and its cultural and political legacy, which structures global film industries as well as academic film studies.' They ground this assertion in Hardt and Negri's summary of imperialism as 'an extension of sovereignty beyond national boundaries'. (2022: 2).[1] Mayer and Roche suggest that Western film genres engage in a conversation on the 'endurance of imperial and/or colonial histories and cultures in the present' (Ibid.: 3). Becoming a metonym for imperialism-cum-sovereignty, the toponym 'west' loses much of its potency as a term of economic and political analysis in their framing of the connection between popular genres and discourses of power.

According to such terms of analysis, the film western also thereby encompasses the transnational. However, rather than a floating signifier, the 'west' must at the very least signal either a geographically linked concept or a set of ideologies – or, even more potently, some combination of the two – but the book stops short of developing this kind of thesis by conceptually fusing imperialism and film industries (and studies). Instead of a cardinal direction, or a subset of hegemonic nation-states, 'west' becomes a metonym for abuse of sovereign power that can retrofitted and redeployed in any global context. Rather than a critical concept, the 'west' and 'western' double back on their function as genre in the manner of the Bahktinian chronotope in this formulation (essentially, isomorphic with genre) as 'a relation between text and the world – of the model of the world put forward by the text . . . [with] two constitutive elements . . . space and time' (Todorov 1984: 83). In other words, a genre trope endowed with mobility but mystified by critical and historical abstraction. In exploring westerns as encounters of genre with ongoing processes of cultural and political signification, Mayer and Roche's collection presents a compendium that plumbs the political and economic shaping of genre. However, an effective critical notion of the transnational that is not metonymous is not fully established. In expanding the critical concept of crime through the series of transnational genealogies in this book, we see Mayer and Roche's collection and others like it as a foundation and point of departure for more fully uncovering what makes a cinematic mode transnational in modality and mobility.

As described in the 'Introduction' to this volume, our contributors share a commitment to alternatives to genre-based approaches to film history and analysis that instead proceeds from a genealogy of genre and form. In the same spirit, Neil Campbell's *The Rhizomatic West* offers a prismatic concept of the 'west' in cultural productions deemed 'westerns', a concept which 'travels between cultures and "uses" [as] it reveals similarities and differences, cultural overlaps, and misunderstandings, and ... rethink[s] the West transnationally disturbs any idea of homogeneity ... displacing it from the center of American consciousness and replacing it within a wider, global domain' (2008: 78). Instead of taking genre as a map of definitive socio-political features, or reiterating the 'west' as chronotope, Campbell views the boundaries and borders contingently holding together the West as markers of descent in a Foucaultian effective history. Campbell describes the book as 'a mobile genealogy of westness, a cultural discourse constructed through both national and transnational mediations, of roots and routes' (Ibid.: 7). Our volume shares strong affinities with Campbell's critique of the transnational constructedness of generic markers, and studies in the book proceed through scrutiny of the roots and routes of generic discursivity in each transnational social context. Each chapter of *Transnational Crime Cinema* is, thus, a mobile genealogy of crime that aims to uncover cinema's presentation of the urgency of the discursive formations of morality, order and power.

Note

1. Mayer and Roche find overlap in cultural expressions of the sources and effects of imperialism and settler colonialism in representations of power and domination in international westerns and films that resemble US-produced westerns.

Works Cited

Campbell, Neil. 2008. *The Rhizomatic West: Representing the American West in a Transnational, Global, Media Age*. Lincoln, NE: University of Nebraska Press.

Mayer, Hervé and David Roche. 2022. *Transnationalism and Imperialism: Endurance of the Global Western Film*. Bloomington, IN: University of Indiana Press.

Paryż, Marek and John R. Leo. 2015. *The Post-2000 Film Western: Contexts, Transnationality, Hybridity*. London: Palgrave Macmillan.

Teo, Stephen. 2017. *Eastern Westerns: Film and Genre Outside and Inside Hollywood*. London: Routledge.

Todorov, Tzvetan. 1984. *Mikhail Bakhtin: The Dialogical Principle*. Translated by Wlad Godzich. Minneapolis: University of Minnesota Press.

INDEX

Note: *f* indicates figure

Abacha, Sani, 247
Abel, Richard, 13–14, 184–5, 188, 195
Accused/Acusada (Tobal, Gonzalo), 158, 170, 171, 173, 174, 175
Affect Poetics of the New Hollywood: Suspense, Paranoia, and Melancholy (Lehmann, Hauke), 204–5
Agier, Michael, 82
Aguayo, Angela J.
  Documentary Resistance, 212
Ajnabee (Samanta, Shakti), 109
Albania, 125–9
  gjyqe të popullit (the people's trials), 135–6
  Ideological and Cultural Revolution, 126, 128, 129
  revolutionary vigilance films, 128–37
  Sigurimi i Shtetit (Albanian secret police), 130, 131, 132, 133–5
Alfonsín, Raúl, 160, 165

Altered Carbon (Kalogridis, Laeta), 231–2
Altman, Rick, 6, 8
Alton, John, 25–6, 27
Alvaray, Luisela, 225
America, 12–13; *see also* Hollywood
  cowboy girl films, 188–9, 191
  dominance, 232
  female adventure heroines, 183–4, 191, 193–4
  female detectives, 189, 191
  film noir, 24, 63–4, 65
  French films, 195
  frontier, the, 188–9
  highways, 224, 225
  New Woman, 188
  realism, 195
  serial queen heroines, 187–8
'Americanization', 50
Andrew, Dudley, 5–6, 7–8
Andriot, Josette, 185, 191–2*f*, 194, 197
Ángel, El (Ortega, Luis), 231

257

INDEX

Anxiety/Delhoreh (Khachikian, Samuel), 62, 68
Appadurai, Arjun
  Disjuncture and Difference in Global Cultural Economy, 202–3
Arabs, 84–5
Archer, Neil
  Road Movie: In Search of Meaning, The, 202
Architecture of Neoliberalism, The (Spencer, Douglas), 229
Archive Effect: Found Footage and the Audiovisual Experience of History, The (Baron, Jamie), 210
Argentina, 23–5, 36–40, 157, 229–31
  avenger, the, 161–4
  bank heist, 155–6
  Bauer, James, 27, 28, 30–6
  Buenos Aires, 224–5
  censorship, 159
  complicity, 166–73, 175–6
  crime fiction, 37–9
  culpability, 166–73, 174
  culture, 39, 40
  Década Infame (Infamous Decade), 158
  foreignness, 39
  highways, 224–5
  history of *policial* cinema, 25–9
  hope, 174–5
  human rights, 164–5, 169, 171, 175–6
  justice/law, 157–8, 159–65, 174–6
  justiciero (justice seeker), 161–4
  lighting, 174
  masculinity, 234n
  Moreira, Juan, 162–3
  neoliberalism, 219, 220, 223–4, 230, 231
  Nuevo cine argentino (New Argentine Cinema), 156
  paranoia, 229–31
  protests, 225f
  redemocratisation era, 158–61
  rural–urban dichotomy, 218–19, 221
  society, 38, 178n
  state crimes, 157–8, 159
  thieves as heroes, 155–6
  vida verde, la ('the green life'), 219, 220–1
  see also gated communities
Argento, Dario
  Bird with the Crystal Plumage, The/L'Uccello dalle Piume di Cristallo, 143, 151
  Cat with Nine tails, The/Il Gatto a Nove Code, 151
  Four Flies on Grey Velvet /4 Mosche di Velluto Grigio, 151
  Tenebrae, 143
Aristarain, Adolfo, 159
  Last Days of the Victim/Ultimos días de la víctima, 159
  Lion's Share, The/La parte del león, 159
  Time for Revenge/Tiempo de revanche, 159
Arlt, Robert, 37, 39
  Trescientos millones, 37
Ash is Purest White/Jiang Hu Er Nü (Jia Zhangke), 93, 96, 101–3, 104, 105
Ashes of Paradise/Cenizas del paraíso (Piñeyro, Marcelo), 156, 163
assemblage, 240
At the Edge of the Law/Al filo de la ley (Desanzo, Juan Carlos), 160
At the End of the Tunnel/Al final del túnel (Grande, Rodrigo), 157–8, 163, 164
Audiard, Jacques, 81
  Dheepan, 81–2
  prophète, Un, 79–80, 81, 83–9
audience, 3, 4, 13
  paranoid spectatorship, 232
  participation, 10
  reaction, 227

thrill of, 9
see also show trials
Aura, The/El aura (Bielinsky, Fabián), 156, 221
Australia, 100
authority *see* power
avenger, the, 161–4
Avery, Tex
 Who Killed Who, 69

Baholli, Sami, 128
bandit heroines, 108–10
Bandit Queen (Kapur, Shekhar), 107, 110, 112, 115, 118
Baron, Jamie
 Archive Effect: Found Footage and the Audiovisual Experience of History, The, 210
Barthes, Roland, 12
Bauer, James, 27, 30–6
 Don't Kill Me!/¡No me mates!, 31
 Escape to Nice, The/Flucht nach Nizza, 31
 Explosivo 008, 30, 31–6f, 38, 40
 Incest/Blutschande, 31
 Mask of Death, The/Die Maske des Todes, 31
 Mystery of the Grey Lady, The/El misterio de dama gris, 28, 30, 31
 Paraguay, Land of Promise/ Paraguay, tierra de promisón, 30
 Singing Comes My Love/Cantando Ilegó el amor, 30
 Witches' Night/Walpurgisnacht, 31
Bell from Hell, The/La Campana del Infierno (Guerin, Claudio), 145, 148
Belsunce, García, 234n
Benjamin, Walter, 186, 189
Besson, Luc
 Femme Nikita, La, 197
Betibú (Cohan, Miguel), 156, 219, 220–2, 223, 224, 232

circulation, 231
paranoia, 227–9, 230
Spanish language production/ distribution, 226
threats, 228
Bhadrakaali, 115
Bicycle Thieves/Ladri di biciclette (De Sica, Vittorio), 46, 54
binge watching, 232–3
Bioy Casares, Adolfo (pseud. Bustos Domecq, H.)
 Seis problemas para don Isidro Parodi, 37
Bird with the Crystal Plumage, The/L'Uccello dalle Piume di Cristallo (Argento, Dario), 143, 151
Bitter Rice/Riso amaro (De Santis, Guiseppe), 57
Black Mirror (Brooker, Charlie), 231
Black Snow/Nieve negra (Hodara, Martin), 158, 168–70, 171, 172, 174
blood money ritual, 248, 249–50
Blood Will Tell/La misma sangre (Cohan, Miguel), 158, 170, 171, 174
Blue Angel, The (Sternberg, Josef von), 34
Blue Eyes of the Broken Doll, The/Los Ojos Azules de la Muñeca Rota (Aured, Carols), 145, 151
Blue Velvet (Lynch David), 206
body, the, 2, 10, 227, 249
'body genres', 227
Bollywood, 108
bolsa de huesos, La (Holmberg, Eduardo), 38
borders/boundaries, 80–1, 82, 87, 88, 202, 206, 246, 254
 imperialism, 255
 paranoia, 229
 west, the, 256

Borges, Jorge Luis (pseud. Bustos Domecq, H.), 37, 39
  'Leyenda Policial', 37
  Seis problemas para don Isidro Parodi, 37
  Universal History of Infamy, A, 12
Bouchareb, Rachid
  Hors-la-loi, 90n
boundaries/borders, 202, 206, 246, 254
  paranoia, 229
  prophète, Un, 80–1, 82, 87, 88
Brah, Avtar, 86
Breathless(Goddard, Jean-Luc), 202
Breu, Christopher and Hatmaker, Elizabeth A., 18n
  Noir Affect, 2
Buenos Aires, 224–5
Buffalo Bill's Wild West show, 188
bureaucratisation, 125–6, 127–8
Burgin, Victor
  'Paranoic Space', 229
Burnt Money/Plata Quemada (Piñeyro, Marcelo), 156
Bustos Domecq, H. (Borges, Jorges Luis and Bioy Casares, Adolfo), 39
  Seis problemas para don Isidro Parodi, 37

Cahiers du Cinéma (Hiller, Jim), 44–5
Cai, Shenshen, 99
Cain, James
  Postman Always Rings Twice, The, 24
Camorra, the 52–7; *see also* organised crime
Campanella, Juan José, 177n
  Secret in their Eyes, The/El secreto de sus ojos, 156, 163, 173, 230
Campbell, Neil
  Rhizomatic West, The, 255–6
Candle for the Devil, A/Una Vela para el Diablo (Martin, Eugenio), 146, 147

capital, 3
  globalised, 2, 7–8
capitalism, 48, 50, 57
  China, 96
  France, 186
  Italy, 142
  Lagos, 249
  see also consumerism
Cara de queso/Cheese Head (Winograd, Ariel), 221
Cardona, Georges, 201, 202, 203, 206, 207–16
  'Shirkers 1992', 201, 202, 203–4, 206–7, 211, 213, 214, 215–16
Carnaro, Erwin, 26, 27
Carter, Nick, 184–5
caso de García Belsunce, El ('The case of García Belsunce'), 221
Cassiday, Julie A.
  'Why Stalinist Cinema Had No Detective Films or How Three Becomes Two in *Engineer Kochin's Mistake*', 131, 133–4
Cat with Nine tails, The/Il Gatto a Nove Code (Argento, Dario), 151
Catcher in the Rye, The (Salinger, J. D.), 202
Catholicism, 151
Cawelti, John, 12
Cazorla-Sánchez, Antonio, 143
Çela, Arianit, 127
censorship, 25
  Argentina, 159
  India, 119
  Iran, 70
  Singapore, 206
  Spain, 144, 147
Chahar-rah-e Havades/Crossroads of events (Khachikian, Samuel), 71
Chang, Justin, 97
Chang, Sylvia, 101, 104
chastity, 119–20

Cheah, Pheng, 7
Chenal, Pierre, 24, 25
   Death by Appointment/El muerto falta a la cita, 24
   Denier Tournant, Le, 24
childhood trauma, 151
Children are Watching Us, The/I bambini ci guardano (De Sica, Vittorio), 54
China, 93, 95, 101
   capitalism, 96
   tropes, 31
   see also Jia Zhangke
Chisum, W. Jerry and Turvey, Brent E. *Crime Reconstruction*, 209
Chow Yun Fat, 103
cinematography, 25
   crowd shots, 46–7
   Dark Buildings/Las grietas de Jara, 172
   Earth Trembles, The/La terra trema, 49
   film noir, 64
   Gomorrah/Gomorra, 55
   Huttula, Gerhard, 26–7
   Jia Zhangke, 98–9, 104
   Khachikian, Samuel, 68
   long shots, 46, 49, 58n
   Relentless, 245, 248, 249
   Suffering, The/Los padecientes, 168
   see also lighting
cities see urban space
citizenship, 186–7
ciudad que huye, La / 'The City that Flees' (Martel, Lucrecia), 220–1
Clam Magazine, 241
Clan, The/El clan (Trapero, Pablo), 156
co-productions, 103
comedy, 23; *see also* crime comedies
communism
   Albania 125–9, 130, 133
   Italy, 45, 48, 50, 51
   Stalinist Cinema, 132
   revolutionary vigilance films, 130
   show trials, 128–9, 135–6
communist noir, 137
complicity, 166–73, 175–6
Con el dedo en el gatillo (Moglia Barth, Luis), 24, 28–9
Consent of the Damned: Ordinary Argentinians in the Dirty War (Sheinin, David), 176
conspiracy theories, 233
consumerism, 143–4, 186, 189, 242, 248; *see also* capitalism
'corredores que pisan fuerte, Los' (Gioberchio, Graciela), 224
Corrigan, Timothy and Duarte, José *Global Road Movie, The*, 206
Corruption of Chris Miller, The/La Corrupción de Chris Miller (Bardem, Juan Antonio), 141, 148
Corsicans, 80, 82–3, 85–7
costume, 192–3, 194
counterculture, the, 147–51
countries see gated communities
cowboy girl films, 188–9, 191
Crime at Three O'clock/Crimen a las 3 (Saslavsky, Luis), 26
crime, organised *see* organised crime
crime comedies, 30, 31, 33
crime fiction, 37–9, 140
crime films, 95–6, 209–10, 253
   definitions, 94–5, 107, 222
   as metaphors, 95
Crime Reconstruction (Chisum, W. Jerry and Turvey, Brent E.), 209
crimen del otro, El (Quiroga, Horacio), 39
criminal profiling, 209
criminal psyche, 4
criminality, 13
crowd shots, 46–7
culpability, 166–73, 174

INDEX

Cutting the Ties/Fijet që Priten (Fejzo, Muharrem), 129, 130, 131–2, 133–4, 137n

dacoity, 109–10
Damages (Kessler, Todd, A.; Kessler, Glenn; Zelman, Daniel), 232
Dark Buildings/Las grietas de Jara (Gil Lavedra, Nicolás), 158, 170, 171, 172–3, 174, 176
De Palma, Brian
  Scarface, 53, 56, 57, 79
De Santis, Guiseppe
  Bitter Rice/Riso amaro, 57
  Tragic Pursuit/Caccia tragica, 57
De Sica, Vittorio
  Bicycle Thieves/Ladri di biciclette, 46, 54
  Children are Watching Us, The/I bambini ci guardano, 54
  Shoeshine/Sciusià, 54
  Umberto D, 46
Death by Appointment/El muerto falta a la cita (Chenal, Pierre), 24
Death in Buenos Aires/Muerte en Buenos Aires (Meta, Natalia) 231
Delirium/Sarsam (Khachikian, Samuel), 62–3, 64–5, 66, 67–71, 72, 73
Delorme, Stéphane, 89
Demare, Lucio, 24
democracy, 14–15, 146
  Argentina, 157, 158–61
Denier Tournant, Le (Chenal, Pierre), 24
Desanzo, Juan Carlos
  At the Edge of the Law/Al filo de la ley, 160
descent, 12
Desperate Hours, The (Wyler, William), 63
Desser, David
  'Global Noir', 243

detective films, 131–4
  Stalinist, 133, 134, 135
  thirdness, 132–4, 135
Detour (Ulmer, Edgar G.), 45
deviations, 9
Dheepan (Audiard, Jacques), 81–2
diaspora, 80–1, 82, 84, 86, 87, 100; *see also* migration
diegesis, 24
Dimendberg, Edward, 222, 224, 225
disguise, 192–3, 194
Disjuncture and Difference in Global Cultural Economy (Appadurai, Arjun), 202–3
distinction, 240
D'Lugo, Marvin and Dapena, Gerard, 226
documentary films, 136, 203, 207
  true crime, 204, 207, 209, 212
Documentary Resistance (Aguayo, Angela J.), 212
Dolly of the Dailies (Edwin, Walter), 196
domestic violence, 121
Don't Kill Me!¡No me mates! (Bauer, James), 31
Downpour/Turbión (Antonio Momplet), 24
Dragonfly for Each Corpse, A/Una Libélula para Cada Muerto (Klimovsky, Leon), 141, 149, 150, 151
Driving Visions Exploring the Road Movie (Laderman, David), 205

Earth Trembles, The/La terra trema (Visconti, Luchino), 45–6, 47, 48–51
Eastern Westerns: Film and Genre Outside and Inside Hollywood (Teo, Stephen), 254
Éclair, 183, 184, 195, 196–7
'ecology of expertise', 239–40

262

'effective history', 12
Elsaesser, Thomas, 73, 212
emotion, 227, 232, 246; *see also* paranoia
Engineer Kochin's Mistake (Macheret, Aleksandr), 133
Escape to Nice, The/Flucht nach Nizza (Bauer, James), 31
ethnicity, 81–2, 83, 84–5, 88
European cinema, 24–5, 36
Exiled/Fong Juk (To, Johnnie), 99, 104
expertise, 239–41
Explosivo 008 (Bauer, James), 30, 31–6f, 38, 40
expressionism *see* German expressionism

Facundo (Sarmiento, Domingo Faustino), 218
failure, 47
family, the, 121, 186
Fantômas films (Feuillade, Louis), 190–1
Far from the Land of the Ancestors/ Fern vom Land der Ahnen (Huttula, Gerhard), 26
Farar/Escape (Shabaviz, Abbas), 68–9
Faryad-e Nime-shab/Midnight Cry (Khachikian, Samuel), 63
fascism, 48, 50–1, 55, 143
fatalism 49, 58n
Fay, Jennifer, 222–3
Fay, Jennifer and Nieland, Justus, 243,250
'fear figures', 228
female detectives, 189–90, 191
female revenge drama, 108, 110–20, 121–2
femininity, 69, 107, 109, 120
 bandit heroines, 108–10
 Bollywood, 108
 chastity, 119
 macho, 108–10
 Malayalam cinema, 111
 Protéa, 193
 revenge, 110–20, 121–2
 see also women
feminism, 185
Femme Nikita, La (Besson, Luc), 197
Fenster, Marc, 233
Feuillade, Louis
 Fantômas films, 190–1
 Vampires, Les, 193
film noir, 24, 44, 45, 46, 47–8, 222
 characters 64, 69
 Desser, David, 243
 Fay, Jennifer, 222–3
 femininity, 69
 globalisation, 238
 influences on, 65
 Lagos, 238, 239, 243, 247
 pessimism, 70
 Spain, 144
 realism, 64
 urban space, 222–4, 238
 visual style, 63–4
film training, 240–1
Fish with the Golden Eyes, The/El Pez de los Ojos de Oro (Ramírez, Pedro Luis), 141, 145, 146–7, 151
flâneurs, 186, 189
flashbacks, 166–7, 171
Flight, The/La Fuga (Saslavsky, Luis), 26, 27, 158
forced disappearances, 157, 165
foreign films, 14
foreignness, 39
formalism, 71–2, 73
Foucault, Michel, 8, 9–12
Four Flies on Grey Velvet /4 Mosche di Velluto Grigio (Argento, Dario), 151

263

INDEX

France, 79–80, 183
  American reception of French films, 195
  American serial queen heroines, 188
  citizenship, 186–7
  co-productions, 103
  consumerism, 186, 189
  Corsicans, 80, 82–3, 85–7
  cowboy girl films, 188–9, 191
  French New Wave, 202
  integration, 83
  masculinity, 186–7
  minorities, 88, 89
  morality, 186–7
  New Woman, 184, 185–7, 191, 196
  social class, 185, 186–7
  women 183–4, 185–7
  see also Audiard, Jacques
Franco, Francisco, 143–4, 146, 147, 151, 152
Freeman, Daniel and Freeman, Jason, 227, 228
Freud, Sigmund, 230

gangster films, 50, 56, 97, 103
Ganti, Tejaswini, 240
García, González, 31
Garrone, Matteo, 47
  Gomorrah/Gomorra, 45–6, 47, 51–7
Gaslight (Cukor, George), 214
gaslighting, 214–15
gated communities, 218–21, 223–5, 232
  threats, 228
  paranoia, 229–30
Gates, Philippa, 190
genealogy, 8, 9–12, 255, 256
gender, 111, 150–1
genre, 5–11, 117–18, 119, 226–7, 231–3, 239, 250, 255–6
'Genre, Genre Everywhere: the Netflix Effect Spreads' (Rubin, Peter), 231–2
George, KG, 112–13

Yavanka ('Stage Curtain'), 112–14
German expressionism, 65, 66, 73
Germany
  cinema, 31
  emigration, 26, 27, 31–2
  krimi films, 140
  studio system, 5–6
  theatre, 26–7
Germany Year Zero/Germania anno zero (Rossellini, Robert), 54
gialli cinema, 140–1, 142–3, 144–52
Giallo Canvas: Art, Excess and Horror Cinema, The (Heller-Nicholas, Alexandra) 141
Giallo!: Genre, Modernity, and Detection in Italian Horror Cinema (Alexia Kannas), 141
Gilda (Vidor, Charles), 46, 63
Giovacchini, Saverio and Sklar, Robert
  Global Neorealism: The Transnational History of a Film Style, 2
Girl from Shiraz, A/Dokhtari az Shiraz (Khachikian, Samuel), 67, 72
gjyqe të popullit (the people's trials), 135–6
glass ceiling, The/El Techo de Cristal (de la Iglesia, Eloy), 141
Gleber, Anke, 189
Global Neorealism: The Transnational History of a Film Style (Giovacchini, Saverio and Sklar, Robert), 2
Global Road Movie, The (Corrigan, Timothy and Duarte, José), 206
global, the, 238
'Global Noir' (Desser, David), 243
globalisation, 53, 156–7, 202–3
  film noir, 243
  Lagos, 248–9
globalised capital, 2, 7–8
Godfather, The (Coppola, Francis Ford), 79

Godmother (Shukla, Vinay), 110
Goga, Lefter, 127
Gomorrah/Gomorra (Garrone, Matteo), 45–6, 47, 51–7
Gonda, Ilse, 34f
Gothic films, 65
Grieveson, Lee, 12–13
Grimson, Alejandro and Kessler, Gabriel, 220, 223
Guerra Gaucho (Demare, Lucas), 29
Guest, The/Mysafiri (Hakani, Hysen), 129, 130
Gulab Gang (Sen, Soumik), 107, 110, 115, 118
guns, 101, 102
Gutiérrez, Eduardo, 162

Hands of Orlac, The (Weine, Robert), 33
Hare, Robert D.
　Without Conscience: The Disturbing World of the Psychopaths Among Us, 213, 214
Harrison, Ben, 216
Haseena Parkar (Lakhia, Apoorva), 110
Haunted Castle, The (Murnau, F. W.), 33
Hazbiu, Kadri, 126–7
Heller-Nicholas, Alexandra
　Giallo Canvas: Art, Excess and Horror Cinema, The, 141
heroes/heroines, 107, 108
　American female adventure heroines, 183–4, 191, 193–4
　American serial queen heroines, 187–8
　Argentinian thieves as, 155–6
　bandit heroines, 108–10
　female spy films, 183–4, 190–7
　prophète, Un, 79–80
　Touch of Sin, A (Tian Zhu Ding), 99
Higbee, Will and Lim, Song Hwee, 1–2
highways, 224–5
Hiller, Jim
　Cahiers du Cinéma, 44–5

Hindi filmmakers, 240
'Hippie' (*Pueblo*), 147
Hispanic market, 226
Historias mínimas / Intimate Stories (Sorín, Carlos), 221
history, 11–14
　Argentina, 25–9
Hitchcock, Alfred, 63
　Shadow of a Doubt, 19n
Hjort, Mette, 94
Hollywood, 6, 44
　Chinese tropes, 31
　gangster stereotypes, 50, 56
Holmberg, Eduardo, 37
　bolsa de huesos, La, 38
Holmes, Amanda, 218
Hong Kong, 103, 104
Horak, Laura, 189
Horeck, Tanya
　Justice on Demand: True Crime in the Digital Streaming Era, 204
horror films, 65, 68, 227
　rape-revenge dramas, 119
Hors-la-loi (Bouchareb, Rachid), 90n
Hosseini, Hasan, 66
House of Psychotic Women (Aured, Carlos), 146
Hoxha, Enver, 126
human rights, 164–5, 169, 171, 175–6
human sacrifice, 248–9
Huttula, Gerhard, 26–7
　Far from the Land of the Ancestors/ Fern vom Land der Ahnen, 26

I Spit on Your Grave (Zarchi, Meir), 112
identity, 81, 82, 84–5, 87
　national, 15, 45, 81, 84–5, 87
ideology, 14
immobility, 83–4
immorality, 12, 13; *see also* morality
imperialism, 255
Incest/Blutschande (Bauer, James), 31

Incident at the Port, An/Një ndodhi në port (Hakani, Hysen), 129, 130
India, 107; *see also* Malayalam cinema
　Bollywood, 108–10
　censorship, 119
　dacoity, 109–10
　domestic violence, 121
　Hindi filmmakers, 240
　nurses, 118
　rape in, 118–19
　revenge films, 110–20
　women, 108–12
　see also Kerala
Inglourious Basterds (Tarantino, Quentin), 112
integration, 83
interpretation, 233
intertextuality, 202, 238, 249
Intuition/La corazonada (Montiel, Alejandro), 158
Investigation Continues, The/Hetimi Vazhdon (Topallaj, Mark), 129, 130, 131
Iran, 61
　censorship, 70–1
　originality, 72
　see also Khachikian, Samuel
Italian Film in the Light of Neorealism (Marcus, Millicent), 46
Italy, 44–5, 142
　Camorra, the 52–7
　culture, 142
　Earth Trembles, The/La terra trema, 45–6, 47, 48–51
　economy, 141–2
　fascism, 48, 50–1
　gialli cinema, 140–1, 142–3, 151, 152
　Gomorrah/Gomorra, 45–6, 47, 51–7
　Mafia, the, 52–7
　modernity, 142
　neorealism, 45–8, 49, 52, 57–8

neorealismo nero, 46, 47, 52, 55, 57–8
neorealist *noir*, 45–8
Spain, link with, 141–2, 151–2
tourism, 141, 142–3

Japan
　co-productions, 103
Jasset, Victorin, 183, 184
　Nick Carter films, 184–5
　Protéa see *Protéa*
　Zigomar, 185
　Zigomar, Eel Skin/Zigomar, Peau d'Anguille 183
Jewkes, Yvonne
　Media and Crime, 203
Jia Zhangke, 93–4, 95, 96, 103
　Ash is Purest White/Jiang Hu Er Nü, 93, 96, 101–3, 104, 105
　co-productions, 103
　collaborations, 104
　honour codes, 96–7
　inspiration, 104
　Mountains May Depart/Shan He Gu Ren, 93, 96, 100–1, 102, 103, 104
　Pickpocket (*Xia Wu*), 98
　themes, 104–5
　Touch of Sin, A (*Tian Zhu Ding*), 93, 97–9, 100, 102–3, 104, 105
　24 City, 97
　Unknown Pleasures (*Ren Xiao Yao*), 98, 99–100
jianghu, 96, 103, 104
'Jòvenes melenudos' (*Mataro*), 147–8
Juan Moreira (Favio, Leonardo), 162, 221
'Juramento' (Carnaro Francisco and Amadori, Luis César), 32
justice, 4–5, 37
　Albania, 125–6, 127–9, 135
　Argentina, 157–8, 159–66, 174–6
　avenger, the, 161–4
　justicia por mano propia (justice by one's own hand), 161

266

Moscow Trials, 135
Nollywood films, 244
'on-site trials', 128–9
rape, 118–19
show trials, 128–9, 135–6
Justice on Demand: True Crime in the Digital Streaming Era (Horeck, Tanya), 204
justiciero (justice seeker), 161–4

Kannas, Alexia
  Giallo!: Genre, Modernity, and Detection in Italian Horror Cinema, 141
Kannezhuthi Pottum Thottu ('Eye-lined and Wearing a Pottu') (Rajeev Kumar, T. K.), 114–15, 118
Ke Jinde, Kelvin, 97
Kerala, 110–11, 112, 118
  rape in, 118–19
  spousal violence in, 121
Khachikian, Samuel, 61–3, 69, 71
  Anxiety/Delhoreh, 62, 68
  censorship, 70
  Chahar-rah-e Havades/Crossroads of events, 71
  cinematography, 68
  criticism, 72
  Delirium/Sarsam, 62–3, 64–5, 66, 67–71, 72, 73
  expressionism, 73
  Faryad-e Nime-shab/Midnight Cry, 63
  formalism, 71–2, 73
  Girl from Shiraz, A/Dokhtari az Shiraz, 67, 72
  inspiration, 65–7, 69, 70
  language, 71
  lighting, 66, 67–8, 72
  locations/sets, 68–9
  Mardi dar Ayeneh/A Man in the Mirror, 68
  originality, 72
  Osyan/Rebellion, 63

  Qased-e Behesht/The Messenger from Paradise, 70
  realism, 64, 70, 71
  social culture, 71
  Storm in Our City, The/Tufan dar Shahr-e Ma, 68, 70
  Yek Qadam ta Marg/One Step to Death, 64
  Zarba/Strike, 68, 71–2
Khoshbakht, Ehsan, 64, 70, 72
Kill Bill (Tarantino, Quentin), 112
Killer is One of 13, The/El Asesino está entre los 13 (Aguirre, Javier) 145, 148, 150, 151
Kinostudio 'Shqipëria e Re' (New Albania Film Studio), 129
Kirchner, Néstor, 165, 166, 175–6
Koven, Mikel, 140, 142–3
krimi films, 140
Kuruppinte Kanakku Pusthakam/Kuruo's Ledger (Menon, Balachandra), 111

Lacan, Jacques
  'Seminar on "The Purloined Letter"', 132–3
Laderman, David
  Driving Visions Exploring the Road Movie, 205
ladrón del siglo, El (*The Thief of the Century*) (Vitette, Luis Mario), 156
Lagos, 237, 238, 239, 242, 244, 245, 247, 250
  expertise, 241
  film noir, 238, 239, 243
  globalisation, 248–9
  human sacrifice, 249
  port, 247–8
landscapes, 229
Lang, Fritz, 3, 5
  M, 3–5, 9, 35
  Nibelungen, 66
  Spies, 33

267

INDEX

Last Days of the Victim/Ultimos días de la víctima (Aristarain, Adolfo), 159
Lattuada, Alberto
   Mafioso, 57
law, the 9–10, 126
   Argentina, 157–8, 160–1, 164–6
   retribution outside of, 160–1
   see also justice
Lefebvre, Martin
   'On Landscape in Narrative Cinema', 229
Lehmann, Hauke
   Affect Poetics of the New Hollywood: Suspense, Paranoia, and Melancholy, 204–5
Leitch, Thomas, 94–5
ley y el crimen: Usos del relato policial en la narrativa argentina, La (Mattalía, Sonia), 38
'Leyenda Policial' (Borges, Jorge Luis), 37
Life is Beautiful/La vita è bella (Benigni, Roberto), 167
lighting, 24, 25, 27–8, 166
   Argentina, 174
   Con el dedo en el gatillo 29f
   film noir 63–4
   Huttula, Gerhard, 26–7
   Khachikian, Samuel, 66, 67–8, 72
   mystery, 67
   Relentless, 245
   Weimar cinema, 25, 33, 66, 67
Lim, Song Hwee, 254
Lion's Share, The/La parte del león (Aristarain, Adolfo), 159
long shots, 46, 49, 58n
Losada, Matt, 223, 228
Lost For Lost/Perdido por perdido (Lecchi, Alberto), 157–8, 161, 173
Lights of Buenos Aires, The/Las luces de Buenos Aires (Migliar, Adelqui), 23

literature, 37–9
local conditions, 250
local events, 247
location, 46, 68–9, 145–6, 169, 173;
   see also landscapes
Lost/Perdida (Alejandro Montiel, Alejandro), 158, 170, 171, 173
Ludmer, Josefina, 162

M (Lang, Fritz), 3–5, 9, 35
MacDonald, Megan C., 83–4
Mafia, the, 52–7, 79
   stereotypes, 50
   see also organised crime
Mafioso (Lattuada, Alberto), 57
Malayalam cinema, 107–8; *see also* India
   female revenge films, 110–20, 121
   'middle cinema', 112
Maniac mansion/La Mansion de la Niebla (Lara Polop, Francisco), 145
Mann, Anthony
   T-Men, 26
Mansker, Andrea, 186
Manzi, Homero, 24, 28–9
   '¡Salud Salud!', 24
Marcus, Millicent, 47
   Italian Film in the Light of Neorealism, 46
Mardi dar Ayeneh/A Man in the Mirror (Khachikian, Samuel), 68
marginalisation, 81, 88
Marziano, Los / 'The Marzianos' (Katz, Ana) 220–1, 223
masculinity, 107, 108, 109, 116, 120
   Argentina, 234n
   France, 186–7
Mask of Death, The/Die Maske des Todes (Bauer, James), 31
mass culture, 13
Massumi, Brian, 228
Mataro
   'Jòvenes melenudos', 147–8

268

Mateo (Tinayre, Daniel), 26
matrilineality, 111
Mattalía, Sonia
  ley y el crimen: Usos del relato policial en la narrativa argentina, La, 38
Mayer, Hervé and Roche, David
  Transnationalism and Imperialism: Endurance of the Global Western Film, 2, 255
Mazur, Grace Dane, 214
Media and Crime (Jewkes, Yvonne), 203, 209
Mello, Cecília, 104
melodrama, 3–4, 69, 227
  Yavanka ('Stage Curtain'), 113
memory, 212–13
men, 109; *see also* masculinity
Menem, Carlos Saúl, 160, 165
'middle cinema', 112
Migliar, Adelqui
  Lights of Buenos Aires, The/Las luces de Buenos Aires, 23
migration, 118; *see also* diaspora
Millennial Cinema (Sihna, Amresh and McSweeney, Terence), 212–13
mimesis, 24
minorities, 88, 89
Mission Across the Sea, The/Misioni Përtej Detit (Malaj, Lisenko), 129, 137n
mobility, 83–4, 104, 144–5, 202, 245–6
'Modas Modernas' ('Modern Fashions') (*Alba*), 150
modernity, 142, 143, 144–5, 146
Moglia Barth, Luis
  Con el dedo en el gatillo, 24, 28–9
  ¡Tango!, 23
  With His Finger on the Trigger/Con el dedo en el gatillo, 23
Momplet, Antonio, 30, 40n
  Turbión, 27f, 30
Monte Criollo (Mom, Arturo S.), 158

morality, 9, 11, 12, 14, 59n, 143
  Argentina, 160, 161–4
  avenger, the, 161–4
  France, 186–7
  Spain, 146, 147
  see also immorality
Moreira, Juan, 162–3
Moscow Trials, 135
Mossello, Facián Gabriel and Melana, Marcela, 39
Mother India (Khan, Mehboob), 108
motherhood, 108
Mountains May Depart/Shan He Gu Ren (Jia Zhangke), 93, 96, 100–1, 102, 103, 104
Murder by Music/Las Trompetas del Apocalipsis (Buchs, Julio), 149–50
Murnau, F. W.
  Haunted Castle, The, 33
music, 23–4
musicals, 23–4
Mystery of the Grey Lady, The/El misterio de dama gris (Bauer, James), 28, 30, 31

narrative, 230
nation, the, 6, 12, 13–14
national identity, 15, 45, 81, 84–5, 87
nationalism, 29, 156–7
Nationalsozialistische Deutsche Arbeiterpartei/Auslands-Organisation (NSDAP/AO), 26
Nazi Party, 26, 41n
Needham, Gary, 142
neoliberalism, 219, 220, 221–6
  expertise, 239–40
  paranoia, 229–30, 231
neorealism, 45–8, 49, 52, 57–8
neorealismo nero, 46, 47, 52, 55, 57–8
Netflix, 204
NFI (Nigerian Film Institute), 240, 241
Nuevo cine argentino (New Argentine Cinema), 156

INDEX

New Nollywood, 237, 238, 239, 241, 242–6, 250; see also Nollywood
New Woman, 184, 185–7, 191, 196
New York Film Academy, 241
newsreels, 136
Ng, Jasmine, 201, 202, 207, 210, 211, 215
Nibelungen (Lang, Fritz), 66
Nichols, Bill, 207
Nigeria, 247; see also Lagos *and* Nollywood
Nigerian Film Institute (NFI), 240, 241
Nigerian Television Authority (NTA), 240
Nine Queens/Nueve reinas (Bielinsky, Fabián), 156, 157–8, 161, 163, 173
noir affect 19n
Noir Affect (Breu, Christopher and Hatmaker, Elizabeth A.), 2
noir films *see* film noir
noir sensibility, 45, 47, 50, 58
Nollywood, 237, 240–1, 242, 244, 246, 249; see also New Nollywood
  film noir, 246–50
  North–South divide, 246
  production/distribution, 238–9
'nostra storia, La' (Raffaello), 52
Nothing Is Forgotten/Asgjë nuk Harrohet (Ibro, Esat), 129, 137n
Nova, Koço, 135
NSDAP/AO (Nationalsozialistische Deutsche Arbeiterpartei/Auslands-Organisation), 26
NTA (Nigerian Television Authority), 240
Nuevo cine argentino (New Argentine Cinema), 156

occult rituals, 248–9
Office Kitano, 103
Official Story, The/La historia oficial (Puenzo, Luis), 162

Okoroafor, Andy Amadi, 241
  Clam Magazine, 241
  Relentless, 237–8, 239, 241, 242–6, 247, 248, 249, 250
Old Cartridge, The/Gëzhoja e vjetër (Kumbaro, Saimir), 129, 130, 134
Olivari, Carlos, 24
'On Landscape in Narrative Cinema' (Lefebvre, Martin), 229
'on-site trials', 128–9
101 Ranch Wild West show, 188
Ong, Aihwa, 239–40
organised crime 45–6, 47, 50, 51–7, 79, 97
  Mafia, the, 50, 52–7, 79
  triad films, 97, 99, 103, 104
originality, 72
Ossessione (Visconti, Luchino), 49, 51, 57, 58
Osyan/Rebellion (Khachikian, Samuel), 63
othering/otherness, 79, 80, 82, 84, 85, 143, 184; see also racism
outlaws, 82
Outside the Law/Fuera de la ley (Romero, Manuel), 23, 26, 27, 158
Ovanessian, Arby, 71

Palacios, Rodolfo
  Sin armas ni ladrones (*Without Weapons or Thieves*), 156
Paraguay, Land of Promise/Paraguay, tierra de promisón (Bauer, James), 30
paranoia, 219, 227–33
'Paranoic Space' (Burgin, Victor), 229
paranoid spectatorship, 232–3
patriarchy, the, 116
Peña, Fernando M., 26, 29
perspective, 114
Petit de Murat, Ulyses, 24, 28–9
Pickpocket (*Xia Wu*) (Jia Zhangke), 98

Piñeiro, Claudia, 221
policing, 13
pornography, 227
Porteño Shadows/Sombras porteñas (Tinayre, Daniel), 158
Post-2000 Film Western: Contexts, Transnationality, Hybridity, The (Paryż, Marek and Leo, John R.), 254–5
Postman Always Rings Twice, The (Cain, James), 24
power, 2, 14–15, 86–7, 88, 89, 95
  Altman, Rick, 8
  opposition to, 37
  prison, 80, 82, 83–4
prophète, Un (Audiard, Jacques), 79–80, 81, 83–9
Protéa (Jasset, Victorin), 183, 184, 185, 187–8, 189
  distribution, 195, 196
  legacy, 196–7
  marketing, 190–6
  reviews, 195–6
Protéa II (Faive, Joseph), 196
psychopathy, 204, 213–14
Pueblo
  'Hippie' 147
Puthiya Niyamam ('New Law') (Sajan, A. K.) 117, 118
Putlibai (Roy, Ashok), 110

Qased-e Behesht/The Messenger from Paradise (Khachikian, Samuel), 70
Quayson, Ato and Daswani, Girish, 80–1
Quesada, Nya, 176
Quiroga, Horacio, 39
  crimen del otro, El, 39

Rabinowitz, Paula, 24, 25, 58n
Race (Abbas-Mustan), 109
Race 2 (Abbas-Mustan), 109
racism, 83

Raffaello
  'nostra storia, La', 52
Rafter, Nicole, 95–6
Ranch Girls, The book series (Vandercook, Margaret), 188
rape-revenge dramas, 118–20; *see also* sexual violence
realism, 44–5, 55
  America, 195
  film noir, 64
  Khachikian, Samuel, 64, 70, 71
  see also neorealism
Registro Unificado de Víctimas del Terrorismo de Estado (RUVTE, Unified Registry of Victims of State Terrorism)
regulation, 13, 14, 25
Reiber, Ludwig, 31
Relentless (Okoroafor, Andy Amadi), 237–8, 239, 241, 242–6, 247, 248, 249, 250
repetition, 226–7
retribution *see* revenge
revenge, 160–1
  avenger, the, 161–4
Revenge (Fargeat, Coralie), 112
revenge films, 110–20, 121–2
  rape-revenge dramas, 118–20
revisionism, 126–7
revolutionary vigilance films, 128–37
Rhizomatic West, The (Campbell, Neil), 255–6
'Río Bank: the Robbery that Turned into Legend' (Aguirre, Osvaldo), 156
Ríos, Sixto Pondal, 24
Road Movie: In Search of Meaning, The (Archer, Neil), 202
road movies, 201, 202, 203–4, 205, 206, 208–9; *see also* highways
Roberts, Joan Warthling, 190
robo del siglo, El (*The Robbery of the Century*) (Winograd, Ariel), 156

271

INDEX

Rocco and his Brothers/Rocco ei suoi Fratelli (Visconti, Luchino), 49
Rome Open City/Roma citta àperta (Rossellini, Robert), 57–8
Romero, Manuel, 23
  Outside the Law/Fuera de la ley, 23, 26, 27
Rossellini, Robert
  Germany Year Zero/Germania anno zero, 54
  Rome Open City/Roma citta àperta, 57–8
Rubin, Peter
  'Genre, Genre Everywhere: the Netflix Effect Spreads', 231–2
rural space, 246
  rural–urban dichotomy, Argentina, 218–19, 221
RUVTE (*Registro Unificado de Víctimas del Terrorismo de Estado*/Unified Registry of Victims of State Terrorism), 165

Sadr, Hamid Reza, 64–5
'¡Salud Salud!' (Manzi, Homero), 24
Sarlo, Beatriz
  Technical Imagination: Argentine Culture's Modern Dreams, The, 41n
Sarmiento, Domingo Faustino
  Facundo, 218
Saro-Wiwa, Ken, 247
Saslavsky, Luis
  Crime at Three O'clock/Crimen a las 3, 26
  Flight, The/La Fuga, 26, 27
Sazie, Léon, 183
  Zigomar crime novels, 183
Scarface (De Palma, Brian), 53, 56, 57, 79
Schlasy, Adolf, 27–8f
Schreber, Daniel, 230
science, 38

Secret in their Eyes, The/El secreto de sus ojos (Campanella, Juan José), 156, 163, 173, 230
Seis problemas para don Isidro Parodi (Bustos Domecq, H.), 37
semana solos, Una / A Week Alone (Murga, Celina), 220–1
'Seminar on "The Purloined Letter"' (Lacan, Jacques), 132–3
sets, 68–9
  Weimar cinema, 25, 33, 66, 67
7th Floor/Séptimo (Amezcua, Patxi), 230–1
Seventh Seal The (Bergman, Ingmar), 202
Sex, Lies and Videotape (Soderbergh, Steven), 202
sexual violence, 118–20, 166–9, 170
sexuality, 119–20, 147
Shadow of a Doubt (Hitchcock, Alfred), 19n
Shapiro, Ann-Louise, 187
Sheinin, David
  Consent of the Damned: Ordinary Argentinians in the Dirty War, 176
Sherni (Malhotra, Harmesh), 110, 112
Shirkers (Tan, Sandi), 199–202, 203–10, 212, 213, 214, 216
'Shirkers 1992' (Cardona, Georges), 201, 202, 203–4, 206–7, 211, 213, 214, 215–16
Shoeshine/Sciusià (De Sica, Vittorio), 54
show trials, 128–9, 135–6
Sicily, 48–9
Siddique, Sophie, 201, 202, 210, 211, 213–14, 215
Sigurimi i Shtetit (Albanian secret police), 130, 131, 132, 133–5
Sihna, Amresh and McSweeney, Terence
  Millennial Cinema, 212–13
Silent Duel/Duel i Heshtur (Anagnosti, Dhimitër), 129, 130–1
Silverman, Debra L., 185–6

272

Sin armas ni ladrones (*Without Weapons or Thieves*) (Palacios, Rodolfo), 156
Singapore, 201, 205, 206, 240
Singer, Ben, 187–8
Singing Comes My Love/Cantando Ilegó el amor (Bauer, James), 30
Snider, Zachary, 232–3
social class, 49, 65, 100, 101, 102, 105
   Albania, 126, 127, 130
   France, 185, 186–7
   gated communities, 223, 224f
   global, 238
   revolutionary vigilance films, 130
social justice, 99–100
social media, 98
society, 71, 80, 95, 178n
   decline, 186–7
   France, 186–7
   global, 238
   relationships, 163–4
Sorrento, Matthew, 207
sound, 23, 24
   Explosivo 008, 35
   see also music
sound-bridges, 33
soundtracks, 23–4
Soviet Union, 135
Space of Memory and Human Rights museum, 165
Spain, 31, 141, 143–4
   counterculture, the, 147–51
   economy, 141, 143–4
   gialli cinema, 141, 144–52
   Hispanic market, 226
   Italy, link with, 141–2, 151–2
   mobility, 144–5
   modernity, 143, 144–5, 146
   tourism, 141, 143, 146
Spencer, Douglas
   Architecture of Neoliberalism, The, 229

Spies (Lang, Fritz), 33
Spiral Staircase (Siodmak, Robert), 65
spousal violence, 121
spy films, female, 183–4, 190–7; *see also* revolutionary vigilance films
Stalinist Cinema, 132, 133, 134
state crimes, 157–8, 159
stereotypes, 56
   Arabs as criminals, 84
   Chinese, 31
   gangster, 50, 56, 97
Storm in Our City, The/Tufan dar Shahr-e Ma (Khachikian, Samuel), 68, 70
streaming services, 231–3
stunts, 188, 191–2f, 194
Sublime Object of Ideology, The (Žižek, Slavoj), 228
Suffering, The/Los padecientes (Tuozzo, Nicolás), 158, 166–8, 171, 172
surveillance, 13, 85–6, 134
suspense, 204–6

T-Men (Mann, Anthony), 26
Tan, Sandi, 199, 200f, 201, 202, 206, 207, 213–14, 215
   Cardona, Georges, 210–11
   Shirkers, 199–202, 203–10, 212, 213, 214, 216
   as unreliable narrator, 209, 211, 212
¡Tango! (Moglia Barth, Luis), 23
Tarantino, Quentin
   Inglourious Basterds, 112
   Kill Bill, 112
Tassara, Mabel, 158–9
Technical Imagination: Argentine Culture's Modern Dreams, The (Sarlo, Beatriz), 41n
technology, 38
'Tehran Noir' retrospective, 61, 63
television, 240
Tenebrae (Argento, Dario), 143

INDEX

Teo, Stephen
   Eastern Westerns: Film and Genre Outside and Inside Hollywood, 254
terrorism, 228
Thesis on a Homicide/Tesis sobre un homicidio (Goldfrid, Hernán), 230
thirdness, 132–4, 135
Thompson, Kirsten Moana, 222
Threat, The/Kërcënimi (Topallaj, Mark), 129, 130
threats, 228, 230, 231
thrillers, 95
Thursday Night Widows/Las viudas de los jueves (Piñeyro, Marcelo), 219, 220–1, 222, 223, 224, 225f, 232
   circulation, 231
   highways, 224–5
   paranoia, 227, 228–9
   Spanish language production/distribution, 226
   threats, 228
Tierney, Dolores, 156–7
Tiersten, Lisa, 186
Time for Revenge/Tiempo de revanche (Aristarain, Adolfo), 159
To, Johnnie, 99
   Exiled/Fong Juk, 99, 104
Touch of Sin, A (Tian Zhu Ding) (Jia Zhangke), 93, 97–9, 100, 102–3, 104, 105
tourism
   Italy, 141, 142–3
   Spain, 141, 143, 146
Trace, The/ Gjurma (Dhamo, Kristaq), 129, 130, 134
Traces in the Snow/Gjurmë në Dëborë (Tare, Edmund), 129, 130
Tragic Hero/Ying Hung (Wong, Taylor), 103
Tragic Pursuit/Caccia tragica (De Santis, Guiseppe), 57
training, 240–1
trans prefix, 254

transcription, 2–3, 7
transgression, 2, 3, 7
Transnationalism and Imperialism: Endurance of the Global Western Film (Mayer, Hervé and Roche, David), 2, 255
transvaluation, 2, 3, 7
Trap, The/Gracka (Kumbaro, Saimir), 129, 130
trauma, 212–13, 215, 216
trauma-bond, the, 215
travelogues, 145, 146
Trescientos millones (Arlt, Robert), 37
triad films, 97, 99, 103, 104
tropes, 56
   Arabs as criminals, 84
   Chinese, 31
   gangster, 50, 56, 97
true crime, 204, 207, 209, 212
Turbión (Momplet, Antonio), 27f, 30
22 Female Kottayam ('22 Female Kottayam') (Abu, Aashiq), 115–16, 118, 119
24 City (Jia Zhangke), 97
Tyler, Stephen, 214

Ulmer, Edgar G.
   Detour, 45
Umberto D (De Sica, Vittorio), 46
uncanny, the, 66, 68
Universal History of Infamy, A (Borges, Jorge Luis), 12
Unknown Pleasures (Ren Xiao Yao) (Jia Zhangke), 98, 99–100
urban space, 64–5, 173, 187, 189
   Benjamin, Walter, 186, 189
   Buenos Aires, 224–5
   emotion, 246
   Fay, Jennifer, 222–3
   film noir, 222–4, 238
   highways, 224–5
   Nollywood, 242

rural–urban dichotomy, Argentina, 218–19, 221
women, 189–90
see also gated communities

Vampires, Les (Feuillade, Louis), 193
vida verde, la ('the green life'), 219, 220–1
violence, 51–2, 98–9, 103, 116
  Argentina, 157, 159, 165, 166–7
  blood money ritual, 248, 249–50
  human sacrifice, 248–9
  India, 121
  police, 149
  revolutionary vigilance films, 130–1
  sexual, 118–20, 166–9, 170
  spousal, 121
  state, 157, 159, 165
  see also guns
Visconti, Luchino, 47
  Earth Trembles, The/La terra trema, 45–6, 47, 48–51
  Ossessione, 49, 51, 57, 58
  Rocco and his Brothers/Rocco ei suoi Fratelli, 49
Vitette, Luis Mario
  ladrón del siglo, El (*The Thief of the Century*), 156

Warshow, Robert, 12
wealth, 101, 102
Weimar cinema, 4, 31, 32, 35, 40, 65, 66
  lighting/sets, 25, 33, 66, 67
Weine, Robert
  Hands of Orlac, The, 33
Welcome Danger (Bruckman, Clyde), 31
west, the, 255
western films, 99, 188, 254–6
  cowboy girl films, 188–9, 191
  see also Moreira, Juan
Who Is the Killer?/Kush Është Vrasësi? (Topallaj, Mark), 129, 130
Who Killed Who (Avery, Tex), 69
'Why Stalinist Cinema Had No Detective Films or How Three Becomes Two in *Engineer Kochin's Mistake*' (Cassiday, Julie A.), 131, 133–4, 135
Wild Horses/Caballos salvajes (Marcelo Piñeyro, Marcelo), 157–8, 161, 162, 163–4, 173
Williams, Linda, 227
Witches' Night/Walpurgisnacht (Bauer, James), 31
With His Finger on the Trigger/Con el dedo en el gatillo (Moglia Barth, Luis), 23
Without Conscience: The Disturbing World of the Psychopaths Among Us (Hare, Robert D.), 213, 214
women, 107–8
  American female adventure heroines, 183–4, 191, 193–4
  American serial queen heroines, 187–8
  bandit heroines, 108–10
  bodies, 227
  Bollywood, 108–10
  cowboy girl films, 188–9, 191
  female detectives, 189–90, 191
  feminism, 185
  flâneurs, 189
  France 183–4, 185–7, 191
  India, rights in, 110–11, 119
  Kerala, 110–11, 112, 18–19
  Malayalam cinema, 110–12
  matrilineality, 111
  motherhood, 108
  New Woman, 184, 185–7, 191, 196
  nurses, 118
  revenge films, 110–20, 121–2
  sexual chastity, 119–20
  sexual violence, 118–20, 166–9, 170
  social class, 186–7

women (*cont.*)
　spy films, 183–4, 190–7
　stunts, 188, 191–2f, 194
　urban space, 189–90
　see also femininity
women-oriented films, 120
World War II, 36

Yakuza films, 103
Yavanka ('Stage Curtain') (George, KG), 112–14, 119, 120

Yek Qadam ta Marg/One Step to Death (Khachikian, Samuel), 64

Zarba/Strike (Khachikian, Samuel), 68, 71–2
Zigomar (Jasset, Victorin), 185
Zigomar crime novels (Sazie, Léon), 183
Zigomar, Eel Skin/Zigomar, Peau d'Anguille (Jasset, Victorin), 183
Žižek, Slavoj
　Sublime Object of Ideology, The, 228